The Long Divergence

Timur Kuran

The Long Divergence

How Islamic Law Held Back the Middle East

PRINCETON UNIVERSITY PRESS   PRINCETON AND OXFORD

Published by Princeton University Press, 41 William Street, Princeton, New Jersey 08540
In the United Kingdom: Princeton University Press, 6 Oxford Street, Woodstock,
Oxfordshire OX20 1TW
press.princeton.edu

Library of Congress Cataloging-in-Publication Data
Kuran, Timur.
The long divergence : how Islamic law held back the Middle East /
Timur Kuran.
p.   cm.
Includes bibliographical references and index.
ISBN 978-0-691-14756-7 (hbk. : alk. paper)
1. Middle East—Economic conditions.   2. Middle East—Economic policy.
3. Economic development—Religious aspects—Islam.   4. Islamic
law—Economic aspects.   5. Islam—Economic aspects.   I. Title.
HC415.15.K87   2011
330.956—dc22
2010017346

British Library Cataloging-in-Publication Data is available

This book has been composed in Sabon LT Std text with Footlight MT Light display
Printed on acid-free paper. ∞
Printed in the United States of America

1 3 5 7 9 10 8 6 4 2

For Wendy,
with love and gratitude

Contents

Preface

I f randomly selected intellectuals were asked to explain why the modern economy took shape in northwestern Europe and not the eastern Mediterranean, the typical answer would contrast western flexibility with Muslim rigidity. Through the Reformation, the Renaissance, and the Enlightenment, many would say, western Christendom liberated itself from Church dogma and gave free rein to creativity. For its part, the Islamic world failed to free itself from the fetters of religious custom. Islam opposes innovation, it is often claimed, so Muslim social structures resisted adaptation and advancement.

Although this common interpretation carries grains of truth, it leaves unexplained why the degree of adaptability may have differed. If the economically regressive elements of Christianity were trumped, what kept the Middle East from overcoming Islam's retarding influences? Why did religious reinterpretations essential to economic modernization diffuse to the Middle East with a lag? The conventional wisdom is also imprecise about the mechanisms through which Islam supposedly blocked economic development.

As I set out to ponder the mechanisms at play, there existed no single work to which readers interested in a broad analytical treatment could turn. Generations of distinguished scholars had studied particular periods, episodes, institutions, or regions. There had also been admirable attempts to measure the Islamic world's economic performance, some by comparative economic historians, others by specialists on Islam or the Middle East. But insofar as attempts had been made to explain observed economic patterns, the emphasis, with few notable exceptions, was on symptoms rather than causal mechanisms. To observe that Muslims of the sixteenth century were indifferent to European advances in publishing is to identify a symptom of trouble, not to explain the unfolding process of retardation.

Past accounts described the problem but did not identify what caused it

A legitimate explanation requires exploring why no sufficiently powerful constituency arose for borrowing particular innovations. Likewise, observing that the Middle East fell prey to European imperialism pinpoints a late symptom of underdevelopment without accounting for the economic inertia that resulted in political subjugation.

This book aims to make sense of the Middle East's transformation from an economically advanced region to an economic laggard. It does not limit itself to describing rigidities. Trying to build a parsimonious argument focused on several critical mechanisms, I have avoided overwhelming the reader with details found in specialized sources. Some historians, including ones whose distinguished works proved indispensable to the research reported here, may find the generalizations unsettling. I ask them to recognize that this book's purpose is different from that of most history books. Particularities and variations are relevant here only insofar as they illuminate why the Middle East experienced a reversal of fortune.

The timing of the slip in the Middle East's global standing is part of the grand puzzle. It has become fashionable to locate the turning point in the nineteenth century, by which time the region was clearly behind in terms of per capita production and consumption. But gaps in such measures of economic performance did not open up in an institutional vacuum. Noticeable differences were preceded by a long period during which the West adopted modern economic institutions and the rest of the world, including the Middle East, remained wedded to commercial and financial institutions characteristic of the Middle Ages. In the economically powerful countries of the nineteenth century, production and commerce involved the pooling of resources within units far larger and far more complex than was possible in the contemporaneous Middle East, or, more precisely, its sectors still isolated from western influences.

The premodern economic institutions of the Middle East, which served identifiable economic ends, were grounded largely in the dominant law of the region, Islamic law. By no means was Islamic law a static construct; it was reinterpreted, in some contexts repeatedly. Nevertheless, in certain areas critical to economic modern-

Middle East lagged behind long before colonialism began in the 19th century

ization, change was minimal during the millennium when the West gradually made the transition from medieval to modern economic institutions, including organizational forms suitable to impersonal exchange on a large scale. Thus, the challenge ahead is to elucidate why classical Islam's distinct combination of economic institutions, obviously compatible with success in the medieval global economy, failed to produce the transformations necessary for keeping the Middle East globally competitive.

All good social science is at some level comparative, for to interpret findings and measure achievements one must have a context larger than the social unit under focus. Comparative analysis also generates intellectual puzzles by isolating the unusual. Throughout the book, therefore, institutions of the Islamic Middle East and their trajectories are compared with those of other places, particularly their often varied counterparts in northern Italy, France, England, and the Low Countries. The West serves as the primary basis for comparison because it is where the modern economy gradually took shape. The restricted menu of organizational forms available to merchants in seventeenth-century Syria presents a conundrum only when viewed in relation to the organizational dynamism of contemporaneous England. Also, it is in competition with the West that economic vulnerabilities of the Middle East became alarming and prompted institutional reforms.

Identifying the long-term effects of selected economic institutions does not amount to evaluating the wider social system. To find that certain features of classical Islamic law turned into economic handicaps is not to deny the vast accomplishments of Islamic civilization; nor does it presuppose that economic productivity is the sole measure of a society's worth. I recognize, of course, the risks inherent in exploring links between economic failures and a religion now widely viewed as a source of backwardness, ignorance, and oppression. Although few people today condemn Islam as explicitly as the anti-Islamic polemicists of the Middle Ages, Islamophobia is hardly dead. But the prevalence of anti-Islamic prejudice is no reason to limit balanced and dispassionate thinking about Islamic history. To refrain from asking questions, pursuing leads, or drawing honest conclusions because the work might be misused would be akin to abandoning technological development on the ground that some innovations facilitate crime.

Insofar as Islam is facing unfounded criticism, scholars aware of the misconceptions have an obligation to correct them through careful argumentation based on demonstrable facts. One of the most virulent ideas of our time, promoted independently by movements as diverse as militant Islamism and the politicized Christian right, is that Islam is inherently incompatible with the liberties, attitudes, and efficiency standards characteristic of the modern West. In the hands of ideologues, this perception of an unavoidable "clash of civilizations" is being used to heighten global tensions. Honest analysis of Middle Eastern history will do nothing to restrain those ideologues, whose minds are closed to evidence at odds with the caricatures they espouse. They will continue to think of civilizations in terms of fixed attributes and of grading them hierarchically, with their own permanently at the top. By the same token, it may help vast numbers of confused people within and outside the region to develop a nuanced understanding of why the Islamic Middle East became relatively poor. It may serve to cultivate an appreciation for the unintended consequences of institutions that, for the most part, are peripheral to current understandings of what Islam represents.

Nowadays, reluctance to critique institutions is commonly driven by a desire to avoid offending people presumed to draw their self-esteem and collective identity from indigenous laws, norms, and customs. But institutions—certainly all economic institutions—have potential benefits that transcend communal bonds and inner comfort. They also shape patterns of cooperation and association, incentives for creating wealth, and market efficiency. Therefore, intellectual restrictions motivated by paternalistic concerns about communal pride may deprive their intended beneficiaries of material self-improvement. Besides, prosperity and self-respect are not competing goals. In an increasingly interconnected world, economic underachievement is itself a source of shame and indignation. Therefore, keeping a community economically unsuccessful might do greater damage to its self-esteem than demonstrating why certain components of its rich institutional heritage are obsolete.

Furthermore, anxieties about causing offense rest on the faulty presupposition that Muslims are inherently hostile to intellectual debate and uninterested in self-improvement. Although there exist Muslims who favor cultural isolationism and protectionism, they do not speak for the rest. Large numbers want to know what elements of their social systems might have contributed, if inadvertently and unpredictably, to developmental bottlenecks. They want to know whether institutional traps, insofar as they existed, have been overcome. In trying to reconcile Islam with the exigencies of modern life, they want to understand the Islamic heritage, if only to distinguish between what remains usable and what is best appreciated without being preserved or revived. Although this book focuses on understanding historical phenomena, it yields insights into the practical implications of Islamist efforts to restore lapsed economic institutions.

In writing this book, I have drawn on the studies of literally hundreds of scholars whose data and insights proved indispensable to the story told here. In some instances, of course, I used past works to identify new linkages, or to provide interpretations that their authors refrained from drawing, or even, in some cases, to prove them wrong. A large group of individuals, many of them authors of valuable works referenced in my bibliography, contributed to the book's development with suggestions, leads, caveats, and criticisms. Though it would be impractical to list all my intellectual creditors, a few of them deserve special acknowledgment. I am grateful to Eli Berman, Murat Çizakça, Michael Cook, Robert Cooter, Mahmoud El-Gamal, Boğaç Ergene, Avner Greif, Murat İyigün, Noel Johnson, Eric Jones, Daniel Klerman, Deepak Lal, Claire Morgan, Mustapha Nabli, Robert Nelson, Douglass North, Şevket Pamuk, Jean-Philippe Platteau, David Powers, Jared Rubin, and John Wallis for reading one or more chapters in draft form and suggesting modifications; Ali Akyıldız, Lloyd Armstrong, Kenneth Arrow, Murat Birdal, Fahad Bishara, Ali Çarkoğlu, Paul David,

Hanming Fang, Fethi Gedikli, Mehmet Genç, Ron Harris, Laurence Iannaccone, Kıvanç Karaman, Murat Koraltürk, Naomi Lamoreaux, Ghislaine Lydon, Donald Miller, Joel Mokyr, Jeffrey Nugent, Virginia Postrel, Frederic Pryor, Gary Richardson, Kimon Sargeant, and Zafer Toprak for stimulating conversations and helpful leads; Mehmet Âkif Aydın for providing access to critical data; Hania Abou Al-Shamat, Banu Birdal, Sinan Birdal, Iva Božović, Debbie Johnston, Feisal Khan, Scott Lustig, Charles Miller, Alvaro Name Correa, Fırat Oruç, Anantdeep Singh, Murat Somer, and Sung Han Tak for dedicated research assistance over the long period when this book was being researched; Müslüm İstekli and Ömer Faruk Bahadur for undertaking painstaking archival searches and providing transliterations; Seth Ditchik, Karen Verde, Sara Lerner, Dimitri Karetnikov, and Janie Chan, all of Princeton University Press, for making it easy to produce this book out of what was a manuscript with many loose ends; and, finally, Christof Galli of the Duke University Library and Joanne Bloom of the Harvard University Library for extended assistance with finding sources and illustrations. These individuals bear no responsibility for the uses I have made of their assistance. None should be presumed to share my conclusions.

The work that found its way into this book began during the 1996–97 academic year, when I held the John Olin visiting professorship at the George J. Stigler Center for the Study of the Economy and the State, Graduate School of Business, University of Chicago. Other components of the initial draft were prepared in June 1997, when I was a visiting professor at the Center for Economic Studies, University of Munich; in June–August 1999, when I held a visiting fellowship of the Social and Political Theory Group, Research School of Social Sciences, Australian National University; in 2002–3, when I was a fellow of the Center for Interdisciplinary Research, University of Southern California; and in 2004–5, when I held a visiting professorship in the Department of Economics, Stanford University.

The Earhart Foundation supported the research through a 2003–4 grant and the John Simon Guggenheim Memorial Foundation through a fellowship in 2004–5. The Metanexus Institute's Spiritual Capital Research Program, funded by the John Templeton

Foundation, provided extended research support at the stages of data gathering, conceptual refinement, and statistical testing. The entire project was supported by the King Faisal Professorship in Islamic Thought and Culture at the University of Southern California, which I held between 1993 and 2007, and by the Gorter Family Professorship in Islamic Studies at Duke University, which I have held since 2007.

In April 2008, when the first full draft of this book came to fruition, the Mercatus Center at George Mason University honored it through a beautifully organized pre-publication conference. Over two days of discussions, an intellectually diverse group of distinguished scholars, all thanked above, subjected the organization and interpretations of the manuscript to critical scrutiny. Both the substance and the presentation of the argument benefited measurably from the comments provided. My only regret is that it proved impossible to pursue every suggestion offered at the conference. In some cases, I am doing so elsewhere, in work that complements the present volume.

Portions of certain chapters draw on one or more of my published articles. They are: "The Provision of Public Goods under Islamic Law: Origins, Impact, and Limitations of the Waqf System," *Law and Society Review*, 35 (2001), pp. 841–97; "The Islamic Commercial Crisis: Institutional Roots of Economic Underdevelopment in the Middle East," *Journal of Economic History*, 63 (2003), pp. 414–46; "The Economic Ascent of the Middle East's Religious Minorities: The Role of Islamic Legal Pluralism," *Journal of Legal Studies*, 33 (2004), pp. 475–515; "The Logic of Financial Westernization in the Middle East," *Journal of Economic Behavior and Organization*, 56 (2005), pp. 593–615; and "The Absence of the Corporation in Islamic Law: Origins and Persistence," *American Journal of Comparative Law*, 53 (2005), pp. 785–834. I thank the publishers of these articles for permission to use them here.

In producing a book about a region featuring several major languages that changed significantly over time, absolute consistency in transliteration is impossible. But I follow some basic rules. Within notes and the bibliography, author names and titles are spelled as in the original source. In the main text, words found in English dictionaries (such as bazaar, kadi, and pasha) are not transliterated.

For simplicity, terms with English equivalents are generally rendered in English (for example, Quran for *Qur'ān*, pilgrimage for *hajj*, Cairo for *Al-Kāhira*); however, wherever confusion is possible, at the first usage of such an English word, the corresponding non-English term is given in parentheses. The transliteration of Arabic and Farsi terms is simplified to show only the glottal stops of the ayn and hamza, and even they are omitted for proper names. All non-Anglicized words from languages that use the Latin alphabet are rendered as in the original. Thus, non-Anglicized Turkish words, including loan-words from Arabic or Farsi that assumed a specific meaning under the Ottomans, are transcribed according to the rules of modern Turkish. Quotations from the Quran are drawn from N. J. Dawood's classic translation; and biblical quotations come from the New Revised Standard Version.

In references to individuals, regardless of their creed or nationality, terms of reverence and status signifiers are omitted, except where necessary to make an analytical point. For expositional convenience, Gregorian dates are used throughout. The acronyms CE and BCE stand for "Common Era" and "Before the Common Era." They correspond to the Latin abbreviations A.D. and B.C.

Timur Kuran
Durham, N.C.,
December 2009

PART I

Introduction

1

The Puzzle of the Middle East's Economic Underdevelopment

At the start of the second millennium, around the year 1000, a visitor from Italy or China would not have viewed the Middle East as an impoverished, commercially deficient, or organizationally primitive region.[1] Although the region might have seemed enigmatic, its oddities would not have painted a picture of general economic inferiority. Now, at the start of the third millennium, it is widely considered an economic laggard, and a plethora of statistics support this consensus. More than half of its firms consider their limited access to electricity, telecommunications, or transport a major obstacle to their business, as against less than a quarter of those in Europe. In the region, life expectancy is 8.5 years shorter than in high-income countries, consisting mainly of North America, western Europe, and parts of East Asia. Its per capita income equals 28 percent of the average for high-income countries. Only three-quarters of the adults in the region are literate, as compared with near-complete literacy in advanced countries (table 1.1).

As of late 1750, the picture was different. Around that time the purchasing power of the average worker in London or Amsterdam was only twice that of the average worker in Istanbul, the largest metropolis and leading commercial hub of the eastern Mediterranean.[2] The gap between Middle Eastern and western living subsequently widened, until World War I. Since then aggregate growth has been roughly equal. Measured as a ratio, in the early twenty-first century the per capita income gap between the West and the Middle East remains what it was a century before.[3]

TABLE 1.1
Comparative Indicators of Economic Performance (2007)

Region, country, or country grouping	Human Development Index (United Nations)	Life expectancy at birth	Adult literacy rate (%)	Gross Domestic Product per capita (US$)
Middle East	0.73	69.4	74.7	9,418
Arab League	0.70	68.5	69.6	8,103
Iran	0.78	71.2	82.3	10,955
Turkey	0.81	71.7	88.7	12,955
OECD (except Turkey)	0.94	77.8	99.0	33,755
China	0.78	72.9	93.3	5,383
India	0.61	63.4	66.0	2,753
African Union (excluding Arab League members)	0.49	51.5	62.3	2,029

Source: United Nations Development Programme, *Human Development Report 2007–8* (http://hrdstats.undp.org).

Notes: As of 2007, the Arab League had 22 members; the Organization for Economic Cooperation and Development (OECD) included 30 of the world's industrialized countries; and the African Union included 53 members, of which 10 also belonged to the Arab League. Gross Domestic Product is measured at purchasing power parity in 2007 dollars. Regional and organization averages are population-weighted. Certain indexes were unavailable for three Arab League members (Iraq, Palestinian Authority, Somalia) and four African Union members (Democratic Republic of the Sahara, Gambia, Seychelles, Zimbabwe). These countries were omitted from calculations of the relevant weighted averages. Hence, the number of countries included in the Arab League and African Union averages vary slightly across columns.

What caused the Middle East to lose economic standing toward the end of the second millennium is not an absolute decline in economic performance. On the contrary, its present living standards far exceed those of a millennium earlier. From 1820 to1913, per capita income grew by about two-thirds; following a period of modest growth between the two world wars, it then tripled in 1950–90.[4] There has been only a *relative* decline caused by slower

Relative, not absolute decline in economic standards

growth than in countries that are now the world's richest.[5] It remains much richer than sub-Saharan Africa, and even India, a star performer since the 1990s.

The Middle East fell behind the West because it was late in adopting key institutions of the modern economy. These include laws, regulations, and organizational forms that enabled economic activities now taken for granted in all but the most impoverished parts of the globe: the mobilization of productive resources on a huge scale within long-lasting private enterprises and the provision of social services through durable entities capable of transformation. Well into the nineteenth century, the private sectors of the Middle East were composed of atomistic enterprises that did not outlive their founders. When individuals pooled resources in profit-making enterprises, their cooperation was meant to be temporary, often no more than a few months. By that time, most of the now-advanced countries had developed institutions essential to the mass mobilization of savings, the lengthening of individual planning horizons, and the exploitation of new technologies through structurally complex organizations. Therein lies a key reason why the Middle East fell behind in living standards and why it succumbed to foreign domination.

In a nutshell, that is the thesis of this book. We shall see that around the year 1000, commercial life in the two regions did not differ palpably. The contractual forms available to Middle Eastern merchants and investors would have seemed largely familiar to their counterparts in western Europe, and vice versa. The differences identifiable in hindsight were not yet of major significance to the rhythms of commercial life, or to economic productivity, or to living standards. Nevertheless, those differences harbored the seeds of a long divergence in organizational development. As the institutional complex of the West gave rise to progressively more advanced commercial and financial institutions, that of the Middle East produced organizational stagnation within those sectors beyond direct state control. The institutions under which Middle Easterners borrowed, invested, and produced did not spawn more advanced institutions; they did not galvanize structural transformations that enabled those functions to be performed more efficiently, over longer time spans, or on a larger scale. In failing to generate major organizational innovations from within, the Middle Eastern institutional complex also hindered opportunities to benefit from innovations produced elsewhere.

Chapters ahead substantiate all these claims with a focus on key economic institutions of the Islamic Middle East prior to its period of intense institutional reform, the late nineteenth and early twentieth centuries. Important clues will emerge from cross-regional comparisons involving the bloc of countries now considered advanced.

Until recently the core of that bloc was known as "western Christendom." Now we call it simply "the West." For our purposes here, the West consists of European societies that, from the twelfth to the early sixteenth century, shared a common political, legal, and religious subordination to the papal hierarchy of the Roman Catholic Church. Some of these countries later experienced a "Reformation" directed partly at Roman Catholicism.[6]

The term Middle East itself is subject to many definitions. In the historical sweep of this book it is used in an elastic sense to include the entire Arab world and Iran, but also Turkey, along with the Balkan peninsula, which Turks ruled during a period when key Islamic institutions remained stagnant. Spain belongs to the region up to the Reconquista—its reversion, by the end of the fifteenth century, from Muslim to Christian control. The term excludes India, central Asia, East Asia, and sub-Saharan Africa, all regions where Islam struck roots. As figure 1.1 shows, most of the territories that I am including in the "Middle East" at one time or another remained under Muslim governance from at least 800 to 1880. By 1300, the region expanded to include much of modern-day Turkey, and by 1500 most of the Balkans.[7]

Islamic Institutions and Their Mutability

Institution is another slippery concept that requires definition. By institution I mean a system of socially produced regularities that shape, and are in turn shaped by, individual behaviors.[8] This definition encompasses consciously created social regularities, such as state-imposed litigation procedures and tax regulations. It also encompasses patterns that emerge as byproducts of other choices, such as procedural expectations based on history, customary contractual practices, and organizational norms.

During the period of interest, an institution of great importance to Middle Eastern daily life was the holy law of Islam (*sharī'a*), also known as Islamic law. In principle, Islamic law covered all human activity. As a matter of practice, certain spheres of life were governed by rules divorced from religious considerations. In the political discourse of the Ottoman Empire (1299–1922) there was even a category of laws known as "ruler's law" (*kanun*), as distinct from Islamic law, and also a third category, customary law (*örf*), which rested on precedent rather than religious scripture or learning.[9]

In commerce and finance, two areas in which the Middle East fell conspicuously behind, right up to modern times Islamic law played a key role. People entered into contracts that followed an Islamic template and were enforced through Islamic courts. They apportioned estates according to Islamic inheritance rules. Residents of the region's great cities obtained services mostly from waqfs, which were trusts formed under Islamic law and supervised by officials with religious training. Almost all lawsuits involving at least one Muslim were litigated by Muslim judges, under Islamic legal principles. Cracking our puzzle thus requires close attention to the practical consequences of Islamic law.

The domains of the three bodies of law were not immutable. Where Islamic law created identifiable handicaps for investors, merchants, artisans, or moneylenders, efforts might have been made to facilitate the circumvention of problematic provisions. Such groups might have sought, for instance, to establish specialized commercial courts operated, without much attention to religion, by judges drawn from their own ranks. Thus, commerce and finance might have become secularized. Yet, until recently no such reforms took place. Prior to the nineteenth century the commercial and financial institutions characteristic of the medieval Middle East did not give way to more complex institutions resembling those of the modern global economy.

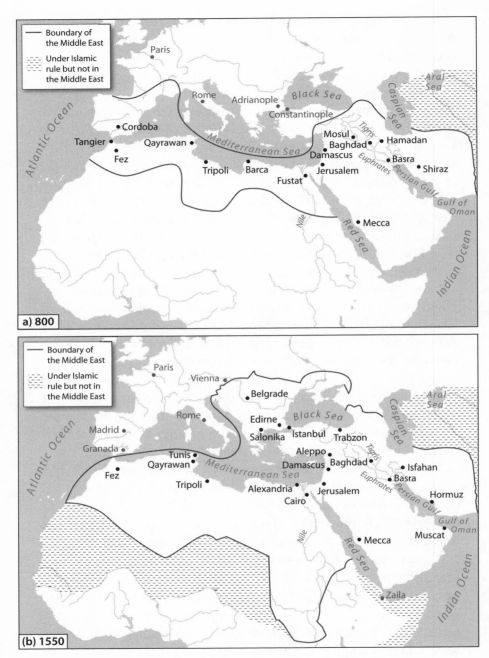

Figure 1.1 Boundaries of the Middle East in 800, 1550, and 1880

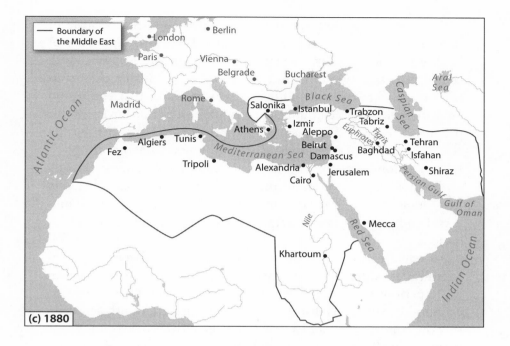

The relevant segments of Islamic law did not remain frozen in a literal sense. Historians of the Middle East identify numerous legal reinterpretations that occurred before the modern era. For instance, they offer the long tenure of Ebussuûd, chief judicial officer of the Ottoman Empire in the mid-sixteenth century, as a shining example of Islamic legal adaptability. Ebussuûd did indeed reinterpret the law on many occasions, often subtly, and typically with an eye toward eliminating ambiguities, facilitating interactions, and preventing conflicts.[10] However, he did not alter the substance of the law in ways that laid the foundations for revolutionary changes in the scale or scope of economic activity. In relation to the ongoing process of global economic modernization, which was to turn into a typhoon leaving no coast untouched, his legal adjustments appear as mere ripples in a pond. If a man born in Cairo in 1000 came alive a few decades after Ebussuûd's death, no aspect of this city's commercial life would have surprised him. Major changes in the scale and scope of Egyptian commerce had to await the 1850s.

Islamic law was not static but the fundamentals of it did not change. Major changes only occured in the 1850s

When an institution appears stagnant, it could be because of personal attachments to the status quo. Thus, the exponents of "modernization theory," which held sway in the mid-twentieth century, cite traditionalism and conservatism as Muslim characteristics inimical to reform.[11] Other writers invoke anti-scientific and fatalistic attitudes as cultural elements harmful to Muslim economic progress.[12] However, fatalism is widespread in today's scientifically advanced countries as well, especially among devout people.[13] Likewise, conservatism is commonplace even in countries growing at dazzling speed; no one wants to live in a relentlessly changing environment lacking fixed points of reference. By themselves, universal and permanent social traits cannot explain variations across societies.

An equally serious problem with ascribing explanatory power to attitudes is that societies governed under Islamic law have enjoyed periods of remarkable structural dynamism. With respect to economic institutions, for instance, the eighth and ninth centuries saw the emergence of an Islamic law to govern the trusts known as waqfs as well as the refinement of the Islamic law of partnerships.[14] In some areas, such as tax collection, innovations and cross-cultural borrowings never ceased. Evidently, precedents were relatively less constraining at certain times and in certain domains. What requires elucidation, then, is not that the Middle East cannot free itself of tradition, or that it lacks creativity. It is that over much of the second millennium, traditions exhibited more resilience in private economic life than in public policy.

A related pattern, also at odds with the central premise of old modernization theory, is that in contexts critical to economic development, satisfaction with the status quo appears to have varied. Egyptian merchants and financiers of the sixteenth century did not find it problematic that their commercial contracts looked much like those of their forefathers. By contrast, in the nineteenth century growing numbers of Egyptian businessmen considered traditional commercial and financial institutions inadequate.[15] By that time foreigners were encouraging local communities to change their business practices. Although some of their advice fell on deaf ears, the local business community was remarkably receptive to reforms

Critique of modernization theory as applied to ME

aimed at modernizing the region's commercial and financial infrastructure. When banking was introduced to Ottoman realms, diverse communities started clamoring for a branch office in their own localities.[16]

Increasing contacts with foreigners constitute a proximate cause of the attitudinal transformation. In the mid-nineteenth century, a period of reforms, major cities of the eastern Mediterranean contained upscale districts filled with European expatriates. Indigenous residents could see that these foreigners lived better and that their lavish lifestyles reflected higher productivity. They sensed that it would be profitable to adopt new business practices. Successful imitation of foreigners would require the transplantation of alien institutions, such as stock markets, municipalities, and laws supportive of large companies capable of outliving their founders. Such transplants did occur eventually—proof that conservatism and fatalism, insofar as they played roles, were hardly decisive.

Evidence of Institutional Underdevelopment

In the early nineteenth century, right before the Middle East's first structural reforms aimed at modernizing its private sectors, local economic life looked primitive in relation to emerging western practices. Whereas commercial partnerships formed under Islamic law typically involved a few partners who pooled resources for short-lived ventures, westerners were forming indefinitely lasting enterprises with tens, hundreds, and even thousands of shareholders. In traditional Middle Eastern credit markets, suppliers typically were individuals capable of making small loans. Westerners had access to commercial banks that could channel capital mobilized from the masses into large-scale productive ventures. No stock markets existed for trading shares of indigenous Middle Eastern companies, which tended to be ephemeral. Stock markets were gaining prominence in the West, where investors in long-living enterprises liquidated shares at will.

The supply of urban social services offers another contrast. In the Middle East, the traditional provider was the waqf. In the face of breathtaking technological advances, this form of trust proved inadequate as a vehicle for keeping services up to date. The municipality, a standard instrument of local governance in western Europe, was better suited to the rapidly changing needs of cities.

From the mid-nineteenth century onward, in Egypt, Turkey, and elsewhere in the region, institutional transplants curtailed the domain of dysfunctional Islamic institutions. The commercial courts established in the mid-nineteenth century offer an example. These courts adjudicated cases according to the French commercial code. Although Islamic courts continued to handle commercial disputes, their share of the legal workload declined precipitously. Because such legal reforms involved the spread of western commercial patterns and a waning of traditional Islamic ways, they are often characterized as economic westernization. However, transplants did not always amount to replicating western institutions. Institutions borrowed from the West were used also to limit western influences, preserve old customs, and even invent new traditions.

A striking example of creative borrowing lies in the development, beginning in the mid-twentieth century, of Islamic banks. From a historical perspective the concept of an "Islamic bank" is a contradiction in terms. An Islamic bank operates on a scale far larger than any private enterprise the Middle East knew before the nineteenth century. It is a corporation, an organizational form alien to Islamic law. Islamic banking thus constitutes an "invented tradition."[17] Its architects have used western institutional models not to make Muslim economic life more "western" but, rather, to encourage saving, investing, borrowing, and lending in ways at least cosmetically "Islamic."[18]

In view of the motives behind the transplants in question, their collective accomplishments are better described as "economic modernization" than "economic westernization." The modernization theorists of the mid-twentieth century, already criticized for treating conservatism as an explanation rather than an observation requiring elucidation, erred also in equating these two concepts. To them, economic modernization entailed the wholesale adoption of western institutions and beliefs. Here the concept has a narrower meaning. Consisting of institutional changes to support economic

transactions of rising scale, duration, and complexity, and to provide economic actors greater flexibility, modernizing economic
reforms are vehicles for catching up with the wealthiest countries
in productivity and consumption. They need not amount to blind
imitation or eradication of differences.

Author's definition of modernization

This narrower meaning accords with the agendas of various
Turkish, Arab, and Iranian reformers of the past two centuries.
None wanted to erase the cultural distinctions of his own country.
Borrowing selectively, each adjusted transplanted institutions to
local circumstances.[19] Their shared goal was to replicate specific
western achievements, not to appropriate western culture indiscriminately. In the traditional economies that they sought to modernize, people borrowed from moneylenders, usually for short periods at a time. Credit contracts often involved no more than an
oral promise, and the adjudication of commercial disputes did not
necessarily rely on documentation. The banks established in the
1850s under the auspices of Turkish and Egyptian reformists could
not operate on the basis of oral agreement. Their transactions, far
more numerous and often much larger than those of a traditional
moneylender, had to be documented according to standardized
procedures. One function of the new commercial courts established
outside the Islamic legal system was to resolve disputes involving
the nascent banking sector.

reformists & banks in ME

By the mid-nineteenth century, which marks the initiation of
major reforms, the world had entered a new economic epoch, that
of modern economic growth.[20] As the designation suggests, its chief
characteristic is self-sustaining economic expansion at an unprecedented rate; although contractions can occur, they amount to temporary reversals along an upward path. This epoch has additional
characteristics: rapid technological change, a doubling of life spans,
massive urbanization, and the means of mobilizing abundant capital through complex private organizations. Muslim reformists of
the nineteenth century may not have understood the origins of these
characteristics, or their connections. Nevertheless, they sensed that
the characteristics had become critical to economic advancement.

modern economic growth = constantly growing growth, albeit w/ occasional faults

The view that modern economic growth depends on certain organizational capabilities does not presume a unique path to high

economic productivity or high living standards. It *does* assume that these ends require fundamental institutional transformations to enable savers, investors, lenders, borrowers, merchants, and producers to operate on much greater scales than ever before, through organizations incomparably larger, and over time horizons far longer than would have made sense in the Middle Ages. If this is granted, it is simply a matter of record that until well after 1750, considered the start of modern economic growth, the Middle East lacked the organizational forms and techniques that distinguish the present epoch from two previous epochs—prehistory to 8000 BCE and settled agriculture from then to 1750.

Other Sources of Underdevelopment

The first *Arab Human Development Report*, issued in 2002 by a commission composed entirely of Arab thinkers, points to a "freedom deficit" and a "human capabilities/knowledge deficit" as two characteristics of the Arab world today.[21] The former deficit refers mainly to governance patterns inimical to civil and political freedoms and the latter to low educational attainment, access to information, and intellectual creativity. Though the terms are new, the handicaps themselves are not. Two centuries ago, observers of the region would have recognized instantly what they meant. Far-reaching reforms were launched partly because the Middle East had become a technological laggard, its states discouraged investment, its inhabitants were poorly educated, and its intellectual life lacked vigor.

If the crisis of the nineteenth century was multidimensional, one may reasonably question whether focusing on deficiencies of private economic organization provides the most fruitful approach to solving our puzzle. Might some other problem be the fundamental cause of underdevelopment, and organizational stagnation merely its byproduct? Might governance patterns, for instance, have limited the menu of organizational forms available to entrepreneurs?

A credible account of the region's economic misfortunes could be developed by focusing on the state's role as a provider of economic infrastructure and enforcer of property rights. As another alternative, one could direct attention to the production of knowledge, investigating its transformations and the ways in which intellectual life constrained responses to economic challenges. In truth, the many patterns associated with the Middle East's troubles all affected one another. To consider one factor the root cause of the Middle East's historical trajectory and all the rest as derivatives would be to commit the "fallacy of absolute priority."[22] This is the illusion that any causal sequence must have a first term. In the proverbial relationship between chicken and egg, there is no absolute starting point. Each entity serves as both source and product, making the relationship bidirectional.

A bidirectional causal relationship existed between any two of the variables that reformers of the nineteenth century endeavored to shape. Each was endogenous to a social system whose variables were all interlinked. General knowledge, technologies of production, commercial institutions, and state structures all evolved together. For a genuinely independent factor of consequence for economic performance we would need to fall back on geography or climate, which Jared Diamond uses to explain global patterns spanning tens of millennia.[23] However, the near-fixity of those factors rules them out as determinants of the institutional trajectories of interest here. A stable climate cannot explain the development of Islamic contract law in the early Islamic centuries, or the adoption, a millennium later, of the French commercial code. If we stick, then, to the socially constructed patterns called institutions, none will be independent of the rest. Legitimate concerns about endogeneity, known in casual discourse as circularity, will emerge whether we focus on technology, knowledge, the state, or private organization. Hence, the starting point for an inquiry is ultimately arbitrary. Whatever causal relationship starts the analysis, sooner or later a relationship in the opposite direction will emerge. Feedback effects will come into play, transforming what started as a linear and unidirectional model into a complex system harboring circularities of the chicken-and-egg type.

Nevertheless, even in studying a complex system there may exist analytical reasons to spotlight initially, and thus to privilege, one particular cluster of variables. In the case at hand, the variables in play did not contribute equally to the *persistence* of the region's underdevelopment. Consider technology and organizational capacity. In the nineteenth century the Middle East was a laggard on both counts. It lacked the know-how essential for mass production as surely as it lacked a law of corporations. England, Germany, and France had both, which enabled their entrepreneurs to form huge companies capable of exploiting new technologies. Hence, Middle Eastern entrepreneurs had trouble competing in the global economy because of both technological and organizational stagnation.

However, these two forms of backwardness did not pose equally intractable problems. A steam engine could be shipped to Cairo, along with the technicians and raw materials needed to make it productive. Transplanting the organizational means to exploit mechanization proved far more difficult. A viable stock market could not be established overnight. It required an intricate legal system, various specialized occupations, and schools to train and certify relevant experts. Only some of the required skills could be supplied by foreigners lacking familiarity with local cultures and vernaculars. Hence, the absence of markets for trading company shares posed a more intractable obstacle to the Middle East's economic advancement than its delays in mechanizing. That is what justifies giving analytic priority to institutional transformation.

It bears emphasizing that organizational capacity affected both technological creativity and the ability to exploit foreign technologies. Just as Middle Eastern schooling patterns affected the region's scientific and technological progress, so its organization of production shaped incentives for technological change and intellectual activity generally.[24] Hence, the region's organizational history is among the factors responsible for its current knowledge deficit.

Private Organizational Development versus Evolution of the State

The foregoing logic would not justify the privileging of private organizational development over the evolution of state structures,

TABLE 1.2
Comparative Indicators of Political Performance (2008–2009)

Region, country, or country grouping	Civil liberties 1 (most) to 10	Political rights 1 (strongest) to 10	Corruption perceptions 1 to 10 (least corrupt)	Rule of law −2.5 to 2.5 (best)
Middle East	5.1	5.6	2.9	−0.3
Arab League	5.4	6.1	2.8	−0.6
Iran	6.0	6.0	1.8	−0.8
Turkey	3.0	3.0	4.4	0.1
OECD (except Turkey)	1.4	1.1	6.8	1.2
China	6.0	7.0	3.6	−0.3
India	3.0	2.0	3.4	0.1
African Union (excluding Arab League members)	4.1	4.2	2.6	−0.8

Sources: Freedom House, *Freedom in the World Report*, 2008 (http://www.freedom house.org), first two columns; Transparency International, *Corruption Perceptions Index*, 2009 (http://www.transparency.org); World Bank Rule of Law Indicators, 2008 (http://info.worldbank.org/governance).

Notes: For the country groupings, see table 1.1. The population figures used in computing the averages are for 2005.

for institutions of governance are no easier to transplant than those of commerce or civil society. Witness the Arab Middle East's persistently low international rankings relating to civil rights, government effectiveness, and rule of law, in spite of political reforms over the past century (table 1.2). Nevertheless, there are three reasons for starting with private organizational capabilities.

The first is pedagogical. Historians of the Middle East have devoted incomparably more attention to the state than to private organization.[25] This is because official archives, loaded as they are with documents pertaining to state functions, exaggerate the state's role in people's lives and lend themselves to state-centric historical accounts that have been fashionable among historians. Whatever the reasons for the distortion, starting with private economic life raises the likelihood of advancing the debate on why the region fell behind. It makes it possible, as we shall see, to identify complex social interdependencies that states do not, and cannot, control.[26]

The second rationale for starting with private organization pertains to institutional flexibility. Among students of the Middle East a popular view is that traditionalism was a basic principle of governance. This view appears, for example, in Mehmet Genç's influential works on Ottoman economic history.[27] Genç considers traditionalism an integral element of the mind-set of Ottoman elites; his followers link this orientation to Quranic verses that counsel moderation. Yet Middle Eastern administrative history offers abundant examples of adaptation to new circumstances. As already noted, tax rates and collection methods changed repeatedly in the face of new challenges and opportunities.[28] Contrary to a common interpretation, this does not signify efficient administration. A state can react to threats by treating symptoms of trouble rather than addressing the deep causes. To be sure, enough flexibility existed to keep dynasties in power for centuries. When the Ottoman state succumbed to European imperialism at the end of World War I, it was in its 622nd year. Such longevity could not have been achieved through policies chained to the past.

It is in turning our gaze to segments of the social system beyond direct state control that stagnant practices become salient. Subsequent chapters will show that the commercial contracts registered by Ottoman courts of the seventeenth century were essentially identical to those prevalent in the region around the year 1000. Likewise, the system through which communities supplied social services was present many centuries earlier. Hence, insofar as inertia explains the Middle East's failure to keep up with western Europe, it is private economic life, not public administration, that calls for primary attention. To put it in terms of the tripartite legal categorization familiar to historians, religious law and customary law merit analytic priority over ruler's law.

The final justification for giving priority to private organization is that it is among the key determinants of state capabilities.[29] If in the nineteenth century European states lent to Middle Eastern states, and not the other way around, the key reason is that Middle

Eastern credit markets were far less advanced than those of Europe. Their organizational handicaps, including the absence of banks and stock markets, limited the supply of domestic capital to Middle Eastern states. Again, at issue is not what mattered to economic advancement in the Middle East. In an interconnected social system everything influences everything else, so state capabilities and private economic life are interdependent. The issue is the start of the inquiry, not where it leads.

[handwritten margin note: limited supply of capital]

Interactions with Other Regions

In discourses on why the Middle East became underdeveloped, a commonly articulated explanation points the finger at outsiders. The machinations of Europeans, it says, turned the region into a "dependent," "plundered," and "self-doubting" part of the world. Certain variants of the argument rest on the illusion that all social interactions have a "zero sum" quality: if the French and British gained, the Syrians and Iraqis must have lost.[30] The Europeans who colonized much of the Middle East by World War I certainly pursued their own agendas, which were sometimes misaligned with those of local communities. Still, interpretations that attribute the region's underdevelopment to foreign meddling miss vital ingredients of the historical record. They leave unexplained why the region succumbed to imperialism at that time, and not before. The relevant questions of causality and responsibility are addressed in later chapters. What needs recognition here is that the Middle East's economic evolution was indeed linked to that of the wider world.

For several reasons, interactions with western Europe deserve special scrutiny. At least initially, it is in relation to the West that the Middle East became underdeveloped. Also, when this divergence turned into a crisis for the region, it is primarily to the West that leaders looked for institutional responses. Finally, the ensuing reforms instituted practices that were introduced to the Middle East by western merchants who operated under the protection of trade treaties. Known as capitulations, these treaties allowed westerners to trade under institutions of their own.

Certain puzzles concerning the Middle East's economic lag present themselves starkly with regard to the capitulations. Treaties of the seventeenth century allowed traders operating under a foreign flag to have their estates handled according to the inheritance laws of their homelands. Through this privilege, they prevented the fragmentation of their estates, a common occurrence under Islamic law. The capitulations also protected foreign merchants from undocumented claims in local courts. Perplexingly, these and other privileges were withheld from local merchants.

Although the underlying motives are complex, one is that foreign privileges enhanced commercial efficiency. Thus, the protection against undocumented lawsuits replaced dispute resolution procedures characteristic of personal exchange with those of impersonal exchange. As works on European economic modernization have demonstrated, in the period when the capitulations gained increasing significance, Europe was making the transition from personal to impersonal exchange. In other words, economic relations based on personal connections were giving way to ones dependent on complex organization. Under personal exchange, gains depend on expectations of future interactions with the same exchange partners, or on knowledge of past behavior, or on ability to disseminate information about misconduct. As exchange becomes impersonal, we know from the works of Douglass North and Avner Greif, the gains from trade rest increasingly on organizations specializing in contract enforcement.[31] In the period when foreigners won protections against undocumented financial claims, Islamic courts commonly decided commercial cases on the basis of oral testimony alone. That betrays the prevalence of personal exchange.

Hence, investigating institutional dimensions of the Middle East's interactions with the West can yield insights into the global realignment of interest here. Organizational differences between western and Middle Eastern traders emerged at least a half-millennium before the Middle East showed signs of general economic backwardness. Although their impact on living standards was initially minor, they set the stage for the sharp divergence recorded under modern economic growth. The growing gap in economic performance then led, beginning in the nineteenth century, to institutional transplants that also facilitated the transformations that enabled the Middle East to start growing at rates unseen in its history. To be sure, not all foreign institutional influences have been beneficial. Certain capitulary privileges, such as exemptions from various user fees, yielded no obvious gains to the region. Nevertheless, viewed from a long perspective, and with a focus on production and consumption, the balance sheet has been overwhelmingly favorable.

During the second millennium the Middle East benefited also from interactions with other regions, including sub-Saharan Africa, central Asia, India, and China. The difference is that in these other cases the Middle East was often the source of institutional transplants, rather than a recipient. Exchanges with these regions were accompanied by mass conversions to Islam and the diffusion of Islamic institutions. There were resource outflows from Islamicized regions, including tributes sent to rulers in Cairo or Istanbul. But what stands out are the institutional benefits that these regions reaped from Islamization prior to the industrial era, when global economic competition fostered incentives to discard Islamic institutions.

Religious Minorities

The reason that premodern conversions to Islam went hand in hand with the diffusion of Islamic institutions is that Muslims were expected to live according to the dictates of Islamic law. Non-Muslim subjects of Islamic states were compelled to follow Islamic law only on matters of taxation and security. Ordinarily they were free to do business under rules of their own selection.[32] Hence, they could have escaped the commercial provisions of Islamic law simply by restricting their dealings to other non-Muslims and resolving disputes through their own communal organizations.

In 1844, the first date for which comprehensive population figures exist, Christians and Jews comprised at least 45 percent of the population of the Ottoman Empire, the region's largest state. Three centuries earlier, they formed 35 percent of the population in Istanbul, and 18 percent in Damascus.[33] Hence, the privileges of

Religious minorities could operate outside of Islamic law
if they did not deal w/ Muslims

non-Muslims are relevant to the conundrum of whether Islamic law hindered economic advancement. If the priviledges in question constituted a significant factor, non-Muslims need not have been affected, at least not equally. Specifically, any rigidities of Islamic commercial institutions might have been overcome with respect to transactions among non-Muslims. In fact, prior to the eighteenth century commercial practices did not differ fundamentally across religious communities. Only at that time did critical differences emerge. It is then that major religious minorities, including Greeks, Armenians, and Jews, pulled ahead of the Muslim majority.

The foregoing patterns add a twist to the puzzle of why the Middle East's global standing deteriorated. Suppose that the rigidities of Islamic law somehow harmed Muslims economically. If communities free to reject the problematic institutions were held back as well, one of two inferences may be drawn. Either Islamic law was less significant than supposed, or something kept non-Muslims from developing different institutions. These possibilities will be considered, but only after long-term consequences of the Islamic institutional nexus have been identified. Before the eighteenth century, later chapters show, religious minorities had incentives to exercise their commercial freedoms in favor of Islamic business practices. Starting in the eighteenth century, changes in the global economy motivated Jews and Christians to favor practices developed abroad, within different legal systems. The freedom of legal choice that allowed the switch was itself integral to the Islamic legal system.

What Is to Be Explained

Evidently there was an extended period when Middle Eastern institutions pertaining to production, finance, exchange, conflict resolution, and governance were considered reasonably efficient, even worth adopting. Whatever their handicaps, visible in hindsight, prior to the modern era these could not have been significant enough to make the Middle East seem economically dysfunctional.

The distinction between static and dynamic advantages is critical here. The former refer to gains obtainable immediately, the latter to benefits available over the longer run, through induced transformations. Around 1500, a quarter-millennium before the start of modern economic growth, the Middle Eastern mix of institutions provided static advantages to regions that deployed them. Those same institutions proved disadvantageous dynamically, in suppressing the structural creativity necessary to preserve competitiveness. Consequently, wherever Islamic law struck roots the nineteenth and twentieth centuries witnessed far-reaching reforms aimed at stimulating the local economy.

The preceding distinction helps us to identify four broad historical patterns in need of explanation. First of all, we must make clear why the Middle East's economic system was long successful in the static sense of providing living standards similar, if not superior, to those elsewhere. This task requires uncovering the logic of the region's economic institutions grounded in Islamic law. We need to analyze, for example, how Islamic partnerships facilitated long-distance trade.

Second, we must uncover ensuing structural rigidities to identify why those institutions were less successful dynamically than in static terms. Certain Islamic institutions of the premodern Middle East now appear strikingly stable because western institutions performing the same functions *did* give rise, in stages, to the more complex institutions of modern global capitalism. Hence, understanding the factors responsible for the West's dynamism will help to isolate obstacles to self-generated development in the Middle East. They will elucidate also why Islamic institutions well adapted to medieval conditions seemed impoverished a millennium later.

No region as large as the Middle East or western Europe has uniform institutions. Variations must be considered, but only insofar as they help to identify fundamental causes of region-wide underdevelopment. It would hinder our goal to catalogue colorful differences irrespective of dynamic significance, in the manner of a butterfly collector exhibiting variety for its own sake. A key difference is that between the institutional trajectories of western Europe and the Middle East's own Christian communities. The latter, like the Muslims among whom they lived, were institutional stragglers. They may have embraced modern banking faster than Muslims, but the early banks that they formed, served, and used were built on western models, and some were also western-founded and -owned.[34] Our third task, then, is to link these temporal relationships to the pattern of primary interest, namely, the region's loss of economic prominence. Put differently, in interpreting why the Middle East as a whole became underdeveloped, we must make sense of the fortunes of its religious minorities—latecomers to economic modernity themselves, but quick adapters relative to Muslims.

Finally, in explicating interactions between the Middle East and the West, we must recognize that these developed under special rules enshrined in trade treaties. Insofar as the Middle East's structural evolution stalled in contexts critical to economic performance, these rules could have alleviated the resulting handicaps. Examining them will bring to the fore certain key characteristics of the Middle Eastern paths to sustained growth.

The heart of the agenda is to examine the dynamics of private economic organization in the premodern Middle East. Why critical transformations failed to occur is the question we seek to answer. Where the particulars involve religion, it is to religion that the argument must lead.

2

Analyzing the Economic Role of Islam

For Middle Eastern intellectuals the mid-nineteenth century was a time of humiliation and anxiety. Once considered backward, Europeans were now living more prosperously and subjugating Muslims. Although none developed a coherent explanation for this shift in fortunes, many sensed that it had something to do with religion.[1] There are several reasons to think that their intuition had a basis in fact.

One has already been given: certain key economic institutions of the Islamic Middle East were intertwined with Islam's holy law. These institutions emerged in the early centuries of Islam, when temporal and spiritual matters were not sharply divided. The laws of the time did not distinguish, as they now effectively do, between the secular and religious realms of life. Rules and regulations could gain identification with Islam even if their origins lay in the pursuit of power and wealth. Thereafter, to attempt institutional reform would be to risk a confrontation with religion. The risk could vary across contexts. The Islamic inheritance system was based on the Quran, and it differed palpably from some of its alternatives. By contrast, the rights and duties of shoemakers, even where rationalized through scripture, carried little spiritual significance. The rules of footwear production did not differentiate Muslims from Christians in any meaningful way. Nevertheless, certain institutions of great significance for investment, productivity, and exchange *were* grounded in Islamic teachings.

A second reason to investigate Islam's economic role is that from the seventh century onward, religion constituted an overarching marker of identity and social status. For legal and administrative purposes the rights and responsibilities of Muslims were differentiated from those of non-Muslims. There also existed identities that we now classify as ethnic, linguistic, or cultural. But these were all secondary identities akin to today's lower-level identities based on profession and neighborhood.

Nationalist historiography obscures the historical importance of religion by reading into the distant past secular classifications that began to emerge in the nineteenth century. Yet, at least in the Islamic world, even ardent nationalists have had to accommodate religious sentiments. At the end of World War I, before setting out to create a Turkish nation out of peoples who defined themselves primarily in religious terms, Kemal Atatürk presented his mission as repelling foreign invaders to save the Islamic caliphate. If he went on to repress traditional Islam, it was because devout Turks formed a potentially powerful conservative bloc.

A third reason to investigate the economic effects of Islam is that successive governments of the region upheld Islamic institutions. The Umayyad, Abbassid, Fatimid, Mamluk, Safavid, Seljuk, and Ottoman dynasties all consulted Muslim scholars, even as they responded to challenges creatively. They carried Islamic economic structures to places that came under their rule. Middle Eastern cities of the fourteenth century harbored similar economic structures. None enjoyed legal personhood, as thousands of cities did in the West. They all deployed Islamic courts for formal dispute resolution.

At no time was every facet of economic life ruled by Islam. The tenth-century sultans who governed the Abbasid Empire from Baghdad did not consult the Quran on every policy decision. But religion could leave a mark even in contexts where no conscious effort was made to follow it. The administrations of all premodern dynasties included clerics. Also, the prevailing Islamic institutions constrained every policy option.

Institutional Frontiers of Economic Life

The constraints imposed by any given Islamic institution could differ among regions, and between cities and the countryside. If for no other reason, the complexity, scale, and other characteristics of economic activity exhibited diversity. Some variants of a particular Islamic institution could support exchanges that were too complex for others. Given our central objective—to pinpoint obstacles to economic modernization in the Middle East—it makes sense to focus on the region's most advanced institutions. It is the most sophisticated institutions of a civilization that determine the frontiers of its economic capabilities, not the simpler, more primitive variants.

In the sixteenth century the bazaars of Istanbul and Cairo offered much more variety than those of Manisa or Qus. The former pair also offered access to a wider range of specialized craftsmen, greater chances of meeting entrepreneurs looking for partnering opportunities, and more exposure to foreign merchants. Hence, the Middle East's economic efficiency relative to other regions depended more critically on the characteristics of commerce in big cities than on those in small towns. It is the former that defined the region's institutional frontiers.

Institutional transformations that would advance those frontiers were more probable in the region's largest trading centers, because that is where entrepreneurs were most likely to feel constrained by existing organizational options and seek more complex alternatives. In some ways, economic life in lesser known settlements was more representative of the region as a whole. But leadership, not representativeness, is what matters here. To determine why the Middle East failed to modernize on its own, one must identify the obstacles present in places most likely to have spearheaded innovations. When modern economic institutions were transplanted to the region, the main economic centers led the way. This is because their existing institutions were relatively advanced and their residents were more accustomed to novelty and diversity.

The institutional frontiers of the Middle East were not fixed, of course, in a geographic sense. In the early decades of Islam, Mecca was among the leading commercial centers of the emerging Arab Empire, and among its sources of institutional creativity. By the ninth century Baghdad, Cairo, Qayrawan, and Córdoba were all far more significant economically. Much later, Istanbul, as the Ottoman capital, became the region's leading commercial center; the other major centers included Cairo, Alexandria, Aleppo, and Salonika, all by then under Ottoman rule. These patterns require us to focus on the Arab empires in relation to the first six or so centuries of Islamic history, and the Ottoman Empire for the period between the fifteenth and nineteenth centuries.

Like every other premodern state under Muslim rule, the Ottoman Empire failed to generate key institutions of the modern economy organically. However, not all of its institutions stagnated. Besides, it was the first Muslim polity to recognize and then seek to overcome its organizational handicaps. Egypt, nominally still under Ottoman rule at the initiation of mid-nineteenth century reforms, usually followed the Ottoman lead. So did Iran, the only major Middle Eastern country never integrated into the Ottoman fold. Precisely because they were relatively quick to adapt, the Ottomans ruled longer than the other two major Muslim dynasties present at the start of modern economic growth: the Safavids of Iran and the Mughals of India.[2] These patterns reinforce the rationale for paying close attention to the Ottoman institutional trajectory in exploring why the Middle East modernized with a lag.

In principle, the roots of Ottoman economic difficulties could have lain in departures from Islam, rather than in a failure to abandon Islamic economic institutions. Modern Islamists make this point to discredit works that rely on the Ottoman experience to demonstrate the inefficiency of Islamic institutions. But Ottoman secularization came mainly after the empire became economically underdeveloped, not before. Prior to the mid-nineteenth century, the Ottomans tried to extend the reach of Islamic institutions and raise awareness of them. With increasing vigor after Syria and Egypt submitted to their rule in 1517, they sought popular legitimacy by claiming to obey Islamic strictures.[3] So links between Islam and economic performance, where present, should be observable in the Ottoman context.

The institutional frontiers of the Middle East determined its capacity to produce and exchange. Whether that capacity amounted to underdevelopment depended also on the institutional frontiers of western Europe, which ushered in the modern economy. As in the Middle East, in the West institutional frontiers shifted over time. In the early Middle Ages, the Italian city-states offered the most advanced markets and established most foreign colonies in the eastern Mediterranean. By the twelfth century, northern Europe had become a center of innovation through the Champagne fairs. Eventually, primacy in market expansion passed to England, France, and the Low Countries. That is why in accounts of the economic ascent of the West, the focus migrates over time from Italy to Holland and England.[4] The following analysis exhibits a similar move. In searching for clues regarding Middle Eastern organizational stagnation, we will focus primarily on Italy in the early Islamic centuries, but almost exclusively on northern Europe subsequently.

Our inquiry will involve comparisons, then, between the Middle East's institutional frontiers and those of western Europe. In both regions the locus of institutional creativity shifted geographically during the period of interest. In successive contexts, we shall be tracking both movements, staying focused on the most advanced institutions of each region.

Unintended Consequences and the Potency of Minor Distinctions

Explaining why the institutional frontiers of two regions advanced at different rates requires the identification of social mechanisms responsible for the observed patterns. A social mechanism is usually more than a causal relationship between variables. It may incorporate feedback effects, such as conservative reactions to cries for reform. But it is less general than a "social law," in that it may represent a constellation of social forces unique to a place and time.[5]

Until modern times Middle Eastern cities lacked a corporate status; none had standing before the law as an organization, as thousands of Europeans already did in the Middle Ages. To make sense of the Middle Eastern pattern, we need to pinpoint a social mechanism that kept them wedded to a traditional form of administration. Likewise, explaining why their financial markets remained atomistic requires finding one or more mechanisms that prevented

Middle Eastern cities lacked corporate status, unlike cities in Europe

the emergence of banks. Ordinarily, the mechanisms at play will have universal elements, such as efforts to shelter wealth against taxation. But the mechanisms themselves could be unique to Islam, the Middle East, or even a single economic sector. Some of the mechanisms identified in later chapters have analogues in China and India. Others do not, because they depended on conditions particular to the Middle East.

The actors who drive a social mechanism through their decisions may well anticipate and intend the consequences. Successive sultans who banned the export of strategic commodities must have understood that their policies would tempt smugglers, and also that the required monitoring would leave fewer personnel to enforce other regulations. However, in interpreting the motion of a complex social system one must avoid exaggerating what individual actors could have foreseen and willed.

That is a common error. Observing that in the nineteenth century the Middle East's banking and insurance sectors harbored disproportionately few Muslims, certain scholars claim that this pattern is rooted in Muslim aversion to interest or in policies designed to weaken Muslim merchants.[6] Each claim treats the observed participation deficit as an intended and anticipated outcome. Even if some actors wanted minorities to dominate the financial sector, neither claim withstands scrutiny. The first leaves unexplained why credit users and providers abided by an interest ban, if in fact they did. The second fails to elucidate why Muslim merchants accepted limitations on their advancement. Neither claim addresses why Middle Eastern actors behaved differently from similarly situated actors elsewhere, for example, English kings, merchants, financiers, and borrowers.

Actually, there is no evidence that Muslim rulers wanted to marginalize their co-religionists in the most lucrative sectors of the emerging modern economy, or that the founders of Islam's canonical schools of law intended to handicap their descendants in financial markets. The troubling patterns of the nineteenth century emerged through processes unimaginable in earlier times. Moreover, the institutions of early Islam had unintended effects. Shortly we shall see that the Islamic inheritance system lowered the Muslim

share of global commerce and delayed Middle Eastern industrialization. The effects were not planned, and neither became an issue
during the rise of Islam, as its inheritance rules took shape. They
are among the unintended consequences of institutions meant to
spread wealth, strengthen families, and promote political stability.[7]

It is often noted that the Islamic inheritance system benefited
wives and daughters, who lacked inheritance rights in pre-Islamic
Arabia. Typically overlooked is that, regardless of its distributional
benefits, it also contributed to organizational stagnation. This
failure illustrates the pervasive tendency to focus on first-order
effects, in other words, the immediate consequences for particular
groups. Dubbed the "fallacy of overlooking secondary consequences," it makes analysts neglect broader social effects over
longer periods.[8] A full-blown inquiry into the economic effects of
a religion must look beyond short-run and direct effects to longer
and indirect consequences. Apart from examining the effects on
targeted groups, it must explore those on others, including generations not yet born. Second-order effects are often more significant for economic modernization than the corresponding first-order
effects.

Another common fallacy is the perception that major social
phenomena, such as the decline of a civilization, must have major
causes. It manifests itself in works that attribute the Middle East's
enfeeblement to huge flaws in its dominant religion. According to
an influential historian, the Arabs who shaped Islam feared innovation and disdained knowledge originating from outsiders; by
contrast, Europeans were generally receptive to inventions, regardless of their origins.[9] This contrast is overblown. At least initially
the Arabs borrowed widely from civilizations that they encountered.[10] In any case, a chain of responses to a minor initial distinction can produce a cumulatively huge effect.

Middle Eastern history offers many examples of small differences
that proved significant. One lies in trade privileges bestowed on
western merchants. Initially these privileges were targeted at specific
commercial ventures. They were also revocable at will. Over time,
they broadened in scope and became practically irrevocable. Although no observer of Mamluk Egypt would have considered the

privileges of Venetian traders relevant to the region's future economic standing, in fact they placed the Middle East on a slippery slope toward economic subjugation. Limiting Muslim participation in cross-Mediterranean trade, the privileges made local rulers dependent for trade on foreign merchants. They also dampened states' incentives to upgrade domestic commercial capabilities.

That social phenomena may have consequences disproportionate to their immediate significance poses analytical complications. It implies that to explain the great divergence of interest here we cannot look simply for distinctions that were, or should have been, considered significant early on. Identifying initial institutions, relationships, and incentives without prejudging whether they affected later developments, we must look for social mechanisms that made certain factors self-amplifying, triggered chain reactions, and fostered rigidities.

Path Dependence

A common theme in historical analyses featuring unintended consequences is path dependence—the dependence of future outcomes on past trajectories.[11] Confronted with identical circumstances, two societies may respond in unique ways because of historic contingencies. In the late sixteenth century, large and durable commercial companies assumed a critical role in the expansion of intercontinental trade, and they promoted global institutional homogenization, the process now called globalization. These early overseas companies originated in the West, where merchants had a history of forming durable organizations; western rulers supported the overseas companies to share in their profits through taxation. Middle Eastern intercontinental traders of the period had no formal organizations, not even guilds. Hence, they were ill-prepared for forming large and durable global trading companies, and rulers lacked a motive to assist them in international markets. The organizational histories of the two groups were critical, then, to the subsequent organizational divergence.

If past failures can limit future options, so can past successes. In the premodern Middle East, sundry social services were provided in a decentralized manner, without reliance on huge bureaucracies. The instrument of delivery was an Islamic form of trust known as a waqf. This magnificent institution limited incentives to develop alternative organizational forms for supplying social services. If autonomous urban governments did not develop until the nineteenth century, this is partly because waqfs already served many of their functions. The inflexibility of waqfs became an obvious handicap only with industrialization, whose new technologies created a need for reallocating vast resources quickly. The observed inflexibility also contributed to rigidities in other areas by limiting organizational know-how. As we shall see later, the development of the waqf from the eighth century onward placed the Middle East on a path that produced massive economic difficulties in the age of industrialization.

Historical analyses involving path dependence share a basic characteristic with theories of "endogenous" economic growth. In these theories, innovations are generated through the prevailing stock of ideas. Because new ideas come from combining existing ideas, innovations feed on themselves by expanding the repository of knowledge. The process of discovery thus entails increasing returns to scale—the economist's way of saying that as the stock of discoveries grows the cost per new discovery falls. Societies that achieve a critical mass of ideas experience self-sustaining growth; others stagnate.[12] Endogenous growth theory illuminates the geographic divergence that characterizes the epoch of modern economic growth. Regions that were modernizing at its start have generally continued to lead the modernization process. By virtue of leading the transition from personal to impersonal exchange, and having experience at solving the organizational challenges of this transition, they have played a vastly disproportionate role in expanding the frontier of organizational techniques. Regions that started to modernize defensively, and largely by imitation, have tended to remain organizational laggards. In forthcoming chapters we will see that the social mechanisms responsible for keeping the

Middle East an organizational follower mirror those of endogenous growth theory.

To identify instances of path dependence is not to pinpoint why societies started out on different paths. Among our challenges is to elucidate why the Middle East and western Europe placed themselves on divergent paths with regard to organizational capacity. The farther we step back, the less the economic institutions of the two regions appear different. Early on in the second millennium the institutional matrix was geared to personal exchange throughout Eurasia. We must locate the small distinctions that induced self-reinforcing institutional differences.

Institutional trajectories are related to distributions of political power. Where states pursue mercantilist policies, the proximate reason is that merchants can use the state to their advantage. Likewise, where states pursue anti-mercantilist policies, as those of the Middle East long did, it is because merchants are politically weak. The political clout of merchants is itself path-dependent. They can remain powerless by operating under institutions inimical to capital accumulation.[13] Explaining how the political weaknesses of merchants and the atomism of their enterprises proved mutually reinforcing is part of our agenda.

Self-Transformation

Our main charge is thus to identify why private economic life in the Middle East did not transform itself in the course of a millennium when another part of Eurasia exhibited sustained dynamism. Previously, in the early Islamic centuries, the commercial and financial institutions of the Middle East displayed remarkable flexibility. Part of the challenge is to reconcile that history of Middle Eastern dynamism, along with west European institutional creativity in the second millennium, with the more recent history of organizational stagnation in the Middle East. The broader task, then, is to account for change as well as stagnation.

Uncovering mechanisms that illuminate both change and stagnation is a mission that numerous thinkers have pursued. Karl Marx sought to explain how self-reproducing economic systems could give rise, over time, to more advanced systems. Charles Darwin invoked natural selection to reconcile the co-existence of species with their origins and evolution.[14] Each thinker proposed mechanisms that drive a broad system's internal dynamics. That is what we are seeking here. It will not suffice to show how outside forces affected economic life in the Middle East. Events such as the Mongol invasions of the mid-1200s and the Black Death of the mid-1300s devastated certain places.[15] But the particulars of economic life depended also on choices made in response to local institutions. In fact, the region's own institutions slowed its recovery from the calamities of the Middle Ages, and the stagnation of those institutions led, centuries later, to economic disappointments that necessitated massive reforms.

Identifying the global implications of Europe's dynamism is the essence of the "world-systems" approach to modern history. In historical accounts that exemplify this literature, the Middle East appears as a passive player situated within the West's "periphery." Like other peripheral regions, it follows the rhythms of western industrialization and conquests. Before the West begins to dominate the world, Middle Eastern institutions are stable; in the course of the expansion, they adapt to western needs.[16] This interpretation leaves unexplained why nothing akin to the western self-transformation unfolded in the Middle East. It also ignores adaptational variations within the periphery. By itself the western trajectory does not explain why Christians and Jews of the Middle East were quicker to pursue mass manufacturing than its politically dominant Muslims.

Where institutions are stagnant, the induced behaviors are self-reproducing. The equilibrium could be upset by an external shock of the sort that world-systems theorists highlight. A major external threat, or new opportunities created by an outside discovery, could have made Middle Eastern merchants upset long-standing commercial patterns through their reactions. However, institutional transformation does not require an external shock. What initiated the transformation of western economic institutions in the early Middle Ages was not shocks emanating from China or the Middle

East. Rather, the institutions themselves induced responses that weakened the incentives to reproduce them.[17]

Hence, the key to the West's observed process of modernization is that its institutions were *self-undermining* and ultimately *self-transforming*. The corresponding institutional complex in the Middle East proved generally *self-enforcing*, if not *self-reinforcing*.[18] If the Middle East reacted to global economic modernization with a delay, this is precisely because over the preceding centuries its indigenous economic institutions gained immunity to outside shocks.[19] Chapters ahead will substantiate this claim.

Shifts in Institutional Efficiency

Insofar as the Middle East's capacity for self-transformation is at issue, it will not do to list its economic institutions at a point in time and tally their economic benefits and drawbacks. An institution hospitable to bilateral trade may turn into an inhibitor of market expansion by blocking more complex forms of exchange. The usefulness of a stable institution will vary over time, depending on the evolution of other institutions, relative prices, and technology. This may seem obvious. Yet, works that consider Islam a source of unmitigated economic strength treat the effects of institutions as fixed. So do certain rival works that portray Islam as a steady impediment to progress. In each case, a presumption of fixity makes it impossible to explain variations in the Middle East's relative performance.

To start with the apologetic literature, consider "Islamic economics," the modern school of thought that offers a distinctly Islamic variant of economics. The first Islamic society in seventh-century Arabia, observes Islamic economics, was a mercantile society. Its leader, Muhammad, was a successful merchant who understood the creation of commercial wealth. Various recollections of his words and deeds (*hadīth*) promoted trust in the marketplace and strengthened private property rights, as did certain verses of the Quran. Having found attributes favorable to exchange and accumulation in early Islam, the promoters of Islamic economics reason that the benefits would have been permanent.

What explains, then, why the Middle East became underdeveloped? Islamic economics invokes factors that blocked the attainment of Islamic ideals. One contributor explains that Muslim economic practices have seldom matched Islamic teachings, and that European intervention worsened the consequences: "The gap separating Muslims from the ideal of Islam's economic doctrine widened considerably when the Muslim world fell under European occupation and when the colonial masters replaced traditional Muslim systems with their own legal and economic institutions. This unhappy situation lasted for too long and caused deep stagnation and the spreading of ignorance and poverty."[20]

The last sentence gets several facts backward. For all its discontents, the Middle East's colonial period brought fundamental transformation, not stagnation; rising literacy and education, not spreading ignorance; and enrichment at unprecedented rates, not immiserization.[21] But it is the underlying thinking that requires attention here. In lamenting the demise of traditional institutions, the Islamist interpretation invokes a timeless and context-independent concept of efficiency. Traditional Muslim institutions performed ideally, it asserts, until inferior European institutions took their place. It thus overlooks that useful institutions might become dysfunctional as the global economy evolves. Likewise, it denies that foreign institutions can broaden capabilities. The Islamist logic leaves unexplained, of course, why the Middle East "fell under European occupation" when it did; why "colonial masters" promoted institutional reforms that not even Islamists themselves want to undo; why peoples of the region allowed, even welcomed, foreign initiatives; and why a "gap" between Muslim economic life and the "ideal of Islam's economic doctrine" opened up centuries before European colonization.

Analogous flaws are present in writings focused on the shortcomings of traditional Islamic institutions, as opposed to their effectiveness. Among these works, those of Max Weber have been the most influential. One of Weber's claims is that the lack of an

Islamic concept of corporation handicapped Middle Eastern cities by hindering urban self-administration.[22] As far as the industrial era is concerned, this is a sound observation. In itself, however, it sheds no light on the Middle East's reversal of fortune. In the sixteenth century the public services available to residents of Istanbul and Cairo were not noticeably inferior to those available to Parisians. Three centuries later, Middle Eastern cities looked relatively disorganized and poorly administered. Evidently the disadvantage of lacking corporate law had grown. The worsening handicap cannot be explained through a static model predicated on fixity.

Although Weber recognizes that the handicap grew over time, he does not explain its persistence. He simply asserts that the irrationality of Islam inhibited any thought of reform.[23] Yet, the Middle Eastern social system never became frozen, as Weber's writings imply. As the taxable capacities of economic sectors changed, tax systems were modified in ways that make sense to modern scholars. Evidently, rationality was not lacking across the board. Given that the Middle Eastern social system harbored fluid elements, it is hardly obvious why its vehicle for delivering urban services was not overhauled before the nineteenth century; nor is it obvious why reforms that brought corporate law to the Middle East had to await the early 1900s. Perturbations in the broader system might have destabilized established urban structures much earlier. A full explanation for the Middle East's historical trajectory must include reasons why the decline in the efficiency of its traditional institutions took so long to elicit reforms.

Local vs. Global Optimality

The residents of cities that delivered services primarily through waqfs at a time when self-governing municipalities offered a superior alternative did not necessarily understand the inefficiencies that are plainly visible now. Many of them must have considered the existing structures optimal. In fact, the residents who financed fountains, schools, and charities through waqfs were using the most advanced of only the locally known means of supply. Had they known of better means of delivery, they might have channeled resources differently. These observations highlight the distinction between local and global optimality.

This distinction is easiest to recognize with respect to topography. South of Mecca is Mount Taif, which towers over lesser mountains in the area. To a person confined to Mecca's environs, it appears as the top of the world. In fact, higher mountains exist farther south, in Yemen, and they themselves are dwarfed by the highest peaks of Ethiopia, across the Red Sea. What appears highest thus depends on the area in view. So it is with locally optimal institutions—social arrangements that maximize efficiency within particular constraints. A person facing those constraints will consider the institutions indispensable. Likewise, an analyst narrowly focused on his particular locality will find the institutions in question advantageous. The same institution need not impress an analyst who studies a broader area and is familiar with alternatives developed elsewhere. The scholar with a greater geographic range will understand that locally optimal institutions can be suboptimal in a global sense. Global optimality is itself a variable property. An institution that is globally optimal in one period may become globally suboptimal as a result of new institutions developed somewhere else.

In chapters ahead, I point to dynamic disadvantages of institutions that distinguished scholars have characterized as evidence of economic success. Likewise, I identify as globally inefficient practices that, from a strictly local perspective, look very useful. Two examples will illustrate how my comparative analysis differs in scope from popular historical traditions in Middle East studies.

Maxime Rodinson's *Islam and Capitalism* shows that the Quran is replete with praise for commerce. Indeed, Islam's holy book goes so far as to encourage combining worship with material pursuits.[24] Rodinson also documents that the recollections of Muhammad's life contain innumerable laudatory comments about merchants. "At the Day of Resurrection," Muhammad reportedly said on one occasion, "the trustworthy merchant will sit in the shade of Allah's throne."[25] In the same vein, an early caliph is reputed to have muttered: "Death can come upon me nowhere more pleasantly than where I am engaged in business in the market, buying and selling on behalf of my family."[26] Mecca, where Muhammad began spreading his message, was a commercial society, Rodinson also stresses, and the young Muhammad made a living as a merchant. He infers that early Muslims were not lacking in commercial encouragement or motivation. Legitimating the development of capitalism, Islam facilitated the Middle East's economic growth, he says.[27]

By the standards of the Middle Ages early Islam *was* hospitable to commerce. In addition to attitudes favorable to enrichment, it supported flourishing commercial centers. As needs evolved, Muslim jurists of early Islam developed the partnership types already known at Muhammad's birth. Their refinements contributed to the Middle East's subsequent commercial successes. By the same token, early Islam's commercial institutions appear simple in relation to those of any modern economy, rich or poor. The commodity exchanges, stock markets, and banks of Saudi Arabia—all contributors to its present wealth—had no analogues in the Prophet's time. Did the institutions of early Islam carry the seeds of institutions suited to the complexity and volume of trade today? There are reasons, all developed ahead, for doubting that they did. Suffice it to note here that modern economic institutions were transplanted to Arabia centuries after their emergence elsewhere.

Following Rodinson's footsteps, historians of later periods laud the trade and production carried under the Islamic legal system. "The legal system was not a barrier to carrying out business," writes Nelly Hanna, the author of a well-crafted biography of Abu Taqiyya, a seventeenth-century Egyptian merchant. "Quite the contrary," she says, merchants "could turn it into an asset."[28] In fact, the possibilities open to an Egyptian merchant of the seventeenth century did not include operating within a joint-stock company, such as the Levant Company, already active in the eastern Mediterranean. Nor could an Egyptian imagine investing in corporations of the sort included in the Dow Jones-Egypt index of the Cairo and Alexandria stock exchanges. Even a merchant at the pinnacle of pre-industrial Egypt's commercial possibilities had a horizon that excluded the higher peaks known to his contemporaries based across the Mediterranean, and discovered much later by his own descendants. Why Abu Taqiyya's business practices were suboptimal in a global sense is something in need of explanation.

Overarching Analytical Themes and Principles

The many analytical themes and principles introduced in this chapter make repeated appearances in the inquiry that follows. Comparisons between the Islamic Middle East and the region that overtook it focus on localities most advanced in economic terms, in other words, on economic frontiers. The analysis aims to uncover the social mechanisms responsible for observed patterns of change and stagnation, not simply to identify trajectories. The explored policy effects include both intended and unintended consequences. Again and again we shall see that history constrains opportunities, that institutions can transform themselves, and that their efficiency can change with evolving conditions. Finally, the distinctions between global and local optimality will come up frequently.

I suggested above that the emergence of Islam stimulated commerce. The particulars will provide an appropriate entry point to the broader analysis. What was the cutting edge of commerce in the seventh century, and in what ways did Islam matter?

PART II

Organizational Stagnation

3

Commercial Life under Islamic Rule

Although little is known about Muhammad's early years, historians generally believe that he worked as a commercial agent for a powerful clan in Mecca. Among the people he served was a wealthy widow named Khadija, whom he later married.[1] Muhammad's trading career is sometimes invoked as evidence of Islam's compatibility with free enterprise and with commercial cooperation across groups defined by descent.[2] The underlying logic is strained. It is akin to stating that because Jesus was a carpenter, Christians must have a special knack for making furniture. Nevertheless, it is significant that the founder of Islam was a successful merchant. His familiarity with markets and commercial risks predisposed him to strengthening mercantile institutions. A polity under his leadership would have granted merchants influence. It was unlikely to equate profit making with exploitation, as the thinkers of antiquity usually did.[3]

Unsurprisingly, the Quran endorses private property, encourages commerce, and supports personal enrichment. Some of its verses characterize profit as Allah's bounty to humanity.[4] Others allow the believer to combine piety with profit seeking. There is even a passage that legitimates commerce during the annual pilgrimage (*hajj*).[5] The last provision bestowed approval on a prominent pre-Islamic practice of Arabia, thus encouraging its continuation. Once every lunar year, pagan tribes visited the Kaba, Mecca's cuboidal shrine. There they suspended their endemic quarrels temporarily, to worship and conduct business in peace. Ridding the Kaba of its idols, Muhammad redefined it as Islam's most sacred sanctuary and the focal point of its main commercial forum.

This was only one of the steps that early Muslim leaders took to promote commerce within the Middle East and across regions. After reviewing the economic significance of the Islamic pilgrimage, we shall see how, in its early centuries, Islam stimulated global commerce also through distinct commercial partnership rules. The institutional creativity of early Islam is particularly significant in view of the subsequent stagnation in commercial organization.

Trade during the Islamic Pilgrimage

Islam requires every Muslim, regardless of proximity to Mecca, to participate in the annual pilgrimage at least once if his or her circumstances permit. Accounts of this event usually characterize it as a magnificent ritual.[6] However, until recently it also served a major economic function. Performed during three specified days, it provided an occasion for lively trade. Many pilgrims financed their pilgrimage through trade alone. Fortunes were made by repeating the journey year after year.[7]

The pilgrimage to Mecca is the Islamic equivalent of pilgrimages undertaken by Jews and Christians. But neither Judaism nor Christianity considered the pilgrimage an economic event, certainly never the backdrop for a trade fair.[8] By contrast, the Quran treats the economic side of the Islamic pilgrimage as inseparable from its religious side. Immediately after a passage describing the pilgrimage duty, it reiterates the legitimacy of commerce: "It is no sin for you to seek the bounty of your Lord by trading."[9] In practice, too, the pilgrimage was intertwined with commerce. At the start of his journey a pilgrim would be blessed through the formula: "May Allah accept your pilgrimage, condone your sins, and let you find a good market for your wares."[10]

The Islamic pilgrimage brought buyers together with sellers, coordinating their bids and offers. In broadening each side of the market, it fostered competition among distant regions. It also helped to legitimize profit-driven commerce, raising the bar for groups pursuing an anti-market or redistributionist agenda. In all these ways, it stimulated long-distance trade and wealth accumulation. By the same token, until aviation the pilgrimage to Mecca was an arduous and expensive affair. It required aspirants to accumulate wealth, which must have stimulated work. Significantly, the financial burden was lightest for merchants. Unlike craftsmen and farmers, whose work had to be performed on site, merchants could perform the pilgrimage as a byproduct of lucrative commercial activity.

Before Islam, Mecca had served as a link in the trade between Byzantium and India.[11] Evidently Muhammad understood the significance of commerce to Mecca's prosperity. After emigrating to Medina with early converts, he broke Mecca's resistance by disrupting the caravan trade on which it depended even for food.[12] Only when the city's leaders joined the fold of Islam did he restore its commercial prominence. Bedouins living along the routes to Mecca were accustomed to being paid for allowing caravans safe passage.[13] The practice of buying them off continued after most converted to Islam. Right up to the twentieth century tribes along pilgrimage routes received regular payments in exchange for exercising restraint.[14]

Quantitative data on the pilgrimage are unavailable for the early Islamic period, but estimates exist for later times. According to an Arab observer of the thirteenth century, 40,000 Egyptians made the journey each year, along with an equal number of Iraqis and Syrians. In the sixteenth century a Portuguese witness estimated that 200,000 people gathered in Mecca, accompanied by 300,000 animals, some for sacrifice, others for trade.[15] If even a quarter of these pilgrims conducted commerce, the pilgrimage would have constituted a vast economic enterprise. Until the nineteenth century the pilgrimage to Mecca remained the Islamic world's leading commercial event. Today it holds economic significance only for western Arabia, whose merchants look to the pilgrimage period much as American retailers await the Christmas season.

The Islamic pilgrimage created wealth directly by fostering opportunities for safe commerce, and indirectly through the exchange of news among pilgrims and the spread of customs and canons of thought. On the downside, its success as a vehicle for concentrated commerce probably hindered the development of secular fairs to link together merchants from across the Islamic world. In fact, the

Middle East developed no nonreligious fairs as important as the Champagne fairs of medieval northern Europe.[16] Initiated as seasonal events, the Champagne fairs turned into essentially permanent pan-European markets. They fueled the evolution of various institutions critical to modern capitalism.[17] Considered a sacred tradition, the Islamic pilgrimage could not have evolved as freely as secular fairs. An attempt to modify its location, duration, frequency, or timing according to the solar year would have provoked charges of sacrilege. Thus, an unintended consequence of the Islamic pilgrimage may have been the foreclosing of an important stimulus to economic modernization.

Cooperative Ventures across Families

Many of the merchants who performed a pilgrimage were self-financed. As such, they shouldered all the concomitant risks, but also claimed any profits in full. Others drew on the resources of family members, who shared in both gains and losses. During the pilgrimage season, as at other times, preexisting bonds of trust facilitated cooperative ventures among family members by attenuating problems of common ownership, supervision, and profit sharing. Kinship substituted for markets also with regard to insurance and credit.

Precisely because they obviated third-party regulation through laws, partnerships among family members were, and remain, common in the Middle East, as elsewhere. Yet a kin-based cooperative venture has glaring limitations. Its access to capital is bounded by the wealth of a single family. It offers a restrictive capacity to disperse risks. Family ties can cause seniority and sentiment to dictate decisions, trumping knowledge and competence.[18] Hence, social gains can flow from institutions supportive of cooperative ventures across kin groups.

A great achievement of world religions has been the cultivation of trust and the facilitation of cooperation among non-kin. Like Judaism and Christianity, Islam served these ends, and thus laid the groundwork for a commercial expansion, by promoting religious brotherhood. Of course, strengthening religious ties carries the risk of limiting exchanges with outsiders. More trust among Muslims could imply less trust between Muslims and non-Muslims. However, Islam strove also to promote exchanges across confessional boundaries. It instituted laws to regulate partnerships among possibly unrelated individuals, including not only non-kin but also the adherents of different faiths.

These laws sprung, some analysts believe, from Quranic commandments. Here is an often-invoked passage: "When the prayers are ended, disperse and go in quest of Allah's bounty." And another: "Believers, do not consume your wealth among yourselves in vanity, but rather trade with it by mutual consent."[19] But the implied institutional associations are tenuous. In promoting commerce, such directives say nothing specific about commercial organization or about cooperation across communities. In any case, the partnership per se was not an Islamic innovation. At the dawn of Islam, partnerships among non-kin were common in the Mediterranean region. Hence, the Muslim jurists who developed an Islamic law of partnerships did not start from scratch. They built on established customs of Arabia, Mesopotamia, Persia, and Greece, and also Jewish and Christian traditions.

Early Muslim jurists gave various preexisting commercial rules an Islamic identity by recasting them as deriving from moral principles found in the Quran. They also undertook successive refinements, usually to accommodate the needs of merchants. That Muslim jurists pursued commercial efficiency is not surprising, because at the time, according to one study, 75 percent of all jurists and other religious scholars (*'ulamā'*) earned a living primarily from business.[20] Remarkably, this exercise of mercantile power was under way two centuries before the merchants of northern Europe developed a common mercantile law (*lex mercatoria* or "law merchant") enforced by commercial courts composed of judges selected from their ranks.[21] The overlap between Muslim religious scholars and merchants is reflected in the course of study required to become a certified scholar. It included mathematics at a level needed to become a competent merchant.[22]

Although Islam's major schools of jurisprudence were not equally hospitable to merchants, they all adopted rules to strengthen mutual trust among unrelated individuals. The most widely followed school, the Hanafi, was particularly eager to accommodate mercantile needs. Three of the four major Sunni schools, including the Hanafi school, allowed partnerships between Muslims and non-Muslims. True, one of those three required every active party of an inter-faith partnership to be a Muslim, ostensibly to prevent the diversion of Muslim capital into un-Islamic pursuits such as the pig trade.[23] But it, too, recognized the usefulness of confessionally mixed cooperative ventures.

The development of Islamic partnership law did not make Middle Eastern commerce impersonal. Merchants and investors generally drew their partners from networks consisting of individuals who dealt with each other repeatedly. As Abraham Udovitch stresses, exchanges continued to be based on multifaceted personal relations.[24] Nevertheless, the development of partnership law was a giant step on the long road from kinship-based exchange to impersonal exchange—the type of exchange that now takes place between a bank and a depositor, between corporations, and between consumers and mail-order sellers. In helping to emancipate the individual from kinship-based networks, Islamic partnership law set the stage for replacing the "limited group morality" characteristic of tribal societies with a "generalized morality" consisting of abstract rules applicable to a broad range of social relations.[25]

Studies of Middle Eastern partnerships between the eleventh and eighteenth centuries show that most were formed between members of the same ethno-religious group—Turks with Turks, Arabs with Arabs, Jews with Jews, Greeks with Greeks, and so on. But in some places and periods, inter-faith partnerships were not uncommon. In seventeenth-century Istanbul, 14.9 percent of all partnerships included at least one Muslim and one or more non-Muslims. Even kadis, or Islamic judges, formed partnerships with non-Muslims.[26]

Islamic Partnerships

Cross-family partnerships played a critical role in premodern commercial life because families sought to diversify risks, and many merchants lacked the capital to venture out on their own. Capital-poor merchants sought financing from investors who preferred to leave the physical work to others. In the premodern Middle East, the Islamic law of partnerships regulated relationships formed between active merchants and passive investors. One option was to have the capital of the enterprise provided in its entirety by one or more sedentary investors, who would eschew a role in its management. This form of partnership was known as *mudāraba*. As an alternative, the merchants, too, contributed to the financing. The resulting partnership went by the name of *mushāraka* or *inān*.

The term "Islamic commercial partnership," or simply "Islamic partnership," serves as an umbrella term for all such contracts formed under Islamic law, including the variants just defined. Whatever the exact specifications, the partners split the profits, if any, according to a formula negotiated in advance. A passive investor's liability for losses was limited to his own investment. Liability for damages to third parties fell entirely on the merchant who caused the harm. Thus, an investor could not be blamed for the infractions of merchants that he was financing. In addition to carrying unlimited liability, a merchant faced an investment risk: his labor could come to nought.[27] However, he was not liable for loss of a passive partner's investment.[28]

Parties to an Islamic partnership enjoyed latitude in setting profit shares. A merchant could claim an advantage on the basis of intangibles such as reliability, geographic knowledge, and commercial expertise. Ordinarily investors gave their active partners broad freedoms to transact according to emerging opportunities. But an investor seeking to lessen his risk was free to constrain a merchant's mandate. He could limit the merchant's mission, geographic range, duration, expenses, and contacts. He could also make profit shares contingent upon the merchant's commercial choices.[29] Such restrictions served to economize on transaction costs—to minimize, that is, the resources spent on negotiating, monitoring, and enforcing exchanges. They thus reduced the possibility of the investors feeling ill-served or cheated. Legal treatises instructed partners to keep their agreements clear, encouraging the use of formulaic agreements designed to limit surprises and misunderstandings.[30]

The partnership forms used in the maritime cities of medieval Italy were motivated, similarly, by the efficient allocation of risks and expected returns.[31] They, too, recognized two classes of partners: active partners who ran the enterprise and carried unlimited liability, and passive partners who contributed capital and shared profits, without participating in management or carrying a risk beyond their investment. The most popular variants, *commenda* and *societas maris*, resembled *mudāraba* and *mushāraka*, respectively. Like Islamic partnerships, those of the Latin world drew into commerce individuals who could not run a business themselves.[32]

Both the *commenda* and the *mudāraba* offered more flexibility than the closest contractual form found in the Talmud, the Jewish *'isqā*. The *'isqā* required equality between the investor and merchant in terms of either profit shares or shares of liability. Although Maimonides' (1135–1204) codification of Jewish law, the *Mishneh Torah*, relaxed this condition, it still required the merchant to accept liability for part of the principal; in addition, it required his profit share to exceed his share of liability.[33] Meant to promote fairness, these restrictions often conflicted with the risk preferences of commercial partners. Two conclusions may be drawn. First, Islamic partnership law allowed the preferences of merchants and investors to trump certain fairness concerns that Islam shares with other religions. Second, at its emergence, it posed no handicap in the Mediterranean world. If anything, it offered identifiable commercial advantages over the known alternatives. People who entered into an Islamic partnership during Islam's first few centuries were using an organizational form that was, arguably, globally optimal.

Contributions to Global Trade

Given the foregoing account, it is unsurprising that Islamic partnership law saw use in medieval long-distance trade. Indeed, it struck roots in emporia that stretched beyond the Mediterranean basin. From the rise of Islam to the industrial era, it supported trade also in parts of tropical Africa and the rest of Eurasia. As Islamic partnership law was taking shape, but also after the Middle East passed its period of heightened institutional creativity, Arabs,

Persians, Turks, and other Muslims participated heavily in trade networks stretching from Spain to China and from the Black Sea to Zanzibar. In the process, they helped to develop the institutional foundations for long-distance trade in regions poorer than the Middle East. Carrying commercial regulations into places previously without written laws, they also introduced arithmetic, which simplified accounting, and metal coins, which facilitated payments and wealth accumulation. Further, they spread Arabic as a commercial *lingua franca*—a facilitator of communication, and thus exchange and cooperation, among areas previously segregated by linguistic differences.[34] In short, Islamic institutions integrated vast territories on three continents. They promoted, as we might say today, wealth-enhancing globalization (fig. 3.1).

In parts of tropical Africa, among other places, Islam spread first to the commercial class and only afterward to the broader community. It is primarily through merchants operating under Islamic law that Islam was carried to China and Indonesia, now home to huge Muslim populations; neither was conquered by an Arab army.[35] Scribes, physicians, teachers, and preachers also contributed to the spread of Islam. However, typically it was commerce that brought such literate professionals to the conversion sites in the first place.[36] Where Muslim merchants penetrated, Muslim judges, known as kadis, went in tow to adjudicate disputes; scribes to record contracts; teachers to provide instruction; and imams to lead prayer services. Sometimes one person performed several functions. A literate merchant could serve as a kadi and also help his fellows draft contracts. Whatever the patterns of occupational specialization, towns with Middle Eastern, or specifically Muslim, trading colonies became centers for Islamic education.[37] The commercial expansion of the Middle East thus triggered chain reactions through which conversions started occurring through multiple channels, including one peripheral to trade. Intermarriages formed a major vehicle of conversion.[38]

In lands that attracted Muslim traders, native converts gained access to established commercial networks based on a shared religion, language, and legal system. Converts did not necessarily observe Islam strictly; many maintained native religious observances.

Figure 3.1 The cupolas and roofs of the Grand Bazaar, Istanbul. This bazaar opened in 1461 as one of the biggest in the world. For centuries, it offered commodities from all over the known world, and travelers marveled at its opulence. (Photo: İzzet Keribar)

By the same token, they tried to establish a Muslim identity by attending communal prayers, socializing deliberately with Muslims, and performing a pilgrimage. Through such acts they distinguished themselves from the unconverted, and gained acceptance by local Muslims.[39]

Their demonstrations of commitment served the function, it has been said, of a "membership fee to an ostensibly religious club."[40] Payment of the "fee" made them more trustworthy in the eyes of other members. This is because, having secured access to a lucrative commercial network, they would not want to forfeit the benefits by letting down another member. Mutual trust among "club" or network members thus enhanced opportunities for mutually profitable exchange.[41] It provided these benefits without necessarily blocking opportunities to conduct exchanges outside the network. Just as Muslims of the Middle East established partnerships and traded with the Jews and Christians in their midst, so converted traders in Africa, India, and China maintained relationships with unconverted natives.

Certain giant commercial centers of premodern Asia and Africa owed their prominence to Islamization. They include Mombasa, Calicut, Malacca, and Canton (to Arabs, Khanfu). In many such centers Islam became the dominant religion. Middle Eastern merchants, mostly Muslims but also Christians, Jews, and Zoroastrians, were usually well-received, even welcomed by the local population, sometimes because they obtained support from a ruler eager to benefit from their skills. Typically they were allowed to have a kadi adjudicate their internal disputes, if not also their conflicts with others. The influx of Middle Easterners led to immense waves of conversion. According to contemporary Arab sources, when bandits captured Canton in 878 and slaughtered its population, the victims included 120,000 Middle Easterners, mostly Muslims.[42]

The establishment of Muslim-dominated trading centers in South and East Asia is noteworthy especially because the Chinese did not establish colonies in the Middle East or export their commercial institutions beyond East Asia. This asymmetry in commercial expansion has been attributed to cyclical rhythms of the monsoon winds and seasonal crop patterns.[43] Yet, the Chinese could have overcome any climatic disadvantages by establishing trading colonies in the Middle East. Another view, often appended to the climatic argument, is that China did not need foreign trade to maintain its standard of living, or finance its government.[44] These assertions assume what needs to be explained, namely, that few

Chinese merchants sought to exploit commercial opportunities in the Middle East. If Chinese rulers and subjects pursued riches in southeast Asia, they might have done so elsewhere. There is no empirical basis for considering their ambitions bounded. Starting in 1405, in fact, the Chinese launched seven expeditions to the western Indian Ocean, each involving a few hundred ships.[45] These voyages belie the claim that the Chinese lacked ambition.

A more plausible explanation for the observed asymmetry is that Islam reached India and the Indonesian archipelago before the Chinese saw the advantages of capturing the trade with those regions. Where Islam had already achieved a significant presence, commercial institutions were sufficiently advanced to deflate receptivity to Chinese alternatives. If in 1433 the Chinese halted their westward expeditions, a key reason is that Islamic institutions were already well-entrenched along the Asian and east African coastlines, and China had no superior institutions to offer.

In the famous account of his voyage across Eurasia, Marco Polo (1254–1324) refers to many Muslim merchants involved in the trade between the Middle East and regions farther east. Describing his visit to what is now Indonesia, he writes: "many of those who dwell in the seaport towns have been converted to the religion of Mahomet, by the Saracen merchants who constantly frequent them."[46] To Polo's European contemporaries, "Saracen" designated an Arab or a Muslim. Most of the "Saracen merchants" in question were Indian Muslims whose forebears were trading in the Indian Ocean even before their conversion to Islam. But Arabs, too, had established a presence in the archipelago.

For centuries after Marco Polo, Muslim merchants retained a major role in Eurasian caravan trade, which remained lucrative until Central Asia's political instabilities made it prohibitively expensive to protect caravans (fig. 3.2).[47] Just a few decades after Polo returned to Venice, the Arab traveler Ibn Battuta (1304–69) wrote a narrative of his own journey through the eastern Islamic world. Like Polo, he speaks of prosperous towns teeming with Muslim merchants. What he intended to be a sojourn in Delhi turned into an eight-year residence when Sultan Muhammad Tughluq appointed him as one of the town's kadis.[48] At his other stops, Ibn

Figure 3.2 In the Middle Ages, commercial caravans of the Middle East included multitudes of merchants who traveled together for security. (Photo: Tom Pfeiffer/www.volcanodiscovery.com)

Battuta did not try cases. But in both Asia and Africa he encountered kadis where he ran into Muslim merchant colonies—evidence that, as Muslim merchants moved, Islamic institutions went with them.[49]

Muslims were active, and in some sectors dominant, also in the Middle East's maritime trade with regions to its east and south (fig. 3.3). Between the eleventh and fourteenth centuries merchants identified as "Karimis," almost all Muslim, heavily dominated the spice trade between the Middle East and India.[50] At the end of the fifteenth century, Vasco da Gama, who initiated the sea route from western Europe to South Asia via the Cape of Good Hope, found that the coastal natives of East Africa and India traded with Arab merchants. Seizing the wares of Arabs whenever he could, he killed thousands of them with legendary cruelty.[51] The episode suggests that in this period Muslim traders remained competitive with Europeans in third markets. In establishing a Portuguese commercial presence in the region, da Gama relied on force rather than superior commercial institutions.

Figure 3.3 A substantial share of the trade within and through the Middle East occurred over water. Cairo, which is situated on the Nile, served as a hub for maritime commerce. Its global significance as a commercial center shrunk in the course of the second millennium. (Photo: Lehnert and Landrock, © Lehnert and Landrock, Cairo. Courtesy of Special Collections, Fine Art Library, Harvard College Library)

Vasco da Gama's mission was part of a campaign to control the highly lucrative trade with the East. The leading Muslim governments of the time hardly remained indifferent to the Portuguese challenge. The Ottoman Empire and Safavid Iran launched campaigns against the Portuguese and each other to preserve, if not augment, their revenues from the Asian trade.[52] Although neither succeeded in repelling the Portuguese, their resistance shows that during the European voyages of discovery Muslim statesmen remained committed to keeping eastern commercial lanes open to their own merchants. Evidently they did not consider Middle Eastern merchants institutionally handicapped vis-à-vis their eastern competitors. Islamic partnership law was not yet a source of commercial disadvantage in the global marketplace. On the contrary, it allowed diverse peoples to conduct trade in vast regions.

The largest collection of documents concerning medieval Middle Eastern trade was found in the storeroom (Geniza) of a Cairo synagogue. They consist mostly of letters, price lists, contracts, and partnership records belonging to merchants active between about 1000 and 1250 in the trade covering an area from North Africa and Spain to India and beyond. Although some of the great merchants mentioned in these "Geniza documents" are Muslim, most are Jewish. The latter often did business according to Islamic rather than Jewish law, using partnerships called *qirād al-gōyīm* in the Jewish legal terminology of the period (literally "partnership of the gentiles," meaning *mudāraba*). The last observation will be interpreted in a later chapter. Critical here is that in the early second millennium Islamic partnership law benefited non-Muslim merchants, too. Indeed, Jewish and Christian traders operating between Cairo, Qayrawan, Palermo, and Córdoba frequently formed Islamic partnerships, and they had some of their disputes resolved in Islamic courts.[53]

Limitations of Islamic Partnership Law

For at least a half-millennium after the birth of Islam, then, Islamic partnership law was adopted by peoples located in far corners of the world as the institutional basis for commercial cooperation. Invoking that impressive achievement, modern Islamists want to restructure economies according to Islamic principles. Thus, the architects of Islamic banking wish bank deposits and loans to be treated as *mudāraba* partnerships, with the bank serving as the active party in the first case and as a passive investor in the second.[54] In truth, by modern standards Islamic partnerships are very simple organizations. They are meant to support ventures of finite duration, not to open-ended ventures without an expected settlement date. They are poorly suited to projects requiring a huge sunk investment and delivering returns over many years. Because they lack legal personhood, before the law their members deal with third parties as individuals, rather than as employees of a firm.

All contemporary economies, even the least developed, harbor firms with thousands of employees who act daily on behalf of an organization that has an indefinite life span and enjoys legal standing. If these employees were made personally liable for obligations incurred through their professional duties, they would find the risks intolerable. For their part, the firms themselves would have difficulty finding outsiders willing to do business. Recognizing the costs of collecting from individual employees as well as the meagerness of most personal portfolios, third parties would seek advance payment for their services. A modern firm uses legal personhood to make the commitments of its employees credible in the eyes of third parties. As a legal person, it becomes a collective body capable of acting as a unit.

But let us not leap ahead of the narrative. Islamic partnership law presented limitations even by medieval standards. Most of its variants required a partnership's principal to consist of currency; they prohibited investing merchandise directly, ostensibly to prevent unjust enrichment, more plausibly to forestall conflicts over the value of the initial investment and the division of profits.[55] Moreover, the merchant's mission was incomplete until he reconverted all merchandise bought on behalf of the partnership into the selected currency.[56]

Where these rules were followed, they could drive partners to sell merchandise, or trade currencies, at an inopportune time or place. True, as in other economic contexts, the rules could be circumvented through legal ruses (hiyal).[57] By one such ruse, a person wishing to invest in a partnership in kind would sell his goods to a trusted third party and pass the proceeds to a merchant, thereby formally establishing a partnership; and the new partner would then repurchase the same goods on behalf of their joint venture. This procedure accomplished in two individually legitimate steps a task that would violate Islamic law if performed through a single step.[58] Although ruses of this sort saw frequent use, partnerships generally conformed to the spirit of the law.[59] In seventeenth-century Istanbul, only 1.5 percent of the partnerships mentioned in court registers had capital consisting of commodities.[60] In any case, even if the ban on investing merchandise was honored mostly in the breach, it need not have been inconsequential. The costs of overcoming its drawbacks through roundabout ways would have discouraged some potentially profitable partnerships.

Because an Islamic partnership lacks legal personhood, obligations arising from its dealings fell on its members as individuals. Although this condition was not crippling, it imposed constraints that third parties would have worked into their cost-benefit calculations. A person who performed services for the partnership, or suffered harm from its activities, could press claims only against a partner with whom he dealt directly. Likewise, an active partner who settled a claim arising from his work for the partnership had to seek restitution from his fellows individually, according to their shares of liability; he could not sue the partnership itself. The same principle applied to the partnership's own claims against third parties. Partners could demand compensation as individuals, never as a collective enterprise.[61]

The Waning of the Middle East's Golden Commercial Age

In the early Islamic centuries, none of these limitations of Islamic partnership law posed a serious handicap for the Middle East in its dealings with other regions. The world knew of nothing substantially better. Although one might point to advantages enjoyed in one context or another by the Chinese or the Italians, on the whole Muslims could pool resources and exploit the prevailing technologies relatively well. This is evident in the contributions that Middle Easterners, including its Muslims, made to commercial expansion on three continents. It is reflected, too, in the diffusion of Islamic institutions to far corners of Asia and Africa.

By the time the Portuguese established themselves in the Indian Ocean, the Middle East's golden commercial age was over. Its trade with South Asia was already past its prime. In the late sixteenth century, some Arabs still went to India; few traveled as far as China. Within a century and a half, even the region's spice trade with India lost its global significance. As late as 1585, three times more spices were transported to Europe via the Middle East, partly by Middle Eastern caravans, than were carried around Africa on Portuguese ships.[62] But by 1750, the round-the-Cape spice trade had extinguished the caravan-based spice trade between the Indian

Ocean and the Mediterranean.[63] Middle Easterners continued to dominate certain trade routes in Africa a while longer. However, in the nineteenth century Europeans made inroads even into Muslim-dominated areas once commercially connected to the Middle East.

A maritime or caravan route could plummet in relative importance without any absolute loss in trade volume. But one thing is unmistakable. The Middle East's share of global trade was declining. In retrospect it appears that the region was on its way to becoming economically underdeveloped. Remember that underdevelopment refers to *relative* economic performance. The Middle East was becoming underdeveloped not because it was becoming poorer in absolute terms, or trading fewer goods, but because its global economic significance was on the wane. According to Angus Maddison's calculations, its share of world gross domestic product, 10.3 percent in 1000, fell to 3.8 percent by 1600 and only 2.2 percent a century later. Over the same seven centuries, the west European share jumped from 9.1 percent to 21.9 percent.[64]

This decline is apparent also in institutional advances. In the early Islamic centuries, Muslims turned a pagan ritual into the world's largest commercial fair. They also developed a law of partnerships that helped to integrate territories stretching from the Atlantic to the Pacific. At the time that Europeans gained a foothold in the Indian Ocean, the Middle East was no longer contributing to the global economic infrastructure. Insofar as economic life was changing, the critical innovations were originating elsewhere, at the initiative of others.

Do the commercial institutions introduced in this chapter account for the decline in the Middle East's role in global commercial expansion? If they once worked admirably, why might they have become sources of underdevelopment? It is those puzzles that we take up next.

4

The Persistent Simplicity
of Islamic Partnerships

I n the tenth century, exchange was essentially personal everywhere, in Italy and India no less than in Iraq. An investor
would finance a merchant known to him as trustworthy, or
known as dependable to trustworthy friends. He would not place
trust in strangers, as we now do when investing in the stock market or buying merchandise through the Internet. Courts existed to
adjudicate commercial disputes. Because judges treated economic
relations as resting on personal ties, these disputes amounted to
contractual conflicts among individuals. If Islamic partnership law
spread to places far from Islam's heartland, this is because prior to
the last two centuries of the Middle Ages, generally considered to
have ended in 1453, it provided an advanced solution to the universal problem of supporting cooperation among non-kin. In the
tenth century nowhere in the world was the regulation of impersonal exchange a pressing concern.

It was around that time that Islamic partnership law assumed its
classical form. From then until the era of industrialization, it underwent no major changes. Up to the nineteenth century it served
as the basis for commercial cooperation among non-kin throughout the Middle East, except, as we shall see, in sectors that came
under foreign domination. It did not give rise to structurally more
complex commercial organizations with indefinite time horizons.
Meanwhile, western Europe saw the emergence of more durable
and much larger organizations. Although simple and short-lived
partnerships continued to be formed all across Europe—as is still
the case, in the twenty-first century—complex enterprise forms were

added, in steps, to the options available to the business community. In the process, exchanges became progressively more impersonal.

We already know that early in the second millennium the partnership rules of the Middle East resembled those of the West. Why, then, did western Europe go on to produce increasingly impersonal solutions to the problem of generating trust outside the family when the initial solution in territories under Islamic governance proved self-reproducing? Identifying the roots of this divergence calls for comparative institutional analysis across geographic regions, for it is only in relation to institutional changes recorded in western Europe that the stagnation of certain Middle Eastern institutions appears puzzling. Clues to the Middle Eastern trajectory will emerge from comparing key elements of Islamic law with their western analogues.

Scale and Longevity of Islamic Partnerships

Whatever its exact form, an Islamic partnership could be terminated at will by any partner, acting unilaterally. He simply had to inform the co-partners of his choice.[1] The death of a partner, whether or not the surviving members learned of it, rendered the partnership null and void. Subsequent gains and losses belonged solely to the responsible partner. The heirs of the deceased did not automatically replace him. If the enterprise was to continue, a new partnership had to be negotiated.[2]

Every additional partner thus increased the risk of premature termination by raising the probability of a partner dying, or simply opting to withdraw, before fulfillment of the contract. That risk increased also with the partnership's expected duration. An Islamic partnership was poorly suited, then, to large and long-lasting business ventures requiring the active or passive participation of many people. Not surprisingly, the typical partnership formed under Islamic law consisted of just two members. In seventeenth-century Istanbul, 77.1 percent of the partnerships mentioned in court records consisted of just two people.[3] Only 7.6 percent had five or more members, the largest two being a thirty-three-person partner-

TABLE 4.1
Size Distribution of Partnerships Mentioned in the Istanbul and Galata Court Registers, 1602–1697

	Number of partners (with percentage of each category)										
Years	2		3		4		5 or more		Total known		Un-known	Total
1602–19*	180	75.6	28	11.8	9	3.8	21	8.8	238	100	9	247
1661–97**	133	79.2	20	11.9	5	3.0	10	6.0	168	100	2	170
Total	313	77.1	48	11.8	14	3.4	31	7.6	406	100	11	417

*Court registers: Istanbul 1 (1612–13), 2 (1615–16), 3 (1617–18), 4 (1619), and Galata 24 (1602), 25 (1604), 27 (1604–05), 41 (1616–17), 42 (1617).
**Court registers: Istanbul 9 (1661–62), 16 (1664–65), 22 (1695–96), 23 (1696–97), and Galata 130 (1683), 145 (1689–90).

ship and a twenty-one-person partnership (table 4.1).[4] No trend toward larger partnerships is detectable from the first- to the second half of the century (fig. 4.1).[5] These findings suggest that the commercial sector remained institutionally stagnant at least until 1700. By this time, we shall see shortly, the English, the Dutch, and other west Europeans were on their way to developing modern commercial organizations.

This is the book's second reference to evidence from "seventeenth-century Istanbul," and many more will follow. The source is a very

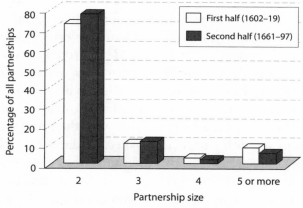

Figure 4.1 Size distribution of Istanbul partnerships, 1602–1697

large data set formed by studying all 10,080 cases found in fifteen Islamic court registers that span the years 1602 to 1697. The registers belong to the courts of central Istanbul and Galata, each located in a bustling commercial district of the Ottoman capital, the region's leading commercial city of the period. Of these cases, 9,074, or 90.0 percent, involved commercial matters. They include 6,494 registrations of a contract or settlement, 2,291 accounts of an adjudicated lawsuit, and 289 records of an imperial edict or ruling.[6] These entries provide information on the commercial practices of the period and on whether they changed in the course of the seventeenth century. The rationale for focusing on Istanbul, rather than a lesser commercial center, is worth restating. Just as advances in European commercial organization were generally observable first and foremost in its main commercial hubs—in the seventeenth century, London and Amsterdam—so the Middle East's dynamism, insofar as it was present, should have shown through most clearly, and before anywhere else, in its most advanced areas.

When an Islamic partnership was formed for commerce alone, with no production intended, it pooled resources for a single trade mission.[7] Although the mission could last a year or two, ordinarily it ended within a matter of months. This was true even if the partners had a long-term personal relationship. Their formal partnerships were for short periods and limited to specific undertakings.[8] As for the principal invested, it tended to be quite small, because risk-averse investors dispersed their capital among multiple trade ventures. Consequently, even a merchant performing a trade mission financed by a dozen investors could be carrying merchandise of limited value. Participants in the caravan trade of the pre-industrial Middle East consisted largely of peddlers who bought and sold small quantities as the convoy moved from market to market.[9] Like the caravan trade, maritime trade was the province of small traders traveling with packs and baskets loadable on a single animal. Major commercial investors diversified their risks by contracting with many merchants traveling in different directions.[10] Surviving records point to merchants who commanded loads valued at many times those of a typical peddler; usually they were financed

Figure 4.2 Bazaar for leather goods, Tunis. Built in the seventeenth century, it brought together many dealers selling similar products. Each operated out of a tiny store. Most were self-financed or had a single commercial partner. (Photo: Compagnie Alsacienne des Arts Photomécaniques)

by high officials.[11] But such officials pursued risk diversification themselves by splitting their resources among many partnerships. Even elite merchants generally belonged to partnerships with few members.

Studies of premodern Middle Eastern cities provide evidence of traders, Muslim and non-Muslim, who built huge households and financed major public services.[12] Taken as a whole, they confirm also that neither the scale nor the organization of commerce changed appreciably over time. In seventeenth- and eighteenth-century Istanbul, Aleppo, Tunis, and Cairo the pooling of commercial resources generally took place through partnerships structurally identical to ones common almost a millennium earlier (fig. 4.2). Moreover, commercial businesses involving resource pooling across families rarely survived their founders; ordinarily heirs to commercial fortunes did not retain, let alone develop, businesses established by deceased relatives. Scholars describe contracts found in records of the seventeenth, eighteenth, and even early nineteenth century with reference to legal treatises of a millennium earlier.[13]

Within Middle Eastern studies very few works exist on organizational dynamics of the private sector, which is a vast subfield of European economic history. This is not for lack of talent. Rather, it reflects the organizational stagnation of Middle Eastern commerce, precisely what this book has set out to explain.

The Beginnings of Institutional Stagnation

To make sense of the stagnation in question, let us step back to the year 1000. There are two reasons to use the early second millennium as our starting point. First, in the preceding several centuries the Middle East witnessed remarkable institutional creativity, including refinements helpful to commerce. Had a need for further refinements been widely felt, they might have followed. Second, the Middle East and western Europe did not differ significantly with regard to business scale or longevity. Around 1000, the *commenda* was no more hospitable to large and durable enterprises than the *mudāraba*. Finally, Middle Eastern commerce was poised to lose its organizational creativity, even as the region's state-controlled sectors remained structurally dynamic.

The last observation draws on a study by Maya Shatzmiller, which compares the number of distinct occupations in Arab-Islamic lands stretching from Iraq to Spain during two consecutive periods: 701–1100 and 1101–1500. In the former period, which encompasses the formative centuries of Islamic law, the Arab-Islamic world had 233 distinct commercial occupations, including sellers, middlemen, brokers, weighers, appraisers, and financiers. In the latter period the number of occupations was 220, roughly the same (fig. 4.3). Remarkably, the number of unique commercial occupations in the bureaucracy and military tripled, and that of educational, legal, or religious occupations more than quintupled.[14] At least since Adam Smith, we have known that division of labor is among the correlates of rising productivity.[15] So these figures point to inertia in regard to commercial organization and also to stagnant commercial productivity. This inference is consistent with the persistent smallness and simplicity of the typical Middle Eastern partnership.

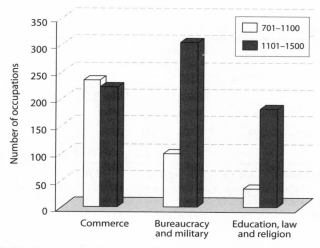

Figure 4.3 Distinct occupations in Arab-Islamic world, 701–1500. *Note:* For commerce, the two numbers are statistically equal at the 99.9 percent confidence level ($t = 7.42$). For the other two categories, the second number is statistically greater, again at the 99.9 percent confidence level ($t = 3.66, 4.11$). *Source*: Shatzmiller, *Labour in Medieval Islam*, pp. 255–318.

Had merchants of the Middle East started forming structurally more complex enterprises, new commercial specializations would have accompanied the organizational innovations.

In and of itself, having an unchanging number of occupations does not point to stagnant commercial life. New occupations could have replaced old ones. Yet, in the second of the periods under consideration the proportion of new commercial occupations was relatively low. Whereas more than four-fifths of all occupations in the bureaucracy, military, education, law, and religion were new, only half of the commercial occupations were (table 4.2). Relatively low occupational turnover in private commerce is consistent with its loss of organizational dynamism. In places and times when private economic life is undergoing radical change, commercial occupations do exhibit high turnover. Of the commercial occupations present in 1903 in Manchester, the heart of English industrialization, 77.2 percent had emerged over the past century.[16]

The public sector, one might observe, includes occupations that support commerce in one way or another. The new bureaucratic

TABLE 4.2
New Occupations in Arab-Islamic World, 1101–1500

Sector	Preexisting occupations (% of total)	New occupations (% of total)
Commerce	42.7	57.3
Bureaucracy, military	10.9	89.1
Education, law, religion	16.1	83.9
All	22.2	77.8

Source: Shatzmiller, *Labour in Medieval Islam*, pp. 255–318.
Note: Occupational turnover in commerce is statistically lower than the average for the economy at the 99.9 percent confidence level ($t = 4.10$). In the bureaucracy and military, turnover is higher, at the same confidence level ($t = 2.89$). In education, law, and religion, it is statistically indistinguishable from the average ($t = 1.20$).

occupations created in the Arab-Islamic world between 1101 and 1500 included the scribe, who helped to register contracts, and the master of the mint, who stimulated commerce by promoting monetization. Likewise, the new legal occupations included the teacher of property law and the legal contract maker, both of whom facilitated the drafting and enforcement of contracts.[17] However, even under the most liberal criteria, the number of commercially beneficial new public occupations is limited. As many as 64.2 percent of the new public occupations promoted the welfare of the ruler, raised taxes, or advanced religion, with no discernible benefit to commerce.[18]

In addition to a wide range of secondary literature, Shatzmiller's figures are based on manuals prepared for the supervisors of urban markets (*hisba* manuals for *muhtasibs*) and treatises concerned with economic life.[19] She did not use court records, which might have furnished additional commercial occupations. Also absent from her sources are documents left by private merchants. The table is probably biased, then, against commercial occupations. However, biases would have operated similarly across the two periods, and it is the temporal trend that matters here, not absolute magnitudes. In any case, the merchants of these periods, whether sedentary shopkeepers or itinerant traders, left few written records. If the Geniza documents receive enormous attention, it is because they form the exception that proves the rule.

The paucity of records prepared by businessmen is itself an indication of stagnation. If commercial occupations were becoming increasingly specialized, this probably would have reflected growing organizational complexity. Merchants would have chosen increasingly to write elaborate contracts, and also to establish archives. A demand might have emerged for manuals focused on running a complex business. Further evidence of organizational stagnation in the private sector lies in legal writings of the Middle Ages. They deal exclusively with small, ephemeral, and structurally simple businesses—proof that more sophisticated organizations were not being formed or even contemplated.[20]

In the centuries following the second of Shatzmiller's periods, the Middle East saw the emergence, or expansion, of ethnically based networks that coordinated activities in various cities. In the seventeenth and early eighteenth centuries, prominent among these was an Armenian network that extended from the Netherlands to China. It was centered in New Julfa, Iran.[21] However, from an organizational standpoint these commercial networks achieved nothing comparable to the accomplishments of business conglomerates based in western Europe. They consisted of family enterprises that cooperated episodically, and usually through *mudāraba* or *inān*, rather than under the aegis of a centralized and essentially permanent multi-family organization. Before the twentieth century, in fact, the region did not produce a single case of mass financial mobilization through non-governmental channels for a major business venture, except insofar as foreigners were involved.[22] Evidently, the institutional stagnation that began around 1000 lasted at least three-quarters of a millennium.

Evolution of Partnerships in the West

During that long period, the commercial infrastructure of western Europe underwent gradual, but cumulatively very important, changes. A long chain of developments transformed the *commenda* into a rich variety of partnership forms, including ones suitable to broadly financed and durable commercial enterprises. Remember that the *commenda*, like the *mudāraba*, dissolved with the death of a partner. In the thirteenth century the Italians sought to overcome the consequent problems through the "family firm" (*compagnia*)— a partnership formed mostly by kin, with each partner assuming unlimited and joint liability. Although a family firm would be liquidated at the death of a partner, it would immediately be reconstituted, usually retaining the name as well as the capital. The largest family firms accumulated assets comparable to those of rulers.[23]

Critical to the family firm's success is that its contractual provisions gained credibility from its longevity and liability rules. It helped that cities could enforce the obligations of local firms and, because a default by one firm would cast doubt on the commitments of others, that they were also motivated to do so.[24] The family firm's lasting contribution to organizational development lies in its demonstration of the value of large and durable enterprises. Yet its reliance on kinship bonds limited its applicability. So did its liability rules, which made cooperation across families more risky than cooperation among relatives. Understandably, people were reluctant to invest in an enterprise that included strangers who might encumber them, or the enterprise itself, with unplanned obligations. Nevertheless, certain family firms turned into enterprises whose family members contributed only a minority of the capital and were outnumbered by outside shareholders.[25]

Another Italian innovation was the hub-and-spoke system devised to link legally independent partnerships. The famous Medici enterprise (1397–1494) consisted of a controlling partnership (the hub) and numerous subsidiary partnerships (spokes), each with a branch manager who assumed joint and unlimited liability for debts of his own branch. In principle, that branch manager was liable also for the debts of other branches. However, because each partnership kept separate books, and because of transportation and communication costs, as a practical matter the creditors of each branch office had first claim on its assets. Hence, creditors treated the Medici partnerships as independent, thus limiting the liabilities of any one branch. By reducing the risks of individual investors, such partitioning of assets promoted investment in the overall enterprise. This is because investors needed to trust only the controlling parties; the trustworthiness of the manager in Bruges was of limited relevance to an investor in Pisa.[26]

The subsidiary partnerships of the Medici enterprise dealt with one another on the same basis as with outside customers, charging them commissions and interest. They reported to the center, which coordinated their activities to make them operate as branches of a single enterprise.[27] This coordination enabled the exploitation of interest differentials across cities included in the network. The enterprise stimulated refinements in double-entry bookkeeping, which served to depersonalize accounting and make records both transparent and comparable.[28] Surviving financial statements of the Medici headquarters in Florence are sufficiently systematic and detailed that modern scholars use them to reconstruct Medici business practices. Particularly significant is that the dissolution of one partnership through a death or retirement left the rest of the enterprise intact. The Medici enterprise, which lasted ninety-seven years —by medieval standards an eternity—thus foreshadowed the modern holding company. Its innovations included the facilitation of clearance operations among subsidiary partnerships.[29]

The joint effect of these institutional changes was that business enterprises far larger and more durable than the typical *commenda* or *mudāraba* came to play an increasingly important role in European economic life, including relations with other regions. In the major Italian trading states of the era, the scale of commercial enterprises grew in the fourteenth and fifteenth centuries. The Medici conglomerate had a permanent staff of 57 in 1470, spread across eight cities, including three outside Italy. The Bardi and Peruzzi conglomerates of a century earlier had even larger staffs; the latter had around twenty shareholders and a staff of ninety spread across fifteen cities.[30] The German Fugger conglomerate, which in the fifteenth and sixteenth centuries practically monopolized the northern European trade in certain commodities, controlled enough resources to make it a major player in continental politics. Though a family partnership, it drew in outsiders through marriages with members of wealthy families. In 1546, the Fuggers possessed the equivalent of 13,000 kilograms of gold as their combined capital, a sum exceeding the resources of any European monarch. Like the large enterprises of Italy, they employed secretaries, accountants, and advisers trained to keep records and maintain correspondence with partners, depositors, suppliers, and clients. The presence of the

Fugger conglomerate all across the continent gave wealth holders some protection against confiscation, for certain investments could be moved across borders simply through a transfer on paper.[31]

The family partnerships of the Middle Ages are the ancestors of the unlimited partnership, known also as a general partnership or *société en nom collectif*. The members of an unlimited partnership, who need not be related, are responsible as individuals to all creditors of the partnership. As for the commenda, it survives in the form of the limited partnership, known also as *société en commandite simple*. A limited partnership has two types of partners: general partners, who manage the enterprise and bear unlimited liability, and special partners, who have no managerial authority and are liable only up to their own investments.[32] These two partnership forms with medieval roots form just a subset of the organizational options now available to the business community. Far more complex organizational forms emerged after the fifteenth century.

Overseas Trading Companies

One such organization was the joint-stock company, a partnership with transferable shares. Joint-stock companies could have many members—some had hundreds—so reorganization became a daily matter. Courts took steps to simplify the reorganization process, thus lowering the costs of maintaining continuity.[33] Among the early joint-stock companies were the English Levant Company and the Dutch, French, and English East India Companies. All had horizons much longer than a single voyage. Their individual shareholders could invest in a particular voyage or commit resources for a number of years; and the companies themselves had some capital considered permanent.[34] The number of merchants within any given company was small by the standards of a modern multinational firm. In 1592, only fifty-three merchants were affiliated with the Levant Company.[35] However, this was a massive number for the time.[36] In addition to merchants, each company attracted passive investors who accepted dividends in cash and played minor roles, if any, in strategy and day-to-day management. In the course of these developments, the act of buying shares became deperson-alized, and stock markets emerged. These markets are the precur-sors of today's giant stock exchanges.[37]

The size of the companies facilitated information acquisition. It also gave them influence over prices. Moreover, where small trad-ers secured merchandise through innumerable and sometimes un-foreseeable payments in the form of tributes and customs duties to monarchs, dignitaries, pirates, and brigands, the companies limited such costs by appointing consuls to represent them and by organiz-ing their own protection.[38] Consequently, the companies retained profits that would have fed the coffers of officials and bandits.

Neither the rise of large companies nor the increasing prevalence of impersonal exchange implies the disappearance of small-scale or per-sonalized exchange. Even modern cities have self-financed street ven-dors and neighborhood stores that serve mostly repeat buyers.[39] But it is not the lower end of the size distribution that matters here. Rather, it is the upper end, which consists of the largest companies. The upper tail of the European size distribution grew longer as enterprises of historically unprecedented size came on the scene. As we saw earlier in this chapter, the two largest enterprises found in the seventeenth-century court registers of Istanbul had thirty-three and twenty-one members. In the late sixteenth century, the Levant company was al-ready much larger, and its membership was destined to grow.

The lengthening of the western distribution's upper tail was made possible by new organizational forms, including ones suited to pool-ing extensive capital for multiple commercial missions. Through myriads of organizational innovations, western business commu-nities gradually overcame the obstacles to growth that continued to limit commercial enterprises in other regions, including the Mid-dle East. This expansion went hand in hand with greater longevity. Whereas even the largest partnerships in Istanbul were established for a finite mission, the Levant company was meant to have an indefinite existence.

By no means were the new organizational forms problem-free. One member of a large partnership could impose losses on the rest. Moreover, at least initially a joint-stock company lacked a legal identity independent of its partners; every partner became a party to legal suits involving third parties, and also to those among other partners.[40] Although the consequent costs could be reduced through constraints on individual partners, it was hardly practical to micromanage the membership. However, such difficulties spawned further organizational creativity. By the seventeenth century Europe had an alternative organizational form that avoided the drawbacks just mentioned: the business corporation. Chapters ahead discuss the advantages of the corporate form and explore its failure to emerge in the Middle East.

Beyond the functions of the new organizational forms, what is remarkable is the sheer diversity of the options that became available to European businesses. Through side contracts, entrepreneurs managed to mix and match the characteristics of the basic organizational forms, broadening their possibilities even further. For example, they modified partnerships to give them greater permanence.[41] The outcome was nothing less than an organizational revolution that made western economies increasingly efficient at pooling resources, monitoring their uses, and exploiting commercial opportunities.

Causes of Organizational Divergence

No single development proved indispensable to the subsequent organizational trajectory. Each represented one of many uncoordinated attempts to accumulate capital and gain longevity while protecting joint assets, limiting risks, and achieving transparency. Two aspects of the European record are particularly significant.

One is the dynamism itself. Given our central puzzle—the stability of the Middle Eastern organizational menu at a time when that of the West expanded steadily—it calls for exploring whether certain structural factors hindered organizational innovation in the Middle East. The other striking characteristic of Europe's trajectory is that the engine of its organizational dynamism consisted of multitudes of private agents, generally operating independently. Indeed, initiatives came from private businessmen acting without coordination; although states facilitated certain arrangements, they did not direct them. This justifies our focus on Islamic partnership law, which regulated transactions among private parties.

We are not interested in why any particular western development —the Medici conglomerate, the Levant Company—was not replicated in the Middle East. The question at hand is why the region's private commercial organizations remained atomistic for centuries on end. Part of the answer lies in the Islamic inheritance system, which tended to fragment the estates of successful businessmen.

5

Drawbacks of the Islamic Inheritance System

Of all the economic rules in the Quran, the most detailed are those on inheritance. Restricting the individual's testamentary privileges to one-third of his or her estate, the Quran reserves the unbequeathed portion to children, spouses, parents, and siblings of both sexes, according to rules dependent on the exact composition of the legally recognized heirs.[1] The rules were understood to provide shares also to more distant relatives under certain circumstances. For certain special cases, the applicable rule differs across the two major denominations and principal schools of law. Only under the Shii interpretation may the testator make bequests to a relative already entitled to part of the estate as a "Quranic heir."[2]

The degree to which the Islamic inheritance system departed from the norms of pre-Islamic Arabia is a matter of controversy.[3] Whatever the extent of historical continuity, its testamentary restrictions clearly subordinated personal preferences to the extended family's need for financial security and predictability. They also strengthened the inheritance rights of females. Although a female heir's entitlement normally amounts to only half that of a male in the same class of inheritors,[4] in seventh-century Arabia this right enhanced the economic security and social status of women.

The assignment of inheritance shares to a wide class of family members reduced wealth dispersion. Also, at least Sunni variants of the law dampened intra-family tensions by preventing wills from favoring certain heirs. More significant for our purposes is that every variant of the mandatory sharing rule made it difficult to keep property intact across generations. Studies of premodern Anatolia, Syria, and Palestine show that fortunes often got fragmented. It was not uncommon for a dwelling or shop to have more than a dozen co-owners. The sudden death of a wealthy person could trigger legal battles among heirs and business partners.[5]

The difficulties of keeping wealth undivided are evident also in statistics concerning the intergenerational transmission of wealth. The descendants of prosperous Ottoman families of the sixteenth century rarely remained wealthy beyond one or two generations. In contrast to Europe, no aristocracy developed in Turkey, or the Arab world, or Iran. Although the prevailing inheritance system was not the only factor at work—expropriations and opportunistic taxation played important roles—what matters is that it contributed to wealth fragmentation. In regard to enforcement of the Islamic inheritance rules, wealthy Ottomans, including the military-administrative elites, were treated like ordinary Ottoman subjects.[6]

Measures to Limit Asset Fragmentation

One would expect the emergence of institutions to prevent the fragmentation of productive assets. Indeed, from the early days of Islam, rulers recognized that property fragmentation could cause efficiency losses and limit the tax base. Islamic jurisprudence sought to minimize the losses by classifying most arable land as state property (initially *ard al-mamlaka*; under the Ottomans, *miri*). The cultivators of state-owned land enjoyed tenancy rights and paid a land tax in return. However, they could not sell or grant their plots, except by permission. Although ordinarily their rights could be passed on to descendants, the land itself was not subject to Islamic inheritance law, and usually it could not be partitioned.[7] The system thus aimed to keep agricultural plots as viable units of production.

Insofar as rulers could enforce their will, this system of ownership limited land fragmentation. But it did nothing to prevent the fragmentation of other property, and it is movable wealth that is primarily relevant here. The wealth of a commercial partner, whether an active merchant or a passive investor, consisted partly of cash and merchandise. At least to that extent, it was subject to Islamic inheritance rules.

Additional responses came at the initiative of communities and families. In certain places local norms allowed families to deny women their legally mandated inheritance shares. The Islamic inheritance system was circumvented also through pre-mortem gifts to a relative, bequests to a minor child of the person targeted for favors, arranged marriages between legal heirs, and side payments to induce the surrender of inheritance rights. Another method of circumvention was to postpone the estate's division by taking advantage of the Quran's imprecision about its timing.[8] The imprecision permitted powerful men to keep estates intact for years without formally denying legal heirs their rights.[9] However, to identify opportunities for circumventing a law is not to establish that law's irrelevance or to prove that the opportunities were commonplace. Take the last circumvention method. Most groups of heirs lacked a powerful person capable of consolidating control over the estate and delaying its division.

Still another method for keeping wealth undivided was to convert it into real estate, for reconversion into the endowment of an Islamic trust, or a waqf. A waqf was statutorily indivisible, and its beneficiaries could include or exclude anyone the founder desired. Hence, establishing a waqf allowed the selection of who would control a property after one's death.[10] It enabled a prosperous merchant to pass his wealth to a single son, thus limiting the benefits accruing to his parents, wife, daughters, and other sons. For that reason, it might seem that the waqf offered a perfect solution to the problem of wealth fragmentation.[11] However, it created other problems, which chapters ahead will lay out, in stages. The waqf restricted the use of assets in ways that hindered adaptations to technological change, the pooling of capital, and organizational development. Hence, it was poorly suited to profit-oriented commerce.

Inheritance Practices in Western Europe

Since our challenge is to explain why in the Middle East self-induced modernization did not take place, it makes sense to review the inheritance practices of premodern Europe, where it did. Bewildering variations could exist even within a politically unified region as small as Moravia or Saxony. Moreover, rules and customs could change over a matter of decades. Given this variability, it is unsurprising that certain European inheritance systems of the Middle Ages were as inflexible as the strictest Islamic variants. In parts of England, one-third of a deceased man's movable property was reserved for his wife and another third for his children, who had to be treated equally. Under medieval Germanic law, a father had no testamentary powers at all; the post-mortem disposition of his property followed a fixed formula.[12]

For all their variations, practically every inheritance system of premodern Europe differed from the Islamic system in one critical respect. Because Christian canon law did not standardize inheritance requirements, practices were relatively easy to modify, and attempts at reform were less likely to be resisted as sacrilegious. Advocates on all sides of the debate could ground their positions in biblical principles, so arguments could not be won through religious rhetoric alone.[13] For both reasons, barriers to keeping estates intact across generations were lower than in the Middle East. Thus, from the Middle Ages onward, the un-Islamic—and un-modern—devices of primogeniture (preference in inheritance given to the oldest son) and ultimogeniture (preference given to the youngest son) enjoyed legal recognition in many parts of Europe. In the sixteenth and seventeenth centuries, when western commercial institutions underwent profound changes, primogeniture was the dominant inheritance practice in Britain, the Low Countries, Scandinavia, and parts of Austria and France.[14] In the late seventeenth century the practice spread also within Germany.[15] Its supporters marshaled more than a dozen biblical verses to give primogeniture a Christian foundation.[16] This continent-wide trend allowed wealthy families to keep assets intact without resorting to such costly methods as establishing a trust.[17]

Certain European practices favoring one child were accompanied by compensatory measures for the others. For example, where a family's land was reserved for the oldest son, daughters might receive dowries and a younger son might be trained to take over its commercial operations. Such egalitarian measures were consistent with the goal of enterprise continuity. Although European families did not always resort to primogeniture, at least the device was available, or could be created where the need was felt widely.

Since the Industrial Revolution, European inheritance patterns have tended to become more egalitarian.[18] The French Civil Code, established under Napoléon in 1804, requires the division of property among all children.[19] This modern transformation is of no consequence to the argument in progress, because by the nineteenth century Europe was already familiar with modern organizational forms. The issue at hand is not whether an egalitarian inheritance system is compatible with large, long-living, and complex business enterprises. Rather, it is whether the Islamic inheritance system might have blocked the indigenous development of modern organizational forms and delayed their adoption once in existence elsewhere. In the period when western Europe but not the Middle East generated modern organizational forms, the former was far more hospitable to inheritance practices designed to keep property intact across generations.

Origins of Inheritance Systems

Why did the Islamic inheritance system rule out primogeniture while European laws proved flexible enough to allow it? Shelomo Goitein offers an answer. In ancient western Arabia, the birthplace of the Islamic inheritance system, most wealth belonged to traders and nomads whose possessions consisted of movable and easily partitioned goods, such as animal herds and precious metals. So Islamic inheritance rules took shape in a society unconcerned with asset fragmentation.[20] By contrast, the Roman and Germanic legal systems, founts of the inheritance systems prevalent in the West, developed in agricultural societies whose members sought to keep land in units large enough to sustain a family. By this logic, as the primary source of wealth shifted from land to easily divisible industrial capital, primogeniture should have given way to "partible" and more egalitarian forms of intergenerational wealth transmission.[21] As we just saw, this inference mirrors the historical experience. European inheritance practices became more egalitarian in the course of the Industrial Revolution.

However, the details of the Islamic inheritance system took shape not in a nomadic milieu but in Syria, seat of the Umayyad Caliphate, and Iraq, from which the Abbasids governed. In both Syria and Iraq agriculture played a greater role than in western Arabia. Might the same factors that motivated the architects of the Roman and Germanic inheritance systems to limit asset fragmentation have made Muslim jurists sympathetic to escape clauses conducive to the preservation of successful enterprises? If history unfolded differently, a basic reason may be that in the region's pre-Islamic past, state power in agriculturally productive areas depended on control over large-scale irrigation systems, which are inessential in areas with adequate rainfall. To keep control over water supply systems, without which the land would remain barren, the states of antiquity strove to weaken independent sources of wealth and power, partly through laws mandating the equal sharing of estates. Pharaonic Egypt, Babylon, and Assyria all had essentially egalitarian inheritance laws.[22] Thus, the Quran's early interpretations emerged, and the building blocks of Islamic law took shape, in a region already accustomed to more or less egalitarian inheritance practices.

Once egalitarian inheritance practices became identified with Islam, groups with a stake in their preservation, including women and younger sons, would have resisted moves toward primogeniture. They would have had the Quran on their side. In brief, the hand of history first shaped the selection of Islam's inheritance system and then limited opportunities for adopting less egalitarian rules conducive to keeping successful enterprises undivided for multiple generations. There is still the question of why merchants did not develop methods of circumvention of particular relevance to themselves. A key factor is that successful merchants tended to have multiple wives.

Polygyny and the Persistence of
Egalitarian Inheritance Rules

The Quran allows polygyny, with the limitation that men can have no more than four wives at one time. Another limitation is that polygynous men must treat their wives fairly, spending equal time with them and giving each the same resources.[23] Historically, the vast majority of married Muslim men had a single wife; polygyny was the preserve of the very powerful and very rich.[24] As such, it provided status and helped to broaden trade alliances by fostering trust among families. Against these advantages, it had a serious drawback: every new wife, by adding herself and her children to the list of potential heirs, compounded the already serious difficulties of keeping an estate undivided. By the same token, the legality of polygyny created new constituencies for keeping inheritance practices egalitarian. If primogeniture were the norm, a family would be reticent to let its daughter marry a man with a son from a previous marriage. However wealthy the man, the marriage could condemn the daughter and her children to future poverty.

Islam's egalitarian inheritance system and Islamic polygyny were thus mutually supporting institutions. The former facilitated the latter; and the latter reinforced obstacles to favoring one child over his or her siblings, or one surviving wife over the others. The two institutions formed, then, a self-reinforcing institutional complex. It is noteworthy that under most interpretations of medieval Christianity, polygyny is sinful.[25] In pre-industrial Europe, primogeniture went hand in hand with a revulsion at polygyny. According to canon law, marriage rested on mutual consent of the two spouses. Hence, the power of the male head of household was more circumscribed than in other parts of the world, reducing his ability to take additional wives.[26] In any case, a woman was particularly unlikely to marry an already married man, for she would lack material security in the marriage.

Further reasons why the Islamic inheritance system proved so stable will be presented in due course. Taking it as given that Middle Eastern merchants could not escape the fragmentation of their estates, let us now inquire into the implications for commercial organization and performance.

Untimely Death and Enterprise Continuity

To identify the effects of the inheritance system, it will be instructive to compare the workings of a hypothetical five-person partnership in two separate jurisdictions: one that allows primogeniture and another that does not. The partnership consists of three investors and two merchants. After its formation through a cash transfer from the investors to the merchants, the latter convert the cash into merchandise and begin their voyage. A few weeks later, one of the two merchants drops dead.

In the jurisdiction where primogeniture is in force, each member's designated heir is common knowledge. After the untimely death, the partnership dissolves, and the dead partner's share passes to his eldest son. In principle, the son may use his windfall gain on some other venture. He may also renegotiate the terms of the interrupted enterprise. Alternatively, he can agree to the original terms, letting the venture proceed as though no death had occurred. In practice, the initial terms were often reproduced automatically, for the partners and their heirs agreed in advance to preserve the venture in the event of a death. Such an agreement was credible because the typical partner had a single alternate who was trained to take over his father's business. Raising expected profits, this practice benefited all concerned parties.

Now suppose that the original partnership is formed in a region under Islamic law. Again, one of the two merchants dies. The dead partner's share must be divided among his possibly numerous relatives and, if he left a will, one or more non-relatives. Imagine that there are four heirs. They may agree to join the partnership's four surviving members to establish a new, eight-person partnership. They are also free, with or without side payments, to reconstitute the divided share by having three of them relinquish their inheritance rights in favor of the fourth. Hence, there is no formal barrier to the venture's continuation under a partly renewed membership. Nevertheless, a single financially strapped heir may create problems by insisting on liquidation of the old partnership. Two factors raise the likelihood of liquidation. First, the heirs will not have been groomed for carrying on the business, as they often were wherever primogeniture was the norm. Second, under the Islamic inheritance system the set of heirs and their shares can change substantially following the birth of a new heir or the death of an existing one. The consequent uncertainty dampens every heir's commitment to an established enterprise.

In the Middle East, then, the probability of premature dissolution was particularly high. A further problem was that each heir was entitled to a fraction of every asset in the estate.[27] Recall that contributions to an Islamic commercial partnership must be in currency, and that its dissolution requires the division of its tangible assets. An heir seeking his share of the partnership's assets may demand part of each good owned at the time of death, whether divisible, as with a load of wheat, or indivisible, as with a slave or a cow. Insofar as indivisible assets are involved, surviving partners may be forced to make sales at an inconvenient time and place.

Commercial Success and Number of Heirs

The number of heirs was not always large. If a merchant died intestate, and he was survived by one wife and a single son, there would be just two heirs, with the wife entitled to an eighth of his estate and the son to the remaining seven-eighths. Yet, successful and wealthy merchants—precisely those who might have pressured the courts to recognize increasingly complex commercial organizations —tended to have more surviving children and were more likely to have multiple wives.[28] Ordinarily, then, they had larger households. Moreover, it is with large estates that the wealth at stake made it particularly worthwhile to launch a lawsuit. Reviewing the court records of Galata from the sixteenth and seventeenth centuries, Fethi Gedikli found numerous suits by heirs demanding their shares of a prematurely dissolved partnership's assets.[29] Some of the merchants included in these records had so many heirs as to make serious fragmentation inevitable.

In the same vein, Abraham Marcus points to two eighteenth-century merchants based in Aleppo.[30] The fortune of the first was split among his wife and thirteen children from consecutive marriages; and that of the second was divided among his four concurrent wives, seven sons, and six daughters. When the dead merchant had no surviving sons, many secondary relatives could gain entitlements. The cases reviewed by Marcus illustrate the possibilities: wife and four nephews; sister, uncle, and aunt; sister and three sons of a cousin; wife, two sisters, and seven cousins; wife, daughter, maternal grandmother, and two sisters.

Another instructive example entails the Egyptian entrepreneur Ismail Abu Taqiyya, who was active between 1580 and 1625. A leading merchant of his time, Abu Taqiyya made a fortune by importing coffee, whose use was just beginning to spread across the Middle East, from Yemen to Egypt.[31] Anticipating Starbucks by several centuries, he also promoted coffee consumption by building scores of coffeehouses. Abu Taqiyya exhibited similar entrepreneurial acumen in reviving the local sugar industry. Sensing a potential for dramatic market expansion, he financed sugarcane production, established refineries, and sold sugar both domestically and in the broader Mediterranean market.[32]

For our immediate purposes here, two elements of his record are noteworthy. First, in his long career Abu Taqiyya operated through myriads of small and independent partnerships involving geographically dispersed people. Each partnership was based on a separate contract designed for a narrowly defined purpose, such as financing a farmer's sugarcane farm for one season, or transporting a load of coffee beans from Mocha to Alexandria, or operating a coffeehouse in Damiat. These partnerships were short-lived, or they pooled limited resources, or both. Second, Abu Taqiyya's conglomerate did not outlast him. After his death, some of his associates took over certain components of his conglomerate. Although many of his coffeehouses probably lived on under different owners and new financial arrangements, his decades-old web of connections disappeared with him, and no person or organization inherited his region-wide commercial reputation. His commercial capital, too, got dissipated. His heirs did not maintain the conglomerate, to say nothing of enlarging it. The number of claimants must have mattered. Abu Taqiyya's heirs included eleven surviving children and four surviving wives. A few of them tried to consolidate their shares of the estate. However, within a decade family squabbles, illnesses, and additional deaths took their toll.[33]

When a partner died, the resulting inheritance claims were usually limited to his own kin. But because the co-owners of an inherited asset could sell, rent, or donate their shares of any partnership asset, the surviving members of a lapsed partnership could be confronted with persons unrelated, even unknown, to their deceased ex-partner.[34] This would compound the costs of premature termination, making merchants and investors try even harder to keep their partnerships small and short-lived.

Inheritance Regime and Partnership Size

It is worth reiterating the rationale for focusing on partnerships: their conduciveness to supporting cooperation among non-kin. In principle, a *mudāraba* or *inān* can pool vastly greater resources than an enterprise restricted to a single family. But the cost of reconstituting a dissolved Islamic partnership could be prohibitive. Particularly relevant is that restarting costs were higher for an Islamic partnership than for its European counterparts. A death could force the liquidation of an Islamic partnership that would easily be reconstituted had it been formed in, say, an English town that practiced primogeniture. In the Middle East, then, investors and merchants would have been relatively more eager to avoid a premature dissolution. They thus had stronger incentives to limit the size and duration of their partnerships.

If costs are borne by surviving members of a partnership that loses a member, irrespective of the prevailing inheritance regime, anything that shortens expected life spans will diminish the attractiveness of large partnerships. Thus, in Tuscany average partnership size shrank temporarily during the Black Death. Here is an explanation by Edwin Hunt and James Murray: "High mortality from the recurring plagues made long-term commercial associations very tenuous, especially when many heirs had become more interested in spending their inheritance than in perpetuating the business. And [large multiple partnerships] had become increasingly risky, requiring the close and dedicated attention of the owner-managers."[35]

To this logic one may add that the risk of expanding a partnership depends, in addition to natural factors, on the prevailing inheritance system. With mortality held constant, as the difficulty of keeping property undivided rises, average partnership size will fall. Hence, a society that fragments estates will have smaller partnerships than one that allows estates to be kept undivided. It will also have less experimentation involving partnerships. The hub-and-spoke system of the Medicis would have been difficult to establish in the Middle East, because the inheritance system limited the credibility of promises to pool resources over long periods. Insofar as the "hub" is vulnerable to fragmentation, it will have difficulty forming a durable network of "spokes."

Dynamic Consequences

The larger and more durable partnerships of Europeans unavoidably generated problems of their own, and the ensuing responses extended well beyond the accommodation of impatient heirs. To track resource flows and facilitate coordination, it became necessary to develop sophisticated accounting systems. By the fifteenth century, manuals of commercial arithmetic appeared to help investors and merchants monitor their enterprises. Among the problems addressed in these manuals was the allocation of profits from partnerships whose capital included investments made at different times.[36] The new rules facilitated the operation of enterprises financed by a continuous flow of funds rather than a simple infusion of cash at the beginning. Meanwhile, the growing volume of stock trading gave rise to formal equity markets, making it easier to raise new capital. Larger and longer-lasting partnerships instigated the creation of hierarchical control systems to economize on deliberation and decision costs.[37] Each of the European innovations reviewed above—linked partnerships, conglomerates, the joint-stock company—added to the organizational complexity of the modern global economy.

With the spread of larger and longer lasting enterprises, commerce became increasingly impersonal. Exchanges among mutual strangers became more and more common. A need thus emerged for information unobtainable from acquaintances, which then stimulated the founding of periodicals featuring commercial information. Hence, between the 1590s and 1640s, regular publications maintained by subscription fees from wealthy merchants appeared in every major European city. Their focus was on commercially useful information, especially prices, shipping schedules and rates, and diplomatic developments.[38] The emergence of a business press facilitated the formation of complex commercial organizations by lowering the cost of information needed to monitor agents and employees efficiently.

Like the general partnership used in medieval Northern Europe, the *commenda* thus turned out to be a self-undermining institution. In creating new opportunities for wealth creation, it also set the stage for enterprises of greater size, scope, and durability. More complex partnerships then generated new problems, stimulating further organizational innovations, along with new markets and services.

The emerging organizational forms did not necessarily meet with sweeping approval. As in other contexts, vested interests put up resistance. Consider the thirteenth-century Italian attempt at increasing longevity through the posting of resident partners in distant lands. Instead of returning home at the conclusion of a contracted trading mission, a resident partner would send a share of accumulated capital to his inactive partners at home as a dividend, receive authorization to reinvest the remainder, repatriate some profits again, and so on indefinitely. Through serial *commenda* these spatially separated partners thus acquired a lasting commercial identity. The arrangement presaged a key characteristic of the commercial enterprises that are now central to economic life: durability. A durable enterprise can make long-term commitments more credibly than one vulnerable to early termination. Before the law, however, Italian partnerships with resident partners were treated as temporary. In 1271, Venetian authorities drove home the point by limiting the duration of a partnership to two years and banning the sending of profits without a personal appearance. From their standpoint, the problem was that reducing the frequency of capital repatriation limited tax revenue.[39]

Despite the roadblocks, advantageous organizational innovations eventually saw wide adoption. Their successes then paved the way for institutions conducive to even larger and even more complex business enterprises. Thus, the stimulus that institutional development received from the variability of inheritance rules generated an institutional chain reaction through which commercial efficiency fed on itself.

The persistently small partnerships of the Middle East did not face the accounting, coordination, information, and liability problems that demanded innovative solutions in Europe. Their members felt no urge to develop or use standardized accounting methods. They did not seek improvements in bookkeeping of the sort that become necessary to facilitate communication and coordination among large numbers of shareholders, and to keep track of assets and liabilities spread across generations. By the same token, the privilege of trading enterprise shares was of limited value to the owners of an ephemeral profit-making enterprise. The brevity of their commitments already provided the liquidity that shareholders of a long-term enterprise obtained through tradability. Finally, merchants and investors of the premodern Middle East had no urgent need for a business press. Since they cooperated mainly with acquaintances, they already had access to reliable commercial information.

Thus, several fundamental innovations of western organizational history—standardized commercial bookkeeping, stock markets, the business press—are conspicuous in premodern Middle Eastern commerce by their absence.[40] They did not even become an issue until the crises of the nineteenth century. Among the legacies of the delays in question is that the local sources used by students of Middle Eastern history consist almost exclusively of records prepared by state agencies, including courts, jurisconsults, and palaces. As we already know, no private sources remotely comparable to the records of the Medicis or the Levant Company have come to light.[41]

True, the Geniza archive contains eleventh-century documents with evidence that some Jewish merchants of North Africa used rudimentary forms of double-entry accounting. It is also true that a 1363 treatise on state finances, the *Risale-i Felekiyye* of Abdullah Ibn Mohammed Ibn Kiya al-Mazandarani, contains tables with debit and credit columns.[42] But these are the exceptions that prove the general rule.[43] Even if double-entry accounting was invented in the region early on, it failed to gain wide adoption and disappeared from use until reintroduced in modern times. These patterns are consistent with the interpretation given above. Small and short-lived partnerships whose members know one another intimately have no pressing need for standardized accounting.

To recapitulate, Islam's essentially uniform inheritance system, by discouraging the formation of larger and more durable partnerships, closed off one path to economic modernization. The resulting organizational stagnation then prevented the Middle East's mercantile community from remaining competitive with its western counterpart. In the fifteenth century the resulting gap in commercial capabilities remained small. However, it was bound to grow. Successive adaptations had an enormous cumulative effect.

Alternative Paths to Modernization

In principle, the Middle East could have developed modern organizational forms through some alternative path. Noticing the western successes in Mediterranean trade, Middle Eastern merchants might have adopted one western innovation or another, thereby jump-starting a modernization process, which could then have followed a course of its own. However, not until the eighteenth century did trade with Europe loom large in the Middle East's external economic relations. Until then its trade with other regions was more important, as measured by volume. Moreover, Middle Easterners remained competitive in trading emporia lacking merchants backed by advanced institutions. In some of them, including South East Asia and East Africa, Islamic commercial institutions offered palpable advantages over their indigenous counterparts, as evidenced by their diffusion to far corners of the old world. For all these reasons, emulating western business practices did not become a pressing need until the eighteenth century. Once that point was reached, within a century reforms were undertaken to enable all Middle Easterners to trade under western-based legal codes.

The most obvious alternative to the modernization path actually followed—the wholesale adoption of certain European institutions —would have involved liberalizing the marriage and inheritance rules that constrained enterprise growth and longevity. However, the explicitness of the relevant Islamic scriptures would have discouraged open resistance. In any case, the prevailing marriage and inheritance practices were mutually reinforcing. Each fostered constituencies with a stake in the other. Jointly they lowered the likelihood of indigenous organizational modernization. Whereas the *commenda*'s successes undermined its popularity, not even the limitations of the *mudāraba* induced fundamental institutional reforms in the Middle East. On the contrary, the *mudāraba* turned out to be self-reinforcing. Indeed, by spreading to regions beyond Islam's heartland, it limited the trading emporia in which Middle Eastern traders encountered difficulties. The ensuing organizational stagnation gradually diminished the competitiveness of Middle Eastern merchants vis-à-vis their western counterparts.

Comparison with Received Explanations

There exist other explanations of why Islam's commercial institutions did not develop in tandem with those of the West. The commodities that Middle Easterners wanted from abroad, says Claude Cahen, were found primarily in the East. Also, in the Middle Ages Middle Eastern markets were large enough to absorb the region's entire production.[44] From these premises, Cahen infers that it was natural for Middle Easterners to pursue trade with Central Asia, India, and East Asia, leaving the Mediterranean emporium largely to westerners. They had no need, he claims, to keep up with western commercial capabilities.

Cahen's thesis does not treat Islamic institutions as inherently static. However, it is premised on a fixed volume of production. Granted that trade with the East was more important, profit opportunities might have induced certain local merchants to seek their fortunes in the Mediterranean emporium. Their commercial successes would then have stimulated the production, and perhaps also the institutional adaptations, necessary to meet the western demand. Hence, there is no necessary link between the initial size of the western market and Middle Eastern commercial competition with westerners. In any case, the organizational stagnation of interest here also afflicted Middle Eastern merchants active in eastern markets. The Cahen thesis does not illuminate why their commercial institutions, too, remained stagnant.

K. N. Chaudhuri offers an explanation that confuses cause and effect. As a rule, he observes, the Middle Eastern and East Asian traders active in the Indian Ocean wielded little political power. The consequent brake on their earnings denied them the scale economies necessary for effective competition against European companies.[45] But why, when earlier merchants were powerful enough to be represented significantly among the shapers of Islamic law, was the requisite political influence lacking? Merchants lost influence precisely because, even as state-controlled sectors of the social system evolved, the region's commercial infrastructure stagnated. Had Islamic law made it easier to keep commercial fortunes intact across generations, Middle Eastern merchants might have gained the clout to achieve further institutional changes. Unlike Chaudhuri's interpretation, the causality proposed here is consistent with the observed trends in occupational specialization.

This criticism of Chaudhuri's thesis applies also to Mehmet Genç's theory of the Ottoman failure to keep up with Europe.[46] The concept of helping merchants to prosper was alien, maintains Genç, to the ideology of the Ottoman ruling class. True enough, but why, say around the seventeenth century, were Ottoman merchants too weak to reshape the dominant ideology in their own interest? The answer, the foregoing chapters have shown, lies partly in the institutions that governed Middle Eastern commercial contracting and the transmission of commercial wealth across generations.

Every religion affects economic performance by helping to shape the legal framework for economic exchange. But religious interpretations are changeable, as are the laws that they legitimize. If they stagnate, one must identify the underlying causes. In the Middle East, common knowledge about the risks of forming large partnerships led merchants and investors to keep enterprises small and ephemeral. The simple organizational form typically used to conduct long-distance trade, the *mudāraba*, was thus self-enforcing. It was also self-reinforcing, not only because it diffused across the globe but also because its stability contributed to the political and ideological handicaps described by Chaudhuri and Genç. Specifically, the social standing of merchants weakened over time, facilitating the spread of anti-mercantile ideologies.

The point is not that commercial organization drives economic ideologies and political evolution, and never the other way around. In a system of interdependent institutions, every institution affects the others. Anti-mercantile policies and beliefs must have affected the organizational opportunities of merchants. But to identify such effects is not to explain their persistence. Impediments to forming large partnerships and preserving successful businesses would have supported attitudes and beliefs harmful to private commerce simply by limiting the resources of major businessmen and commercial dynasties.

Unintended Secondary Consequences of Early Islamic Institutions

The stagnation of Islamic commercial institutions is an unfortunate consequence that could not have been intended or foreseen a millennium earlier. The Islamic law of partnerships was well suited to the medieval economy in which it developed. The Islamic inheritance system spread wealth by providing mandatory inheritance shares to all sons and daughters, and Islamic polygyny had the same effect by enabling the wealthiest merchants to have unusually numerous heirs. What could scarcely have been understood in the early Islamic centuries is that, in the face of outside developments, these institutions would eventually incapacitate Muslim merchants in their dealings with the West, in third markets, and even at home.

To observe that Islam's marriage, inheritance, and partnership rules blocked organizational modernization is not to assert that these institutions are incompatible with a modern economy. Institutions inimical to modernization need not interfere with the operation of modern organizational forms, once those forms have been transplanted from elsewhere. Consider an owner of 1,000 shares in Orascom Telecom, a modern Egyptian corporation listed on both the Egyptian Stock Exchange and the London Stock Exchange. At her death, the shares are divided among her husband and five children. This distribution is of no consequence to Orascom's survival. By diffusing the company's ownership and giving its management a freer hand, the estate's fragmentation could even facilitate its continuity.

The business corporation is critical to the modern global economy. Hence, it is natural to wonder whether the Middle East might have overcome the handicaps identified thus far, and made the transition from personal to impersonal exchange, through some alternative organization rooted in corporate law. Yet Islamic law lacks a concept of corporation. Our next task is to explain why no institution analogous to the business corporation emerged and why this mattered.

6

The Absence of the
Corporation in Islamic Law

The year 1851 saw the founding of the first predominantly Muslim-owned joint-stock company of the Ottoman Empire: the Şirket-i Hayriye marine transportation company, literally the "Auspicious Company." Headquartered in Istanbul, its ownership was divided into 2,000 tradable shares. At the time, the empire was just beginning to install the requisite legal infrastructure. Commercial courts established to enforce the newly adopted French commercial code were in their infancy, and the opening of an organized stock exchange was not even on the drawing board. Nevertheless, Şirket-i Hayriye began operation under the patronage of sultan Abdülmecit, its largest shareholder. The remaining shares were purchased by Turkish officials and a few prominent financiers, almost all Armenian.[1]

For lack of a suitable Turkish word, Abdülmecit characterized Şirket-i Hayriye through a neologism derived from the French *compagnie* and English "company": *kumpaniye*. What was his motive for favoring an organizational form alien to Islamic law, the traditional basis for commercial contracts? The Ottoman economy was now dominated, he observed, by large and permanent enterprises, in other words, *kumpaniyes*. The emerging banking, mass transportation, and manufacturing sectors consisted of *kumpaniyes*, all owned by foreigners and minorities; it was time for Muslims to join the trend of pooling resources within modern enterprises.[2] Evidently Ottoman elites of the mid-nineteenth century considered Islamic partnerships ill-suited to the new economy that was unfolding before their eyes. They could see that Islamic partnership law, generally unchanged since the tenth century, did not measure up to the organizational forms that had become prevalent in the global economy.[3]

From the standpoint of the region's organizational development, Şirket-i Hayriye's key contribution lies in the tradability of its shares. As we already know from earlier chapters, the continued existence of a traditional Islamic partnership was dependent on its partners; it became null and void at the withdrawal, incapacitation, or death of even a single member. Authorized to issue tradable shares, Şirket-i Hayriye could survive changes in membership; the shares of exiting partners would simply switch hands, without recontracting. As significant is that Şirket-i Hayriye was not declared a corporation. It was established as an *unincorporated* joint-stock company. Why the sultan did not charter Şirket-i Hayriye as the first Ottoman-recognized corporation is unknown. However, a corporate charter would have lacked immediate practical value, because the empire's Islamic courts, even its nascent secular courts, lacked familiarity with the corporation. By contrast, the tradability of Şirket-i Hayriye shares was a credible characteristic, for a few Ottoman cities already had informal markets in government bonds and the shares of foreign companies.

A critical characteristic of the corporation is legal personhood: before the law, it is a fictitious person. Today, of course, almost any large company in the region—Turkish Airlines, Suez Steel, Saudi Telecom—can sue and be sued as though it were a person, in both its home country and internationally. Legal personhood simplifies litigation. It also shields jointly held assets from the liabilities of individual shareholders. A distinction must now be introduced between "owner shielding" (limited liability for shareholders) and "entity shielding" (limited liability for the company itself).[4] An unincorporated joint-stock company and certain Islamic partnerships could provide owner shielding: the protection of partners' personal assets from the creditors of other partners. But neither offered entity shielding. Precisely because Şirket-i Hayriye lacked entity shielding, the creditors of a single shareholder could force it to liquidate. Only if established as an entity with legal standing and assets of its own—as a corporation—would it have enjoyed both forms of protection.

Knowing of Abdülmecit's personal commitment to Şirket-i Hayriye's success, a shareholder's creditors would have thought twice before pursuing its dissolution. Unincorporated joint-stock companies lacking sultanic patronage would have been more vulnerable, and this would have hindered their ability to raise capital. Indeed, in the half-century following the founding of Şirket-i Hayriye the *kumpaniyes* established in the Ottoman Empire were mostly foreign corporations with headquarters in London or Paris, and their major disputes were settled in foreign courts. Ottoman corporations were owned overwhelmingly by non-Muslims enjoying foreign legal protection, in other words, the right to do business under the laws of a foreign power.[5] The explosion in domestic, and particularly Muslim, *kumpaniye* formation that Abdülmecit tried to trigger through a visible prototype occurred only after 1908, when the Ottoman parliament passed a law of corporations (fig. 6.1).[6] A similar pattern held in Egypt, where until the 1920s most

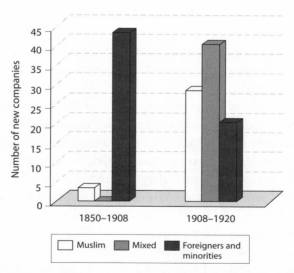

Figure 6.1 Publicly traded new Ottoman companies: 1850–1908 and 1908–20. For explanations, see endnotes 5 and 6. *Note:* The distributions are statistically different at the 99.9 percent level of significance (χ^2 (2) = 61.43). *Source:* Akyıldız, *Ottoman Securities*, pp. 93–185 and 186–301.

heavily capitalized companies consisted of corporations headquartered abroad.[7] This history of the region supports the view, derived from experiences elsewhere, that the unincorporated joint-stock company is an inferior substitute for the business corporation.[8]

Our present challenge is to unlock the mystery of why the corporation entered the Middle Eastern menu of organizational options only recently, in the twentieth century. The task may be divided into three subtasks, of which the last two will be left to the next chapter. The first is to explain why, early on, Islamic law closed itself off to the corporation. The corporation need not have been invented from scratch, for its essential elements were present in pre-Islamic legal systems. The second subtask is to determine why associations that approximate the corporation and that embodied a concept akin to an artificial person did not emerge after the first few Islamic centuries. And the third is to explain why, as western Europe profited increasingly from the corporation, this organizational form was not transplanted to the Middle East.

Roman Origins

The association of individuals into groups pursuing a common goal extends to time immemorial. So does the concept of a collective entity, critical to the family and the state. Under the Romans, who developed this concept further, the state was empowered to hold property and transact with natural individuals as though it was itself a person.[9] Collectively held Roman tax farms could outlive their individual partners; organized as special partnerships called *societas publicanorum*, they separated ownership from management, had representatives who acted for the company as a unit, and were treated as tradable.[10] *Corpus Juris Civilis*, the law code compiled during the reign of Justinian (527–65), allows the imperial treasury to sue and be sued in court.[11] However, not even Justinian's code articulated a precise definition of the corporation, to say nothing of identifying its rights and obligations in general terms. It does not elucidate the relationship between the ensemble and its members. It does not specify whether the collective rights enshrined in a corporation come from a public charter or merely the will of its founders.[12] Even the terminology used in the code (*universitas, collegium, persona*) is nebulous.

These ambiguities betray the conflicting motives of Roman officials. Allowing groups to have representatives, own property jointly, and have a collective life beyond the lives of its individual members could make society more productive and enlarge its government's tax base. However, the same capabilities could also sow instability by facilitating the organization of disgruntled collectivities. Jurists who wanted incorporation to be a state-granted privilege tried to balance these considerations.[13] From their standpoint, regulated incorporation had the further advantage of enabling the state, as the issuer of corporate charters, to claim some of the resulting rents.

In opposing all permanent associations other than the family and the state, these jurists rejected freedom of association. Nevertheless, over the next half-millennium diverse private associations—burial clubs, craft guilds, charities, cults, churches, monasteries—gained general recognition as a corporation in the eastern Roman Empire and, more prominently, in former territories of the western Roman Empire. To varying degrees, each exercised self-governance. Typically they could own property, elect representatives, enter into contracts, and act as a legal person.[14] In seeking to sharpen the boundary between themselves and the outside world, some of these early corporations made a point of withdrawing from local politics.[15]

There is a reason why this decentralized incorporation movement was stronger in western Europe than in Byzantine territories. In the West, states were relatively weak. Charlemagne, who purported to govern as "emperor" of the Holy Roman Empire (800–14), exercised meaningful authority over only a small area. Most of his ostensible subjects were probably unaware of his rule, if they even knew of him.[16] Associations thus declared themselves a corporation to establish order within their own microcosm and compensate for the absence of a central authority capable of enforcing contracts. The proliferation of self-declared corporations undermined the Roman principle of regulated incorporation. Without states capable of dictating terms, associations took matters into their own hands, claiming the right of self-governance and endeavoring to impose their will on individuals and other corporations with whom they interacted.

Emergence of Formal Corporations

The centuries of weak state authority in the West coincide with the formative period of Islamic law. Muhammad was born just six years after Justinian's death, and some of Islam's leading early jurists were contemporaries of Charlemagne. Around 1000, as Islamic partnership law was assuming its classic form, the West was continuing to experiment, in uncoordinated fashion, with the corporation. A critical step was taken about two centuries later. Following the split of Christianity in 1054, and during the struggle to emancipate religion from the control of emperors, kings, and feudal lords (1075–1122), the Roman Catholic Church began calling itself a corporation and running its affairs according to a new canon law (*jus novum*).[17] Dealing with sundry issues, including jurisdiction, property, and contracts, canon law built on innumerable concepts and rules belonging to preexisting secular and ecclesiastical legal systems. But unlike its forerunners, it emerged as a systematized body of law articulated in texts.[18]

During the incorporation wave of the sixth through eleventh centuries, all across western Europe the clergy had developed a collective self-consciousness and formed effectively autonomous religious organizations. Now, by claiming a corporate identity of its own, the entire Church differentiated itself from the secular world, separated its assets from those of its members, and wove detached clerical collectives into a transtribal and transnational organization with an autonomous chain of authority. The move would also enhance the power of the Church over clergy by weakening clerical bonds to competing sources of authority, such as the family. Where states regained power, the assertion of legal personhood, too, began to matter. Meanwhile, other attempts were made to form corporations with elaborate legal systems. Thousands of towns in northern Italy, France, England, and Germany acquired a corporate identity, in some cases through a royal charter, in others simply through the will of their residents.[19]

Several economic factors fueled the rise of the modern city in western Europe: the revival of commerce, rising agricultural productivity, and population growth through migration from the countryside.[20] Insofar as individuals and other collectivities viewed a city as an entity likely to outlast its representatives, it could enter into long-term contracts, borrow at low cost, and threaten punishment credibly. As an autonomous entity, it could also lower its governance costs by making its own bylaws. These benefits would have risen with city size, making large cities especially likely to incorporate.

However, this cannot be the whole story, for the towns that incorporated in this period varied greatly in population.[21] Whatever its known applications, corporate law constituted a public good. Hence, the broader incorporation movement must have facilitated the incorporation of towns. People from all walks of life could learn from the experiences of, say, religious groups. They could transfer to non-religious realms know-how concerning such processes as running elections within the Church and appointing Church representatives. The general incorporation movement also promoted tolerance with regard to the incorporation of new groups.

The evolution of the European corporation depended, then, on the weakening of central authority following the demise of the western Roman Empire. The consequent power vacuum provided incentives as well as opportunities to enhance organizational efficiency by instituting private legal systems. The process of incorporation thus fed on itself, as new corporations increased experience and familiarity with decentralized governance. By the time strong states re-emerged, corporations were firmly embedded in the fabric of daily life.

Also critical was a characteristic of Christianity, namely, that it developed in a milieu featuring, paradoxically, a strong state. This made it focus on matters of faith, morality, and community, generally ignoring the challenges of economic and political organization. Early Christians usually followed Roman law in their daily interactions even as they tried to live as good Christians. A precedent was thus set for the coexistence of multiple legal systems, each with its own limited jurisdiction, and with possibly overlapping constituencies. During the incorporation wave that culminated in the development of canon law, this precedent facilitated acceptance of numerous distinct legal systems, some religious and others secular. When the waning of Roman power in the West stimulated the incorporation of innumerable overlapping groups, Christians were already accustomed to non-religious legal systems. Significantly, the developers of canon law did not address all domains of life. They took for granted the existence of secularized domains governed by legal systems developed, and subject to modification, outside their own purview.

The Formation of Islamic Law

During Islam's formative period the peoples of the Middle East, including Muslims, had exposure to the Roman institutional heritage. Subjects of the early Arab empires, especially Syrians and Egyptians, studied and practiced Roman law, though usually in forms supplemented and modified by local customs. Converts brought into Islamic discourse legal concepts with which they had familiarity. Islamic law thus borrowed from Roman law directly as well as indirectly, through the region's indigenous communities.[22] Hence, an Islamic variant of the corporation could have been developed simply by transplanting existing concepts into the emerging legal system.

True, relative to their counterparts in western Europe, the corporations established in eastern Roman lands enjoyed less autonomy. By the sixth century, cities under Byzantine rule had lost much of their financial independence, and their town councils had lost effectiveness.[23] Laws governing monasteries were formulated centrally, and with an eye toward uniformity and discipline. Monasteries were banned from merging, lest they create centers of political power.[24] Insofar as early Muslims gained exposure to Roman legal culture through interactions with the inhabitants of formerly Roman territories, they encountered, then, more than permissive attitudes toward the corporation. They gained familiarity with the view that the corporation should serve state power rather than decentralized local governance. To these factors that shed light on why Islamic law spurned the concept of a corporation, one may add that in schools that trained Muslims to join the learned class (*ulamā*), Roman law was left out of the curriculum.

But even collectively these factors leave much unexplained. During the seventh through tenth centuries, as classical Islamic law was taking shape, any Muslim jurist concerned with organizational efficiency would have known that the Roman legal tradition offered relevant, if fragmentary, ideas. Besides, pertinent concepts were present also in Persian law, with which Muslim jurists were also familiar. A Zoroastrian temple could hold property and make loans as an organization.[25] It is all the more puzzling, then, that the corporation was excluded from the corpus of Islamic law.

One clue lies within the communal organization of pre-Islamic Arabia. At the birth of Islam, inhabitants of the Arabian peninsula were divided into tribes bound together by real or fictitious blood ties. The individual was expected to support his fellow tribesmen and assume responsibility for their acts. This system promoted unending feuds. Moreover, intertribal alliances formed for defensive purposes were inherently unstable; a routine conflict could trigger escalating violence and a scramble for new alliances.[26] Because of the resulting insecurity, people stood to gain from an ideology capable of unifying peoples through all-inclusive bonds of solidarity.[27]

Islam responded to this broad need by promoting communal bonds based on religion rather than descent. "Cling one and all to the faith of Allah and let nothing divide you," says the Quran. "Remember the favors He has bestowed upon you: how He united your hearts when you were enemies, so that you are now brothers through His grace; and how He delivered you from the abyss of fire when you were on the very brink of it."[28] The community-building referenced in this verse was critical to Islam's rapid diffusion. It fostered an ideology conducive to weakening kinship ties, reducing intertribal violence, and enhancing material security. It also facilitated collective action against outsiders, as evidenced by the early conquests.

Islam's initial emphasis on community-building is reflected in the duties enunciated in the Quran. Eight of its verses call for "commanding right and forbidding wrong."[29] Four of these assign this obligation to individuals, the remainder to the collectivity of Muslims (*umma*).[30] None imposes the duty on a subgroup such as an assembly of elders. In fact, the Quran says practically nothing on the internal organization of the Muslim brotherhood. Although it does not ban associations formed to pursue legitimate ends, neither does it mention any by name. No collective economic actor appears in the Quran, let alone a collectivity considered a legal person. Islam's most authoritative source of guidance harbors nothing obvious, then, that might have inspired or supported the corporate form of organization, or justified borrowing it from an outside source.

At the point when the Quran became a closed book, tribal bonds remained strong. The evidence lies in several patterns: the commonality of marriages among kin, the practice of holding extended kin of a criminal collectively responsible for paying blood money (*diyya*) to the victim's kin, the tribal alliances formed in subsequent succession struggles, and the prevalence of mistrust between Arabs and non-Arabs.[31] Over the next few centuries, as the medieval Church weakened tribal bonds among Christians through the prohibition of marriage within kin groups, tribalism remained a potent social force among Muslims.[32] Nevertheless, Islam had unleashed a counter-force that now denied tribalism legitimacy and forced Muslims to cloak nepotism and clannishness in a rhetoric of religious unity and brotherhood. It provided the means to resolve disputes through courts committed in principle to the equality of all Muslims before the law, as opposed to inherently biased tribal structures.[33] Though by no means extinguished, tribalism had ceded the high moral ground to a pan-tribal religious ideal.

Obstacles to Subcommunal Self-Governance

Christian scripture is not lacking in passages that decrie divisions within the faith. Here is Paul of Tarsus, in his first Epistle to the Corinthians: "I appeal to you, brothers, in the name of Lord Jesus Christ, that all of you agree with one another so that there may be no divisions among you and that you may be perfectly united in mind and thought."[34] In any case, at the time that Europe converted to Christianity, it was divided along tribal lines, as Arabs were at the rise of Islam. Latins, Germans, Slavs, Celts, Avars, and others provided identities that competed with Christianity. Hence, Christian leaders would have felt the same urge as Muslim leaders to block divisions within their religion. Yet, Christianity also harbors teachings that may be used to legitimize subcommunal autonomy. The Biblical injunction to "render to Caesar the things that are Caesar's, and to God the things that are God's" offers the most salient example.[35]

This injunction has no analogue in Islamic discourse. Muhammad was both a religious and a political leader, and Islamic law was meant to regulate all spheres of life, without ceding ground to secular legislation.[36] On the face of it, the presumed comprehensiveness of Islamic law ruled out self-governance on the part of subcommunities; one could not replace divine law with human-made law even in limited domains. Like the commitment to a union of tribes in one great family, the lack of a formal separation between the religious and the secular thus conflicted with the concept of incorporation, and all the more so with the ideal of incorporation at will.

The development of Islamic legal interpretation supported the communal vision embodied in the Quran. The interpretation of legal texts was entrusted to trained individuals rather than an organization or office capable of exercising impersonal political power. Acts of a mufti (jurisconsult) were mere opinions. Another mufti could issue a different, yet equally legitimate, opinion. Likewise, a kadi adjudicated on the basis of his own reading of the law. In principle, his judgments did not create precedents for later judges, not even his own judgments in the future. New cases would be decided through fresh interpretations of the same texts, again by kadis acting as individuals.[37] In practice, conformist pressures homogenized judicial opinions and decisions. Yet the learned class achieved common positions without the benefit of a hierarchy. In keeping religious interpretation decentralized, Islam thus denied the Muslim community a corporate prototype.

The tradition of resting legal authority on texts provided rents to individuals with legal training, which they would want preserved. Allowing the formation of self-governing organizations could have diminished those rents by depressing the demand for judgments based on Islamic law. Hence, the learned class had reason to spurn the concept of a corporation. In western Europe, one might object, literate professions found ways to benefit from the proliferation of corporations. They did so by helping corporations to develop legal systems of their own, thus contributing to the co-existence of multiple jurisprudential traditions, canonistic as well as civilian.[38] Why would their Middle Eastern counterparts not have viewed corporations in the same light? One difference is that in the West the literate professions were not backed by a centralized state capable of enforcing a unified law. Political power was divided among emperors, kings, and cities, which is why corporations flourished in the first place. In much of the Middle East the learned class was integrated into centralized states capable of suppressing assertions of self-governance. Another difference is that the Muslim learned class already enjoyed a monopoly over adjudicating all disputes involving even one Muslim; it played an important role also in the adjudication of lawsuits among non-Muslims. By encouraging incorporation, it would not have achieved any obvious economic gain.

Islam's communal vision is reflected in classical Islamic political theory. This largely normative discourse generally recognizes no political boundaries except that between the abode of Islam (*dār al-Islām*), consisting of Muslim-ruled territories, and the abode of war (*dār al-harb*), governed by non-Muslims.[39] Tribal loyalties having given way, in theory, to religious brotherhood, the global community of Muslims was to be undivided.[40] This principle of a unitary community constrained the grouping of individuals for purposes of administration. Non-Muslims could be categorized according to their relation to Muslims, as with the distinction between protected religious minorities (*ahl al-dhimma*) and unprotected foreigners; and either group could be divided further, as necessary. For example, the Venetians could be classified as "friendly" and accorded rights denied to Spaniards. By contrast, all Muslims of similar social status had to have essentially equal political and economic rights, regardless of ancestry, language, or place of residence.

There existed practices in conflict with this broad ideal. Precisely because ancestry remained a source of legitimacy, many rulers claimed descent from Muhammad. The extension of inheritance rights beyond the nuclear family strengthened kinship ties, as did limits on testamentary freedoms. Yet, the ideal was not honored only in the breach. Up to modern times trade tariffs distinguished in the first instance between Muslims and non-Muslims. Whereas the latter could pay duties at various rates, a single rate applied to all Muslims, including the subjects of unfriendly rulers. In spite of a long history of Turkish-Iranian rivalry, the Ottoman and Safavid Empires charged each other's Muslim subjects the same duties that they charged their own. The procedures of premodern Islamic courts offer a second example. Whereas a Greek or Armenian would be identified as such, a Muslim Arab, Turk, or Albanian would be identified simply as a Muslim. That is one reason why national self-awareness developed more slowly among Muslims than among non-Muslims.[41]

The early interpreters of Islam had several reasons, then, for spurning a concept liable to facilitate factionalism. Most critically, they wanted to avoid stimulating rival forms of solidarity, such as tribalism. The life of the community was never cleansed, of course, of characteristics we now associate with the corporation. A form of legal personhood emerged in practices such as collective punishment for murder and collective responsibility for taxation.[42] A measure of self-governance appeared in the legal autonomy granted to Jews and Christians on civil matters, although mechanisms covered later on constrained their political powers. For yet another example, both limited liability and some separation of ownership from control were inherent in the most common forms of the Islamic partnership. From such elements, motivated legal scholars could have derived the corporation.

Emergence of the Waqf

Early Muslims, including the learned class, were motivated to develop some organization capable of indefinite existence. The huge start-up costs of providing certain durable social services created a need, as elsewhere, for an organizational form able to spread those costs over a long horizon. Mosques, fountains, and schools offer examples of structures that are both expensive to build and perpetually useful. One possible organizational solution is the corporation. By virtue of its perpetuity, an incorporated town may build a fountain and then manage it indefinitely. That solution was adopted widely in western Europe.

There were alternatives. In the Islamic Middle East diverse services, including ones with high start-up costs, came to be provided by an institution already mentioned, the unincorporated trust known as the waqf. At one level, this institutional choice, which appears to have been made about a century after Muhammad, was stunningly successful.[43] In the Middle Ages, waqfs financed innumerable services in cities far larger than any western town; and they did so without direct state involvement.[44] Ibn Battuta's fourteenth-century account of his journeys through Muslim-ruled lands speaks of a dazzling variety of waqfs, including ones that provided drinking water, pavements, assistance to travelers, support for pilgrimages, and wedding outfits to impoverished brides.[45] Outside of cities, most of the caravanserai (fortified inns) used by traveling merchants were funded by a waqf (fig. 6.2).

A waqf was established by an individual owner of immovable property to supply in perpetuity a function deemed legitimate under Islamic law. Like a corporation, it could be fine-tuned to specific needs. It shared with the corporation also the capacity to outlive its founder, employees, and beneficiaries.[46] There were also major differences. First, whereas an association could turn itself into a corporation through the collective will of its members, ordinarily the founder of a waqf had to be an individual.[47] Second, whereas a corporation was meant to be controlled by a changing membership, a waqf was to be controlled forever by its founder, through directions contained in the deed (*waqfiyya*) he had filed when endowing his property. Thus, a

Figure 6.2 Zazadin Han, a fortified inn for merchants near Konya, Turkey. Completed in 1236, it was financed for centuries through a waqf. Merchant caravans stayed in it for a nominal fee. It lost its usefulness as the transit trade through Anatolia dried up. (Photo: İzzet Keribar)

waqf's mission was irrevocable; not even its founder was authorized to alter its purpose retroactively. To drive home the point, after filing the waqf deed in court, a founder would customarily ask the kadi for a change in the terms, and the latter would deny the request on the ground that revered jurists considered waqf stipulations irrevocable.[48] A third difference concerned self-governance. Unlike a corporation, which could remake its rules of operation at will, those of a waqf were meant to be fixed; the founder's instructions were enforced through judges and, where the deed was silent, according to local custom.

Just as the Church did not invent its corporate identity from scratch, so the waqf did not emerge in an institutional vacuum. The concept of a trust was present in Roman law; and pre-Islamic peoples of the Middle East, including the Persians, used it in various forms.[49] The recollections of Muhammad and his companions include references to arrangements akin to a trust. For example, the second caliph Umar I (586–644) allegedly immobilized certain properties for the benefit of orphans and the poor, pledging not to donate, bequest, or sell them.[50] Why would early Muslims have found the concept of trust congenial, even as they spurned the corporation? Although no records concerning the motivations of its originators have survived, the waqf accords with Islam's communal vision, discussed above. Insofar as leaders considered factionalism a threat, they would have favored an institution with a single founder and a fixed mission to one involving self-governance by an organized group. Unlike the statesmen of medieval Europe, they had the power to block the legitimation of self-governing units.

To identify a reason for rulers to favor the waqf over the corporation does not explain why individuals founded waqfs. Two common motives were generosity and prestige. Even jointly, however, these motives would not have accounted for the range of services supplied. Another, sometimes the main, inducement for endowing a waqf is that it provided pecuniary gains to the founder and his family. The founder could appoint himself the waqf's caretaker (*mutawalli*), set his own salary, hire relatives to paid positions, and even designate his successor, thus bypassing Islam's inheritance regulations. In endowing assets as waqf, a founder also made them more secure. Distressed rulers were less likely to confiscate waqf assets than private property. Hence, the waqf served as a wealth shelter. The credibility of this insurance depended on its presumed sacredness, based on its absorption into Islamic law and also on the emphasis in public discourse on the piety motive of founders. The belief that property becomes sacred upon being endowed as a waqf is what discouraged the confiscation of waqf property, for rulers could lose legitimacy.

Just as the founder of a waqf sought a credible commitment to the security of his endowment, so a ruler who gave up opportunities to expropriate sought to have the founder commit credibly to supplying the designated social services. Requiring the caretaker to follow the waqf deed to the letter was an attempt to ensure that commitment. Like other types of trust, the waqf was designed as inflexible in order to mitigate the agency problem inherent in delegating implementation of the founder's instructions to successive individuals liable to divert assets to their own uses. The typical deed stated the services to be performed and the employees to be hired, often down to minute details, such as the ingredients in the meals to be served, and the salaries of individual employees.

The "static perpetuity" principle of the waqf emerged, then, through an implicit social bargain between rulers and the owners of private property. That the bargain could result in inefficiencies must have been understood, for escape valves were instituted to enable pressing changes. But the flexibility was strictly limited. In some places and times, the standard formulary for establishing a waqf contained a list of allowable operational modifications.[51] However, only one set of changes could be made; once the right was exercised, static perpetuity would apply forevermore. Hence, eventually the judgments and preferences of caretakers, employees, and intended beneficiaries would cease to matter; both the waqf's mission and its mode of operation would become frozen. What if there came a point when the mission could no longer be met? If changing trade routes made a waqf-financed caravanserai fall into disuse, could the endowment be reallocated? As the law was commonly understood, the caretaker lacked the necessary authority. He could abandon the caravanserai, in which case its supporting assets would accrue, by default, to the poor. Yet another manifestation of static perpetuity is that multiple waqfs could not pool their resources to benefit from economies of scale. This limitation became a serious handicap in the age of industrialization, when emerging technologies raised the optimal scale of production in many sectors.

By tradition, the establishment of a waqf was construed as the withdrawal from circulation of its corpus and the assignment of its revenue to the designated service.[52] Understandably, the service had to be commensurate with the expected revenue. A larger endowment was needed to finance a congregational mosque than, say, a water fountain (fig. 6.3); in the event of a perceived mismatch between projected income and expected expenditures, the courts might disallow the waqf. Against this background, static perpetuity seems to have been designed also to safeguard the waqf's capacity to meet its recorded social obligations. As a matter of practice, maintaining the capacity over a long period was a challenge.

Figure 6.3 Sabil-kuttab of Nafisa Al-Bayda, Cairo. Endowed in 1796 as a waqf by a wealthy Egyptian woman, it had a fountain below and a Quran school above. Water was brought to the fountain daily from the Nile. (Photo: Nasser Rabbat)

Sooner or later conditions would change sufficiently to make the waqf's goals unattainable without an infusion of new resources or changes in its mode of operation.

Whatever the motives underlying the waqf's characteristic features, they produced inefficiencies. These are visible in contrasting the colleges established as waqf-financed madrasas with those founded contemporaneously as universities. The early universities of Europe, including Paris (1180) and Oxford (1249), were founded as trusts.[53] But they quickly became self-governing and self-renewing organizations through incorporation. By contrast, the Islamic colleges known as madrasas continued to be constrained by the directives of their founders. Over time, therefore, the curriculum changed less in madrasas than in universities, helping to turn the Middle East into an intellectual backwater.[54] Although many factors contributed to the region's lack of intellectual prominence after several bright centuries under Islamic rule, a basic cause lies in the waqf's organizational limitations.

Madrasas and universities were both non-profit organizations. Their differences late in the second millennium may be traced to a fateful divergence of paths initiated soon after the birth of Islam. The waqf became Islam's main organizational form for providing social services at a time when western Europe deployed the corporation for many of the same ends. The organizational gap widened in the late sixteenth century, when the West began applying the corporate form of organization to profit-oriented production, finance, and commerce.

Early Institutional Choices, Late Handicaps

We now have initial insights into the constraints that Sultan Abdülmecit faced as he decided to launch the Ottoman Empire's first indigenous joint-stock company. If he did not charter the Şirket-i Hayriye as a corporation, a basic reason is that Islamic law lacked such a concept. Like a corporation, a waqf could outlive its founder, employees, and beneficiaries. However, it was not meant to be self-governing. On the contrary, it was conceived as an essentially frozen entity with a fixed endowment and an unchanging function carried out under given rules. By the early second millennium, then, the Middle East and western Europe were already on divergent paths with regard to corporate development.

Profit-oriented businesses were not yet organized as corporations even in Europe. The first business corporations emerged in the middle of the second millennium. Hence, by itself the identified institutional divergence does not explain why the Middle East was relatively late in applying the corporate concept to business. Making sense of this particular delay requires a two-pronged investigation. We must understand, first, the institutional dynamics that produced the business corporation in Europe, and, second, the barriers to its emergence in the Middle East. Several possible distinctly Middle Eastern paths to the corporation can be identified. The waqf offered one potential starting point, Islamic partnership law another, and there were more.

7

Barriers to the Emergence of a Middle Eastern Business Corporation

I t was in the late sixteenth century that European commercial enterprises started being organized as corporations. The voyages of global discovery and the consequent invigoration of overseas trade formed the impetus for this development. The commercial expansion relied on capital outlays for unusually long periods and from growing numbers of investors. However, various practices essential to the workings of the business corporation had already emerged over preceding centuries. The early variants of the business corporation combined known organizational features, though in novel ways.

Some of those features did not emerge at all in the Middle East. Others did, but their applications were suppressed for political reasons. The resulting deficiencies explain why Şirket-i Hayriye could not have been founded as a corporation and why, in instituting their corporate laws, Turkey and Egypt looked abroad for a model. Equally telling is that the Turkish and Egyptian transplants were accompanied by complementary institutional reforms. Evidently there were multiple obstacles to the indigenous emergence of the corporation.

As a prelude to developing these points, we must familiarize ourselves with the European path to the modern business corporation. Its most salient aspect is the organizational dynamism of various business communities. Diverse organizational forms were tried, by combining organizational features in distinct ways. Why analogous organizational dynamism was lacking in the Middle East requires investigation. The key issue is not why any particular

development, such as the overseas trading company, was not replicated. It is that the private commercial sector lacked the dynamism
that might have allowed local merchants and investors to form
self-governing and long-lasting organizations of their own. Had
they been more creative, sultan Abdülmecit would not have needed
to establish an organizational prototype from above, as an initiative of the Ottoman administration. He took the lead precisely
because organizational modernization had not come from below,
through innovations of local commercial players.

Overseas Trading Companies and the Maturing of the Business Corporation

For all their organizational creativity, the Italians stopped short of
applying the corporate concept to profit-making enterprises. But
they did develop precursors of the business corporation. One was
the Genoese Bank of San Giorgio, founded in 1407. The shareholders of this chartered bank received dividends tied to profits.
Management was controlled by the largest shareholders; the smallest did not even vote in the general assembly.[1] This arrangement
advanced the separation of management from ownership, which is
a characteristic of the business corporation. In a simple partnership
any member, through his power to force liquidation, can veto any
decision. By concentrating authority in large shareholders, certain
Italian enterprises of the fourteenth and fifteenth centuries deprived
lesser members of unilateral power. Hence, they could grow without sacrificing governability. Insofar as their shares were tradable,
they also enjoyed greater longevity than a simple partnership.

The novel organizational features and techniques of the Bank of
San Giorgio and similar businesses spread slowly. The same can be
said of other commercial innovations, such as double-entry bookkeeping and owner shielding.[2] Nevertheless, they demonstrated
how features destined to become united in the business corporation could benefit production, finance, and commerce. They also
broadened the options of risk-averse investors and merchants.

The earliest business corporations were founded in the late six-teenth and early seventeenth century by English and Dutch mer-chants seeking to broaden access to capital and monopolize over-seas markets. Their evolution entailed three patterns of interest here. First, an advance could occur through multiple paths. Second, organizational innovations were induced, as in earlier times, by identifiable economic goals, such as entity shielding and reduced governance costs. Finally, they often generated unintended prob-lems, which made creativity feed on itself.

The key challenge of the Levant Company, the East India Com-panies of the Dutch and English, and other overseas companies was to raise abundant fixed and working capital. This objective produced a deal among three sets of players: active traders, inves-tors who passively awaited returns, and the state, which chartered companies and helped to enforce agreements among their mem-bers. The state's involvement was immediate in England, where the lack of a legal tradition of owner shielding required incorporation from the start. It came later in Holland, where enterprises formed as commenda took to coordinating activities within a single com-pany.[3] Whatever the exact pattern, the state shared in the profits through taxes and cheap loans. It also benefited from certain com-pany assets: embassies, consulates, trade facilities, and ships deploy-able in warfare.[4]

In both countries the overseas companies stimulated the devel-opment of secondary markets for shares, though the circumstances differed. Initially the shares of English companies were transfer-able only with the consent of other members. These companies provided public goods to their members, including rules in their collective interest.[5] The public goods enhanced share prices, as did the expansion of stock markets. With the emergence of constituen-cies for relaxing restrictions on transferability, the English compa-nies evolved into joint-stock companies. Interest in a joint-stock company could be transferred at will. This evolution induced in-dividual companies to accept more shareholders. Established by twenty merchants in 1581, the Levant Company had two hundred a century later.[6]

To turn to the Dutch case, at its establishment in 1602 the Dutch East India Company's shareholders were required to pledge their capital until 1612. However, the shares were freely transferable. The emergence of a booming secondary market for these shares eliminated the need for a pre-specified liquidation date. At the end of the ten-year period, the Dutch parliament renewed the company's charter, though as a joint-stock company. Thenceforth, it was to have a perpetual existence, and partners would exit simply by selling their shares.[7] From a different starting point than England, then, Holland established one of the prerequisites of a profit-making corporate sector. Both patterns show how problems stemming from novel institutions can trigger new innovations, giving organizational transformation its own momentum.

Simple organizational forms would remain popular even after the spread of unincorporated, and then incorporated, joint-stock companies. The new forms were of little structural consequence to small businesses organized as a sole proprietorship, family enterprise, or simple partnership. Joint-stock companies achieved prevalence only in the early eighteenth century; holding 0.013 percent of England's national wealth in 1560, they held 5.2 percent by 1717.[8] Nevertheless, the reviewed experiences provided the institutional fine-tuning and know-how to deploy the business corporation widely, if ever this became optimal.

As the Industrial Revolution unfolded, the corporate form proved useful especially in sectors where efficiency required thousands of workers to use extensive capital in coordinated fashion. One such sector was international shipping, which grew by leaps and bounds in the seventeenth and eighteenth centuries. Whereas 770 European ships sailed from Europe to Asia in the sixteenth century, 6,661 did so in the eighteenth century, with Dutch and English corporations accounting for three-quarters of the total.[9] The corporate form gave a further stimulus to the mobilization of capital through measures to shield working capital from individual shareholders and their creditors. In encouraging the appropriation of corporate earnings, as opposed to the raiding of corporate assets, it also reduced shareholder risks.[10] The business corporation thus contributed to the financing and management of industrial capitalism.[11]

The evolution of the business corporation would continue, as would that of laws that underpinned it.[12] A key development of the nineteenth century was "free incorporation"—the right to incorporate at will, without the consent of a monarch, president, or parliament.[13] Meanwhile incorporation itself gained flexibility; for example, it became routine to modify voting rules to suit special needs.[14]

Nothing here presupposes that as an organizational form the corporation is necessarily superior to the partnership, regardless of circumstances.[15] Both forms of organization present trade-offs. Whereas in a growing partnership decision making becomes cumbersome, in a numerically equivalent corporation managerial control poses the greater challenge. That is why in industrial economies the incidence of partnerships and corporations varies across sectors. What is undeniable is that the unprecedented prosperity of the modern age, like the economic leadership of the West, has depended on a movement toward larger, more complex, and longer lasting profit-seeking enterprises.[16] And this has required advanced organizational forms. In nineteenth-century France, partnerships remained the most common organizational form, but the larger the enterprise, as measured by either employment or capital, the more likely it was to have corporate-like features or be an outright corporation.[17] The corporation was almost always the organizational form of choice in sectors where efficiency required the prevention of investors, their heirs, and their creditors from withdrawing capital at will. The increase in organizational scale, complexity, and longevity that marked the economic ascent of the West was accompanied by a rise in the use of advanced financial techniques, such as double-entry bookkeeping and the trading of equity.[18]

Missed Middle Eastern Opportunities

The advantages of the corporation bring us back to the stagnation of business organization in the Middle East. In the early Islamic centuries, the previous chapter showed, Islamic law recognized only natural persons, and waqfs provided services supplied in western

Europe increasingly by corporations. By themselves these initial choices do not explain why, more than a millennium later, there were no Muslim-founded corporations, or even unincorporated joint-stock companies. To make sense of the continued absence of organizations conducive to capital accumulation on a large scale, we must identify chains of causation that inhibited their emergence. Insofar as opposing processes were present, we must elucidate also why certain social mechanisms proved decisive.

Although the formative period of Islamic law would have constrained subsequent legal and organizational choices, the barriers were not insurmountable. After the advent of Islam, opportunities arose to reconsider the legal standing of groups and associations. One is the reality of autonomous Muslim subcommunities, which conflicted with the ideal of undifferentiated communal unity. From the dawn of Islam Muslims faced situations that fostered group identities less inclusive than that of the full community. The exigencies of daily life thus exposed the impracticality of keeping the global religious community undivided and undifferentiated. By the end of the seventh century, with Egypt, Syria, and Iraq in the Islamic fold, it was no longer realistic, if it ever was, to expect the full community to get involved in every issue. In practice, the individual Muslim's duty of "commanding right and forbidding wrong" had to be limited to local matters. Of necessity subgroups of the community would enjoy a measure of self-governance.

Further challenges to the ideal of communal unity appeared through political divisions. Just decades after Muhammad's death, even as new rationales emerged for treating the community as undifferentiated, the Sunni-Shii division became a permanent source of discord.[19] Meanwhile, converts maintained tribal, ethnic, linguistic, and geographic loyalties. Nor were these the only signs of entrenched political division. Movements arose to bestow privileges on Arab Muslims, or at least on Muhammad's descendants, along with counter-movements defending the rights of non-Arabs.[20] Every Muslim empire featured at least one politically privileged ethnic group, along with minorities dominant in one economic sector or another. Finally, after Muhammad no Muslim sovereign enjoyed legitimacy throughout the global community of Muslims. In adhering to the ideal of a unified community and withholding legal rights from subcommunities, jurists and political theorists doubtless sought to deny social divisions legitimacy. But established subcommunities need not have accepted the ideal of undifferentiation. Constituencies with a stake in subcommunal autonomy could have raised objections. They might also have pressured states to embrace the corporation, or some analogue, as a useful innovation.

The efflorescence of corporate life in the West created another opportunity to reconsider the legal standing of groups and associations. True, prior to the nineteenth century few Middle Easterners traveled to the West. That would have slowed the diffusion of new organizational technologies.[21] But western traders visited, even settled in, Muslim-governed commercial centers. There was a steady flow of pilgrims to the holy sites of Christianity and Judaism. Moreover, incorporated groups, such as the Hospitallers, participated in the Crusades as both fighters and providers of charity. Thus, it was possible to learn about western organizations without going far.

The most significant opportunity for learning about western organizational advances presented itself with the overseas trading companies. Middle Eastern merchants, financiers, customs officials, and judges came into contact with chartered trading companies; merchants who ventured to India encountered them also outside their own base. For lack of pertinent records, we do not know how Middle Eastern merchants viewed the companies. However, it should have been apparent that these companies benefited from more or less centralized management and that they enjoyed unusual longevity. At the end of the seventeenth century, Aleppo featured dozens of English "merchant houses," each operated by a partnership regulated through the Levant Company. In contrast to the Islamic norm of short-lived business associations, some of these partnerships lasted decades, much like the repeatedly renewed Italian enterprises of earlier centuries. Most houses employed wage-earning factors, whose tenure was indefinite.[22] When an English, Dutch, or French merchant died overseas, his son or widow might take over, preserving his enterprise.[23] Local merchants must have realized that their foreign counterparts enjoyed capabilities that

Islamic law generally denied. Recall that under the Islamic inheritance system a merchant's wealth usually got dissipated after his death, unless he had endowed a waqf, which restricted the use of his assets.

For their part, Middle Eastern statesmen could see that western negotiators of the trade treaties known as "capitulations" valued the privilege of settling estates as they saw fit, disregarding Islamic inheritance rules. By the mid-fifteenth century the capitulations typically gave western consuls sole jurisdiction over the disposition of estates belonging to their countrymen.[24] This right enabled western merchants in the Middle East to prepare enforceable wills that kept their estate undivided; if they died intestate, their own nation's inheritance regulations would apply. As trade with the West gained importance, and Middle Easterners began losing market share to western traders in third markets, connections might have been sought between the content of the capitulations and foreign modes of organization. Yet between the fifteenth and eighteenth centuries, a time when commercial organization advanced by leaps and bounds in the West, the Middle East produced no interpretation of these developments, or of their links to the capitulations. No reports appeared on the management of overseas trading companies, the consuls who represented foreign merchants, or foreign inheritance practices.

This may appear as evidence of general apathy or ingrained traditionalism, especially when coupled with indifference to certain other advances.[25] But attitudinal factors furnish at best a proximate explanation. The Middle East never sealed itself off from the West. It imported western goods, which points to an understanding that the West produced useful things. The region also borrowed military technologies, implying an appreciation of how western innovations were changing the Mediterranean balance of power. Nor was curiosity deficient across the board. Where leaders sensed an advantage to learning about foreign practices or know-how, they managed to become informed. What requires explanation, then, is not Middle Eastern apathy per se. It is why, until the nineteenth century, no notable attempts were made to learn about the value of European advances in capital pooling, enterprise preservation, commercial management, information dissemination, and bookkeeping. Even the exceptions are instructive. Ebubekir Ratib Efendi, the Ottoman Ambassador to the Habsburgs in 1791–92, mentions the Viennese stock exchange in a report to his sultan. It is a bustling market, he says, where diverse bonds are bought and sold. But this is a brief passage tucked among five hundred pages of commentary on the Habsburg military and tax systems.[26] It generated no initiative to facilitate the trading of financial assets.

Two possible explanations for this selective apathy may be ruled out quickly. Islamic law was frozen, so goes a common supposition, by a "closing of the gate of innovation (*ijtihād*)" after a few centuries of creativity. In fact, Islamic law never became literally frozen. Although in principle fixed, it enjoyed flexibility as a matter of practice. For example, from an early period onward the military was reorganized, sundry fines and tolls were imposed, the tax system was altered, and rules governing the inheritance of land were revised, all by decree and with only the flimsiest basis in Islamic law.[27]

The other possibility is that, because of the prevailing legal ethos, fictitious persons could not be promoted without challenging the very core of Islam. Although the Quran would not provide any obvious help to a reformer trying to legitimize corporate entities, with a modicum of imagination a person steeped in Islamic legal history could have found precedents for rudimentary forms of legal personhood. When asked whether property can be donated to a mosque, which is not a natural person, certain early jurists ruled in the affirmative.[28] Likewise, the fourth caliph Ali (d. 661) reputedly ruled that the furnishings of the Kaba belong to itself.[29] Such precedents might have justified granting legal standing to a socially constructed entity.

One might wonder at this stage whether the state blocked the pursuit of emerging opportunities. This possibility will be addressed in due course. What has been established thus far is that if some major constituency had pressured the Islamic court system to grant legal personhood to commercial organizations, religious obstacles could have been overcome.

Lack of Demand for Organizational Innovation

In spite of the many opportunities for introducing advanced organizational forms, until very late no demand emerged for organizational changes of the sort witnessed first in Italy and then in northwestern Europe. Recall that in the West the unincorporated joint-stock company, and eventually the corporation, gained commercial applications only after generations of experimentation with simpler organizations, such as family firms and coordinated partnerships. Management patterns and business techniques evolved incrementally, as innovations induced further innovations. What might have blocked similar chains of innovation in the Middle East?

We have already seen that Islam's relatively egalitarian inheritance system raised the costs of liquidating a partnership prematurely, thereby limiting the size and duration of partnerships, fragmenting the estates of successful merchants, and hindering the preservation of businesses across generations. The dynamic consequences are critical here. Members of small and short-lived partnerships felt no urge to develop sophisticated accounting methods or to obtain greater liquidity through tradability. An unintended consequence of such stagnation is that the business community could not even contemplate using an organizational form akin to the corporation. Without standardized bookkeeping, one cannot measure the net worth of a profit-seeking corporation in a way that will make sense to investors; also, bankruptcy procedures will foster serious conflict. Absent an infrastructure for trading shares, investing in a corporation will amount to relinquishing liquidity. For these reasons alone, any Middle Easterner seeking to incorporate would have had trouble attracting investment. These difficulties help to explain why, until modern times, no efforts were made to transplant the business corporation from abroad or, for that matter, to develop it indigenously. In theory, the business techniques and practices necessary to make the business corporation productive could have been deployed along with the corporation itself. However, the added costs made it less likely that anyone would consider the innovation worthwhile.

Once again, nothing in the evolving argument rests on the alleged fixity of Islamic law. Practices might have surged ahead of doctrine for a while, with individual kadis accommodating organizational forms alien to strict Islamic teachings. Given sufficient incentives for organizational innovation, appropriate doctrinal changes would have followed. If no such sequence of events occurred, the reason lies in a lack of demand for organizational development—itself a reflection of missing institutional preconditions.

New institutions do not emerge individually, independently of other developments. Because the feasibility of any given innovation depends on the broader institutional matrix, they develop as clusters, or "institutional complexes."[30] The case at hand offers an illustration. Europe was able to adopt the business corporation when the need arose because its institutional preconditions had fallen into place through centuries of incremental and interlinked organizational improvements. For the Middle East to develop a private corporate sector to match, say, the overseas companies, it also would have had to develop standardized bookkeeping and markets for trading shares. In other words, the path that the West traversed through myriads of organizational micro-innovations spread across many centuries would have had to be leapfrogged through a macro-innovation encompassing an entire institutional complex. Indeed, when corporate law finally arrived in the Middle East, this happened as part of an organizational surge that included the introduction of stock markets, banks, modern accounting, a commercial press, and even new judicial systems.[31]

If the structural stagnation of commercial partnerships constituted one reason for the dearth of organizational innovation in general, another was that successful merchants tended to convert their wealth into real estate, for reconversion into the corpus of a waqf. They did so for the very reason why founding waqfs gained enormous popularity among high officials: the weakness of private property rights. Like other wealthy groups, prosperous merchants sheltered wealth within waqfs.[32] The consequent outflow of mercantile wealth from the profit-oriented private sector must have limited even further the likelihood of partnerships expanding in size and gaining complexity. This is because the very merchants founding waqfs were those whose successes might have induced organizational adaptations to a larger scale of commercial activity. The availability of the waqf thus dampened the need for organizational modernization in the profit-oriented private sector.

Structural Stagnation of the Waqf

An unintended consequence of the waqf system was the dampening of incentives to develop organizational forms suitable to large and durable commercial operations. Could resources flowing from the commercial sector to the waqf sector have induced structural changes in the latter? This question brings us to the dynamics of the waqf itself. As we already know, the waqf substituted for the corporation, with which it shared the capacity to outlive a founder. Yet the waqf did not generate, or metamorphose into, an organizational form akin to the corporation.

There are four key differences between the waqf and the business corporation. First, the waqf is not a profit-maximizing entity. Second, an individual's share of a waqf's income is not transferable. Third, no clear separation exists between the property of a waqf and that of its caretaker. Finally, the waqf lacks legal personhood. In the face of opportunities for gain, these distinct characteristics could have given way to corporate characteristics. Why did transformations fail to occur?

From the eighth century onward, the waqf was considered a vehicle for providing charity through the "immobilization" of wealth. One of the literal meanings of "waqf" is "to stop," another is "to make dependent and conditional."[33] Immobilization was widely viewed as precluding profit maximization in the manner of a commercial partnership. To be sure, the two goals were not incompatible. Maximizing returns on the waqf's capital would also enhance its capacity to pursue its mission. It is such logic, in fact, that gave rise to the practice of exchanging a waqf asset for another asset deemed more profitable (*istibdāl* or *muʿāwada*).[34] But the practice required the permission of a judge, who would charge for registering the swap and could withhold his permission until bribed.[35]

Even in the absence of corruption, which will be taken up shortly, the exchange process was more costly than it would be for a commercial enterprise. For this reason, it was uncommon. Studying the Waqf al-Haramayn of Algiers, which administered vast properties for the benefit of Islam's holy cities, Miriam Hoexter finds that it conducted 0.06 exchanges per year in the period 1648–1700, and 0.24 in 1700–86.[36]

Why was the caretaker's discretion not extended in order to improve his ability to exploit waqf resources? The state, whose legitimacy depended on waqf-delivered services, had a stake in the stability of waqfs. Greater caretaker discretion, by boosting waqf profitability, would increase the risks taken with waqf assets. During the formative years of the waqf system, statesmen might have reasoned that these risks outweighed the possible gains. In the process, they would have solidified the tradition of limiting the caretaker's managerial discretion.

Such thinking, if indeed it was a factor, would have carried less weight with respect to a "family waqf" (*waqf ahlī*) meant to benefit primarily the founder and his descendants than to a "charitable waqf" (*waqf khayrī*) serving a broader constituency. In practice, the separation between the two categories was more one of degree than of kind; only a small minority of waqfs provided benefits confined to family members.[37] Nevertheless, family waqfs are particularly relevant here. For one thing, where social services were not at stake, the state lacked a compelling motivation to limit caretaker discretion. For another, there is no obvious reason for the state to have prevented family waqfs from turning into family firms. Precisely because the resources of a strict family waqf serve the family itself, its caretaker, a family member himself, would have wanted to maximize its profitability. Moreover, his relatives, both as individuals and as a collectivity, had every incentive to develop ways to align his interests with theirs. Hence, the family waqf might have been the starting point for innovations of the sort that generated the modern firm elsewhere.

Yet, in the public imagination the waqf was intertwined with delivering a designated service. The consequent expectations would have inhibited moves toward making waqfs serve strictly commercial purposes. They would have discouraged caretakers from making trade-offs readily accepted in business. The generic name of this proclivity to separate related issues is "compartmentalization."[38] Just as compartmentalization causes inefficiencies in the modern world, so it would have kept waqfs from maximizing returns on their assets.[39] The only partial exception to this pattern, the "cash waqf," will be considered in the next chapter. Even in that case, the distinction between charitable and commercial organizations was sustained.

This distinction might have eroded if the potential beneficiaries of organizational change enjoyed free organizational choice. In fact, groups with a stake in the status quo limited the available options. They included kadis, who were empowered to supervise waqfs, and risk-averse waqf beneficiaries. Kadis were particularly motivated to resist moves to turn the waqf into a commercial organization, because they derived rents from their duty to enforce the founder's expressed will. Waqf-related corruption, which is a major theme in Middle Eastern legal history, generally involved bribes paid to a kadi in return for his consent to deviations from the waqf deed.[40] One might object to the observation that kadis had a stake in the non-commercial character of the waqf on the ground that they could have negotiated an alternative arrangement beneficial to everyone, including themselves. Two factors stood in the way. First, kadis had no organization capable of collective bargaining on their behalf. Second, the brevity of their tenures and the precariousness of their subsequent appointments encouraged them to make the best of existing opportunities.

The supervisory authority of the kadis contributed, then, to keeping waqfs from acquiring corporate features. One such feature was transferability. Under waqf law, a person's entitlement to the waqf's income was non-transferable, to preserve the connection between the intended and actual uses of waqf resources.[41] Consider a waqf established to provide water to a particular neighborhood. Its residents could not transfer their rights to another neighborhood, because that would violate the express wishes of the founder.[42] In eighteenth-century England, too, limitations were placed on the transferability of trust assets and entitlements, partly to preserve the character of a trust. English trust law required trusts to be managed "prudently," which was understood to preclude entrepreneurial activity.[43] Yet, the waqf played a far greater role in the Middle East than its analogues did in the West, where the corporation was often the organizational form of choice. So rules to preserve boundaries among economic sectors, or among organizational forms, were much more consequential in the Middle East.

Legal personhood is another feature that failed to emerge. A waqf caretaker, regardless of the movability of his waqf's corpus, bore personal liability for the actions he took in fulfilling his duties. Aggrieved parties sued the caretaker, not the waqf itself.[44] There was no clear demarcation between assets of the waqf and those of its caretaker. The courts that adjudicated disputes involving the caretaker's exercise of his fiduciary duties mitigated the consequent personal risks. But this protection exacted a cost. Kadis effectively expected, and usually obtained, payment for these services, too—another reason why they supported the organizational status quo. Therein lies an important reason why the waqf sector saw no transition to legal personhood. A compounding factor is that legal personhood did not exist elsewhere in the legal system. Employees of Muslim-governed states were personally responsible for damage to the equipment they used in performing their duties. For example, the couriers of Ottoman sultans were personally liable for the horses they rode.[45] The transition in question would have entailed a macro-invention, in the sense of requiring supportive judicial reforms.

In earlier chapters we encountered early Islamic institutions that turned out to be self-enforcing. The waqf, too, was self-enforcing. Key constituencies had powerful incentives to maintain the features that distinguished it from the corporation.

Role of the State

An inquiry into the persistent simplicity of the organizational forms used by profit-seeking Middle Eastern enterprises must address more than the incentives of individual subjects. States might have found it advantageous to help the business community develop larger, longer-lived, and more complex organizations. In England and Holland, we saw, revenue-seeking states chartered overseas trading companies and assisted them through administrative and legal measures.

States do not benefit automatically from organizational innovations useful to private groups. Significantly, neither the English state nor that of the Dutch endorsed private organizational innovation indiscriminately. For centuries, each discouraged threatening innovations. In 1279, for instance, an English king issued a "Statute of Mortmain" to regulate the transfer of real estate to the Church and other corporations.[46] Until the nineteenth century, forming an English corporation was subject to government approval, granted selectively.[47] Such facts underscore the political dimension of organizational innovation. Wherever organizational advances occurred, the process involved bargaining among constituencies with conflicting interests.

The Middle Eastern states established after the rise of Islam quickly discovered the advantages of treating certain groups as administrative units for taxation. The craft guilds that emerged around the fifteenth century (in Arabic, asnāf or hirfa; in Turkish, esnaf or loncas) offer a case in point. They submitted to price controls and territorial restrictions, usually in return for state-supported monopolistic and monopsonistic rights. To varying degrees they enjoyed autonomy in setting membership requirements and selecting members. Although taxes were sometimes levied directly from individual members, this authority was often delegated to the head guildsman.[48] Another common method of group taxation was tax farming. Known since antiquity, it entailed auctioning off the right to "farm" a group's tax obligations. If the corporate form of organization was to emerge through indigenous means, the guild or tax farming might have provided the starting point. Let us explore first why the guilds of the Middle East did not evolve into corporations.

A guild could outlive its members. In other respects, however, it differed from a corporation.[49] Though recommended by the membership, a guild's leader was appointed by the state. True, as a matter of practice many guilds enjoyed substantial autonomy in the selection process, and in conflicts between the guild and the state, the latter did not always prevail.[50] However, guilds that produced vital commodities in places critical to political stability (for instance, the bakers and butchers of Istanbul) had leaders chosen directly by the government, usually from among military officers loyal to the sultan.[51] To survive, these leaders had to serve two masters at once. Representing their fellow guildsmen before the state, they also had to safeguard interests of the latter. Hence, the guilds were not organizations likely to work against basic state objectives. They enjoyed self-rule only insofar as the state considered it helpful to revenue generation or harmless to political stability.

Another guild characteristic at odds with the corporate model involves dispute resolution. To solve their internal problems, guild leaders and members often went to state-appointed officials outside the guild system. Still another difference is that the guilds lacked significant assets of their own; guildsmen owned or rented their shops and instruments as individuals.[52] Some guilds formed common funds to provide mutual insurance, but the magnitudes were small. The largest common guild fund in seventeenth-century Istanbul was that of the cauldron makers. In 1640, it held a sum that amounted to what a single skilled construction worker would make in eight years.[53]

Nevertheless, the guilds might have acquired more autonomy over time. If this did not happen, a key reason must lie in political conditions. At the time of their emergence, Anatolia was in turmoil, with weak statelets vying for authority in the face of frequently shifting boundaries—much as in western Europe during the half-millennium that saw the proliferation of the earliest religious and urban corporations. Had the turmoil continued, the consequent political and legal vacuum might have permitted the guilds to develop corporate features. However, the Ottomans managed to unite Anatolia and extend their authority over major commercial centers in the broader region. Opting to make guilds serve state goals, they saw no reason to grant them legal personhood, or the means to manage their resources centrally, or the right to expand their operations at will.

The Obstructed Transformation of Tax Farms

To turn to tax farming, its purpose was to raise taxes from constituencies that the ruler understood poorly. By auctioning off the right to collect their taxes, the state drew help from knowledgeable private parties. Competition among bidders served to maximize tax revenue, which the ruler received partly in advance. Ordinarily, the higher a tax farm's taxable capacity, the larger the winning bid.[54]

Tax farms were formed by the state, rather than tax constituencies themselves. The state was free to alter their boundaries and to switch to direct taxation through salaried officials. Where possible, it opted for direct taxation, resorting to tax farming only where the cost of direct collection was particularly high.[55] A tax farm could provide its operator a financial base for challenging state authority, and its constituency could develop a common identity conducive to collective opposition. Aware of these risks, successive Ottoman sultans kept the tax farm period short enough to enable frequent rotation among tax farmers; depending on the sector, the term was one to twelve years. Sultans also adjusted farm boundaries and persecuted tax farmers showing signs of acquiring a political base. From the start, then, tax farming served as an instrument of state power rather than of collective empowerment on the part of subcommunities. As such, it was unlikely to ignite an incorporation movement.

All else equal, the longer the tax farm period, the greater the bids of aspiring tax farmers. However, as the period lengthened, the winner's ability to acquire political autonomy rose accordingly. The Ottoman state thus faced a risk-return trade-off. How it resolved that trade-off could change in response to a greater risk from another source. In 1695, mounting budget deficits forced the state to convert numerous short-term tax farms into life-term tax farms (*malikane*s). As intended, the amounts required to purchase a tax farm rose.[56] Consistent with the foregoing logic, Ottoman tax farmers gained political clout and began asserting a right to bequeath farms to their descendants. Because of pressing revenue needs state officials turned a blind eye to these developments, but only for a while. Waiting for an opportunity to curb the autonomy of tax farmers, in 1812 they started to confiscate life-term farms. Following a setback, the process was completed in 1842.[57]

This episode illustrates how the Ottoman state arrested political and economic decentralization. More relevant here is the accompanying interruption of organizational innovation. To meet the payments required to win auctions, tax farmers had taken to forming partnerships intended to last for the duration of the farm, possibly decades.[58] Predictably, personal emergencies and new business opportunities prompted partners to withdraw from established tax farms by selling their remaining rights. Under the strict interpretation of prevailing Ottoman laws, such sales were illegal; the existing partnerships needed to disband and have their terms renegotiated by the modified group of partners. However, tax farmers and the state had a common interest in ensuring the viability of the new system of transferability. The former benefited through higher share prices, the latter through the consequent rise in tax farm bids. An officially tolerated market in tax farm shares thus began to flourish. Another induced innovation involved management. Instituting a rotating division of labor for the sake of efficiency, partners started taking turns as managers.[59]

Just as western organizational advances fed on themselves, so these developments might have placed the tax farm sector on a path of sustained organizational modernization. Transactions involving tax farm shares might have generated formal stock markets. Likewise, the managerial rotation system, which imposed costs on individual partners, might have induced the hiring of professional managers, thereby promoting a separation of ownership from management. A demand for partnerships with indefinite lifespans might have followed, for in a professionally managed partnership with changing owners "lifetime ownership" becomes a meaningless concept. One might also have seen advances in bookkeeping practices. In brief, the Ottoman tax farming sector was poised to develop advanced techniques of economic management, generate an indigenous variant of the joint-stock company, and establish the preconditions for the business corporation. Conceivably, tax farmers themselves might have formed the region's first corporations.

Had it run its course, the described dynamic would have been an unintended consequence of a state policy motivated by immediate revenue generation. Alas, prior to the mid-nineteenth century the Ottoman state was unconcerned with the organizational opportunities of private investors, except insofar as they affected tax revenue transparently. For fear of immediate revenue losses, it opted to inhibit innovations. In the early nineteenth century, worried about the growing difficulty of tracking ownership records and afraid of losing the right to re-auction tax farms, authorities restricted the number of outstanding shares per tax farm. Then they took to confiscating tax farms and switching to direct taxation.[60] These moves alleviated the pressures for further organizational innovation.

The shareholders of tax farms were too weak to resist the state-imposed restrictions. Had organizational development not lagged elsewhere in the social system, the outcome may well have been different.[61] In contemporaneous France, where tax farmers were able to pool capital more easily, they also formed a much smaller group. In the eighteenth century, the Ottoman Empire had between six thousand and twelve thousand life-term tax farmers. France had only eighty-eight tax farmers. The difference in numbers helps to explain why, unlike their French counterparts, Ottoman tax farmers were unable to keep the state from violating their rights. It is far harder to organize thousands of farmers than it is to organize fewer than a hundred.[62]

The Absence of Middle Eastern Family Firms

As already noted, the Middle East could have developed durable organizations suitable to large-scale business through a distinct evolutionary path. Enterprises involving the pooling of family resources might have provided yet another starting point. By virtue of the trust that exists among blood relatives, the family served, in the Middle East as elsewhere, as the basis for cooperation over long time periods. Middle Eastern history offers abundant examples of parents who pooled resources with their children, and of siblings who founded and operated a business jointly. However,

few cases exist of what we call a family firm—a business operated by a family for generations, with its reputation maintained
long after the death of its founders. The egalitarianism of the Islamic inheritance system hindered the formation of family firms.
A Quranic heir could easily frustrate efforts to keep a deceased
family member's property under the family's control. Another obstacle was the lack of legal personhood in Islamic law. If a son
challenged an attempt to keep his father's estate undivided, the law
would have sided with him, denying his family legal standing as
a unit.

The advantages of overriding individual rights in favor of the
family did not escape notice. A pertinent institutional model came,
once again, from the waqf system. As we have seen, early in Islamic
history families of means started to endow family waqfs. An unintended consequence was the dampening of pressures for alternative local solutions to the challenge of keeping resources intact
for the benefit of the family as a whole. Alas, the family waqf shared
the key limitation of waqfs in general. The static perpetuity principle made it rather inflexible for commercial purposes. Two other
factors made it a poor substitute for the family firm. Local norms
generally required a portion of its income to be devoted to a charitable purpose.[63] And the rule that assigned its management to a
single caretaker precluded managerial innovations aimed at turning the family into an organization suitable to large-scale business
in a dynamic economy.

There are two notable exceptions to the use of family waqfs as
family enterprises. Already encountered in chapter 4, the first consists of the family enterprises formed in the seventeenth and early
eighteenth centuries by the Armenian merchants of New Julfa, Iran.
These enterprises consisted of repeatedly renewed Islamic partnerships among family members. They appear to have avoided wealth
fragmentation through inheritance practices that departed significantly from Islamic law. As Christians, Armenians were not required
to abide by the Islamic inheritance system. Successive Iranian shahs
tolerated and even encouraged the preservation of New Julfan family wealth across generations, because they shared in the returns
through taxation and attractive loans.[64]

The other case is that of the Karimi merchants, who operated between the mid-twelfth and fifteenth centuries, usually out of Egypt and mostly in the spice trade. Some of them became fabulously wealthy, largely because rulers allowed them to monopolize the supply of spices to the Mediterranean. Many Karimi merchants passed their businesses, contacts, and reputations on to their children, who had been trained through apprenticeships to take over.[65] Some managed to evade the stringent requirements of the Islamic inheritance system. What accounts for these patterns? It has been suggested that a few early Karimis were Jewish, and that others came from the edges of the Islamic world.[66] Although information on their backgrounds is scant, in converting to Islam they may have adopted Muslim practices selectively, avoiding those inimical to capital accumulation. Whatever the history, successive Egyptian dynasties, first the Ayyubids and then the Mamluks, tolerated their unconventional succession practices. They did so for exactly the same reason that Iranian shahs supported the New Julfa Armenians: contributions to the state through taxes and loans.[67]

Evidently it was not impossible to overcome the organizational handicaps grounded in Islamic law. Rulers would not necessarily oppose, and could well support, organizational and financial innovations from which they themselves stood to gain. Yet the cases of the Karimi merchants and New Julfa Armenians are exceptions. Apparently, the legal constraints discussed in the last five chapters were difficult to overcome. Only under special circumstances could steps be taken in the direction of durable and long-lasting commercial organizations. In fact, neither of the two exceptions was replicated in the region, and neither brought about lasting legal advances. Whereas similar developments in western Europe tended to spread and then spawn new institutional transformations, the family enterprises of the Karimi merchants and New Julfa Armenians had no enduring consequences for organizational development in the Middle East. In early nineteenth century Egypt and Iran, durable family enterprises were anomalous and more complex commercial organizations nonexistent.

Mutual Reinforcement of the Obstacles to Developing Middle Eastern Corporations

In the early Islamic centuries, we have seen, the conditions governing organizational evolution differed between the Islamic Middle East and the West. Born in a society torn by endemic tribal warfare, Islam developed a legal system averse to subdividing Muslims politically. This system precluded non-state organizations akin to the Roman corporation. Legal personhood, critical to the empowerment of self-governing private organizations, was thus excluded from Islamic law early on. Meanwhile, the corporation was spreading in western Europe. In a political environment marked by weak central authority, diverse collectivities took to governing themselves autonomously. Thus, the initial organizational divergence between the Middle East and the West reflects legal choices made, in both regions, during Islam's formative period, the seventh to tenth centuries.

In the course of the second millennium, as corporations proliferated in the West, three distinct mechanisms kept the Middle East organizationally lethargic in areas that contributed to economic success during the Industrial Revolution. The first involves the persistent simplicity of partnerships. Until quite late, Middle Eastern producers, merchants, and investors saw no need for standardized bookkeeping, or professional management, or free transferability of shares. This is because the Islamic inheritance system, along with its marriage rules, dampened incentives to form large and long-lived partnerships; and the consequent stagnation in enterprise size and longevity made it unnecessary to develop the institutions of modern economic life. The business community had long been familiar with owner shielding, or limited liability, a feature useful even to ephemeral two-person partnerships, which could be formed at will through contract. However, profit-seeking groups did not develop entity shielding, the ability to protect an organization's assets against claims by individuals. The reason is that entity shielding, which requires new law, is useful especially to long-lived enterprises, which did not emerge. As a byproduct of this institutional stagnation, the region failed also to develop the preconditions for transplanting the business corporation from abroad.

The second mechanism of stagnation worked through the supply of social services. At a time when western charities, religious bodies, universities, and cities adopted the corporate form of organization, in the Middle East analogous functions were served primarily by the waqf, the Islamic analogue of the trust. Like a corporation, a waqf could outlive its founder. But it was not self-governing. Required to follow the founder's directives, its caretaker lacked the discretion necessary to maximize profitability of the endowment. If waqfs failed to turn into self-governing and profit-maximizing organizations, one reason is that vested interests stood in the way. Reforms would have threatened the rents that judges derived from their duty to monitor waqf caretakers.

The third mechanism involved state policies. Notwithstanding early Islam's aversion to factionalism, premodern Muslim rulers treated certain collectivities as groups. Thus, they accorded de facto recognition to guilds and tax constituencies. There was no insurmountable obstacle, then, to the treatment of traders as groups. Had they been organized already within merchant guilds or under consuls, and possessed the know-how to form large and durable enterprises, states might have assisted their continued organizational development. In fact, Middle Eastern merchants developed no permanent organizations. As late as the early nineteenth century, they formed small associations for temporary missions. This lack of organizational longevity must have dampened the motivation to grant them a collective identity. It would also have limited incentives to help them through innovations such as legal personhood and entity shielding.

These three mechanisms were mutually reinforcing. The organizational stagnation of the local commercial sector kept rulers disinterested in assisting them. As chapters ahead will show, it also induced them to strike deals with foreign merchants, thus stimulating the flow of capital into enterprises formed outside of Islamic law. The ubiquity of waqfs dampened the need for corporate law. The absence of non-profit corporations, by keeping courts unaccustomed to legal persons, raised the difficulties of introducing the corporate concept into commercial life. Anyone trying to form a business corporation would have had to start by familiarizing judges with the concept.

We now see why in the 1850s Abdülmecit, contrasting his shrinking empire with the dominant states of the global economy, noticed a vast difference in commercial organization. For a millennium, the West had been developing ever newer organizational forms to suit a panoply of social needs. Its producers, merchants, and investors had learned how to form, operate, and preserve structurally complex organizations. States had contributed to these advances for their own ends. As for Abdülmecit's own region, the organizational options of private businesses operating under Islamic law hardly differed from those of the Middle Ages. Previous Ottoman sultans had not encountered transformations worth stimulating for their own benefit. Moreover, where such transformations had started to unfold, as when the shift to life-term tax farms begat partnerships with tradable shares, his predecessors had seen not opportunities for spiraling social gain but immediate fiscal and political threats.

Inadequacy of the Essentialist Thesis

The Islamic heritage harbors elements that promote conservatism, and generations of Muslims have invoked scripture and perceived precedents to block institutional change. However, Islamic law is not inherently unchangeable, because reformers are able to draw legitimacy from the very same sources. Had a significant demand emerged before the nineteenth century for expanding the organizational options of merchants, religious sensibilities would not have posed an impregnable barrier. Judges could have altered the practice of Islamic law by tolerating deviations and relaxing interpretations. Muftis might have assisted merchants through commerce-friendly opinions (fatwās).[68] That is why this chapter has departed from the "essentialist" interpretations of earlier generations, traveling great lengths to uncover why various possible paths to the corporation were blocked. For the sociologist Max Weber, as for the Islamologists Claude Cahen and Samuel Stern, the lack of an Islamic corporate culture was a defining feature of premodern Islamic civilization. Having located it, they refrained from exploring why it endured.[69]

The most telling reason to reject the essentialist interpretation lies in the legal reforms that followed Abdülmecit's initiative. By the early twentieth century the corporation had been transplanted to the legal systems of the Middle East. Nowhere did legal personhood or entity shielding generate reactions in the name of Islamic purity. Islamist movements of the twenty-first century do not want to limit legal standing to natural persons. They have no qualms about organizational longevity. They do not take issue with the Islamic world's rapidly expanding stock markets, in which millions of shares change hands daily. Certain institutions of early Islam kept the corporation from emerging indigenously. Once borrowed from abroad along with supporting institutions, it was absorbed into local legal systems without notable resistance.

The fact that Middle Eastern economies now benefit from corporations does not mean that the long delay in this adoption has had no lasting effects. Because of the delay the region's university systems and municipalities lack the benefit of centuries of experience. In hampering the development of civil society, the delay also set the stage for the state-led development strategies that still quash individual initiative. Another effect is that the region's financial markets lack sophistication by today's standards. Our next task is to explore how organizational limitations hampered the evolution of credit practices.

8

Credit Markets without Banks

The first two successful banks of the Middle East, the Bank of Egypt and the Ottoman Bank, were founded in the 1850s. In each case, the capital and organizational template came from abroad, and the administration was foreign-dominated. Around the same time, both Egypt, which was nominally under Ottoman suzerainty, and the Ottoman Empire itself established specialized commercial courts that adjudicated essentially according to the French commercial code. These legal reforms restricted the jurisdiction of the Islamic courts on economic matters. Among their novelties was the explicit legalization of interest.[1] If it took foreigners to introduce modern banking to the region, the reason is that indigenous financial institutions failed to keep up with the times. In popular discourses this stagnation is commonly traced to Islam's prohibition of interest. Because of this prohibition, it is said, Muslims had serious qualms about credit markets, requiring foreign intervention to induce financial modernization.[2]

The premises of this claim are open to question. Never and nowhere did the presumed Quranic ban on interest make Muslims withdraw from credit markets either as borrowers or lenders. From the seventh century onward, Muslims found ways to deal in interest without violating the letter of the prohibition. Only in the late eighteenth century did Christians and Jews start playing a conspicuously disproportionate role in credit markets. In earlier times, the region's moneylenders included a more or less proportionate share of Muslims. Besides, the financial successes of minorities did not include the development of indigenous banks. When in the nineteenth century Christians and Jews gained prominence as bankers, they did so through institutions transplanted from the West, not ones developed on their own. Thus, the Middle East's lag in starting to modernize financially was a phenomenon that transcended religious boundaries. In any case, credit markets were subject to restrictions even in western Europe, the birthplace of modern banking.[3] Hence, the Islamic ban on interest could not have been the key reason why its financial development lagged behind that of the West.

Identifying the actual causes requires an examination of relevant institutions. What financial transactions did Islam allow, in principle and in practice? What institutions governed those transactions, and how did they evolve? The lag in question was rooted, as with the region's commercial stagnation, in early Islamic institutions. As we shall see, those institutions did not spell financial backwardness immediately. Early in the second millennium the Middle East's financial markets were advanced by the prevailing global standards. Yet they failed to evolve in ways conducive to mobilizing large amounts of private capital for extended periods, leaving them poorly suited to the exploitation of modern technologies. The foreign banks established in the nineteenth century were among the responses to this failure. Filling a vacuum, they compensated for the lack of indigenous banks.

Given the conventional wisdom that links the Middle East's financial retardation to its interest ban, it makes sense to explore first the ban's actual impact on early Islamic economic life. Though often evaded, this ban did have costs, which could have been eliminated through the legalization of interest. However, for reasons rooted in institutions seldom viewed as relevant to financial development, that step was taken only in the nineteenth century.

The Islamic Interest Ban and Its Rationale

In its strict interpretation, classical Islamic law requires every loan, regardless of size or purpose, to be free of interest. The principal justification is that the ban appears in the Quran. What the Quran explicitly prohibits is *ribā*, an ancient Arabian practice whereby the debt of a borrower doubled if he failed to make restitution on time.[4] *Ribā* commonly resulted in confiscation of the borrower's assets, even in his enslavement. Consequently, it fueled communal tension. In banning the practice, Islam effectively prohibited immiserization and enslavement for debt.[5]

It is not self-evident that a ban on *ribā* requires a general and timeless prohibition of interest. After all, a modern family that borrows at interest to finance a house does not risk becoming the lender's slave. Likewise, no grave danger was present when an affluent medieval farmer financed the planting of a plot through interest-based credit. Precisely because the Muslim community need not benefit materially from a categorical ban on interest, the promoters of a broad prohibition claimed that even seemingly innocuous practices pose hidden harms. Every form of interest, they argued, generates unjustified enrichment by allowing the lender to earn a return without giving the borrower appropriate countervalue. In addition, the borrower bears undue risk (*gharar*) in that he agrees to make restitution even in the event of grave misfortune.[6]

By this logic, the lender should always carry a share of the unavoidable risk associated with a loan. He should be ready to waive his right to repayment in situations where the borrower cannot fulfill his obligation without hardship. If the creditor of a destitute debtor were to insist on restitution, he would be failing to show compassion to a brother or sister in their time of need. Were he to insist, in addition, on making a profit by collecting interest, he would also be guilty of morally unjustified enrichment.[7]

This rationale for a general ban was developed in a society already accustomed to financial restrictions. Well before Islam, legal codes of the Middle East included stipulations to limit borrowers' exposure to risk. The code of Hammurabi capped the interest rate on grain loans at 33 percent per annum and that on silver loans at 20 percent; it also restricted slavery for debt to a period of three years. A millennium later, around 600 BCE, the laws of Solon reduced or annulled most preexisting debts, and they prohibited slavery for overdue obligations. Around 450 BCE the Roman Twelve Tables capped interest at 8.33 percent per annum and imposed fourfold damages on creditors who demanded more.[8] Whatever their particularities, all such financial restrictions were meant to lessen the ubiquitous and socially destabilizing danger of enslavement for unpaid debt. Throughout the ancient world, including pre-Islamic Arabia, defaulters were routinely sold into slavery and often shipped to foreign lands. Such horrible consequences tainted all interest earnings, making profit-reaping lenders appear as greedy exploiters. Thus, the Islamic view that interest produces unjustified enrichment simply re-expresses an ancient prejudice common to the eastern Mediterranean.

Monotheistic precedents for prohibiting interest, as opposed to capping its rate, were set by Judaism and, in stricter form, by Christianity. The Torah prohibited lending at interest among Jews.[9] It also banned collecting interest from the poor.[10] Later, but still centuries before Islam, Christian theologians condemned interest as an instrument of avarice. The blanket prohibition in Christianity was grounded in Old Testament rules but also in a New Testament ban on charging interest even to grave sinners: "Lend, expecting nothing in return, and your reward will be great."[11] It was justified also through an Aristotelian tenet that took on a Christian hue: money being barren, interest amounts to robbery.[12] Medieval Christian qualms about interest are still apparent in European church carvings of the evil usurer dragged by his purse down to hell.

All such precedents for regulating interest applied above all to consumption loans. In the overwhelmingly agrarian economies of antiquity, loans for production or commerce were uncommon, and governments rarely borrowed. The main purpose for borrowing was to meet personal subsistence needs. However, medieval theologians applied the Christian interest ban to both consumption and business loans. In the same vein, many early Islamic leaders interpreted the ban on *ribā* as subsuming all forms of interest.

A corollary to considering interest-based production loans un-Islamic was to make commercial partnerships seem inherently Islamic. Well before Islam, Middle Eastern traders were familiar with partnerships whose members shared both profits and losses. Whatever the merits of forbidding interest, such partnerships offered an alternative to interest-based commercial credit. They made it possible to spread the risks of joint ventures across the suppliers and users of capital. Consider a *mudāraba* partnership to which a sedentary investor supplies capital and a traveling merchant his labor. If brigands sack the caravan carrying the partnership's goods, the investor loses his capital, and the merchant's expended labor goes to waste. Thus, the loss is shared. If instead the merchant borrows from the investor at interest, and the loan contract is enforceable costlessly, any loss falls on the merchant alone.

Evasion of the Interest Ban

Not all financial transactions fit the template of a commercial partnership. Because individuals who borrowed to meet subsistence needs would not aim to reap a return, consumption loans could not be based on profit and loss sharing. In principle, lenders could have been required to make interest-free loans, but that would have dampened their incentive to lend. Hence, as a practical matter borrowers frequently compensated their creditors through payments that amounted to interest. Notwithstanding the prevailing prejudices, these borrowers did not necessarily consider themselves exploited. For their part, moneylenders found interest-based lending sufficiently lucrative to justify the risk of opprobrium.

As far as is known, no Muslim polity has had a genuinely interest-free economy. This is not surprising, for risk tolerance varies widely across individuals. Muslim communities have included credit seekers prepared to pay for the privilege of shifting their risks onto others; they have also included credit providers willing to carry risks for a price. In short, incentives as well as opportunities to participate in interest-based credit deals have always been ubiquitous. Evidence of the persistent appeal of interest is found even in Islam's canonical Age of Felicity. Not even *ribā* itself vanished with its prohibition. The ban on *ribā* is reiterated in a section of the Quran recorded toward the end of Muhammad's life, which suggests that the practice remained alive.[13] To be sure, Islam prohibited enslavement for debt, and this ban was enforced widely even as slavery itself remained legal.[14] Still, even in modern times the least developed areas of the Islamic world have seen compound interest rates of 50 percent or more;[15] like *ribā*, such rates can cause liabilities to mushroom. One may point, of course, to times and places where interest was treated as illegal; and it is easy to cite leaders who depicted interest as horribly immoral. The eleventh-century jurist Sarakhsi characterized the sin of dealing in interest as more grievous than committing thirty-three adulteries.[16] Nevertheless, rarely have offenders endured conviction or even prosecution.[17] Islam does not prescribe a punishment on earth for dealing in interest.

The circumvention of the interest ban has taken two forms: compartmentalization and casuistry. The first relegates practice and ideal to separate spheres of discourse, allowing the ban to be ignored in daily life without rejecting it in principle. Premodern Islamic history offers striking examples of compartmentalization. In the sixteenth century, an Ottoman sultan limited the annual rate of interest to 11.5 percent throughout the empire, though only on transactions that satisfied the letter of the ban through stratagems; this order was duly ratified by a legal opinion (*fetva*).[18] A study of credit practices in seventeenth-century Kayseri, an Anatolian town, shows that interest payments were not only customary but also "condoned, sanctioned, and certified" by religious scholars (*ulema*), notables (*ayans* and *eşraf*), and high Ottoman officials.[19] Remarkably, Kayseri's Islamic establishment considered an annual interest rate of 20 percent a sacred commandment and, provided the mandated rate was respected, it treated neither lenders nor borrowers as impious.[20] A separate study of financial practices in the same century, focusing on Bursa, another Turkish town, also finds evidence of de facto legitimacy. In Bursa the customary interest rate was 10 percent, well below that of Kayseri. The difference probably reflects Bursa's proximity to international trade routes, which enhanced its access to credit. More important, perhaps, only Bursa had professional moneylenders.[21] In supplying credit to many people simultaneously, financial specialists diversify their risks, thereby lowering the premia necessary to keep their operations viable.

In the sixteenth and seventeenth centuries, transactions involving interest were so common that courts frequently adjudicated disputes over whether a contract involved a loan or a partnership.

In the typical case, a merchant returning from a commercial voyage would claim that his load was stolen or lost in a disaster. "We formed a partnership," he would testify, implying that he owed the investor nothing. For his part, the investor would claim that he provided capital at interest, entitling him to a full refund, plus accumulated interest. Numerous such cases exist in the judicial records of seventeenth-century Istanbul.[22] Their very existence, and that some of these cases were resolved in favor of the party demanding interest, confirm the commonness and legality of interest-based credit. Comparable findings have emerged from studies focused on earlier periods. The Geniza documents introduced in chapter 3 show that around the eleventh century peoples of the eastern Mediterranean, including Muslims, often used interest-based credit. On both retail sales and long-distance trade, the same documents also suggest, payments were routinely deferred for an interest charge. The rate, sometimes as low as 4 percent, varied depending on payment terms, goods transacted, and market conditions.[23]

The casuistical method for evading the ban involves legal artifices (*hiyal*) that allow interest to be charged without violating the letter of the presumed prohibition. One such artifice was to conceal interest charges through discounts for advance payment.[24] Another was to lend in one currency and repay in another, burying the interest charge within the exchange rate. A less transparent artifice was the double sale (*'ina* or *mukhātara*). Here is how the double sale could be used to disguise a 100 dinar loan at 15 percent interest from lender L to borrower B. L purchases a blanket from B for 100 dinars in ready cash, then promptly returns the same blanket to B for 115 dinars, payable in one year. By the end of the second transaction, the blanket has returned to its original owner, B has gained 100 dinars, and L stands to receive 115 dinars in a year's time. Together, these transactions amount to a 100 dinar loan at an annual rate of 15 percent. However, neither involves interest when considered in isolation. Yet another common artifice has been the loan with usable collateral. It involves the borrower giving the lender a productive object as collateral, for instance, a horse. There is nothing illicit about lending a horse to an acquaintance. However, in this context the purpose is to disguise an interest payment.[25]

In the court registers of Istanbul, references to interest are made frequently through such euphemisms as "payment for cloth" (*çuka bahası*), "price of fur" (*kürk semeni*), "treating ten as eleven" (*ona onbir hesabı*), "eleven for ten stamp duty" (*ona onbir pul hesabı*), "earning" (*ribh*), "religious achievement" (*mârifet-i şeriyye*), "religious procedure" *(muamele-i şeriyye)*, "religious transfer" (*devr-i şerî*), and "fee for commodity financing" *(murâbaha)*. The euphemisms overcame the appearance of sinful activity.[26]

All such forms of casuistry received religious stamps of approval, although the legality of any given form could vary across Islam's schools of law.[27] Evidently, the unviability of the interest ban quickly gained recognition even among the most influential interpreters of the law. The "simple and rational way" to escape the need for elaborate financial casuistry, says Siadat Ali Khan, would have been to "amend, repeal, or abrogate" all laws that treat interest as un-Islamic.[28] However, over more than a millennium, conservative jurists precluded these options. Their resistance would have discouraged proponents of some type of legalization from transgressing the ban openly. Consequently, reformists chose to meet the steady demand for giving and taking interest through financial stratagems. In avoiding direct challenges to the ban, closet reformers inadvertently sustained the fiction that eliminating interest is both desirable and possible.

Costs of the Interest Ban

Stratagems for circumventing the interest ban allowed the reallocation of risks according to variations in individual risk preferences. However, in the premodern Islamic world, interest was not charged as freely as in today's secular economic systems. Just as partnership contracts could be challenged on the ground that an interest payment was stipulated, so interest-based debt could be disavowed by alleging that the lender had agreed to a partnership.[29] Also, the persistent illegality of interest presented a threat to interest claims. An independent-minded judge could invalidate an interest-based contract.[30] This danger would have raised the prevailing rates, because profit-maximizing lenders would have allowed for potential attempts to avoid restitution. A harmful consequence of the interest ban was thus to increase the cost of credit for everyone, including entrepreneurs seeking capital.

The interest ceilings of economically liberal localities such as Bursa and Kayseri would have imposed economic costs of their own. Although we do not know how well the ceilings were enforced, they could have been circumvented through financial stratagems. A willing lender could have extended credit to a willing borrower at a rate above the ceiling simply through an appropriate double sale or by accepting collateral equivalent to the foregone interest. However, such stratagems would have complicated the financial transaction. If the transaction was being registered at court, each of its steps had to be recorded separately. In requiring two court registrations where one would have sufficed, the double sale thus raised court fees. Besides, every stratagem required safeguards to counter the danger of the borrower or lender using one of a group of linked transactions to his own advantage. A common safeguard was to place documentation in the hands of a trustworthy intermediary authorized to produce, if necessary, a side document to reverse an abused transaction.[31] Hence, although few loan contracts were registered in court, documents generated as part of a stratagem must have raised credit costs.

Adverse consequences of the Islamic interest ban were not limited to added documentation or litigation. Over the long run, a more significant cost was that commercial, financial, and monetary matters could not be discussed honestly and openly. The resulting impoverishment of public discourse would have clouded individual understandings of the time value of money, delaying the development of a capitalist mentality.[32] Where and when interest was openly regulated, one might expect public opinion, including official pronouncements, to have fueled an interest legalization movement. However, even in seventeenth-century Bursa and Kayseri authorities sought to have it both ways: though accepting interest under one name or another, they refrained from objecting to the Islamic teachings that induced casuistry. Breaking what they considered the law where convenient, they left the law itself intact. In the process, they kept public discourse wedded to the ancient view that interest is somehow immoral.

The ethical status of interest remained questionable, then, even at times and in localities where interest-bearing credit was tolerated. Thus, many interest-based loan contracts continued to conform to the letter of Islamic law. A common Ottoman practice, known as *istiglâl*, was to have the borrower sell his house to a lender and immediately lease it back from him; the borrower was expected to repurchase the house at the end of the loan period for the same price.[33] The fictitious rent, which usually obeyed the prevailing interest ceiling, was obviously a pre-specified interest payment, and the courts understood that. Nevertheless, when a borrower failed to repurchase a house sold as part of an *istiglâl* contract, the court would allow the lender to keep it on the ground that every contract must be followed to the letter.[34]

In principle, a bank, assuming it somehow emerged, could disguise interest charges through the same technique. In a default, it might even prefer to have title to the borrower's house, because the cost of liquidation would be lower than if a suit had to be filed first. However, the practice would have raised interest rates by diminishing the bank's flexibility in coping with risks. The net benefit of banks would have been lower than if interest were charged freely and openly.

The persistent illegitimacy of interest affected economic modernization also by discouraging financial practices generally free of interest. Consider the bill of credit (*suftaja*), which a broker issued to a person seeking to transfer funds to another location. At the chosen location the bill holder would receive cash from an agent of the broker. Insofar as the broker matched customers moving cash in opposite directions, the bill of credit eliminated the risk of losing cash in transport. Although the broker received compensation, interest was not necessarily involved because, in principle, the fee was not for the use of money.[35] During the period between purchase and redemption, however, it is the broker, rather than the buyer, who enjoyed the use of funds. Hence, the fee could be lowered by the broker's expected income from the funds. Insofar as such an adjustment was made, the contract involved a disguised interest payment to the buyer. This is one reason why the bill of credit appeared un-Islamic to some enforcers of Islamic law.[36] That the time-value of money affected the contract is obvious from the fact that the broker paid a daily fine if he delayed repayment beyond the agreed date. Another basis for religious opposition was that the broker's service to the buyer eliminated a risk involving money.[37]

As a matter of practice, qualms about the legitimacy of the bill of credit deterred neither its widespread use nor its legal enforcement over large regions.[38] Nevertheless, data from the eleventh century to the eighteenth century show that the controversy made some Muslim merchants, and perhaps most of those in North Africa, accept the risks of carrying large sums on trips over land and sea.[39] At a minimum, then, the interest ban sometimes diminished the use of the bill of credit in contexts where it could have provided benefits. Insofar as frank discussion on the determinants of brokerage fees was squelched, a more serious effect over the longer run would have been delays in the advancement of economic thought, the rationalization of economic morality, and the modernization of economic practices.

How the Western and Middle Eastern Experiences Differed

Much of the foregoing account matches the European experience. At the start of the second millennium, interest was as maligned in Christian Europe as in the Islamic world. Christian moralists justified a ban as essential to protecting the weak, and particularly people facing starvation, from greedy exploiters. As in the Middle East, pragmatic clerics condoned stratagems to circumvent the interest prohibition.[40] Still, banking arrived in the West a half-millennium before locally established banks opened in the Middle East. Barcelona got its first chartered bank in 1401, Genoa in 1407.[41] The early banks, and those that followed, usually paid depositors interest, meeting their obligations through returns on long-term investments. Foreshadowing modern banking, they maintained fractional reserves, which required them to anticipate the demand for money and devise procedures for meeting unexpected withdrawals. As fractional reserves gained legitimacy, they were tempted to invest ever larger shares of their deposits, inevitably leading to bankruptcies.[42] Cities responded by instituting reserve requirements. Every financial innovation thus restructured incentives and spawned new challenges, inducing further innovations.

The development of western banking, and of its broader financial system, did not come suddenly, through a transformation completed within a generation. There was a long evolution, and the path varied across countries.[43] In some places, players other than banks dominated financial intermediation until the late eighteenth century. For instance, up to 1789 the growth of the French credit market owed more to notaries than to organizations we would recognize as banks. Notaries, whose traditional function was to draw legal contracts, contributed to financial development by matching borrowers and lenders unknown to each other, and also by broadening the menu of available credit options to include long-term loans.[44] All such developments facilitated the emergence of banks by promoting familiarity and experience with their key features, including impersonal exchange. In France, between 1660 and 1770, a period when credit was supplied mainly by notaries, the fraction of Parisian loans featuring personal links between borrower and lender fell by more than a third.[45]

Institutional advances went hand in hand with attitudinal changes. It had been common for European financiers to suffer anxiety over the morality of interest.[46] Testaments of the Middle Ages offer abundant examples of instructions to return interest payments or donate interest-tainted wealth to the Church.[47] However, already in the thirteenth century ecclesiastical debates over interest were under way. Contrary to impressions grounded in Max Weber's *Protestant Ethic and the Spirit of Capitalism*, the view that interest is sinful was under fire well before the Reformation. By the fifteenth century most European theologians considered it legitimate as a return on investment. Concomitantly, people of all walks of life were distinguishing between reasonable and unreasonable interest, reserving the term usury for the latter category. The Reformation accelerated this moral transformation by making it acceptable to disobey Mosaic prohibitions harmful to financial efficiency.[48] Thinkers of the eighteenth century, including Adam Smith, David Hume, and Bernard Mandeville, then advanced the process by making interest seem virtuous. By the nineteenth century few western businessmen questioned the morality of interest. This ethical evolution facilitated financial modernization by broadening the license to innovate and by alleviating the fear of sinning in the pursuit of profit.

Insofar as the Middle East took up the question of interest during this attitudinal transformation in the West, discussions were more cautious. Tied to old religious interpretations and increasingly removed from the concerns of merchants and producers, they did little to forge a social climate hospitable to banking. The commonness of interest-bearing credit, even the legitimacy that many courts bestowed on low-interest loans, failed to transform financial morality. Under the circumstances, financiers generally refrained from compensating their depositors and from investing funds provided for safekeeping.[49] Although no restriction was obeyed strictly or universally, the net result was to limit the supply of loanable funds and the growth of lending operations. Consequently, during a half-millennium when western attitudes toward interest underwent progressive liberalization, Islam's formal commitment to the interest ban helped to deprive the Islamic world of a prime engine of growth.

Nothing thus far explains why interest gained legitimacy sooner in western Europe. We have observed that financial markets in the West modernized sooner, without identifying why those of the Middle East lagged. It bears noting that as late as the thirteenth century the Middle East had advanced financial markets by global standards of the day. The Middle Eastern economy was served by currency changers, moneylenders, and pawnbrokers, along with merchant financiers. In the course of their commercial activities Middle Eastern merchant financiers accepted deposits, and made loans and intermediated payments through bills of credit convertible in distant lands and promissory notes honored locally (*ruq'as*). Such financial operations had assumed "fairly complex forms" as early as the mid-eighth century, observes Abraham Udovitch, "at least three or four centuries before anything comparable is recorded for medieval Europe."[50] Why, then, was the Middle Eastern torch of financial creativity subsequently extinguished while that of the West stayed ablaze?

Organizational Roots of Financial Stagnation

The answer lies in differences involving the organization of credit services. Right up to modern times, Middle Eastern financiers provided credit as individuals or through short-lived, small, and generally unspecialized partnerships. These financial partnerships could not pool the deposits of more than a few savers, undertake clearance operations beyond the simplest, or supply credit to the masses.[51] Like commercial partnerships, they were terminable at will. Another limitation of these rudimentary enterprises is their lack of legal personhood, which restricted the financial transactions that others were willing to conduct with them. At the establishment of the Bank of Egypt and the Ottoman Bank, the region lacked organizations able to fulfill their functions. The delayed emergence of Middle Eastern banks mirrors, then, the organizational trajectory of the broader commercial sector. Prior to the mid-nineteenth century, the region's indigenous private enterprises were all small, simple, and ephemeral. Given that pattern, Middle Eastern banks would have been an anomaly.

To see why, let us step back to twelfth-century Baghdad and imagine that fifty individuals form a simple partnership intended to fulfill two basic functions of a modern commercial bank: accepting deposits and making loans. To stay within the law, the bank must disband and reorganize at the death of any given partner. A renegotiation must take place also if a member chooses to withdraw his capital. These requirements will make the operations of the enterprise very expensive. Hence, the financiers of Baghdad will avoid repeating the experiment until liberated from the requirement of recontracting at every loss of a member.

At the time, incentives against forming large partnerships were as strong in Florence as in Baghdad. Modern banking could not have emerged anywhere in the West. The road to modern banking was traversed through many small steps spread across centuries, beginning with renewable and thus effectively indefinite partnerships linked through one or more common partners who coordinated their activities. The Medici enterprise, introduced earlier as an example of multiple partnerships organized in hub-and-spoke fashion across many countries, offers a prominent example. Among the novel functions of the Medici "hub" in Florence was the facilitation of clearance operations.[52] As financial conglomerates capable of increasingly complex undertakings came to dominate European finance, their constituents became more numerous. By the fifteenth century financial partnerships of five to seven investors were not uncommon, and the number could be larger.[53]

Not until the nineteenth century do we find financial enterprises with shareholders in the hundreds or thousands.[54] Until then, credit suppliers cooperated through increasingly complex partnerships.[55] In the meantime, however, the ingredients of modern banking were falling into place. The spread of partnerships with growing numbers of inactive partners smoothed the transition to joint-stock banks whose shareholders knew little about daily operations and could transfer shares at will. Another factor, which gained significance in the eighteenth century, was the increasing acceptance of business corporations; this development facilitated the recognition of rules providing financial intermediaries an existence apart from their founders and employees. Through all these developments, along with the strengthening of private property rights, interest rates declined. In England, rates on long-term borrowing fell from 14 percent in 1693 to 3 percent in 1739.[56]

Until well into the nineteenth century the Middle East saw nothing comparable. The financial sector did not generate indigenous joint-stock companies. Equally significant, there was not a single case of mass mobilization for a major private venture. Along the way certain wealthy families made loans that were large by the standards of the day, usually to individuals, occasionally to the government.

However, there were no private lenders capable of matching the scales attained from the 1490s onward by the Fuggers, whose loans affected the balance of power between princes. None had the capacity to finance missions of global discovery, such as Magellan's 1519 expedition, heavily funded by profit-seeking German merchants.[57]

The Cash Waqf Alternative

To solve the puzzle of why financial institutions of the Middle East followed a distinct evolutionary path is not to establish that financial modernization must follow a trajectory observed in some part of western Europe. The Middle East might have reached the same outcome through a path of its own. It could have established unique organizations that fulfilled one or more functions of a modern bank—receiving demand and time deposits, pooling deposits to make large loans, matching borrowers and lenders unknown to one another, and investing in securities. Moreover, the features of these organizations might have been united eventually in a long-lived organization akin to a bank. A possible starting point for an evolutionary process culminating in a bank was the waqf—Islam's alternative to the corporation.

As we already know, under classical Islamic law a waqf's assets must consist of real estate. In certain places this requirement was relaxed early on to legitimize what gained recognition as a "cash waqf"—a waqf whose corpus consists of cash. The main beneficiaries were the holders of liquid wealth, including moneylenders. They favored relaxing the immovability requirement in order to acquire privileges originally reserved for owners of real estate. A cash waqf produced income by lending at interest. Although cash waqfs were long uncommon, they became prevalent in the fifteenth and sixteenth centuries, mainly in Turkey and the Balkans, where the dominant school of law was relatively respectful of commercial needs. As some of the judges posted in these areas interpreted waqf rules liberally to accommodate the demands of financiers and their clients, they made it easier for others to do the same. Cash waqfs thus spread through a bandwagon process confined to the region's northwestern corner.

Not everyone welcomed this diffusion. In the eyes of conservative clerics, the cash waqf violated both waqf law and the prohibition of interest. Conceding the charges of illegality, its defenders rested their case on pragmatism.[58] However, by the seventeenth century the controversy had run its course, and the cash waqf enjoyed wide legitimacy in areas where it was prevalent.[59] Could it have metamorphosed into the modern bank? Precisely because the cash waqf met important needs, in the sixteenth century more than half of all new waqfs in Turkey held assets consisting mostly, if not exclusively, of cash. Measured by assets, however, cash-holding waqfs tended to be small, and they lent primarily to consumers rather than entrepreneurs.[60] Their popularity stemmed partly from the quest for material security. Like landowners, moneylenders wanted to protect their assets against confiscation and arbitrary taxation. The needs of credit users also contributed to their popularity. Ordinary moneylenders were charging rates commensurate with the risks that they took on account of the interest ban. Wherever the cash waqf enjoyed legal approval, it allowed moneylenders to charge lower rates. The sacredness it acquired through inclusion in the wider waqf system shielded its interest-based activities from charges of sinfulness.[61]

We saw earlier that the static perpetuity principle made the standard waqf of immovables dynamically inefficient. The cash waqf limited the dangers of becoming dysfunctional. Simply by redirecting loans from one set of borrowers to another, it could transfer capital across economic sectors. Where a waqf of immovables might have its capital tied up in an increasingly unproductive farm, a cash waqf's commitment was constrained only by the time-structure of its loan. Nevertheless, the cash waqf itself was subject to operational constraints. Like the founder of a waqf of immovables, that of a cash waqf could restrict its beneficiaries and charges. Thus, the deed of a seventeenth-century cash waqf might require it to lend at exactly 10 percent and only within a particular neighborhood.[62] In addition to the founder's tastes and biases, the restrictions imposed on a cash waqf typically reflected the prevailing interest rates at its inception. Over time, of course, the fixity of its lending rate could limit its profitability. Partly because of this requirement, only a fifth of all cash waqfs survived beyond a century.[63]

Why might the founders of cash waqfs have fixed their lending rates? Static perpetuity being among the defining principles of the conventional waqf system, perhaps such a step was considered critical to having a cash waqf qualify as a waqf. It would have seemed the least a founder should do to meet the requirement of immobilizing the endowment. Indeed, requiring the caretaker to charge a nominal rate commensurate with the waqf's designated expenses might have been viewed as essential to its permanent viability. Such logic presupposed an unchanging economy. In times of escalating rates, it was bound to cause trouble.

Indeed, as nominal rates rose in credit markets outside the waqf system, caretakers discovered opportunities for personal enrichment through arbitrage. Borrowing money from the cash waqfs under their supervision, Turkish caretakers of the sixteenth through nineteenth centuries lent on their own account to the moneylenders (sarrafs) of localities with higher interest rates. The difference could be enormous. In the seventeenth century, when the cash waqfs of Bursa charged interest rates around 10.8 percent per annum, the moneylenders of Istanbul charged between 18 and 25 percent.[64] The latter are known to have obtained capital at 12.5 percent, a rate between the fixed rate of the cash waqfs and the market rate in Istanbul. Evidently, both caretakers and moneylenders benefited from the flow of funds to Istanbul's credit market. Had the deeds of cash waqfs permitted greater flexibility, they themselves could have reaped the gains accruing to caretakers.

It is tempting to view the cash waqf as a rudimentary bank poised to overcome its inflexibilities if only given enough time. However, obstacles to the necessary modifications were not trivial. In contrast to a bank that pools the deposits of the masses, a cash waqf, like a standard waqf, was formed through a single individual's savings. Moreover, the rule of static perpetuity barred cash waqfs from pooling their resources. Rarely was this rule circumvented through a loan or grant to an established waqf.[65] In practice, the requirement to follow the founder's directives exactly was enough to limit the size of the cash waqfs formed. Because each cash waqf diversified its risks by lending to many people at once, the requirement also limited the size of the average loan. Indeed, the distinction between a waqf and a profit-making commercial enterprise carried over to the cash waqf. Whereas moneylenders outside the waqf sector could pool resources within financial partnerships, which they did on a small scale, cash waqfs could not merge in order to supply credit on a larger scale.[66] This handicap helped to keep them from developing into banks. There was nothing to prevent borrowers from pooling capital themselves. They were free to borrow from multiple cash waqfs. However, the transaction costs of numerous small loans exceeded those of an equivalent large loan. Unsurprisingly, evidence of pooling by borrowers is meager.

To evolve into some form of bank, the cash waqf would have had to overcome an additional restriction of Islamic law: lack of legal personhood. Born into a system lacking familiarity with the concept, the cash waqf never became a legal entity. This limitation reduced its capacity to raise capital as well as its ability to take advantage of new market opportunities.

The Arrival of Modern Banking

In most areas on the Middle East, financial markets did not even benefit from the cash waqf. As a consequence of the resulting deficiencies, large-scale finance in the region, including lending to governments, was initially supplied by foreigners. The Middle East welcomed foreign banks in the nineteenth century, when Europe's share of world trade reached around 70 percent.[67] To participate in the global expansion of commerce, Middle Eastern businesses needed more credit. With the region's own financiers unable to accommodate their needs, Europeans stepped in to exploit the emerging opportunities.

The early 1800s saw several abortive attempts to establish small banks, along with a few successes.[68] Dozens of successful attempts followed in mid-century (figs. 8.1 and 8.2). In addition to the Bank

Figure 8.1 Alexandria branch office of the Anglo-Egyptian Bank, founded in 1864.The bank opened 16 branches. (Courtesy of Max Karkégi, www .egyptedantan.com)

of Egypt (Alexandria, 1855) and the Ottoman Bank (Istanbul, 1856), the banks established in this period include the Anglo-Egyptian Bank (Cairo, 1864) and the London and Baghdad Association (1864). All of them were largely, if not wholly, European-owned and -operated. Private banks with predominantly local ownership gained importance in the 1890s, and largely Muslim-owned ones did so in the early twentieth century.[69] Although the foreign banks of the mid-nineteenth century lent primarily to states, whose mounting debts stoked their appetite for credit, they also financed private commercial, agricultural, and industrial ventures. Moreover, they accepted deposits, provided housing loans, and made advances to consumers. Their interest rates stood well below those prevalent in older markets dominated by local financiers.[70] Before long, specialized banks came on the scene, including strictly commercial banks.

These observations conform with the launching of campaigns all across the region to have major banks open new branches. Their purpose was to enable farmers and merchants to escape the exorbitant rates and other draconian requirements of traditional moneylenders.[71] In the second half of the nineteenth century, and in

Figure 8.2   Cashiers' windows of the Ottoman Bank's Izmir branch, which opened in 1856, the year the bank was founded. (Courtesy of the Uğur Göktaş photograph collection)

many places even later, peasants without access to banks paid interest rates varying between 20 percent and 100 percent, with their crops serving as collateral. By contrast, European agricultural interest rates had fallen to around 4 percent.[72] Commercial interest rates, too, were high in traditional markets. In those of Lebanon and Syria they stood at 24 percent in the mid-nineteenth century. Meanwhile the silk guilds of Istanbul were paying 18 percent, as compared with the 5 percent paid by their counterparts in Lyon, France.[73] With the spread of banks, growing numbers benefited from relatively cheap loans. The volume of lending also rose by orders of magnitude, dwarfing that of cash waqfs. In 1909, the state-owned Turkish Agricultural Bank advanced six times as much credit as the total capital of the Ottoman cash waqfs. The Ottoman Bank advanced twelve times as much.[74]

The differences between the new banks and traditional financiers were not limited to scales and rates. Enjoying legal standing, foreign banks could sue and be sued as organizations, though initially only in foreign courts, or in local courts operated by European consulates under long-standing privileges. The procedures and capabilities of these courts continued to evolve in concert with western institutional developments. The consular courts gained familiarity, for instance, with the accounting systems of modern banks. As economic relations between Europe and the Middle East deepened, these courts facilitated the diffusion of modern banking.

Causes of the Lag in Financial Development

This chapter has invoked several institutions that blocked evolutionary paths in the direction of modern banking: the Islamic law of commercial partnerships, the Islamic inheritance system, the waqf system, and the individualism of Islamic law. All were introduced earlier as causes of the region's other handicaps. Like the region's previously discussed symptoms of underdevelopment, delayed financial modernization was an unintended consequence of institutional choices that served laudable objectives. The provision that a partnership ended with the death of a partner provided safeguards for the deceased partner's heirs. Egalitarian inheritance rules dampened wealth disparities and gave women financial security. Restricting the discretion of waqf caretakers enhanced the founders' control over their endowments. Finally, the individualism of Islamic law hindered factionalism. Roughly a millennium ago, as these Islamic provisions were taking shape, no one could have anticipated the evolutionary paths that they would foreclose. Nor could anyone have predicted that the institutional evolution of an economically undistinguished continent would eventually make it disadvantageous to conduct finance under Islamic law.

During the long historical process that culminated in European economic domination over the Middle East, opposition to interest became a proximate cause of the Middle East's failure to modernize its financial institutions. All else equal, entrepreneurs would have felt freer to speak their minds and pursue financial innovations had the legitimacy of interest not been an issue. But Muslim qualms about interest could not have hindered institutional development more seriously than, say, the anti-interest stance of the Church. Whatever difficulties the Islamic interest ban created for financial and commercial development, these could have been surmounted, as in Europe, if the scale and longevity of private enterprises had expanded. For one thing, a need for standardized accounting would have emerged, and new enterprises would have found legal stratagems increasingly inconvenient. For another, in allowing the preservation of successful private enterprises, the transformation would have strengthened the commercial class, enhancing its political leverage over religious conservatives.

If the impetus for financial modernization ultimately came from abroad, the fundamental reason is that the region's traditional institutions blocked indigenous paths to financial innovation. The rise of the cash waqf is the one significant exception, and it supports claims made in earlier chapters. The cash waqf filled the need for a long-living organization capable of lending at interest. However, precisely because it was a waqf, it could not pool deposits to achieve the scale necessary for making large loans; nor could it adjust adequately to changes in market opportunities. As such, it proved inferior to the organizational forms that played central roles in western financial modernization.

Like Judaism and Christianity, Islam could have gravitated to a more liberal interpretation of its teachings on credit transactions. Vast numbers of Muslims have now made this switch, in fact, through economic modernization drives aimed at overcoming underdevelopment. Although Islamist anti-interest movements exist even today, they enjoy little support beyond platitudes. Almost all of the fifty-six members of the Organization of Islamic States treat interest as legal, effectively ignoring the calls of Islamists who favor a stringent interpretation of Islam's financial prescriptions. Muslims who receive a religious education learn that interest is un-Islamic, but almost all proceed to deal in interest, often without noticing the contradiction. In the few countries where interest is formally illegal, the state itself facilitates this compartmentalization through legal loopholes and by treating violations as personal failings deserving damnation but no worldly retribution.[75] Official duplicity makes it easy to give or take interest without reflecting on the morality of the act.

The economic transformation that the Middle East initiated in the nineteenth century involved the emergence of banks dealing in interest openly and unabashedly. Although this event was essential to the region's industrialization, two groups of thinkers have been impressed especially by its costs. Islamic economists view the banks that proliferated in the course of the modernization process as evidence of destructive westernization.[76] For their part, dependency scholars view them as imperialist instruments to make the region chronically reliant on the West.[77]

Neither group of interpreters makes sense of why the observed modernization took place in the nineteenth century rather than earlier. Nor do they explain why diverse local players, including Muslim merchants and financiers, welcomed the institutional transformation. Relative to the prevailing Islamic institutions, the new institutions of the West improved capabilities for pooling resources, and they lowered credit costs. In the process they turned the Middle East's traditional financial system into an economic handicap. As for the timing of the Middle East's economic modernization, it was tied to the structural evolution of western Europe. Hence, the region's financial transformation was a natural response to structural advances abroad.

The last six chapters have suggested that in inhibiting economic modernization, traditional Islamic institutions set the stage for economic underdevelopment. If the articulated logic is correct, groups able to do business under different institutions would have enjoyed an advantage with respect to Muslims, who had to live by Islamic law. Specifically, local Christians and Jews would have benefited from the "choice of law" that Muslim-governed states customarily granted to their non-Muslim subjects. Likewise, foreign merchants would have benefited from treaties that enabled them to do business under institutions of their own. These possibilities will be explored next. First on the agenda is the economic trajectory of minorities. Among the puzzles is that it took more than a millennium for the legal privileges of non-Muslims to produce notable commercial successes.

PART III

The Makings of Underdevelopment

9

The Islamization of Non-Muslim Economic Life

Until the late eighteenth century, no major religious community of the Middle East outclassed others in either commerce or finance. However, in the course of global economic modernization, local Christians and Jews registered advances that Muslims failed to match. By the nineteenth century Greeks and Armenians, and to a lesser extent Jews, were playing strikingly disproportionate roles in the region's commercial and financial life, especially in cities. They had leapt ahead of Muslims also in living standards. That is why over the past two centuries Middle Eastern reforms to restore national economic competitiveness have included policies to improve the relative economic standing of Muslims.

The successes of minorities have been attributed to western favoritism toward non-Muslims, European imperialism, and the clannishness of the minorities themselves. But none of these factors arose in the eighteenth century; for instance, efforts to impose European control over the Islamic Middle East extend to the Crusades. So they leave unexplained why the minorities began to pull ahead of the majority in the eighteenth century, and not before. Also relevant, it is said, is that Muslims shunned interest, looked down on commerce, and had military duties from which non-Muslims were exempt. The first two claims are open to challenge, and all three raise a question of timing. None elucidates the pre- and post–eighteenth century patterns simultaneously. In other words, none makes sense of why no major differences existed before the eighteenth century and also why, at this time, Muslim commercial participation started to recede in relative importance.

A weightier explanation is that minorities benefited disproportionately from opportunities to conduct business within networks including sizable numbers of westerners. These opportunities did indeed prove increasingly lucrative; in time they increased the competitiveness of local Christians and Jews. Yet, we still need to explain why, at least initially, Muslims derived fewer benefits from new opportunities linked to the rise of the West. A related challenge is to explain why it is that around the eighteenth century, and not before, networking with westerners proved so beneficial to non-Muslims. Business networks do not necessarily bring net benefits to their members; they may block advantageous exchanges with outsiders. In the course of economic modernization, western networking itself modernized. It became intertwined with institutions that facilitated impersonal exchange. That is what made interactions with westerners increasingly lucrative.

The key to a comprehensive explanation lies in Islam's distinct form of legal pluralism. Under the Islamic system of governance non-Muslim subjects could conduct business outside the jurisdiction of the Islamic court system and, absent Muslim involvement, seek adjudication in autonomous courts. This choice of law gave Christians and Jews a huge advantage as the West developed the legal infrastructure of the modern economy. They started to advance economically simply by adopting western business methods, forming economic alliances with westerners, and using western courts to settle disputes. Traditionally denied the same choice of law, Muslims could not take advantage of modern institutions as individuals. They had to wait for collectively generated legal reforms, and the delay left them economically handicapped. The observed bifurcation in communal economic standings was thus an unintended and unforeseeable consequence of a pluralistic legal system designed, paradoxically, to help Muslims by giving Islamic courts jurisdiction over all their legal affairs.

Initially, the evidence indicates, Christian and Jewish traders enjoyed no major institutional advantage over their Muslim suppliers, clients, partners, and competitors. If anything, Muslims benefited from greater legal certainty and possibly also from pro-Muslim institutional biases in adjudication. In principle, they could have suffered from lack of access to non-Muslim courts. But for reasons addressed below, the costs in question proved minor until quite late. Minorities gained an advantage, and Muslims started falling behind, only when the former began to exercise their choice of law differently, in favor of western legal systems. This flight from Islamic law, and from the laws of local minorities, took place as hundreds of thousands of Christians and Jews acquired western protection and moved their business dealings, usually in part, outside the Islamic legal system.

We face, then, two related puzzles. The first is that in the eighteenth century the minorities began a rapid economic ascent. And the second is that, despite the choice of law they enjoyed, in contexts relevant to economic performance the earlier legal practices of non-Muslims resembled those of Muslims. We start in this chapter with the second puzzle, because its resolution will help to crack the first.

Islamic Legal Pluralism

When communities differ in their economic accomplishments, the reason often lies in the legal regimes under which they conduct business. The critical comparison here is between the legal rights of the Middle East's Muslims and its dhimmis (*ahl al-dhimma*), as its Christians and Jews were known. Though subject to sundry discriminatory restrictions, dhimmis enjoyed an ultimately critical right denied to Muslims. From the rise of Islam to the secularist reforms of the nineteenth century, they were entitled to choice of law, except on criminal matters, which fell exclusively within the jurisdiction of Islamic courts. Although the doctrinal basis for this choice varied over time, its fundamental principles remained fixed.

Choice of law, which will be treated as synonymous with jurisdictional choice, is not the same thing as choice of forum or court; in principle two courts may litigate a given case under the same law. In the present context, however, choice of law almost always

Figure 9.1 Ananias (Hanani) Church, Damascus. Dating from the first century, it was restored or rebuilt several times under Muslim rule. (Photo: İzzet Keribar)

amounted to choice of forum, because each religion or denomination's courts applied its own distinct law. Known collectively as "denominational" or "communal" courts, the non-Islamic courts were among the institutions that enabled local Christians and Jews to maintain distinct identities (fig. 9.1).[1]

It was not Islam that introduced choice of law into the region. The Romans and Byzantines had granted jurisdictional choice to Jews, assorted Christian communities, and, later, Muslims.[2] But the earliest basis for the form of concern here was a distinctly Islamic inter-communal arrangement known as the "Pact of Umar" (*'ahd 'Umar*) and commonly attributed to the caliph Umar I or his namesake Umar II (d. 720).[3] Over the centuries many rulers invoked it in setting policies vis-à-vis minorities.[4] The pact ceased to serve as a common point of reference as Islamic legal pluralism adapted to changing administrative needs. Consider the *millet* system through which Ottoman ethno-religious communities preserved their customs and languages.[5] Although Ottoman rulers sometimes invoked the Pact of Umar, usually they appealed simply to Ottoman precedents. Yet those precedents upheld rights and responsibilities enshrined in Islamic law through the Pact of Umar. The functional commonalities are unmistakable.

No text of the Pact of Umar has been dated to earlier than the ninth century, so it must have had a long gestation period. Its attribution to a revered era—the first Umar's rule fell within Islam's Age of Felicity—would have enhanced its authority and protected it against challenges. What matters is that it came to be associated with early Islam and that it allowed dhimmis to avoid Islamic courts in contexts relevant here. One variant of the pact instructs Arabia's dhimmis as follows:

> We shall supervise all your dealings with Muslims . . . We shall not supervise transactions between you and your coreligionists or other unbelievers nor inquire into them as long as you are content. If the buyer or the seller among you desires the annulment of a sale and comes to us to ask for this, we shall annul it or uphold it in accordance with the provisions of our law. But if payment has been made and the purchase consumed, we shall not order restitution . . . If one of you or any other unbeliever applies to us for judgment, we shall adjudicate according to the law of Islam. But if he does not come to us, we shall not intervene among you.[6]

According to these provisions, Christians and Jews were subject to Islamic law in all commercial and financial dealings involving Muslims. But in interacting with other non-Muslims they were free to choose among jurisdictions.

Ex Ante versus Ex Post Choice of Law

Jurisdictional choice may be exercised either ex ante (at the stage of contract negotiation) or ex post (after agreement on terms). Necessarily consensual, ex ante jurisdictional choice enhances efficiency; the parties would not agree to law A over law B unless each expected to do at least as well under A and possibly better. By contrast, ex post jurisdictional choice may be exercised unilaterally, to secure an advantage at the expense of others. Suppose that two individuals form a partnership under Jewish law. At the end of the contract period, a dispute erupts over the division of profit, and the first appeals for a resolution under Islamic law. He does so in the expectation of benefiting in a legal game that appears to have acquired a zero-sum quality; he senses that he will gain at the expense of his partner.

The Pact of Umar gave dhimmis *both* forms of jurisdictional choice. It allowed contracts made outside the Islamic legal system to be voided opportunistically simply by appearing before a kadi, or Muslim judge. Such opportunism was impossible in relation to contracts sealed by a kadi. A dhimmi could move a case out of Islamic court only if *all* parties agreed. For their part, Muslims enjoyed no comparable choice of law. As Muslims they could not use non-Muslim courts, whatever the expected benefits. Nor was renouncing Islam a viable option, for apostasy was punishable by death.[7] In some localities and periods Muslims could pick and choose among judges belonging to different schools of Islamic jurisprudence (*madhhabs*).[8] In Ottoman Egypt, for instance, it was possible to rent a shop according to Hanbali law and get married the next day under Maliki or Hanafi law.[9] There existed religious scholars who facilitated school switching by issuing opinions (*fatwās*) according to the teachings of all major schools. Some of them explicitly endorsed switching, even temporary switching, provided the motivation was a belief in another school's superiority on the matter at hand.[10] However, school switching could require a formal change of allegiance. In any case, where it became common rulers took to banning it; or they made it unfeasible by withholding appointments from kadis belonging to unfavored schools.[11]

Differences among the four major Sunni schools of jurisprudence were merely symbolic on most commercial and financial matters. On other matters, they could be significant to potential litigants.[12] For example, whether an estate was divided according to Hanafi or Maliki rules could affect the set of beneficiaries as well as the distribution of shares. Yet in estate divisions judicial chaos was hardly the norm. For one thing, Muslim families were expected to have inheritance cases adjudicated according to their own school of law. For another, judges rarely honored unilateral school switching, and any member of a family belonging to a particular school could block the settlement of an estate according to another school. On commercial matters, too, opportunistic school switching was discouraged. Ex post choice of law was less of a problem, then, for Muslims than for Jews and Christians.

On civil matters Muslims, like dhimmis, could seek informal arbitration. However, all parties had to agree, so arbitration could not provide a predictable advantage at someone else's expense. In practice, therefore, an arbitrator (hakam) could not trump a contract formed under Islamic law; and arbitration was not a source of contractual uncertainty, as Islamic law was for dhimmis who opted to conduct business under an alternative legal system. In any case, an arbitrator's decision was not an enforceable judgment; rather, it was an opinion concerning the facts of a dispute and the relevant rights. It could be appealed before a judge, who was free to annul it as contrary to his own school of jurisprudence.[13] A Muslim seeking a binding decision had no choice, therefore, but to approach an Islamic court. Ordinarily, that court would expect contracts to satisfy Islamic law.

At least in principle, we have seen, Christian and Jewish merchants could choose from larger sets of contractual forms, debt instruments, deeds, and inheritance arrangements. Where they found it convenient, they could follow the rules of their own communities. At the same time, they were free to use Islamic business methods, emulate Islamic inheritance practices, and take disputes to a kadi. Ordinarily a kadi was obligated to try all cases presented, including those initiated by dhimmis.

"Legal pluralism" describes a condition found to a greater or lesser extent in every social system: multiple and possibly conflicting layers of social organization.[14] Like other forms of legal pluralism, its Islamic form allowed legal variety and experimentation. Accordingly, both Muslims and non-Muslims endured tensions between legal requirements and customs, and between the often divergent claims of overlapping social networks defined along geographic, linguistic, or familial lines. Nevertheless, and curiously

in retrospect, Islamic legal pluralism gave Muslims, who were politically and militarily dominant, *fewer* legal options than it did to
subservient communities.

There is a voluminous literature on how jurisdictional choice facilitates the evasion of inefficient rules and arrangements.[15] People
choose among legal systems according to cost-benefit calculations,
it says, disfavoring those reputed to litigate unfairly, inconsistently,
or slowly. Because this logic treats contractual choices as binding,
it does not apply to the case at hand. Only if Islamic legal pluralism limited dhimmi legal choice to its ex ante form would the induced behaviors furnish reliable clues concerning the perceived
merits of Islamic law.

Precisely because dhimmis could appeal to an Islamic court at
any time, even after agreeing to the jurisdiction of a communal
court, minority legal practices did not reveal unambiguous information about relative efficiency. Although the legal choices of a
non-Muslim plaintiff could indicate that he considered Islamic law
more favorable than other legal systems, it could mean, alternatively, that he put a premium on legal certainty and enforceability.
These motives for choosing Islamic law were neither mutually exclusive nor invariant to context. Changes in other legal systems
could turn the advantages of Islamic contractual forms into mani-
fest *dis*advantages. Thus, whether choice of law benefited the Middle East's religious minorities is an empirical matter capable of
yielding a different answer in one domain than another. I turn,
therefore, to the historical record.

Jurisdictional Choices before Economic Modernization

The natural domain of the communal courts consisted of matters
connected directly to religion: marriage, divorce, custody, inheritance, and slavery. However, they were also empowered to litigate commercial and financial disputes. Each religious community's
courts had distinct features—unsurprising in view of their mutual
autonomy. Jewish congregations operated law courts mandated to
base their judgments, including those concerning business, on Jew-

Figure 9.2 Ahrida Synagogue, Istanbul. Built in the late 1400s, it was restored in 1694. For centuries its rabbi adjudicated cases among Ottoman Jews. (Photo: İzzet Keribar)

ish law (fig. 9.2). Their judges helped investors, creditors, and merchants draw up contracts likely to hold up before a Jewish tribunal. Temporary Jewish courts were set up at trade fairs to assist Jewish merchants in establishing partnerships and making credit arrangements.[16] For their part, Orthodox Christians operated ecclesiastical courts headed by a bishop, metropolitan, archbishop, or patriarch. The officials of these courts helped their co-religionists draft deeds, wills, and commercial agreements. When a case came before an ecclesiastical court it was supposed to be settled according to canon law. After 1453, when the Ottoman Empire absorbed the last remnants of Byzantium, the most important of these courts was that operated by the Orthodox Patriarch.[17] Armenian merchants could take their intra-communal disputes to courts that relied solely on Armenian witnesses.[18]

Nevertheless, local Jews and Christians made heavy use of the Islamic legal system. Evidence pertaining to Christian courts in the region is quite limited relative to documentation on Christians appearing in Islamic courts as litigants, witnesses, guardians, and

agents.[19] Non-Muslims often appeared before a kadi with complaints against their co-religionists. Even intra-communal disputes
among Christians of the same denomination, like those among
Jews, were frequently adjudicated by a kadi. This finding is commonplace in the historical literature on Middle Eastern legal practices. Numerous studies show that Ottoman Jews of the fifteenth
and sixteenth centuries used Islamic courts routinely.[20] In the seventeenth century, Kayseri's Greek and Armenian minorities took
financial and commercial disagreements to Muslim courts at about
the same per capita frequency as the city's Turks.[21]

Some studies go so far as to claim that dhimmis used Islamic
courts exclusively. Noticing myriads of minority-initiated cases in
the Islamic court registers (*sijills*) of Damascus for 1775–1860 and
failing to find any reference in these registers to a Christian or Jewish court, Najwa Al-Qattan infers that none existed.[22] She proceeds to question whether the city's dhimmis enjoyed meaningful
legal autonomy. Her logic is strained. First of all, the court registers
could have avoided references to communal courts as a matter of
principle, or to avoid legitimizing competing suppliers of adjudication, or simply out of habit. Second, "frequent use" is not the same
thing as proportionate use. Without population shares, which Al-
Qattan omits, there is no way of knowing whether the minorities
of Damascus used Islamic courts as readily as their Muslim neighbors. Finally, even a finding of proportionate use would not conflict with the evidence of legal autonomy reported here. Just as a
person can refrain from exercising a constitutional right to free
speech, one may be free to file a case in a communal court yet opt
to appear before a kadi.[23] Al-Qattan's data do not establish that
minorities never enjoyed choice of law. They merely call for an
explanation of why the dhimmis of Damascus, like those of other
places, made heavy use of Islamic courts on the eve of the Middle
East's western-inspired institutional reforms.

Studies that do take account of population shares confirm that
minorities used Islamic courts frequently. By the same token, they
show that minorities sued each other disproportionately less in
Islamic courts relative to Muslims suing other Muslims. In the seventeenth century, according to a study by Ronald Jennings, one-

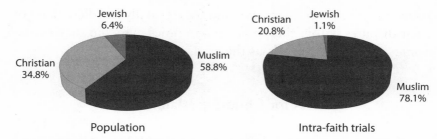

Figure 9.3 Population shares of Istanbul's three religious communities and their shares of all intra-faith trials in Muslim courts. *Note*: The trial shares are from the author's sample of seventeenth-century Istanbul court registers. The Muslim share of the intra-faith trials is disproportionately large at the 99.9 percent level of statistical significance ($t = 16.67$), and the Christian and Jewish shares are disproportionately small ($t = 12.49$ and $t = 9.22$, respectively). The population shares are based on data in Mantran, *İstanbul*, p. 46.

third of all cases tried by the Islamic court in Nicosia, Cyprus involved at least one Christian.[24] At the time, close to half of Nicosia's population consisted of Christians, so it is clear that they were using Islamic courts disproportionately less than the city's Muslims. Of the intra-faith trials, 81.4 percent were among Muslims, and only 18.6 percent among Christians. In seventeenth-century Istanbul, likewise, intra-Christian and intra-Jewish trials in Islamic courts were disproportionately lower than intra-Muslim trials. Although 34.8 percent of the city's population was Christian, only 21.8 percent of the lawsuits among co-religionists were among Christians (fig. 9.3). Absent a reason for believing that Christians were relatively less disputatious or less litigious, we may infer that Christians handled a substantial share of their disputes outside the Islamic court system. The intra-Christian trials included ones that pitted Greeks against Armenians, along with Greek versus Greek and Armenian versus Armenian trials.[25] Hence, the proportion of intra-communal trials limited to Christians was even lower than that of all intra-Christian trials.[26]

The evidence also shows that a sizable share of the minorities somehow found the Islamic court system advantageous. The challenge, then, is to reconcile the principle of Islamic legal pluralism with the evidence of minority legal practices. If dhimmis were free to operate courts of their own, and they actually handled many of their disputes within their own communities, why did they use Islamic courts as frequently as they did?

Motives for Choosing Islamic Courts

Most obviously, dhimmis dealt extensively with Muslims, and kadis had sole jurisdiction over all disagreements in which at least one party was Muslim. Although there exist examples of Muslims agreeing to settle cases before a Christian or Jewish court, the risks made them highly exceptional.[27] Insofar as personal economic success required dealing with Muslims in at least some contexts, a Jew or Christian had to be familiar with Islamic law and prepared for litigation before a kadi. This provided an incentive to use Islamic courts. Interactions among dhimmis belonging to separate religious communities offered additional reasons. Because each side considered the other's court biased, cross-communal lawsuits were usually taken to a kadi in the expectation of relatively impartial adjudication.

Christians and Jews also used Islamic courts to register financial transactions and record ownership claims. If any problem arose, so they thought, the facts could be checked and verified by the most authoritative court of the land, which served as a public notary. Minorities relied on Islamic registration also to safeguard their interests in the event the state or individual Muslims challenged their rights. Consequently, the appropriate venue for suing was often the Islamic court.[28] Variations in court fees must have affected legal choices. Wherever a communal court charged more than the area's Islamic court,[29] some cases may have been taken to the kadi simply to minimize litigation costs.[30] Much more important, perhaps, were the Islamic court's superior powers of enforcement. Most communal tribunals lacked authorization to impose temporal penalties, and they were particularly powerless when the parties belonged to multiple faiths.[31] In this respect, they operated more as arbitration boards than as bona fide courts.

Still other reasons to favor the Islamic courts lay in the substance of Islamic law. As chapter 3 showed, the Islamic partnership rules offered at least as much flexibility as those of the Middle East's Christian communities, and advantages over the Jewish 'isqā. Unsurprisingly, right up to the eighteenth century non-Muslim traders sometimes opted for Islamic partnerships even when their partners were exclusively co-religionists.[32] Here is an example, then, of non-Muslims favoring Islamic law through mutual agreement, at the stage of contract negotiation. In forming Islamic partnerships, merchants and investors also made their agreements binding. There were contexts, of course, in which the substance of Islamic law would have seemed disadvantageous. Matters of inheritance come to mind. A successful Greek merchant with several children might have found the Islamic inheritance system problematic for the challenges it poses for his business. Even in such contexts, however, Islamic law might have been favored as a means of preventing opportunistic jurisdictional switches.

The principles of Islamic legal pluralism are consistent, then, with the record of dhimmi legal practices. Minorities who were free to use an autonomous communal court had diverse reasons to favor Islamic justice. Where no evidence of communal courts has emerged, it could be that the reasons for choosing Islamic courts were sufficiently sound to make communal courts superfluous.

The foregoing logic carries implications for the evolution of the Middle East's entire legal infrastructure. As I will show next, the incentives to use Islamic courts caused minorities to make their legal systems more similar in practice to those of Muslims. Islamic legal pluralism thus galvanized a process of legal homogenization. Paradoxically, then, it lessened the very legal diversity that it allowed and protected in principle. This homogenization carries implications for economic modernization. Like Islamic law, which stagnated in domains relevant here, the legal systems of the minorities would have failed to modernize.

The Dynamics of Islamic Legal Pluralism

Earlier chapters showed that the Islamic inheritance system prevented the Middle East from developing the organizational capabilities essential to remaining globally competitive. By fragmenting the estates of successful merchants, it kept Islamic commercial partnerships small and short-lived; it also dampened pressures to develop complex enterprises. The consequent lack of organizational progress did not pose a major problem as long as no other region had modernized. However, it became a huge handicap for merchants operating under Islamic law as organizational advances in the West brought about larger and more durable enterprises.

Choice of law allowed dhimmi communities to settle estates according to inheritance rules of their own and to develop new forms of commercial organization, including complex partnerships and even the business corporation. In principle, then, non-Muslims could have avoided the organizational stagnation experienced by Muslims. In practice, legal homogenization burdened the entire indigenous population with the same developmental handicaps. The tendency toward legal uniformity is abundantly visible in relation to inheritance practices.

Like the Islamic inheritance system, that of Greek Orthodoxy tied inheritance rights to the combination of heirs. Under the latter, however, legal heirs were generally limited to the nuclear family and surviving parents. In addition, daughters usually lacked inheritance rights.[33] Thus, the estate of a man survived by a wife, two sons, and two daughters would be divided differently depending on whether Islamic or Greek Orthodox inheritance rules were followed. In the traditional Jewish system, a father was entitled to disposal of his property through a will. He could single out one or more children for special treatment. If a parent died intestate, daughters did not inherit when there was a son, although each had to be maintained out of the estate until she attained her majority or got married. When there was more than one son, the oldest received twice the share of any other. A husband inherited from his wife, but a widow was entitled only to maintenance.[34] Hence, an estate settlement could be markedly different under Jewish law than under Islamic law. Consider a married Jewish woman who under Jewish law would inherit nothing from her father. Under an Islamic settlement, she would be guaranteed a portion of the estate. Not surprisingly, Jews and Christians sometimes took inheritance disputes to the kadi in the expectation of personal gain, sometimes after losing in their own courts.[35]

Precisely because the prevalence of such cases was common knowledge, many dhimmi families took steps to keep their members from carrying inheritance matters to Muslim judges. Thus, they allowed daughters to inherit some property and restricted bequests to non-relatives. For that reason, Jewish and Christian families took inheritance disputes to Istanbul's Islamic courts less frequently than Muslim families did. In the seventeenth century only 13 percent of the intra-faith inheritance disputes in the city were among non-Muslim relatives—far less than the 41.2 percent share of non-Muslims in the total population.

The communal courts often condoned concessions to Islamic law; some even encouraged legal Islamization in order to minimize interferences in the affairs of their communities.[36] Nevertheless, rabbis and priests harbored misgivings about granting legitimacy to Islamic practices. The twelfth- and thirteenth-century responsa of Moses and Abraham Maimonides, like the sixteenth-century responsa of Samuel de Medina, are replete with complaints about Jews litigating cases in Islamic courts.[37] Also in the sixteenth century, Orthodox prelates of Bulgaria appealed to Istanbul for help in keeping the local Islamic courts from serving Christians; Bulgarian kadis were encouraging Christians to use their services, the prelates complained, in violation of the judicial authority vested in the Church.[38] The countermeasures of dhimmi leaders included ostracism, even excommunication. The excommunicated were banned from the weddings, funerals, and worship services of their community.[39]

In the Middle East, as in other places, belonging to a religious minority amounted to accepting an implicit contract. The sanctions in question counteracted the temptation to challenge that contract ex post by carrying intra-communal disputes to an Islamic court. Thus, they made the implicit contract between the minority and its individual members relatively more binding. To a degree, therefore, they preserved communal legal norms, thereby enforcing a right enshrined in the Pact of Umar. That is evident in the court use statistics from seventeenth-century Istanbul and Nicosia.

On occasion Middle Eastern rulers took steps to bolster communal courts. For instance, they issued edicts endorsing or reconfirming the legal privileges of religious minorities, sometimes during negotiations with a strategically placed community.[40] For their part, certain kadis refused to accept non-Muslim cases indiscriminately, foregoing litigation fees in the process, probably on orders from above.[41] As with the sanctions minority communities imposed on their own members, such official efforts to uphold legal pluralism enhanced the credibility of contracts made under non-Islamic systems. Nevertheless, only rarely would a kadi deny a subject's right to adjudication under Islamic law. Nor did any Muslim official succeed in preventing Jews or Christians from appealing to the kadi, if indeed any tried to go that far. On balance, therefore, Islamic law exerted a huge influence on both the practices of the communal courts and the evolution of dhimmi legal doctrines. The legal practices of Middle Eastern minorities thus underwent Islamization, weakening whatever reasons might have existed for favoring a non-Muslim legal system in cases among non-Muslim coreligionists. Therein lies a key reason why the religious minorities so often took cases to Islamic courts.

Adverse Effects on Organizational Modernization among Minorities

Against this background, let us reconsider the lack of major differences, until the eighteenth century, in economic achievements of the region's religious communities. Insofar as Islamic law hindered development, people of all faiths would have been held back. In particular, the financial rules and organizational forms of non-Muslims would have stagnated alongside those of Muslims.

Indeed, no group made primogeniture the norm in settling estates; and none developed the advanced organizational structures that the Middle East eventually transplanted from western Europe. In the early eighteenth century, all confessional groups continued to form partnerships according to Islamic law.[42] From an institutional standpoint, then, native Jews and Christians conducted business much like Muslims. In tolerating, even encouraging this institutional standardization, the communal courts contributed to making all groups operate under similar rules in domains critical to material advancement.[43] The similarities of Muslim and non-Muslim business practices help to explain why until this time no minority pulled measurably ahead of Muslims and why none generated modern forms of economic organization on its own.

Responsibility for the dynamic inefficiency of Middle Eastern economic institutions belongs partly, of course, to the inequities of Islamic legal pluralism, including its late variants such as the Ottoman *millet* system. If all communities had choice of law, and court decisions were equally well enforced, the historical record would have differed in several respects. With opportunities for ex post jurisdictional switching curtailed, the legal systems of the minorities might have enjoyed greater popularity. The ensuing legal competition might have induced Muslims to reform the Islamic inheritance system, at least to allow exceptions for merchants. Conceivably, some system conducive to organizational modernization would have gained popularity. Islamic legal pluralism was not a sufficient condition for the dynamic inefficiency actually observed. Also relevant were particulars of the prevailing inheritance system. Had Islamic inheritance practices been more conducive to organizational change, the legal homogenization resulting from Islamic legal pluralism need not have harmed economic development.

Minorities and the Path to the Corporation

In discussing the absence of the corporation, we saw that community-specific state policies created opportunities for organizational change. The taxation of minorities generated organizational prototypes that might have stimulated the development of corporate law. Through the ages, sultans often found it advantageous to relegate tax collection to a communal leader abreast of his constituents' capacity to bear taxes. For Jewish and Christian communities, he was usually a religious authority. The communal leader would negotiate a tax for his "contribution unit" (under the Ottomans, *avârızhane*) and then apportion the burden among the unit's households, presumably on the basis of private information about ability to pay.[44] In negotiating with the sovereign he would often seek to minimize his community's tax burden through tricks such as doctoring birth registers and understating production capacity.[45] With varying success, rulers tried to co-opt communal leaders to serve as their agents. When results were unsatisfactory, they would switch to direct taxation through outside agents. It appears that states would have resisted any move to assert genuine corporate power on behalf of religious minorities. Until the nineteenth century, the era of nationalist awakenings, they were generally powerful enough to prevail.

That minority communities would be recognized as groups only insofar as benefits accrued to the state is clear from a series sixteenth-century dealings between the Jews and Ottoman authorities of Jerusalem. The former sought to lease a plot for use as a cemetery. Because no collective entity had standing before the courts, they could not do so as a community. Three wealthy individuals stepped forward to lease land in their own names, with each assuming personal responsibility for paying one-third of the rent. The Islamic court that registered the thirty-year lease did not treat the trio as a representative body; it addressed each renter as "a member" of the Jewish community.[46] This is significant. Overcrowding in cemeteries was not a pressing concern of authorities. Hence, they would have seen no particular need to grant Jews legal recognition as a community in this particular context.

The same authorities faced different incentives when debt restitution or tax collection was at stake. Around the same time, in 1596, an impoverished Jew appeared before a kadi to complain that he was ordered to repay part of a debt incurred for the collective benefit of his community. Challenging the requirement on legal grounds, he testified that Jerusalem's Jewish community lacked standing before the law. Although the plaintiff was interpreting Islamic law correctly, the judge made him pay his share.[47] In this context, the Jewish community was effectively granted legal personhood. Why the difference between this case and that of the cemetery? The Jews borrowed mostly from Muslims, and some of their creditors were dignitaries. For this reason alone, the restitution of Jewish debts was of concern to officials. In addition, both intercommunal harmony and financial markets benefited from the orderly repayment of debts. The state thus gained from having a communal leader allocate debt burdens among his constituents. As with taxation, he would possess the local knowledge necessary to exact resources; the state's own agents would not.

Insofar as rulers facilitated or promoted communal autonomy for non-Muslims, they provided organizational rights formally denied to Muslims. In an Islamic court a Muslim litigant was rarely designated as a member of a Muslim subcommunity—a Turk, a Shii, a Bektashi, a Maliki. When Muslim groupings were recognized for purposes of efficient governance, as with tax farming, the consequent administrative divisions were treated as temporary. If minorities were permitted to form permanent communal organizations, the reason must have been that this was relatively less threatening to political stability. In the sixteenth century, any non-Muslim community that used its autonomy as a vehicle for resistance to the incumbent regime, or for broad institutional reform, would have faced resistance from Muslims, on the ground that Islam, or Islamic dominance, was under challenge. Mobilizing the masses against an organized Muslim opposition would have been more difficult.

As we saw in relation to guilds and tax farms, premodern Muslim rulers understood the uses of treating communities as self-governing units. But they allowed self-governance selectively and in limited contexts. So although a religious community of the Middle East might have organized itself as a corporation, as western religious communities frequently did, strong states stood in their way. Therein lies another reason why, prior to the eighteenth century, the economic life of the region's minorities resembled that of its religious majority.

Religion and Economic Performance

Much of the existing literature on premodern Middle Eastern history ignores religion on the ground that the region's religious communities adjusted their practices to market realities, rendering it practically irrelevant to actual outcomes. Yet religion could have mattered greatly, because in contexts of interest here, legal rights and obligations depended on faith. If differences in legal opportunities did not cause economic fortunes to diverge, the reason is that Islamic legal pluralism, the source of differences in legal opportunities, proved self-undermining. In particular, it fostered individual incentives that eroded differences in commercial organization, finance, and the division of estates.

Economic historians of the nineteenth century are much less likely to consider religion irrelevant to the relative economic performance of the Middle East's diverse communities. This is because by this time the region's Christians and Jews very obviously performed better. Why their fortunes improved markedly at this historical juncture, and why Muslims were left behind, is the other historical puzzle identified at the start of this chapter. Just as the lack of differences before the eighteenth century was associated with the Islamization of non-Muslim economic life, so the subsequent divergence was linked to its de-Islamization.

10

The Ascent of the Middle East's Religious Minorities

The renowned Turkish journalist Falih Rıfkı Atay witnessed World War I and its aftermath, including the Greek occupation of western Turkey and Armenian collaboration with Russian and French invaders. He attributes the severity of the Turkish responses to a "feeling of inferiority" rooted in the undisputed economic dominance achieved by Anatolia's Christian minorities.[1] The economic successes of the Greeks and Armenians had fueled separatist movements, which then galvanized defensive military campaigns, as well as far-reaching social and economic reforms, to reverse the positional losses of Turks.

Positional losses produced defensive reactions also on the part of nineteenth- and early twentieth-century Arab intellectuals who came in contact with western achievements in science and industry, and observed the minorities living in their midst leap ahead economically.[2] Arab nationalism and pan-Islamism were both driven partly by efforts to improve Muslim economic fortunes.[3] Likewise, mob violence against Christian Arabs, where it occurred, stemmed partly from the economic insecurity that Muslim Arabs developed in the face of steady Christian advances.[4]

The economic ascent of the Middle East's religious minorities, and the concomitant loss in the relative economic performance of its Muslims, thus ranks among the most consequential social transformations of the modern era. Before we explore the underlying social mechanisms, we shall review the evidence on what the transformation entailed.

The Middle East's Great Bifurcation

No aggregate statistics are available on the inter-communal distribution of economic activity in the premodern Middle East. However, historical research is replete with examples of regions whose commerce exhibited substantial, if not disproportionately high, Muslim participation. The Geniza documents indicate that around the eleventh century Muslim merchants controlled, in addition to much of Cairo's transit and long-distance trade, much of its local commerce.[5] Records from fifteenth-century Egypt and Syria and sixteenth-century Turkey paint a similar picture: although Christians and Jews controlled certain mercantile activities, Muslims dominated others.[6]

Equally revealing are judicial records from seventeenth-century Kayseri, Turkey. At the time, its population was 78 percent Muslim. In credit cases handled by the Islamic courts the lender was a Muslim 82 percent of the time—evidence that the town's successful financiers included Muslims.[7] A century later Muslim merchants played a disproportionately important role in the commercial life of Basra, Iraq.[8] In the same period, commercial activity in the Red Sea was in the hands of Ottoman Muslims, especially Egyptians; the Black Sea trade was conducted primarily by Muslim Turks; and at four major Mediterranean ports—Algiers, Alexandria, Istanbul, Canea—Turks were the main charterers of caravaning ships.[9] Between 1779 and 1781, Muslims constituted 64 percent of the Ottoman subjects shipping goods from Istanbul, where the Muslim share of the total population was about 58 percent.[10] True, Muslim participation in the bilateral trade with Western Europe was limited.[11] However, until the eighteenth century, the Middle East's trade with other places carried greater economic weight, and in no other major emporium was the Muslim role insignificant.[12]

The historical literature thus contradicts the once-prevalent view that Muslims habitually left commerce to Jews and Christians.[13] Yet by the nineteenth century, which is when this misperception took hold, Muslim traders and financiers had yielded enormous market share to local non-Muslims. Already in the late eighteenth century, Greek, Armenian, and Jewish merchants dominated the commerce of major cities. Even earlier they formed an overwhelming majority of the brokers who mediated between western and local traders. Familiar with local economic practices and increasingly also with those of westerners, Christian and Jewish brokers distributed European imports, arranged the purchase and transport of goods destined for the West, and harassed local debtors. Studies on Ottoman maritime trade of the eighteenth century find not only that non-Muslim minorities played major roles. During that century, they also show, the Muslim share plummeted.[14]

The trend was to continue. By the end of the nineteenth century the Ottoman Empire's Muslim merchants were decidedly secondary players in its external trade with Europe; and at home, too, they had lost enormous ground to local minorities. To be sure, the imbalance was not as pronounced as the typical European report made it seem. Turkish, Arab, and other Muslims continued to dominate rural-urban trade in many heavily Muslim regions, much of the coastal trade done by small vessels, and, in the international arena, the commerce among certain Muslim countries.[15] Nevertheless, the general picture was overwhelmingly favorable to minorities.

In the Black Sea region, for example, the import and export businesses had come under the domination of Greek and Armenian merchants. According to a British document from 1884, of fourteen major commission agents in Trabzon, three were Persian, one was Swiss, and the rest were Greek or Armenian. Out of thirty-three exporters, three were Turkish, one was Swiss, and the remaining twenty-nine were again Greek or Armenian. Of sixty-three major importers, only ten were Turkish; local Christians made up most of the remainder. At the time, 54 percent of Trabzon's population consisted of Muslims, mostly Turks; Greeks and Armenians formed 40 percent (fig. 10.1).

In the Mediterranean trading emporium, a leading Turkish hub was Izmir. From the late eighteenth century to the early twentieth, ethnic Greeks dominated Izmir's commercial life. Comprising between 20 percent and 38 percent of the population, they formed between 40 percent and 60 percent of the city's merchants. Their domination was especially pronounced in large-scale international trade, which they conducted in cooperation with Greek communities

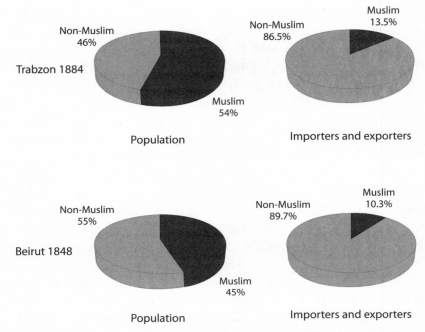

Figure 10.1 Minority shares in the import-export sectors of Trabzon (1884) and Beirut (1848). The population figures are for 1891. *Note*: For both Trabzon and Beirut, the two distributions are statistically different ($\chi^2(1)= 66$ and 49, respectively). *Sources*: On Trabzon: Turgay, "Trade and Merchants," pp. 289–92, 303; on Beirut: Labaki, "Christian Communities," table 11.14.

in other Ottoman centers and abroad.[16] In Istanbul, at the end of World War I Turks constituted just 4 percent of the merchants specializing in exports and imports. They were hardly represented among the suppliers of skilled services to the ports, where Greek, Italian, and French had become the dominant languages. In this predominantly Turkish city, Turks formed only 15 percent of the wholesalers serving the domestic market, and 25 percent of the retailers.[17]

The commercial prominence of the minorities was also evident in major Arab trading centers, where Muslims generally outnumbered other religious communities. In 1826, individuals with names identifiable as Muslim constituted only six of the thirty-four Beiruti merchants doing business with Europe; by 1848 this number had fallen to three (fig. 10.1). For the next three-quarters of a century, the city's foreign trade remained almost entirely in the hands of Christian families.[18] Beirut's lucrative silk trade, too, was almost entirely in European and local Christian hands; between 1904 and 1911, silk exports by Muslim-owned enterprises equaled less than 1 percent of the total.[19] In Aleppo, Muslims maintained a major presence in commerce, but all the wealthiest merchants were Christian.[20] Meanwhile, Baghdad's foreign trade fell largely under the control of local Jews, who benefited from ties to Jewish merchants abroad.[21] In 1837, Alexandria had seventy-two "merchant houses"—clusters of commercial partnerships expected to be renewed repeatedly; forty-three of these belonged to Europeans, twenty-seven to local minorities, and two to Muslims.[22]

These data drawn from European and private local reports are consistent with statistics found in official local publications. In 1912, according to Ottoman yearbooks, the shrinking empire's Muslims, by then 81 percent of the population, played a negligible role in its trade with western Europe. Even in internal trade their significance was much diminished. Muslim Turks comprised only 15 percent of the 18,063 local traders important enough to be listed by name; of the total, 43 percent were Greek, 23 percent Armenian (fig. 10.2).

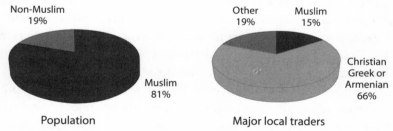

Figure 10.2 Muslim and minority shares of major Ottoman traders, 1912. *Note:* Among the major traders "others" include Jews, Christians other than Greeks and Armenians, and people whose ethnicity or religion is unidentifiable from name alone. *Sources:* Traders from Sonyel, *Minorities*, pp. 258–59; population figures from Behar, *Population of the Ottoman Empire*, table 2.20.

Not Just a Matter of Numbers

The stunning economic ascent of the minorities was not merely a matter of numbers. Standing at the forefront of economic progress, they established a vastly disproportionate presence in various new sectors. The nascent insurance sector provides an example. In the 1890s, European insurance companies drew their agents and appraisers in Trabzon almost entirely from the local Greek and Armenian communities. As such, Turks were practically excluded from the lucrative opportunities generated by the opening of formal insurance markets. In Trabzon, as elsewhere, wealthy Muslims used non-Muslim insurance agents, just as they frequented shops, used shipping companies, and stayed in hotels owned and operated by minorities.[23] In Istanbul, as late as 1922, not one insurance company had been founded by Muslims or counted Muslims among its managers.[24]

The region's religious minorities attained an especially great dominance in finance. Throughout the nineteenth and early twentieth centuries, in Istanbul's Galata district, the financial center of the Ottoman Empire, most owners, managers, and agents of banks and brokerage houses were Greek, Armenian, and Jewish, in that order; foreigners were also prominent, and the language of communication was usually French.[25] The "Galata bankers," as they came to be known, served critical roles as creditors of the state.[26] In Izmir, two-thirds of the major bankers were Greek.[27] In Beirut, all the major indigenous banks were Christian-owned and -operated.[28] In Egypt, Jews were very prominent in financial activities. Serving as lenders, moneychangers, and pawnbrokers, they also won top management positions in various banks.[29]

Minorities achieved dominance also in new industries and public services. In major cities, water, gas, electricity, telephone, tram, and subway services were founded mostly through foreign capital, and the managerial staff was overwhelmingly non-Muslim.[30] In the late nineteenth century, when Muslim Turks constituted 83 percent of Bursa's population, Greeks, Armenians, and foreigners owned thirty-one of its forty-one steam-powered silk-reeling mills.[31] Bursa's chamber of commerce, founded in 1889 in the image of a western business association, reflected the commercial dominance of the city's minorities: 58 percent of its membership was non-Muslim.[32] Replicating the general pattern, practically all the joint-stock companies established under new laws had exclusively non-Muslim founders.[33]

The foregoing transformations need not have affected the distribution of wealth across religious communities. In principle, the Muslim majority could have compensated for its relative losses in commerce and finance through higher participation in other lucrative sectors. In fact, no countervailing trends emerged, and the living standards of minorities rose much faster than those of the majority.[34] In some places widening economic disparities induced massive land transfers to non-Muslims.[35] These disparities were evident also in the vast under-representation of Muslims in the prestigious new neighborhoods of major cities,[36] in the disproportionately low numbers of Muslims among bank customers and buyers of insurance,[37] and in the paucity of Muslim-owned businesses in new commercial centers established outside the traditional guild system.[38]

Popular Explanations

Commonly given explanations for this broad transformation fall into three categories. The first involves Muslim attitudes or practices. A frequent suggestion is that the burdens of conscription and war weakened Muslims at a time when non-Muslims, largely exempt from military duties, prospered through business.[39] As an explanation for the bifurcation under scrutiny, this point admits two objections. First, from the earliest days of Islam onward, non-Muslims were exempt from military service. Second, militarily active communities do not necessarily fall behind.

A related argument invokes the prominence of Muslims in the state bureaucracy. According to many reformers of the late nineteenth century, not to mention later interpreters, Muslims were conditioned to scorn commerce and to treat martial and administrative pursuits as morally superior.[40] Yet Muslims were not always uncompetitive in commerce, so their anti-commercial prejudices, insofar as they were present, could not have been decisive. In any case, the attitudes in question could have changed over time. If there was a transformation, one would have to explain it rather than take it as given. It could have been a rational response to handicaps Muslims began to encounter in the commercial arena.

The Islamic prohibition of interest, it is said, limited Muslim participation in modern commerce and finance.[41] But premodern Muslims routinely gave and took interest, sometimes openly and without apology. It bears reiteration that until recent centuries the profession of money lending included sizable numbers of Muslims.[42] If Christians and Jews gained economic prominence the reason was not, then, that they were inherently readier to ignore qualms about interest common to the three Abrahamic faiths. Explanations centered on Muslim attitudes are not necessarily irrelevant to our central concerns. However, they raise more questions than they answer.

To turn to our second category of explanations, it is said that groups excluded from political power concentrate on business, encourage their young to follow suit, and, precisely because they endure discrimination, display clannishness. In the case at hand these observations carry little weight. For one thing, certain Middle Eastern minorities did less well than Muslims as a whole; the Kurds and the Shiis offer examples.[43] For another, the successes of Middle Eastern non-Muslims far surpassed those of minorities elsewhere. Nowhere in the West did Jewish, Protestant, Catholic, or Eastern Orthodox minorities come to dominate the economically most dynamic sectors as in the Middle East.

The third category of explanations invokes the assistance minorities received from foreign powers, partly in the form of legal privileges.[44] Western policies biased in favor of Middle Eastern Christians and Jews, and against the region's Muslims, lead yet again to questions rarely posed. In view of the long rivalry between eastern and western Christians, why were the latter partial to Middle Eastern Christians? Although special bonds existed between them by virtue of a shared faith, doctrinal differences could make a Christian trust Muslims more than fellow Christians of a rival denomination. The period of the transformation in question is replete with examples of western Christians seeking refuge in Muslim territories, as opposed to places controlled by, say, Orthodox Christians.[45] As for pro-Jewish discrimination, the history of western anti-Semitism raises the question of why the western powers were partial to Jews of the Middle East. To be sure, western anti-Semitism was weakening, and the Jewish diaspora gave Middle Eastern Jews advantages in dealing with westerners. Nevertheless, it is hardly self-evident why Middle Eastern Jews started receiving better treatment from westerners at this particular historical juncture.

By no means do the identified deficiencies establish that networking is irrelevant to the issue at hand. Rather, they show that this networking itself requires explanation. To observe that westerners favored minorities points in the right direction, but without specifying why western assistance became increasingly valuable. After all, the use of networks in cross-cultural trade, even if statically efficient, could be dynamically inefficient.[46] If westerners opted to network with minorities, the reason could be that the latter were better equipped to participate in new markets and to adopt modern business practices. The focus on networking also leaves unexplained why Muslims were relatively slow at emulating the business practices of increasingly successful Europeans.

A fuller understanding of the Middle East's great bifurcation requires focusing, again, on how Middle Easterners conducted business and on how their practices changed. Why did trends vary across communities, and why, from the eighteenth century onward, did differences gain increasing significance?

Middle Eastern Manifestations of the Organizational Revolution in the West

By the eighteenth century the organizational revolution in the West was generating an explosive growth in global commerce. Trade between the Middle East and western Europe was also soaring, and the pace would accelerate in the nineteenth century. This explosion of interregional trade was accompanied by a growing presence of European companies and businessmen in the region. That the European successes rested partly on new organizational forms and business practices would have become increasingly apparent to local businessmen who dealt with them. What European advantages would have caught notice?

European companies and businessmen had access to cheap credit from financial enterprises that pooled the savings of thousands. They could raise capital through stock markets. They could have their disputes resolved by courts familiar with the ongoing organizational advances and accustomed to dealing with legal persons. Because the companies were long-lived, they could establish reputations that would not vanish with the death of a shareholder or employee. Europeans benefited also from the assistance of consuls posted in commercial centers of the Middle East. These consuls gathered information about bureaucratic procedures, local customs, commercial opportunities, and individual reputations. They helped to settle the estates of Europeans who died in the Middle East according to European inheritance systems. They resolved conflicts under the laws of their own countries. As will be shown in later chapters, they enabled foreign merchants and companies to operate, to a degree, within an institutional framework transplanted from Europe.

Exposure to the West's steadily developing commercial culture expanded the jurisdictional choice set of the Middle East's local Jews and Christians. It permitted them to overcome the limitations of indigenous legal systems by exercising their legal choices differently, in favor of the modernizing systems of the West. So it is that their choice of law, which was denied to Muslims, enabled them to pull ahead in the new global environment produced by the West's organizational revolution.

Jurisdictional Shifts

To do business under the laws of a western country, a Middle Eastern Christian or Jew had to acquire its protection, becoming a protégé. Achieving this status initially required a letter of patent (*berat*) that a western representative would obtain from the local ruler. Patent-bearing dhimmis became eligible for many of the fiscal, judicial, financial, commercial, and personal rights that westerners doing business in the Islamic world had long exercised through privileges known as capitulations. They thus acquired rights akin to diplomatic immunity. These patented Ottoman subjects started paying only a 3 percent tax on imports, as against the higher taxes generally required of dhimmis.[47] They also gained the right to be tried in a consular court, even in a court on foreign soil, provided no Muslim was party to the dispute. Accordingly, they could use business methods supported by European courts but unrecognized by either Islamic or communal courts. Consuls spread across the Middle East strove to have local protégés treated like European expatriates.[48] Among the privileges of protégés was immunity from Christian corsairs who preyed on Ottoman ships.[49]

In itself western protection was nothing new. Well before the West achieved economic dominance over the eastern Mediterranean, its consuls were hiring dragomans (Latinized form of *tercümans*, Turkish for interpreters) to serve as translators, negotiators, and advisers. Most of their hires consisted of Greeks, Armenians, and western expatriates. Rarely did consuls hire Muslims, probably because of aversion to confronting an employee in Islamic court, where foreign testimony could be discounted. Dragomans enjoyed the privileges traditionally granted to resident foreign merchants.[50] Until the eighteenth century the typical consul had two or three dragomans. As the demand for protection rose, consuls started hiring them in much larger numbers.

An incentive for meeting the growing demand was that protégés paid consulage fees.[51] These fees were imposed with an eye toward appropriating a share of the rents produced by the rising efficiency of western legal systems.[52] That the consuls sought to extract rents is evident from variations in their fees, which depended on the value of the supplied protection. In 1795, when the Black Sea trade was opened to foreign shipping, the price of English protection doubled.[53] A century later the Russian consul in Trabzon collected 140 times more from a "first-class merchant" than from an ordinary resident.[54] Consuls created and appropriated rents by extending privileges to a widening circle of non-employees. The vast majority of the new hires became "honorary dragomans"—consular servant-interpreters only in name.

It was not by coincidence that the minorities distinguished themselves, especially in banking, insurance, and other distinctly modern economic sectors. Such sectors could not have operated under Islamic law, which is why all of the Middle East's earliest banks and insurance companies were headquartered in Paris, London, or some other western city. Initially, these companies drew almost all of their Middle Eastern agents, correspondents, and managers from local minorities enjoying the status of "honorary dragoman." This hiring pattern served to minimize dealings with Islamic courts. It also created opportunities for forming long-lasting business relationships between foreigners and minorities, including more or less permanent partnerships governed largely by western laws.[55] It is true, then, that the minorities owed their advances to acceptance into networks essentially closed to Muslims. Yet, the value of the networks lay in opportunities linked to modern institutions conducive to impersonal exchange. These networks were lucrative precisely because they provided privileged access to new economic sectors supported by advanced legal codes. In sum, Middle Eastern Christians and Jews did not purchase western protection merely to expand their commercial contacts. They did so to join networks using large and durable organizations, financial techniques, and litigation practices that enabled increasingly impersonal forms of exchange.

Honorary dragomans formed a class of "native foreigners"—locally born and raised functionaries who were integrated into domestic life and spoke local languages, yet held the same legal status as foreign non-Muslims, except possibly in their dealings with Muslims. Before long, European powers began viewing local minorities not only as useful middlemen, brokers, interpreters, and consorts but also as instruments of political influence. France took a special interest in Catholics, Britain in Protestants and Jews, Russia in Orthodox Christians, each claiming a right to protect whole communities.[56] To preserve their tax bases, local rulers took to limiting the numbers of dragoman patents. In response, consuls found a way to grant legal protection without local authorization. For a fee, they would give dhimmis citizenship documents entitling them to foreign privileges, including consular justice. These documents were known as "consular patents," as distinct from the official patents issued by Muslim authorities.[57]

The available figures concerning the size of the patented merchant community can be confusing. Some scholars have estimated the number of officially patented residents of one city or another, generally using Middle Eastern archives; others have estimated the number of protégés of a particular western state, relying on diplomatic records. Only the latter estimates include the holders of consular patents. Collectively, the figures confirm that, starting in the eighteenth century, the total protégé population grew by orders of magnitude. By the end of the eighteenth century, when the Ottoman population was around 30 million, the Austrians alone were protecting 200,000 Ottoman subjects; few of these protégés had ever set foot in Austria, and even fewer served a consul.[58] By 1808, Russia had extended protection to 120,000 people, mostly Greeks.[59] In 1882, "foreign subjects" accounted for 112,000 of the 237,000 residents of Galata, Istanbul's leading commercial district; most were natives.[60] In 1897, half of all the Jews in Egypt were foreign nationals, including both patented natives and European-born residents retaining foreign citizenship.[61] As of the mid-nineteenth century, in Aleppo alone more than 1,500 non-Muslim Ottomans were engaged in international trade under a foreign government's protection.[62]

As the protégé population mushroomed, it became apparent that protégés could compete effectively not only with local Muslims and non-western foreigners but also with their protectors themselves. Thus, from 1770 onward, the growth of Izmir's external trade owed more to the successes of native non-Muslims, particularly the initiatives of local Greeks, than to further western advances.[63] Around the same time, in Aleppo and other leading Arab commercial centers, local Christians and Jews began replacing European merchants, bankers, and insurance brokers.[64] By 1911, only 3 percent of the merchants registered in Istanbul were identifiable

as French, German, or British.[65] In the course of these developments, religious minorities of the Islamic world, including those of
the Balkans, established a salient presence in the commercial life
of Leghorn, Naples, Trieste, Vienna, Leipzig, Amsterdam, and other
western centers.[66]

Motives for Westernization

To acquire western capabilities, patented Middle Eastern merchants
had to learn European languages and familiarize themselves with
European customs. As they took these steps, their consumption
patterns became "westernized," initiating transformations that
would eventually draw in Muslims as well. The changes in their
skill sets and lifestyles enabled them to take advantage of the new
economic opportunities provided by western laws. Thus, western
languages facilitated entry into the class of protégés, and western
lifestyles paid growing dividends as foreigners gained economic
dominance (fig. 10.3). Yet westernized Middle Easterners remained
distinguishable from expatriate westerners. They retained the local
knowledge that kept western traders chronically dependent on
dragomans. Consisting of familiarity with local vernaculars and
customs, this "knowledge of things oriental" enabled patented non-
Muslims to retain influence within commercial networks dominated by indigenous communities.[67] It is thus a combination of two
types of knowledge—"oriental" and "occidental"—that gave patented businessmen a pivotal position in economic dealings with the
West.[68] Their competitiveness grew as an Ottoman diaspora composed overwhelmingly of minorities took hold in western Europe.

That this rise in competitiveness depended on western know-
how and institutions is evident from the organizational choices
of minorities. In the eighteenth century a new type of enterprise
emerged and became increasingly common among minorities: the
merchant house. As we saw in chapter 7, foreign merchants who
settled in the Middle East had introduced this organizational form
to the region at least a century earlier. It consisted of a partnership,
or set of partnerships with overlapping memberships, established

Figure 10.3 Yüksek Kaldırım, a street within a minority-dominated neighborhood of Istanbul, around 1860. The Greek and Armenian signs hanging from the shops testify to the growing economic power of Ottoman religious minorities and to the political confidence that it fueled. The attire of the people passing by captures the Europeanization of Christian and Jewish lifestyles. (From a postcard by Römmler and Jonas, Dresden, 15019 Bh. Courtesy of the Uğur Göktaş photograph collection)

for an indefinite period rather than to carry out a designated mission intended to last a few months. Many merchant houses had collateral branches operated by family members; some were also active in manufacturing.[69] As with a joint-stock company, a merchant house could enlarge or change its membership without loss of continuity. In fact, it could transform itself into a joint-stock company simply by issuing explicitly tradable shares. A merchant house did not conform to long-standing organizational practices based on Islam's partnership rules. Indeed, kadis steeped in traditional Islamic law had trouble grasping the accounting problems and profit allocation disputes that it generated. This is why most merchant houses, and the vast majority of the largest, were formed exclusively by non-Muslims, who could appeal to western courts. True, the merchant houses were not dependent on modern courts. Their members could willingly assume the risks of illegality, agreeing, and having their customers and suppliers agree, to settle disputes through informal arbitration. Nevertheless, access to consular courts constituted an advantage, which increased with the scale of operation.[70]

As western protection became increasingly valuable, Muslim traders too would have had incentives to switch legal jurisdiction. Why did the practice not spread to them as well? For Muslims to accept western legal protection would have represented a radical challenge to the Islamic legal system, which required them to live by Islamic law; this must have dampened their demand for protection. In any case, consuls were reluctant to extend protection to Muslims, lest this anger religious authorities and complicate relations with rulers. It was safer to protect local Christians and Jews, for whom acquiring the status of a "local foreigner" was, in principle, like opting to litigate a dispute in a communal rather than Islamic court. Provided they remained under the jurisdiction of Islamic courts on criminal matters, as well as on civil matters involving Muslims, foreign-protected non-Muslim subjects could be considered as living within the guidelines set by the Pact of Umar and maintained, in the Ottoman Empire, through the *millet* system.[71]

The foregoing interpretations accord with the continued successes of Muslim merchants in overwhelmingly Muslim areas. Few foreigners settled in such areas, partly, it would seem, to minimize encounters liable to land them before the kadi. Consequently, merchants dependent on Islamic law endured no major handicaps in heavily Muslim inland towns. The same logic explains why non-Muslim merchants were relatively unsuccessful in cities without European consuls.[72] We can lay to rest, then, the common argument that the continuation of Muslim successes in some places absolves Islamic institutions of responsibility for Muslim difficulties in leading commercial centers.[73] Geographic variations in Muslim participation—Aleppo versus Damascus, Alexandria versus Asyut, Istanbul versus Sivas—were not due to esoteric factors. They stemmed from systematic practical benefits that western institutions conferred upon foreigners and their protégés.

That western protection was sought for its practical advantages is evident in selections made among the suppliers of western protection. The western legal systems through which patented non-Muslims advanced economically were not identical, and the services of western consuls were not interchangeable. Ordinarily a French consul carried greater influence than one from Piedmont, and many more consuls were French than Piedmontese. Such differences influenced jurisdictional selections; and switches reflected undulations in the European balance of power. In nineteenth-century Beirut, observes Leila Fawaz, "local merchants did not hesitate to switch from one consul's protection to another's, according to the needs of the moment." Evidently, "when it suited their interests best," merchants would give up consular protection. "At those times they claimed to be first and foremost Ottoman subjects, at least until they won the matter at issue, usually a judicial case."[74] Jacob Landau, another historian, relates that Egyptian Jews kept close watch over duties imposed on protégés. The French consular corps was considered undemanding. By contrast, Austro-Hungarian protection appeared a mixed blessing after patented Jews were asked to join the Habsburg military campaign against Italy.[75]

The number of western protégés skyrocketed, it is sometimes argued, because of faltering local security and rising European military strength. These were relevant factors. However, by themselves they explain neither why Muslims lost competitiveness, nor why their handicaps peaked in cities most exposed to the West, nor why European expatriates eventually lost market share to their own protégés.

Unintended Consequences of Islamic Legal Pluralism

The last two chapters have furnished a unified explanation for two broad historical patterns: (1) the absence, before the rise of the West, of striking imbalances among the Middle East's major religious communities; and (2) the ascent of the region's religious minorities in the course of the West's economic modernization process. We have also laid the groundwork for explaining why the nineteenth century witnessed feverish legal reforms to improve local competitiveness, especially the productivity of Muslims. What drove these reforms were the very incentives that made local Christians and Jews seek western legal rights. Significantly, they included the adoption of western commercial codes.

On the surface, the analyzed patterns are emblematic of the social adjustment mechanism named after Charles Tiebout.[76] Known also as "voting with one's feet," the Tiebout mechanism enhances social efficiency as individuals move across legal jurisdictions and, in response, disfavored jurisdictions undertake reforms. In keeping with this mechanism, before the eighteenth century non-Muslim merchants frequently opted to do business and apportion estates under Islamic law, partly because of its superior enforceability. These personal choices induced the Islamization of minority legal practices. When Europe's institutional transformation created new legal opportunities, the same mechanism produced a mass counter-movement away from Islamic law. This helped to publicize the growing inadequacies of Islamic commercial law—much as an exodus from a neighborhood exposes its loss of appeal.

However, each of these adjustment processes—the Islamization of minority legal practices and, subsequently, the westernization of Middle Eastern practices—also had unfavorable economic effects. In the earlier period, Islamic legal pluralism allowed minorities to make jurisdictional switches ex post, imparting uncertainty to their contracts. As such, it undoubtedly discouraged non-Muslims from initiating institutional transformations that might have helped the Middle East to achieve economic modernization on its own. The surest way for Christians and Jews to raise the credibility of their agreements was to make their own legal practices resemble those of Muslims. The consequent Islamization of non-Muslim legal practices did not necessarily produce a net gain in commercial efficiency. Insofar as it was motivated by uncertainty reduction rather than commercial productivity, the Middle Eastern economy may have suffered. There would also have been dynamic losses insofar as legal uniformity extinguished incentives to improve organizational forms. The Islamization of inheritance practices created just such an evolutionary barrier. Had these practices not converged, the region's peoples may well have generated large and durable private enterprises on their own. Moreover, they might have refrained from seeking foreign protection and transplanting foreign laws. The modern history of the Middle East could have been markedly different.

Does the identified rigidity point to a failure of the Tiebout mechanism, which is commonly used to explain why the West took the lead in economic modernization?[77] Such a conclusion is unwarranted, because the Islamic legal system violated two of Tiebout's assumptions. The Tiebout mechanism entails symmetric legal pluralism—equal rights to move across legal jurisdictions. Islamic legal pluralism amounted to asymmetric legal pluralism—broader legal options for some communities than for others. Had Islam given all groups identical legal options, competitive pressures might have rendered Islamic law more responsive to the evolving global economy. Another Tiebout assumption is that individuals can enter into contracts that are binding with regard to jurisdiction. This rules out switches made after contract negotiation. Had ex post switching been blocked, decisions in favor of Islamic law could have been viewed as efficiency-improving. In fact, the contractual decisions of minorities were driven partly by concerns about enforcement. By the same token, legal Islamization was driven by incentives to curb opportunism rather than substantive advantages of Islamic law.

To turn now to jurisdictional switches of the eighteenth and nineteenth centuries, they were motivated largely by identifiable benefits of western law. Legal transformations in the West had raised the advantages of trading with westerners, joining their networks, and using their methods. The realization of the huge new potential depended, however, on extinguishing opportunities for ex post jurisdictional change. Under Islamic legal pluralism, even a westerner could force a change in jurisdiction on associates by fabricating a story of Muslim involvement. Unsurprisingly, western statesmen used their growing diplomatic influence, itself a by-product of economic success, to shield their citizens and protégés from Islamic trials. This contributed to excluding Muslims, considered especially prone to seeking Islamic justice, from the most dynamic sectors of the global economy.

Imposed initially to benefit Muslims, the Pact of Umar, and specifically its provision that gave the kadi sole jurisdiction over cases involving Muslims, thus had the unintended effect, more than a millennium later, of seriously harming Muslim economic opportunities. In reaction, many Muslim merchants and investors sought to remove finance and commerce from the jurisdiction of Islamic courts. The establishment of secular and heavily western-influenced commercial courts in Istanbul and Cairo in the 1850s was partly a response to this groundswell of demand for reform. The economic harm to Muslims also set the stage for intercommunal animosities that, in the twenty-first century, continue to limit exchanges, cooperation, and investment in the Middle East.

Animosities were directed also at western protectors of the minorities that surged ahead economically. Those protections were extended under privileges whose origins stretch back to the Middle Ages. Why were privileges extended to foreigners in the first place, and what drove their evolution? We shall see next that key Islamic institutions were central to the development of the capitulations.

11

Origins and Fiscal Impact
of the Capitulations

s it entered World War I, the Ottoman Empire abrogated all of its bilateral trade treaties known as capitulations. The occasion sparked joyous celebrations across the shrinking empire, whose subjects had come to consider the capitulations demeaning and a terrible fiscal burden. The date of their abrogation became a holiday.[1] Crafted by Muslim rulers and their counterparts in Christian Europe, the capitulations provided extraterritorial privileges to foreign merchants conducting business in lands under Islamic law. That they imposed costs on the local population is undeniable. By the twentieth century the capitulations were exempting foreigners, and to a degree even their protégés, from taxes, tolls, and fees paid by Ottoman subjects. They were also restricting the Ottoman government's ability to raise taxes. On these grounds, many writers hold the capitulations responsible for the Middle East's current economic woes.[2] They also treat the Muslim rulers who issued capitulations as irrational.[3]

However unfavorable the consequences of the capitulations for certain groups in the modern era, they do not explain the emergence of these trade treaties in the Middle Ages. The capitulations emerged because they provided identifiable benefits to constituencies in both western Europe and the Middle East. For many centuries, they facilitated trade relations within the Mediterranean marketplace. It is not self-evident why they turned into sources of abuse.

The westerners trading with the Middle East belonged to societies that were developing institutions to enhance contract credibility, promote impersonal exchange, limit arbitrary taxation, and align individual efforts and rewards. The capitulations allowed them to operate in the Middle East under institutions transplanted from their countries of origin, raising the efficiency of their trades. As the West modernized and pulled ahead of the Middle East economically, the scope of the western privileges expanded accordingly. The Muslim rulers who agreed to successive capitulations expected to gain from the consequent stimulation of commerce. Commodity flows would become more predictable, trade would grow, and tax revenue would increase.

Our goal now is to make sense of the capitulations and to evaluate their role in the economic evolution of the Middle East. We shall see that in imposing costs on certain groups the capitulations also delivered lasting general benefits that have been overlooked. In the long run they served as a vehicle for transplanting various trade-expanding and wealth-producing institutional innovations to the Middle East. As such, they facilitated certain key legal reforms of the nineteenth century. This chapter explores the origins of the capitulations and their Islamic rationale. It also shows how their restrictions on taxation enhanced the predictability of western returns in the Middle East. Their role in promoting impersonal exchange is left to the next chapter.

Early Capitulations

Contrary to a common supposition, the practice of granting foreigners extraterritorial privileges did not originate with Islam. From 1082 onward, Byzantium provided Venetian merchants preferential treatment in trade, freeing them from tariffs incumbent on natives.[4] The Byzantines allowed Venetians also to maintain courts of their own. Over time similar concessions were made to other nations. Predictably, foreigners came to play a key role in Byzantine commerce.[5] Around the same time various French and Italian cities exempted each other's merchants from customary commercial tolls. To one degree or another, they also allowed foreign merchants to base their internal affairs on laws of their own.[6]

As far as is known, Arab rulers of the first Islamic century did not grant extraterritorial privileges to foreigners. After their successors took to giving foreign traders special rights, for a while non-Muslim foreigners were taxed more heavily than local subjects, as required by Islamic law. On passing a customs station in either direction, a non-Muslim foreigner typically paid 10 percent of the value of his merchandise; a Christian or Jewish subject paid 5 percent, and a Muslim, irrespective of political status, only 2.5 percent. The nature of this discrimination suggests that the ruling classes of early Islam intended to favor Muslim traders, whose activities they financed; non-Muslims paying tribute to a non-Muslim ruler were to hold "least favored" status.[7] The rate structure indicates also that Arab rulers, who derived revenue from trade, did not expect to lose from favoring Muslim traders over foreigners. Were Islamic commercial institutions somehow inadequate, this protectionism would have entailed observable costs. Blocking lucrative exchanges, it would have dampened rulers' enthusiasm for pro-local protectionism.

Later Muslim rulers adopted the Byzantine practice of granting foreign communities rights, privileges, and exemptions through treaties (in Arabic, *imtiyāzāt*, meaning privileges; in Turkish, *ahid-nâmes*, meaning covenant letters). In the twelfth and thirteenth centuries the Fatimid and Ayyubid rulers of Arab lands, like the Seljuks of Turkey, were giving Venetian, Genoese, and Pisan merchants rights to trade at customs rates as low as 2 percent, along with judicial privileges to settle disputes with other foreign Christians in courts of their own.[8] At least one subsequent treaty, negotiated in 1337 between the emir of Seljuk Aydın and the duke of Venetian Crete, exempted Venetians from all import duties on most commodities.[9] Significantly, these forerunners of the capitulations include treaties that granted privileges also to Muslims. In the thirteenth century, Arab merchants in Corsica and Sicily could face trial in Muslim courts. And for several centuries preceding the downfall of the Byzantine Empire in 1453, visiting Turkish and Arab traders lived in enclaves known in Italian as *fondacos* and in Arabic as *funduqs*. Although information pertaining to daily life in these enclaves is scant, their residents almost certainly could settle commercial disputes internally.[10]

The early capitulations are aimed essentially at reducing tariff discrimination against foreign traders and allowing them to settle internal disputes through legal procedures of their own choice. In stimulating competition, the first provision enhanced economic efficiency. As for the second, it allowed foreigners to resolve conflicts through arbitration, without involvement of the ruler's own courts. Arbitration requires the consent of all parties, so at initiation it is efficient: each party must expect to do at least as well as in a formal court. A ruler who allows foreign traders legal autonomy can expect, then, to benefit from lower transaction costs. Insofar as adjudication is left to individuals familiar with the litigants, judgments will improve. Also, communal enforcement mechanisms can be brought into play, providing a deterrent to dishonesty without interference from functionaries lacking local knowledge.[11] Internal dispute resolution mechanisms thus raise the profits of foreign merchants, which increases potential tariff revenue.

Initially, the capitulations skirted certain themes that figure prominently in later treaties, such as inheritance practices, collective punishment, and documentation of contracts. These themes are present in treaties that Mamluk sultans made with Venice and Florence in the fifteenth century, and those that the Ottomans negotiated with European nations over a half-millennium. The fifteenth through twentieth centuries thus mark a period of expanding foreign trade privileges. The privileges reflected institutional changes under way across the Mediterranean.

Mounting Foreign Privileges and Their Abrogation

The Ottoman capitulations showered with attention are those negotiated in 1536 between Süleyman the Magnificent and King François I of France.[12] They enabled the French to displace the Venetians as the dominant "nation" in Mediterranean commerce.[13] According to Ottoman political lore, Süleyman granted these capitulations as a gesture of goodwill, and he could revoke them at any time. In fact, the specifics were negotiated, and both sides obtained valuable rights.

Thereafter, the Ottoman Empire found itself on a slippery slope entailing increasingly generous and generally unreciprocated privileges to more and more nations. In 1580, the English secured essentially the same trading rights as the French. Other powers, beginning with Holland and, in a period of rapprochement, Venice, then obtained comparable privileges of their own.[14] Along the way, the Ottoman Empire began to shrink territorially. New capitulations were issued and old ones renewed from positions of diminishing military strength. In line with bargaining theory, foreigners obtained progressively greater concessions. Also, given the Ottoman stake in maintaining trade flows, it became unrealistic to treat the privileges as revocable unilaterally. By the early nineteenth century the capitulations had turned into an instrument for providing foreign nationals and their local protégés broad privileges denied to most Ottoman subjects. They were also giving western powers a say over key economic policies. Eventually the capitulations forced the Ottoman Empire to abolish various domestic monopolies. With the Anglo-Ottoman Commercial Convention of 1838, the Ottoman state agreed to enforce substantially higher duties on exports than on imports. This compounded the disadvantages of domestic producers intent on competing globally.[15]

The foregoing transformation is evident in changes in the meaning of the term "capitulations." The term derives from the Latin *capitula*, which refers to the chapters into which treaties were divided. Thus, at the signing of the early commercial treaties, "capitulations" meant "chapters." That was a time of Arab and Turkish territorial expansion, and the treaties were not perceived as inimical to Muslim sovereignty. Eventually, as the region started to lose soverignty, the term acquired the connotation of "surrender." That the capitulations came to be associated with subjugation is evident also in the refusal of the Ottoman Empire's successor states to recognize them, unless forced by colonial masters.[16]

Mamluk and Ottoman Capitulations

Key economic provisions of the initial capitulations to France had precedents in the commercial privileges granted in 1442 and 1497 by Mamluk Egypt to Venice and Florence, respectively.[17] In fact, the Mamluks provided privileges that the Ottomans withheld from foreigners until the seventeenth century. The Mamluks may have been ahead because they negotiated from a position of weakness: their rule in Egypt faltering, they were desperate for certain imports.[18] In 1536, the Ottomans appeared militarily invincible, which is why Süleyman could achieve his objectives through relatively few concessions.[19] His bargaining strength fostered a perception of unilateralism, which endured at least another century, as successive sultans continued to treat the capitulations as acts of grace deniable to enemies.[20]

Of the sixteen articles that comprise the initial French capitulations, five impose reciprocal obligations on France and the Ottoman Empire; they concern freedom of mobility, security, cooperation against piracy, and state protocol. Each of these articles mirrored earlier capitulations, including ones granted by the Byzantines. Two other articles, though explicitly reciprocal, address special concerns of one side or the other: the return of runaway slaves (of greater importance to Ottomans) and consular authority over handling shipwrecks in foreign waters (of significance only for France, the party that deployed consuls). As for the remaining nine articles, they provide French privileges without reciprocity. French merchants were entitled to consular representation, trials in French courts, wills enforceable by French authorities, and immunity from collective punishment for the offenses of individual Frenchmen.[21] By the seventeenth century the Ottomans were granting capitulations focused even more strikingly on foreign needs. The English capitulations of 1675 consist of fifty-five articles appended to those of earlier Ottoman-English agreements. Every one addresses the concerns of English merchants. True, it was customary to include a clause imposing reciprocal obligations across the board.[22] However, as the economic institutions of the two sides diverged, reciprocity became increasingly symbolic.[23]

The fiscal provisions of the capitulations, including customs duties, underwent their own evolution. Both the French capitulations of 1673 and the English capitulations of 1675 stipulate a 3 percent ad valorem duty on merchandise exported or imported by their merchants, slightly more than the 2.5 percent due from Muslims.[24] From the late seventeenth century to 1914, all capitulary powers enjoyed essentially "most favored nation" status with regard to tariffs.

Definitely critical were provisions concerning the predictability of taxation. Foreigners gained a progressively broader set of exemptions from other charges that Ottoman subjects continued to endure. If the Ottomans traveled down a slippery slope in relation to taxation, it is these non-tariff privileges that made a difference. The expansion of foreign privileges is evident also in the judicial sphere. The early French and English capitulations had stipulated that kadis would adjudicate lawsuits between subjects and foreigners, albeit under special rules.[25] Over time, western traders gained ever greater immunities to Islamic prosecution. This happened as the jurisdiction of western and, after the mid-nineteenth century, secular local courts expanded at the expense of Islamic courts.[26]

To the end, kadis retained jurisdiction over cases involving Muslims. The Ottoman state never ceded the right to try cases involving even a single individual they construed as an Ottoman subject. Nevertheless, foreigners found it increasingly easy to defy the Islamic courts in cases involving Ottoman subjects, often with the connivance of local elites. By the early twentieth century, European diplomats were able to issue effectively unchallengeable rulings. Thus, Ottoman subjects could no longer count on the protection of Islamic courts.

Limits of Received Explanations

No satisfactory explanation exists for the granting of the Middle Eastern capitulations or for their transformation into one-sided privileges inimical to political sovereignty and discriminatory against the religious majority. The invoked factors include two political and three economic objectives.

The most common explanation is that the capitulations served to split Europe, fount of the Crusades, by forming alliances with friendly Christians. In this view, the early Ottoman capitulations were shrewd acts to weaken Christendom. The initial capitulations to the French were expanded in 1569, just as the Ottomans were preparing to conquer Cyprus, then held by Venice, a commercial rival of France. The English capitulations strengthened a rival of two Turkish enemies, the Habsburgs and the Pope.[27] Like the Mamluks and Safavids, the Ottomans did indeed use trade policy to build alliances, making privileges contingent on peaceful relations.[28] In some cases, alliance formation might even have been the dominant motive. But geopolitical objectives do not explain the substance of the capitulations. They do not elucidate why, say, a documentation requirement was imposed for lawsuits against foreigners.[29] Even if alliance formation was a first-order objective initially, other objectives must have gained precedence over time.

The other frequently invoked political factor is the desire to weaken domestic merchants, lest they sow instability. According to Mehmet Genç, who emphasizes the survival instincts of ruling dynasties, premodern Muslim rulers restricted private capital accumulation. To that end, they confiscated the estates of high officials and capped commercial profits through price controls. From this perspective, welcoming foreign merchants was less a response to military threats than a handmaiden of domestic power politics.[30] However, granting foreigners judicial privileges is not the only way to discriminate against domestic merchants. In any case, it is not obvious why local merchants stood by as foreign merchants accumulated rights. What explains their political impotence? One factor, already developed, is the stagnation of domestic commercial institutions. Insofar as the available legal systems inhibited resource pooling within large and long-lasting enterprises, the political power of domestic merchants would have been limited. If this is granted, the growing handicaps of domestic merchants were an independent cause of the capitulations, as opposed to their objective. A ruler might have agreed to capitulations partly because his own subjects were becoming commercially uncompetitive and reversing this trend seemed costlier than allowing foreigners to dominate trade with western Europe. The underlying goal would have been to compensate for the economic limitations of domestic merchants rather than to weaken them politically.

The most common economic explanation is that revenue could be raised more easily from foreign merchants than from domestic ones. Under Islamic law foreigners pay higher duties in comparison to subjects, so foreign traders were welcomed, it is said, in order to stimulate tariff revenue. Further, the cultural particularities of foreign merchants and their concentration in major ports made them easy targets for tax collectors.[31] But if fiscal considerations were paramount, why did the state not impose stiffer tariffs on domestic merchants, who used the same ports? All domestic merchants paid taxes without a basis in Islamic law. Abundant precedents existed for rate adjustments as well as new forms of taxation.[32]

Another economic explanation invokes a geocommercial objective: maintaining the viability of the Middle East as a transit stop. Mamluk Egypt and the Ottoman Empire are said to have granted commercial privileges to maintain the attractiveness of Mediterranean trade routes between Europe and Asia after the circumnavigation of Africa (fig. 11.1).[33] Rival trade routes certainly influenced the strategic thinking of Middle Eastern rulers. But they

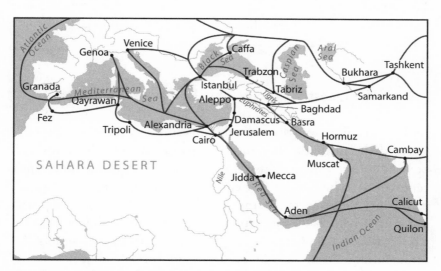

Figure 11.1 Transit trade through the Middle East, c. 1498

cannot have been central to the capitulations, which existed well before Vasco Da Gama reached the Indian Ocean. More critically, the objective of supporting old trade routes did not require pro-foreign discrimination. Transit trade could have been stimulated through commercial incentives blind to faith and nationality.

Finally, there is a provisionist explanation centered on imports. Merchants from Christian Europe were particularly welcome, it has been argued, because they supplied strategic goods such as tin, silver, and gunpowder.[34] However, no necessary connection exists between stimulating trade and privileging foreigners. The desired inflow of strategic commodities could have been induced through non-discriminatory subsidies. By itself, then, the demand for certain commodities sheds no light on the capitulations.

The existing literature thus identifies five distinct motives for the capitulations: coalition formation, limiting the political capabilities of potential domestic rivals, revenue generation, protection of trade routes, and securing strategic goods. Although some of them are integral to the story, even collectively they yield few insights into the reasons why the capitulations gained significance over time. More critically, none explains the substance of the capitulations—why, that is, they provided certain privileges and not others. To fill in the gaps, we turn first to the fiscal privileges given to foreigners. The next chapter will take up the legal privileges that allowed them to do business in the Middle East using their own organizational forms and procedures.

The Quest for Predictable Returns from Trade

As we already know, the capitulations of the seventeenth century lowered the tariff on foreigners to a rate slightly above the 2.5 percent collected from Muslim merchants. Even in the nineteenth century, by which time the capitulations discriminated against merchants required to operate under Islamic law, foreigners enjoyed no privileges on this count. The Anglo-Ottoman Commercial Convention of 1838 stipulates that British merchants will pay the same duties as "the most favored class of Turkish subjects." Commercial regulations shall be "general throughout the Empire" and "applicable to all subjects," implying the inclusion of local Jews and Christians.[35]

If foreigners acquired tax privileges, these stemmed not from tariff reductions but from immunities against other taxes. From the early Arab empires onward, Middle Easterners paid diverse personal taxes, including unanticipated levies imposed to appropriate rents. In the Ottoman Empire, opportunistic taxation was common especially during fiscal emergencies associated with military campaigns. Non-customary taxes were known as *avârız*, literally "accidental" or "irregular" but widely understood to mean "whatever can be extorted."[36] In western sources, extortionate impositions on foreigners are denoted by a similar sounding word: avanias. The term encompassed charges levied over and above what custom, the law, or a treaty dictated.[37] Foreigners felt that extraordinary taxes fell on them disproportionately. Whatever the truth, this perception made them seek protections against ad hoc taxes. Thus, the capitulations of 1673 stipulate that the French are exempt from all obligations other than charges explicitly listed. Likewise, those of 1675 state ad nauseam, presumably to allay ambiguity, that the English shall pay no other fees.[38]

Resistance to taxation is as old as human civilization. It is not unusual, then, that foreigners in the Middle East complained about various charges. However, foreigners objected especially to the unpredictability of their obligations. They objected, for instance, to arbitrary exactions at ports, such as duties demanded whimsically for goods kept on board.[39] Arbitrary taxation raises the cost of capital and discourages trade by making investors demand a risk premium. Hence, restrictions on Ottoman fiscal powers would have enhanced efficiency by making returns from interregional commerce more predictable. That a fundamental function of the capitulations was to enhance the predictability of foreign commercial returns is evident also in clauses that bar collective punishment for the misdemeanors of an individual foreigner. The French capitulations of 1536 state:

> When one or more subjects of the King [of France], having made a contract with a subject of the [Ottoman] Grand Signior, taken merchandise, or incurred debts, afterwards depart from the State of the

Grand Signior without giving satisfaction, [neither] the bailiff, consul, relatives, factor, nor any other subject of the King shall for this reason be in any way coerced or molested, nor shall the King be held responsible.[40]

The text then commits the French king to prosecuting and punishing fugitive merchants. By preventing unscrupulous Frenchmen from heaping liabilities on their co-nationals, this arrangement diminished the risks of traders operating under French protection. Provided they stayed within the law and fulfilled their contractual obligations, their profits would be safe.

The capitulations extended additional privileges to alleviate foreign commercial risks. One involved inheritance. Each treaty of the fifteenth or sixteenth century includes an article giving consuls sole jurisdiction over the estates of their countrymen.[41] By virtue of this right, a Parisian could inherit from a compatriot who died in Damascus. The article also ensured the enforceability of foreign wills at odds with Islamic inheritance practices. If a foreigner died intestate, his consul would follow the inheritance customs of his home town.[42] Confiscation could still occur if the property was acquired illegally or the deceased left unpaid debts.[43] Also, inheritance cases involving both foreigners and subjects led to complications.[44] Nevertheless, consular authority over foreign estates diminished local interference.

In enabling foreigners to avoid the asset fragmentation caused by the Islamic inheritance system, the inheritance articles of the capitulations gave them an advantage in building and preserving commercial enterprises. Equally important, they facilitated partnerships between expatriate merchants and investors at home. Western merchants also benefited, of course, from the evolving financial institutions of Europe. The emergence of increasingly complex financial intermediaries, and eventually banks, enabled them to raise funds more cheaply and for longer terms than anyone could in the Middle East's atomistic financial markets.

Frivolous lawsuits constituted yet another obstacle to predictable returns. In the Islamic system the winner could be asked to pay the expenses of litigation. This encouraged lawsuits, benefiting the kadis who collected fees, whether from victorious plaintiffs or acquitted defendants. The French capitulations of 1740 addressed this problem through a stipulation that when lawsuits are brought "contrary to justice" the kadi must collect fees from the plaintiffs instead of the innocent defendants.[45]

The Onset of Reverse Discrimination

By no means were western negotiators interested only in the predictability of their investments. As their bargaining power rose, they also pursued outright privileges. Already in the early seventeenth century European consuls in Istanbul were exempt from taxation, as were their dragomans.[46] In time the capitulations provided foreign merchants immunity from new taxes. In fact, it became the norm to forbid charges on foreigners unless allowed specifically by a treaty. Of the seventy-five articles that comprise the English capitulations of 1675, no fewer than twenty-eight limit a charge.[47]

In subsequent years western negotiators sought exemptions from paying for services. Ultimately they were so successful that capitulary tax restrictions were interpreted as giving foreigners and their protégés free access to services for which most natives were charged. In the late nineteenth century, for example, western governments invoked the capitulations to exempt their nationals from a municipal fee to finance storage tanks for flammable liquids.[48] Foreigners thereby escaped a charge that European municipalities imposed freely on their constituents. Eventually, western fiscal privileges reached the point where an Ottoman subject could avoid a tax, fee, or fine simply by transferring an asset's ownership to a foreigner. Another method of evasion exploited the principle that foreign-occupied premises could be searched only in the presence of a consular representative. If a consulate was slow to act, the delay enabled the transfer of goods or evidence of liability to a foreigner of different nationality, which then required the involvement of another consulate, further complicating the investigation.[49] Still another method, used by foreign insurance companies charged with breach of contract, was to insist on adjudication in their home country.[50] When foreigners accepted to pay for services, they did not always pay equally. The Ottoman commercial courts established in the 1850s to serve all nationalities adopted two fee schedules, one for natives and another for foreigners. When fines were involved, foreigners paid half as much as natives guilty of the same offense.[51]

These extreme examples come from the nineteenth century, which is when the capitulations turned into instruments of outright pro-foreign discrimination. But even earlier, western representatives sought privileges cloaked as a request for fair and predictable taxation. Upon close consideration, certain charges that contemporaneous negotiators characterized as avanias hardly appear arbitrary. Consider the seventeenth-century claim that merchants who married an Ottoman subject were burdened with unjust taxes. Under Islamic law such merchants became liable for the taxes due from local Christians and Jews. Likewise, they lost eligibility for the privileges of foreign visitors.[52] Such reclassification was common throughout the globe. Yet it is obvious why western expatriates objected stridently. As the capitulations became ever more generous, the benefits of remaining a foreigner rose accordingly. In addition, as visiting European merchants turned effectively into permanent residents, their likelihood of marrying a local woman rose, augmenting the demand for annulling the status reclassification rule.

Whereas contemporaneous western observers complained about real or imagined inequities borne by their co-nationals, Middle Eastern commentators of the century preceding World War I lamented burdens imposed on natives.[53] Each side overlooked significant factors. Local commentators failed to see that the expansion of commerce with the West depended on limiting opportunism and arbitrariness in the taxation of foreigners. In the absence of credible limits, Europeans would have had to charge more for their services. For their part, western commentators generally failed to acknowledge that efforts to achieve commercial predictability and equal taxation spawned pro-foreign discrimination.

No systematic research exists on the magnitude of the average tax advantage enjoyed by foreign merchants. They paid taxes also to their own states, so their total tax burdens could have been heavier. Two things are certain. First, the sweeping fiscal immunities of foreigners raised the attractiveness of working in the Middle East. This is evident from the huge influx of foreigners. Egypt had no more than a few hundred foreign residents in the eighteenth century; by 1878 there were about 70,000, and by 1907 around 150,000.[54] The pattern was similar in Turkey. In 1600 there were a few thousand Christian foreigners in Istanbul, and most were slaves. On the eve of World War I, the city had 130,000 foreign residents—one-seventh of the total population.[55] Second, the fiscal immunities of foreigners gave indigenous minorities added incentives to acquire western legal protection. The fiscal advantages of foreign and foreign-protected merchants came on top of the administrative support they received from ambassadors, consuls, dragomans, and clerks prepared to interfere on their behalf at the slightest dispute with authorities.

Not only did Muslim merchants and unprotected non-Muslims lack such support; as a consequence they became the targets of choice whenever fiscally strapped authorities sought to raise tax revenue. Prior to World War I, the burden of new levies—stamp duties, profit taxes, trade licenses, house taxes, and road labor dues, to name a few—fell largely on unprotected natives.[56] No less significant was the unpredictability of taxes on locals. With authorities introducing new taxes and revising rates continuously, unprotected natives lived with uncertainty over their obligations. Especially in sectors where profitability was hard to conceal, this uncertainty must have discouraged investment and entrepreneurship.

Variations in Enforcement

Disagreements over the effects of the capitulations stem partly from geographic variations in their enforcement. Although a treaty typically enumerated a single set of rights and obligations, these were meant to apply strictly only in the main commercial center—in the Ottoman Empire, Istanbul. Additional agreements proclaimed through sultanic decrees fine-tuned the main treaty. For example, they adjusted certain fees according to the port visited.[57] The consequent variations stemmed partly from differences in the powers of local officials.

A related source of variation lay in imperfect control over officials. Away from the capital, capitulary provisions could be interpreted in self-serving ways, even defied. In the early 1600s officials in Izmir charged Venetians export dues on the local market value of cotton, rather than on the purchase price inland, as was customary. In addition, they required export duties almost double those specified in prevailing capitulations.[58] Around the same time, the tax farmers who collected tariffs in Cyprus refused to accept the reduction that the Dutch obtained in 1612. Only through negotiations, which may have entailed unrecorded side-payments, did Cypriot customs officials agree to implement the reduction.[59]

An Ottoman decree of 1618 prohibited customs officials in Aleppo from overestimating the value of goods belonging to foreigners. Another decree legalized contracts that shifted the tariff burden from Venetian sellers to their local clients.[60] Venice had requested the decrees because of inconsistent implementation. In the following century, an Aleppine dragoman for the British, exercising a capitulary privilege, asked that a dispute between him and a local dignitary be transferred to Istanbul. The local kadi insisted that the matter fell within his own jurisdiction. Notwithstanding the capitulations, the kadi misunderstood his authority; under Islamic law, he functioned as an agent of his sultan, who was free to reclaim any judicial responsibility. Nevertheless, when the British consul complained to the governor, the latter sustained the decision.[61] Even in the mid-nineteenth century, by which time foreigners had enormous leverage over officials in commercial centers, certain provisions of the capitulations went unrecognized in places where the Ottoman government lacked authority. In Mosul, Iraq, the ferry tax was higher for foreign merchants than for local merchants—the opposite of the pattern in Istanbul. Special taxes and tolls tripled the 5 percent import duty stipulated by the Anglo-Ottoman Commercial Convention.[62]

Foreign officials understood that power was decentralized and that the regulatory landscape differed across localities and sectors.

They also grasped the advantages of dealing directly with local notables. Indeed, foreign representatives in commercial centers as important as Aleppo, Alexandria, and Izmir made a point of negotiating also with local governors, pashas, kadis, tax farmers, and even thugs.[63] In view of the unreliability of centralized enforcement, they effectively sought "local capitulations" in contexts where interstate capitulations lacked credibility.[64] To ensure favorable terms they also played competing notables against each other, threatening to relocate their operations if their demands were rejected.[65]

Where capitulary provisions were violated, the perpetrators were not necessarily Muslim officials. The customs officials and other tax farmers accused of transgressions included Christians and Jews. As discussed earlier, by the nineteenth century hundreds of thousands of their co-religionists enjoyed foreign protections that enabled them to compete effectively with foreign companies. Hence, the observed infractions reflect struggles over market share. The same logic applies to violations perpetrated by Turkish, Arab, or other Muslim officials. Although the available records seldom reveal the full scope of official motivations, pro-local commercial protectionism must have been a common factor.

Variability in enforcement helps to explain why, even as capitulary rights turned into instruments of pro-foreign discrimination, foreigners continued to complain about business conditions and to press for institutional reforms. By publicizing, and even exaggerating treaty violations, they sought to tighten enforcement. A byproduct of their campaigns is an abundance of data on violations. The evidence does not imply that the capitulations lacked practical significance. In all commercial centers where foreigners established a major presence, they benefited from tax exemptions denied to local subjects.

Islamic Rationales

The fiscal provisions that exempted foreigners from local taxes and fees limited the reach of Islamic law in Muslim-governed territories.

Yet successive concessions received the blessing of religious authorities, whose understandings of Islam adapted to evolving social realities. The earliest capitulations were easily justified on religious grounds. Under classical Islamic law non-Muslims can be treated differently depending on whether they live in the "abode of Islam" (*dār al-Islām*) or "abode of war" (*dār al-harb*).[66] Specifically, protections afforded to the residents of Muslim-governed territories may be denied to non-Muslim foreigners. By the same token, Islamic law allows the extension of security guarantees (*amān*) to useful foreigners who pledge "friendship and sincere good will."[67] It was legitimate, therefore, to grant privileges to selected Christian nations capable of serving Muslim goals. Thus, as early as 651, Egyptian administrators were incorporating into treaties with Christian rulers "safe conduct guarantees" for foreign individuals and groups.[68]

As for enabling foreign merchants to live by their own laws, it was a short step for a Muslim ruler, having granted them security, to endow them with legal options similar to those of native Jews and Christians. Allowing a Venetian to exercise choice of law could be defended by viewing him as a potential subject. Under Islamic law, a non-Muslim foreigner who resided in an Islamic territory for more than a year became a dhimmi.[69] The term used to designate a "pact" with dhimmis (*'ahd*) also designated some early trade treaties with foreigners.[70] For Islam's interpreters, it seems, these treaties did not involve a radical break with the past.

Eventually the capitulations granted foreigners rights well beyond those found in early Islamic treaties. Those of 1536, like the Mamluk treaties of the previous century, explicitly overruled the principle that a foreign non-Muslim became a dhimmi after a year of residence:

> No subject of the King who shall not have resided for ten full continuous years in the dominions of the Grand Signior shall or can be forced to pay tribute, Kharadj, Avari, Khassabiye [various taxes].[71]

Over the following century other nations, too, obtained the right to retain foreigner status beyond the one-year limit.[72] By the nineteenth century even the ten-year rule was unenforceable. As with so many other modifications, high Islamic authorities allowed each successive extension.

In certain seventeenth-century lawsuits that pitted an Ottoman subject against a foreigner, the latter invoked, along with sultanic decrees, the authority of clerics.[73] Religious functionaries also permitted the lowering of tariffs for westerners to the levels of Muslims. Ultimately they even allowed local minorities to move into foreign legal jurisdictions. Clerics were not of one mind on such privileges. However, they never formed an organized religious opposition to the capitulations. As a group, then, they contributed to the process that gradually placed the Middle East in a tutelary relationship to western powers.

Neither religious leaders nor statesmen could have failed to grasp the economic significance of the capitulations. Scores of decrees and opinions on urban craft guilds betray an appreciation of how commercial privileges affect market outcomes.[74] Authorities could observe that European merchants dominated certain commercial emporia. Broadening their privileges would surely compound the handicaps domestic merchants faced in those markets. If capitulations were granted in spite of these observable costs, and then expanded repeatedly, the ruling classes of the Middle East must have expected to benefit from the activities of foreign merchants, to whom domestic merchants offered no credible alternative. Although the early Islamic practice of security guarantees did not amount to capitulations, various precedents allowed the grounding of foreign privileges in Islamic principles.

Those privileges were not limited to fiscal immunities. Far more significant were privileges that allowed westerners to carry into Middle Eastern markets their evolving organizational forms and business practices. The transplants in question involved restrictions on the operation of Islamic courts. In accommodating the restrictions, we shall see next, clerics unwittingly facilitated initial steps toward the region's transition from personal to impersonal exchange.

12

Foreign Privileges as Facilitators of Impersonal Exchange

O
n May 9, 1665, Mehmet bin Mahmut, a Baghdad merchant, sued Heneage Finch, the English ambassador to the Ottoman Empire, in an Istanbul court. A group of English merchants, complained Mehmet, would not repay a debt. The record is silent on why the ambassador was sued, rather than the merchants accused of default.[1] When the trial began, the ambassador showed the kadi the text of an Ottoman-English treaty, which stipulates that in cases involving even one trader operating under the English flag, neither claims nor witnesses may be heard in the absence of documentary support (*hüccet*). Reminded of this agreement, the kadi asked Mehmet to prove his claim through written evidence. Mehmet replied that he lacked documentation, prompting the judge to throw out the case on procedural grounds.[2]

Had the alleged defaulters been Ottoman subjects, Mehmet would not have been required to document a debt contract. Under the prevailing interpretation of Islamic contract law, oral agreement was sufficient to validate the terms of a loan. By contrast, in English courts the trend was toward rejecting oral financial claims, unless backed by documentation. Evidently in England business was becoming less personal, and the courts were making the requisite procedural adjustments. This 1665 case thus suggests that Ottoman sultans of the late seventeenth century allowed trials involving English traders to accommodate the ongoing legal transformation in England. In the face of foreign demands, they were conceding, in effect, that "impersonal exchange," the hallmark of modern economic relations, requires a different institutional framework than "personal exchange."[3] Written contracts help to provide impartial justice in settings where enforcement mechanisms based on personal relations are ineffective. That is why the requirement constituted a step toward impersonal exchange and, hence, economic modernization. But the requirement that doomed Mehmet bin Mahmut also had a downside. Being limited to cases against foreigners, it also contributed to the unfolding economic marginalization of the Middle East's Muslims and the region's loss of global economic significance.

Foreign Complaints about Islamic Courts

In the correspondence of foreign merchants doing business in the Middle East under the capitulations, a frequent theme is that Islamic courts, which litigated many of their disputes with natives, were biased against non-Muslims, and all the more so against those from abroad.[4] There is nothing surprising here. The traditional procedures of Islamic courts favored Muslims. Non-Muslim, and particularly foreign, testimony was devalued relative to Muslim testimony. This is reflected in the very low share of minorities among the witnesses that appeared in the Islamic courts of seventeenth-century Istanbul. The figures are particularly low in cases involving Muslims, because non-Muslims were prohibited from testifying against them; in cases among Muslims alone, Christians and Jews never appeared as a witness (table 12.1). Foreign litigants suffered also from linguistic handicaps, inadequate local knowledge, and limited connections. In any case, courts throughout the premodern world favored local interests.[5]

The records of Islamic courts are replete with cases in which a kadi treated the word of a non-Muslim as more credible than that of a Muslim opponent.[6] In seventeenth-century Istanbul, Muslim plaintiffs won 57.8 percent of their cases against Christian defendants; for their part, Christian plaintiffs had a win rate of 71.4 percent against Muslim defendants.[7] Nevertheless, both the principle that a Muslim is relatively trustworthy by virtue of his faith and the practice of relying on Muslim witnesses disproportionately

TABLE 12.1
Distribution of Witnesses by Religion in Istanbul Lawsuits, 1602–1697*

Religion of plaintiff	Religion of defendant	Cases without witnesses	Cases with witnesses	Witnesses		
				Muslim	Christian	Jewish
Muslim	Muslim	399	243	741	0	0
Muslim	Christian	84	35	62	12	0
Muslim	Jewish	19	12	42	0	0
Christian	Muslim	37	21	39	16	0
Christian	Christian	90	79	99	76	0
Christian	Jewish	3	2	0	4	0
Jewish	Muslim	13	2	5	0	0
Jewish	Christian	13	5	9	5	0
Jewish	Jewish	2	4	0	0	13
All pairings above		660	403	997	113	13
Other lawsuits**		51	18	50	4	0
Total cases		711	421	1047	117	13

*Court registers in sample: 15 registers of Galata and Istanbul courts, listed in table 4.1.
The cases here include all lawsuits that involve documentation and/or concern one or more of the following issues: commercial partnership, waqf, taxation, guild, communal affairs.
**Category includes lawsuits involving (a) at least one foreigner, gypsy, or recent convert to Islam as either a plaintiff or defendant; or (b) litigants belonging to all three faiths.
Note: 556 Muslim litigants participated in cases with witnesses, as against 221 Christians and 29 Jews (the calculations omit "other lawsuits" and treat each defendant or plaintiff as a single litigant). Muslims are over-represented among witnesses ($t = 21.95$) and Christians and Jews under-represented ($t = 20.15$ and 7.34) in relation to their participation in lawsuits.

sowed anxiety among foreign merchants. They even complicated relations between Muslims and local non-Muslims, who were usually trusted more readily than foreigners, could have Muslim protectors, were accustomed to the Islamic judicial system, and enjoyed the same legal status as Muslims in the protection of life and property. The mere possibility of differentiated evaluation of testimony threatened the enforcement of commercial agreements between Muslims and non-Muslims, thus limiting opportunities for inter-communal cooperation. The frequent rotation of kadis posed another problem: if one kadi adjudicated impartially, his successor might give the benefit of the doubt to Muslims as a matter of principle.

Whatever the nature of local favoritism in the Middle East, nothing suggests that it grew over time. Two other issues became increasingly significant: the predictability and quality of adjudication. As western legal systems developed, foreigners found it increasingly difficult to comprehend the logic behind kadi verdicts. Arbitrariness is the key characteristic of what, centuries later, Max Weber would characterize, condescendingly, as "kadi-justice."[8] Weber's relevant scholarship is misleading. In principle, kadi decisions were based on intricate legal doctrines, and the registers of Islamic courts reveal much consistency. Nevertheless, the key doctrines guiding kadi decisions dated from the early Islamic centuries.[9] The ensuing doctrinal stagnation ensured that foreigners from institutionally dynamic societies would find Islamic law increasingly alien to their daily experiences. In addition to decreasing legal predictability, foreigners were bound to perceive a loss in the quality of kadi verdicts. This is because legal training in the traditional Islamic mode was inadequate for understanding exchanges involving new business techniques and organizational forms.

The incentives to use alternative courts could have grown, then, even as anti-foreign biases remained constant. Indeed, as the economic institutions of the two regions diverged, foreign calls for immunity from Islamic justice grew louder. Successive capitulations responded to the growing demand by broadening the range of cases exempt from the jurisdiction of Islamic courts.

It is relevant again that in Muslim-governed territories anyone could use Islamic courts. Thus, foreigners sometimes registered contracts in Islamic courts, even contracts among themselves.[10] Also, a share of the disputes among themselves came before a kadi.[11] As with minorities, this right undermined another right: legal autonomy in intra-communal affairs. The problem, discussed earlier in interpreting the economic performance of indigenous minorities, was twofold. First, losers of consul-adjudicated lawsuits could reopen the case before a kadi, whose rulings trumped those of other courts.[12] Second, the right to Islamic adjudication remained even in respect to contracts based on another legal system. This rendered legally unenforceable whatever a kadi might find incomprehensible or objectionable. Hence, all commercial contracts of foreigners were subject to opportunistic behavior. In stages, the capitulations enhanced the credibility of these contracts. They did so by enabling foreign merchants to commit themselves to doing business under alien, and specifically non-Islamic, institutions.

The Pursuit of Contractual Credibility

The first significant measure was a ban on kadis adjudicating lawsuits among co-nationals. The French Capitulations of 1536 state:

> The kadi or other officers of the Grand Signior [Süleyman the Magnificent] may not try any difference between the merchants and subjects of the King [of France], even if the said merchants should request it, and if perchance the said kadis should hear a case their judgment shall be null and void.[13]

This was not the first provision of its kind. Mamluk Egypt had given French consuls the right to settle all cases among Frenchmen.[14] Yet the 1536 variant was particularly explicit; and from then on judicial autonomy for foreign "nations" became a fixture of the capitulary system.[15] The restriction would have benefited the French consuls, who charged for their judicial services. As for merchants trading under the French flag, the main advantage was that local judges could no longer undermine contracts drawn according to French legal norms.

The challenge to the supremacy of Islamic law is self-evident. Although the restriction did not concern lawsuits involving Muslims, it curtailed the jurisdiction of Islamic courts within the abode of Islam. In the previous century the Mamluks had not gone that far. According to their capitulations, any case could be tried by a kadi, except that privileged foreigners were free to request a transfer to the ruler's own court.[16] Under Islamic law, the duty to deliver justice fell, in any case, on the ruler, who could delegate responsibility to kadis.[17]

Blocking kadis from hearing cases among foreign co-nationals would have deprived them of the speedy trials for which local courts were widely praised. On the positive side, by enhancing the credibility of contracts among foreigners operating under the same flag, it would have encouraged them to pool their resources in larger amounts and for longer periods. Yet foreign merchants went to Ottoman lands to trade with local residents, not among themselves. They remained exposed to Islamic lawsuits, because Ottoman subjects retained the right to sue a foreigner before a kadi. Besides, the Islamic courts continued to claim sole jurisdiction over cases involving Muslims.

Forum Transfers

Foreign negotiators sought to address the matter through a variant of the Mamluk forum transfer rule. By the seventeenth century, the Ottoman-granted capitulations were stipulating that cases "exceeding the value of four thousand aspers (akçes)" be tried in the capital, before an imperial council (divan-ı hümayun) consisting of high administrators and possibly headed by the sultan himself, with a foreign representative present.[18] In 1675, when the English won this right, the threshold amounted to 174 times the average daily wage of a skilled construction worker. Due to inflation, the range of cases that met this threshold requirement expanded steadily. By 1838, the year of the Anglo-Ottoman Convention, it amounted to just four times that wage (fig. 12.1). Certain late capitulations required cases in places far from Istanbul to be tried by the highest regional authority—in Tunis, for example, "the Council of the Bey, the Dey, and the Divan," as opposed to "ordinary judges."[19]

Local merchants, Muslim or not, had always been free to petition for a hearing before a tribunal of dignitaries.[20] However, rulers heard appeals selectively, and most subjects had neither the resources to pursue a case in the capital nor the clout to prevail. They also lacked an organization to defend them in trials against

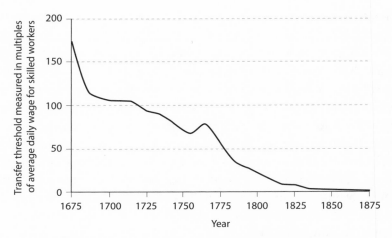

Figure 12.1 Threshold for forum transfer rights of foreigners: 1675–1875. *Note:* Based on data from Istanbul in Özmucur and Pamuk, "Standards of Living," table 1.

foreign adversaries assisted by consular staff. The forum transfer option thus amounted to a foreign privilege. One benefit to foreigners was that their major lawsuits became sensitive to international pressures. Another is that adjudication before a relatively slow-changing administration, whose members could be reminded of their own precedents, made contract enforcement more predictable. Kadis were rotated frequently in order to keep them from establishing local ties. A new appointee could differ from his predecessor in style, temperament, skills, and biases.[21] The resulting judicial uncertainty would have hindered contract enforcement. At least on financially important disputes, foreign merchants could escape that uncertainty through a forum transfer.

The availability of a legal right does not mean that it will be exercised indiscriminately. Eligible cases did not always land before high-level tribunals. For one thing, it was not costless to exercise the transfer right. Initiating a transfer could involve transportation costs. More significant, it could lead to loss of reputation in the eyes of local clients and suppliers favoring speedy kadi justice to lengthy trials conducted by intimidating high officials.[22] For another, foreigners would have preferred the Islamic courts when they felt confident of winning. The latter factor would explain why the alleged anti-foreign bias fails to show up in court records from

TABLE 12.2
Outcomes of Civil Trials Involving Foreigners, 1602–1697*

Litigants	No decision	Total resolved cases	Resolved cases won by foreigner	
			Number	%
Ottoman plaintiff–foreign defendant[a]	2	12	10	83.3
Foreign plaintiff–Ottoman defendant[b]	0	6	6	100
Foreign and Ottoman partners as plaintiffs–Ottoman defendant[c]	0	3	2	66.7
Total	2	21	18	85.7

*Court registers in sample: 15 registers of Galata and Istanbul courts, listed in table 4.1.
[a] No verdict: Galata 25 (1604), 50a/4. Case transferred to a special tribunal: Galata 145 (1689), 48a/1. Won by Ottoman plaintiff: Galata 145 (1689–90), 78b/2, 99b/2. Won by foreign defendant: Istanbul 9 (1661), 19a/1, 222b/1; Galata 130 (1683), 17b/1; Galata 145 (1689–90), 24a/2, 36b/1, 107a/7; Istanbul 22 (1695), 36a/2, 162a/1; Istanbul 23 (1696), 7b/2, 31b/1.
[b] Galata 25 (1604) 71b/3, 71b/4; Galata 145 (1689–90) 45b/1, 96b/4, 98a/1; Istanbul 22 (1695), 2a/1.
[c] Won by Ottoman defendant: Galata 27 (1605), 83a/1. Won by foreign and Ottoman partners: Galata 145 (1689) 57b/4, 67b/3.

the seventeenth and later centuries.[23] Indeed, though few in number, the vast majority of the foreigner-subject cases in our sample of court cases were resolved in favor of the foreigner (table 12.2).

It is not self-evident that foreigners benefited from the forum transfer option. Yes, it gave them further legal protections against opportunistic behavior by local buyers, suppliers, debtors, and creditors.[24] However, the privilege gave them incentives to cheat Ottoman subjects, who would have had to exercise caution in dealings with foreigners and to add a risk premium to their prices. Foreigners would have sought ways to limit these drawbacks. But their benefits from the forum transfer option must have outweighed the costs, for they, and increasingly also their protégés, eagerly demanded the transfer of lawsuits involving Muslims.[25]

The differences in legal status between Muslim and non-Muslim subjects are relevant once again. Recall that in the eighteenth century it became easier for the latter to purchase foreign legal protection. By becoming a French protégé, a Greek-Ottoman merchant could more or less level the legal playing field in his dealings with the French. In the event of conflict, his protégé status would dampen the pro-French bias of the French officials who would step in to adjudicate. The protection system thus reduced the significance of the forum transfer rule with respect to protected minorities. Therein lies another reason why minorities came to play a disproportionate role in dealings with foreigners, and why their economic ascent coincided with the rise in interregional trade. Minorities advanced partly by intermediating between foreigners and Muslims under a dual legal status—operating under Islamic law in interacting with Muslims and under a foreign legal system in dealing with foreigners.[26]

In the sixteenth century, chapter 10 showed, foreigners dealt with Muslims cautiously, to avoid entanglement in lawsuits adjudicated by kadis.[27] For the same reason, European consuls picked their dragomans almost exclusively from among religious minorities. As the judicial rights of foreigners expanded, we now see, the tables turned. At least in the leading commercial centers, it was Muslims who had reasons to avoid international ventures. "No wise Egyptian will ever enter into a partnership with a foreigner, or accept his surety," wrote *The Times* of London in 1870.[28] For their part, foreign merchants and their protégés had progressively less need to avoid interactions with Muslims; consuls gained increasing powers to keep their co-nationals out of Islamic court and, by the nineteenth century, even out of secular local courts. Besides, in the event a local court found them guilty, their consuls could appeal directly to officials beholden to western governments. Muslim legal handicaps became increasingly serious with growing European participation in the Middle Eastern economy. No longer could they be dismissed on the ground that economic relations with India and East Asia were relatively more significant.

Prevalence of Oral Contracting

Foreign concerns about contractual credibility stemmed from more than the biases of local courts. Another source of anxiety was that

Islamic courts relied heavily on oral evidence. From the rise of Islam, oral testimony played a central role in Islamic adjudication. Though documents could be presented as evidence, they were viewed with suspicion, partly because of the possibility of forgery, but also because written texts could be misread to illiterate and innumerate litigants. With low levels of education feeding this mistrust, it became customary to accept a document only if validated by morally upright witnesses.[29] A litigant could invalidate a document by casting doubt on the authenticity of a seal or signature, or by impugning the character of a witness to its creation. Thus, in seventeenth-century Istanbul a written contract was rarely accepted as legal proof without live witnesses to establish its authenticity.[30] In only 3.1 percent of the cases in which a document was presented and contested by the opposite side was a decision reached without testimony from witnesses to its creation.[31]

The function of a document was not to provide evidence but, rather, to facilitate the identification of credible witnesses and to help witnesses remember the relevant facts.[32] Accordingly, a court could refuse to recognize its own records.[33] In 1604, an Istanbul fire consumed the proof of purchase and payment that a man received from the Galata court. Rather than consult its own records for the original copy of the destroyed document, the court called in four Muslim witnesses to the registration process.[34] To ensure the availability of corroborating oral testimony in case of litigation, written contracts had to furnish the attestations of multiple witnesses. Hence, witnesses were always in high demand. Found at every court, certified witnesses (shāhid ʿadl, but usually just shāhid or ʿadl) exercised the function of a modern notary.[35] They assisted and observed the registration of private contracts as well as the recording of kadi judgments.

As the capitulations were being expanded through new judicial provisions, only a minority of all kadi trials turned on documentation. In seventeenth-century Istanbul, a document was introduced in about a fifth of the disputes over property or a sale, and an eighth of those over debt or a partnership (table 12.3). This was so even though introduction of a document massively increased the chances of winning a lawsuit. When only the plaintiff supported

TABLE 12.3
Use of Documents in Civil Trials, 1602–1697*

Source of actual or potential dispute	Registration	Trial performed				
		Document used		Only oral testimony used		
		Number	%	Number	%	Total
All commerce	6494	351	15.3	1940	84.7	2291
Partnership	368	19	11.3	149	88.7	168
Property	756	101	22.2	354	77.8	455
Sale	2296	117	19.1	497	80.9	614
Debt	2180	159	12.2	1142	87.8	1301

*Court registers in sample: 15 registers of Galata and Istanbul courts, listed in table 4.1.
Note: Some cases fall into more than one category.

his case through a document, he won 83.9 percent of the time. When only the defendant did so, the plaintiff's win rate plummeted to 7.2 percent.[36]

In a court hearing based on oral testimony alone, the judge weighs the merits of contradictory testimonies by considering, along with the alleged facts, the credibility of the litigants and their witnesses. This process does not necessarily produce a verdict. So it was in the premodern Middle East. As in other places, such impasses were overcome by asking one side or the other to take an oath. Faced with a dispute unresolvable on the basis of verbal testimony, the kadi would ask the defendant to clear his name, or the plaintiff to establish the veracity of his claim, by swearing on his "book" (Quran, Bible, or Torah). In seventeenth-century Istanbul, 18.7 percent of all civil lawsuits were decided through an oath.[37]

Court Procedures and Impersonal Exchange

The procedures used to litigate disputes involving documentation presumed repeated interactions between court participants and the rest of society. In such a setting plaintiffs, defendants, or witnesses who lost credibility through false testimony would damage their social relations as well as their prospects for doing business; hence, they would tend to testify truthfully. Moreover, if asked to take an oath, they would think twice before lying, to avoid damaging their reputation in the eyes of knowledgeable members of the community. By the same logic, in conflicts rooted in contractual ambiguity, defendants eager to maintain a good reputation would have been reluctant to win on the basis of an oath, rather than a court verdict. In the court records of seventeenth-century Istanbul, one encounters refusals to take an oath even when compliance would almost certainly have resulted in exoneration.[38] This may surprise readers attuned to the behavioral incentives of modern commerce, which is largely impersonal. If the outcome of the trial hinges on an oath, in a society characterized by impersonal exchange a selfish defendant accused of default will swear that he has paid. In an impersonal community, then, an oath is of limited informational value. In communities accustomed to personal exchange, such as that of the premodern Middle East, its informational value can be substantial.[39]

Procedures suitable to a closed community accustomed to personal exchange can lose reliability, then, on matters involving interactions with outsiders. Consider a witness who would be reluctant to testify falsely against an insider for fear of communal retribution. The same witness may speak ill of an outsider without trepidation, knowing that his community will not object. Likewise, a judge who might face communal resistance if his rulings are biased against a local group may tilt the scales of justice against foreigners with impunity. For these reasons alone, litigation procedures based heavily on oral evidence exposed foreigners to greater dangers than ones requiring documentation.

Unsurprisingly, around the middle of the second millennium foreigners on business in the Middle East complained tirelessly about oral legal procedures. They did so in the belief that burdens of abuse fell disproportionately on them.[40] In a letter written in 1567, a Venetian official in Istanbul fumes that the local legal system is unaccustomed to written evidence. "All cases," he suggests contemptuously, "even the most important, are . . . summarily dispatched by verbal evidence."[41] An added problem was that only locally drawn documents were even considered; a Venetian summoned to court could not prove an agency, partnership, or guardianship through a contract notarized in Venice.[42] Still another problem was that litigants could hire witnesses prepared to testify on their behalf. This raised the potential costs of restricting the use of documents.[43]

To repeat, oral court procedures work ideally only in small and closed societies in which everyone knows one another intimately through dense webs of interaction. These conditions were lacking in the major commercial centers that attracted foreigners. Whether in Istanbul, Izmir, Aleppo, Alexandria, Cairo, or Tabriz, professional witnesses could get away with false testimony because the conditions of a small and closed society were *not* satisfied. In every such city, residents knew the members of their own commercial networks, but these represented only subsets of the wider population. To survive and prosper, it was not necessary to be trusted by everyone living in the city.

Judicial corruption is a major theme in Middle Eastern history, and the prevalence of false witnesses is one of its subthemes. Evliya Çelebi (1611–82), author of the most famous Ottoman travelogue, reputedly suggested that twice as much of a particular kadiship's revenue came from injustice as from justice.[44] James Porter, English ambassador in Istanbul between 1746 and 1762, wrote that in Turkey almost all judges were corrupt. "They tell us of some rare examples in Turkey of uncorrupt judges," he quipped. "I have heard of one, but none have come to my certain knowledge."[45] Complaining bitterly of witnesses "who make a professed trade of attending courts of judicature, and live by it," he also observes: "False witnesses should be punished according to the Quran; however, that happens but seldom."[46] Historical records rarely document corruption because its perpetrators have tried hard to cover their traces.[47] But the Ottoman court registers do contain explicit references to bribing by officials and false witnessing.[48]

Kadis were supposed to inquire into the character of any witness presented in court, and to dismiss unreliable testimony. However, because their tenure was short, they were not always motivated to find the truth. In any case, character reading, never an infallible process, weakens when societies grow and interact with outsiders.

Therein lies another reason why contract enforcement was particularly unreliable where visitors or foreigners were involved. Even a fully honest and perfectly unbiased kadi would find it difficult to separate truthful and false testimony in cities with tens of thousands of merchants, including visitors from all over the Middle East and foreign lands.

For foreign merchants active in the Middle East the local court system was problematic, then, for two distinct reasons. In the first place, the rules of evidence appeared stacked against them in lawsuits against local subjects. Second, the weight given to oral testimony devalued the evidence contained in written documents, thus diminishing the quality of kadi judgments. As the use of written contracts gained prevalence among foreign merchants, and documents drawn abroad became more common, the Islamic courts became increasingly disadvantageous.

Absent the quality issue, foreign merchants would have been satisfied with measures to eliminate discrimination. They might have demanded, say, special Islamic courts with "mixed" tribunals on which foreigners had representation. This option had seen use elsewhere. In medieval northern Europe, for instance, alien merchants often were entitled to a "half-tongue" (*de medietate linguae*) trial, in which the jurors would include speakers of the defendant's language.[49] In the same vein, a 1348 treaty between Seljuk Aydın and the Sancta Unio coalition of Latin powers, which included Venice and the Pope, allowed for mixed courts to adjudicate disputes involving Turks and Latins.[50] But the Mamluk and Ottoman capitulations addressed foreign qualms about Islamic courts in a different way. They sought to have kadi courts use special procedures in trials involving foreigners. At least in contexts involving foreigners, the consequent privileges helped to adapt the kadi courts to Europe's ongoing transition from personal to impersonal exchange.

Documentation Privileges in the Capitulations

At the time of the early Ottoman capitulations, commercial trials based solely on oral testimony were the norm also in parts of western Europe.[51] Oral evidence created problems analogous to those in kadi courts. The hiring of false witnesses and judicial corruption were common all across the continent. However, the use of oral testimony and the discounting of written evidence became increasingly controversial as commerce expanded and exchanges became more and more impersonal, in the sense of being conducted between individuals lacking reliable knowledge about each other's character.[52] The growing complexity of commercial and financial organizations compounded the drawbacks of oral evidence. Documentation became more common to facilitate both the tracking of payable and receivable accounts and their communication to others.[53]

During the transition, there was resistance to imposing a documentation requirement, partly because the literate would benefit disproportionately. Moreover, documents were treated with suspicion, and trials often centered on whether a document was authentic. A litigant who appeared to have endorsed a document might claim that his seal was stolen or that, being illiterate, he was tricked into accepting a clause quite obviously detrimental to his interests. For their part, the expected beneficiaries of documentation sought to improve the credibility of their written contracts by having them notarized.[54] But over time, in some places faster and more broadly than elsewhere, reliance on documents grew. Also, financial claims based solely on oral testimony became suspect and eventually legally invalid. The trend culminated in laws that made claims based on oral evidence legally unenforceable. In Venice written contracts became mandatory on matters of importance in 1394, in France in 1566, in Scotland in 1579, and in Belgium in 1611.[55] In England they became mandatory on all contracts with the Statute of Frauds of 1673.[56] These transformations drew strength from the spread of literacy and numeracy (fig. 12.2). One would expect foreigners to try to transplant to the eastern Mediterranean the institutions of impersonal exchange with which they were becoming increasingly familiar. The anti-foreign biases of Islamic court procedures provided an added motive for making documentation mandatory. Insofar as it is the substance of a written contract that decides a case, the religion or nationality of the litigants ceases to matter.

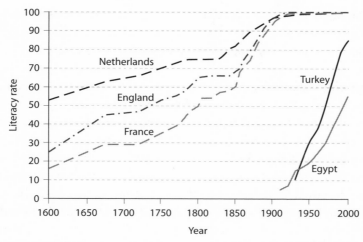

Figure 12.2 The rise of literacy in western Europe and the Middle East: 1600–2000. *Data sources:* Stone, "Literacy and Education," pp. 120–21; Sanderson, *Education and Economic Decline*, pp. 3–5; Spufford, "Literacy, Trade, and Religion," pp. 248–63; Wintle, *History of Netherlands*, pp. 269–70; France, *Annuaire Statistique* 1911–52; Heyworth-Dunne, *History of Education*, p. 360; Egypt, *Recensement Général, 1897*, pp. 20–22; Egypt, *Statistical Yearbook* for 1909, table 12; Egypt, *Annuaire Statistique 1925–26*, table 12; Turkey, *1927 Umumî Nüfus Tahriri*, pp. 39–46; Kazamias, *Education and Modernity*, table 2; *UNESCO Statistical Yearbooks*, 1963–99. For Turkey and Egypt no reliable estimates exist from the period before the nineteenth century.

As early as the fifteenth century some kadis had been required to use special procedures in regard to commercial dealings between local merchants and certain foreigners. In 1486, for instance, the Ottomans imposed a documentation requirement for cases involving merchants from Dubrovnik. These cases were to be heard only if the transactions had been recorded in a court register (*sicil*) and a kadi had issued a document stating the facts of the case (*hüccet*).[57] In the same vein, the Mamluk-Florentine treaty of 1497 required Florentine contracts with Mamluk subjects to be documented in the presence of certified witnesses.[58] A documentation clause is found also in the 1536 Ottoman capitulations given to France:

> In a civil case against Turks, tributaries, or other subjects of the [Ottoman] Grand Signior, the merchants and subjects of the [French]

King can not be summoned, molested, or tried unless the said Turks, tributaries, and subjects of the Grand Signior produce a writing from the hand of the opponent, or a "heudjet" from the cadi.[59]

This clause harbors a striking asymmetry: although French subjects are free to sue locals on the basis of oral testimony, they themselves may not be sued without documentation. Its purpose was to lessen the kadi's reliance on Muslim witnesses whenever the defendant was a Frenchman, focusing attention in such cases more on the written agreement than on matters of probity, piety, faith, and nationality. With documentation, witnesses could still be heard if its validity was questioned.[60] But the burden of proof would fall on the challenger of the document, so the possibility of escaping an obligation, or of fabricating a liability, would diminish. Partly to protect French merchants against the invalidation of documents by paid witnesses, the capitulations of 1536 stipulated also that a kadi "may not hear or try . . . subjects of the King without the presence of their dragoman."[61] As an Ottoman subject in command of local vernaculars, a dragoman was equipped to discredit fraudulent testimony. The requirement concerning his presence, like the documentation provision, became a standard feature of subsequent capitulations.[62]

In our seventeenth-century sample of court cases, seventy-two of the 8,785 commercial cases include one or more foreigners. Of these, forty-nine resulted in the drawing or recording of a written contract, and the remaining twenty-three were trials. In 42.9 percent of the fourteen trials with a foreign defendant, a document was introduced by one side or the other (table 2.4). This figure exceeds the share of all trials involving appeal to documentation: 15.3 percent. The foreign defendant won six of the eight trials in which no document was introduced. Although the smallness of the sample precludes statistical significance, it appears that when foreigners were confident of winning a case without documentation they accepted the traditional procedures, without invoking a capitulary privilege. Also revealing are the two cases that the foreign defendant lost. In one, the Muslim plaintiff, a high official, supported his case through multiple documents.[63] In the other, the for-

TABLE 12.4
Document Use in Civil Trials Involving One or More Foreigners, 1602–1697*

		Document used	
Side of foreigner(s)	*Total*	*Number*	*%*
Defendant[a]	14	6	42.9
Plaintiff[b]	9	5	55.6
Total	23	11	47.8

  *Court registers in sample: 15 registers of Galata and Istanbul courts, listed in table 4.1.
  [a] Document used: Istanbul 9 (1661), 19a/1, 222b/1; Galata 145 (1689–90), 48a/1, 99b/2; Istanbul 22 (1695), 36a/2; Istanbul 23 (1696), 7b/2. No document used: Galata 25 (1604), 50a/4; Galata 130 (1683), 17b/1; Galata 145 (1689–90), 24a/2, 36b/1, 78b/2, 107a/7; Istanbul 22 (1695), 162a/1; Istanbul 23 (1696), 31b/1.
  [b] Document used: Galata 25 (1604), 71b/3, 71b/4; Galata 27 (1605), 83a/1; Galata 145 (1690), 98a/1; Istanbul 22 (1695), 2a/1. No document used: Galata 145 (1689–90), 45b/1, 57b/4, 67b/3, 96b/4.

eigner lost on the basis of oral testimony alone, but the amount at stake was small; in all likelihood the defendant, an English ship captain accused of stealing a roll of iron, reasoned that the reputational hazard of invoking capitulary immunity outweighed the potential gain.[64] All in all, it appears that by the seventeenth century the capitulations provided foreign merchants fairly strong protection against frivolous lawsuits.

For disputes involving foreigners operating under different flags, through the sixteenth century the default rule was that the Islamic courts had jurisdiction. Given foreigners' mistrust of Islamic justice, this may seem odd. Yet the nations competing for commercial influence in the region mistrusted each other as well, sometimes more intensely. Besides, a kadi court offered a neutral forum for adjudication. The word of every foreigner was weighted equally, and in summoning local witnesses none enjoyed an advantage over others. In any case, foreign communities interacted much less with each other than with the local population, which limited the number of "mixed" foreign cases. As interregional trade expanded and gained complexity, both interactions among foreigners and their aversion to using kadi courts would have increased. Predictably, rival foreign communities eventually negotiated ground rules for trying mixed cases without reliance on Islamic courts.[65] Sometimes a mixed tribunal was formed; at other times the case was heard by a mutually agreed foreign judge or consul.[66]

Islam and the Documentation of Contracts

If in the seventeenth century commercial life was based primarily on oral contracts in Istanbul, the same was true in the rest of the Muslim-governed Eastern Mediterranean. Nowhere had written commercial contracts become the norm, and nowhere had they acquired the legal significance that they do in all modern economies, including those of majority-Muslim areas. Tellingly, during that century the use of written contracts actually declined in the one place that moved from western to Muslim rule. After the Ottomans took over Crete from the Venetians in the mid-seventeenth century, written maritime contracts became less common. The Venetians had employed professional notaries to record all maritime agreements. With the Islamic courts of the Ottomans honoring oral contracts, even the use of receipts for monetary transfers became sporadic.[67]

Were these patterns rooted in Islam's traditional sources? Because Islam emerged in a highly illiterate society, one might expect the Quran as well as recollections of Islam's revered initial decades to have legitimized oral contracting and ignored documentation. Endorsed by Islam, the norm of oral contracting and the associated legal procedures might then have lived on in the more literate societies that became Islamicized through either conquest or cultural diffusion. Yet the evidence conflicts with this reasoning. Islam's traditional sources promote oral contracting in only certain contexts; in others, they treat documentation as indispensable. Here is a long verse from the Quran:

> Believers, when you contract a debt for a fixed period, put it in writing. Let a scribe write it down for you with fairness. . . . Call in two male witnesses from among you, but if two men cannot be found, then one man and two women whom you judge fit to act as wit-

nesses; so that if either of them commit an error, the other will remember. . . . Do not fail to put your debts in writing, be they small
or big, together with the date of payment. This is more just in the
sight of Allah; it ensures accuracy in testifying and is the best way
to remove all doubt. But if the transaction in hand be a bargain
concluded on the spot, it is no offence for you if you do not commit
it to writing.[68]

Written contracts are optional, this verse says, when the *quid* and
the *quo* are simultaneous, as when a person buys a camel and pays
instantly. There is nothing surprising here, because requiring the
documentation of spot sales would have raised transaction costs
for little gain. The verse also says that documentation is required—
not just recommended—when the *quid* and the *quo* are separated
in time. A loan must be documented and so must a sale for deferred payment. What if the traders are illiterate? They must hire a
scribe to record the contract for them, says the Quran. Presumably
a literate person can be consulted if a dispute arises over the content of the agreement. Jurists facilitated the work of scribes and
judges alike by developing formularies for use in registering contracts, and these formularies underwent adaptations to suit local
circumstances.[69] Precisely because formularies were available, in
the Islamic court registers of any place and period one finds remarkable consistency in the format of agreements, whether the issue
is marriage, a waqf, inheritance, a partnership, or debt.

Clearly, a large majority of the litigants who faced off in seventeenth-century Istanbul courts were doing business in violation
of a rule stated in the Quran. Few of them documented their contracts involving transactions spread across time. Even debt contracts, explicitly required to be documented, were left undocumented as a rule. Lack of religiosity is probably not the reason. In
all likelihood the benefits of documentation did not justify the
costs involved. At the time, the literacy rate could not have been
much more than 5 percent (fig. 12.2).[70] Although the cost of paper
was not a critical factor, scribes did not work for free.[71] Much
more important was that documentation carried the risk of trans-
mitting information to state officials prepared to grab resources

wherever possible.[72] Oral contracting kept financial information private except in the event of a dispute requiring litigation by a kadi.

For all the drawbacks of documenting contracts, the benefits were limited because of the prevalence of personal exchange. Since merchants, investors, savers, and borrowers usually contracted with people known to themselves or their trusted acquaintances through repeated exchanges, oral private contracts tended to be fulfilled and people had reason to believe that after their passing, obligations toward their inheritors would be honored. These factors limited the value of putting agreements in writing. This interpretation accords with the contracting practices in small Ottoman towns of secondary economic importance. Two such towns were Çankırı and Kastamonu, both in central Anatolia. In the seventeenth century, these towns were less cosmopolitan than Istanbul, and by virtue of their smaller sizes their residents were much less likely to trade with strangers. Boğaç Ergene finds that only 11.1 percent of the cases involved an appeal to written documents—a third less than in Istanbul.[73]

In brief, the Quranic requirement to document contracts involving delayed payment was violated frequently for several reasons, including the limited benefits of documentation under personal exchange and the risk of giving tax collectors information on personal wealth. The oral legal culture that foreigners modified at the margins through the capitulations was grounded, then, in the prevailing political and economic conditions. It did not stem from some essential element of Islamic doctrine.

The verse quoted above also requires the authentication of written contracts by credible witnesses to their preparation. We already know that this requirement tended to be obeyed meticulously. As with violations of the documentation requirement, those of the witnessing requirement are explicable in economic terms. In eleventh-century Spain and North Africa, authentication of a document through a kadi's handwriting was considered sufficient validation whenever the witnessing requirement appeared socially burdensome.[74] The rationalization rested on Islam's necessity principle (*darūra*), which is also based on the Quran: "Allah desires your well-being, not your discomfort."[75] The necessity principle legiti-mizes a normally illegitimate practice to prevent hardship. Writing around 1200, the jurist Ibn al-Munasif explained that it may prove impossible to find two witnesses able to travel to the trial site, de-laying resolution of a conflict.[76] Significantly, where tolerated, the practice of accepting documents lacking oral authentication was treated as abnormal. Ibn al-Munasif did not object to a witnessing requirement per se; where feasible, he supported it.

Appraising the Capitulations

The previous chapter showed that foreign merchants in the Middle East enjoyed exemptions from sundry levies and protections against arbitrary taxation. Whatever the consequent benefits, the gains from carrying western institutions into the region must have been far more significant. In shielding foreigners from undocumented legal claims, the capitulations lowered the costs of interregional exchange. In stimulating document use, they facilitated the intro-duction of organizations that pool the resources of strangers and enjoy legal standing, such as the incorporated banks established in the nineteenth century. They also extended the planning horizons of foreigners and enhanced the credibility of their long-term com-mitments. By virtue of such advances, foreigners in the region were able to exploit the economies of scale and scope inherent in mod-ern technologies. They achieved these successes by operating within enclaves that adapted to institutional advances in Europe, even as local economic institutions stagnated. The advantages of foreign-ers propelled minorities to obtain foreign legal protection. Thus, in enabling the foreign economic domination that gained high vis-ibility in the nineteenth century, the capitulations also contributed to the ascent of the region's indigenous minorities.

Political advantages accrued to the Mamluk and Ottoman rulers who granted capitulations. More critical here, these treaties kept western merchants interested in trading, allowing rulers to appro-priate some of the resulting trade surplus through tariffs and fees. For several centuries, Middle Eastern rulers thus benefited from external productivity gains without having to undertake domestic legal reforms. The capitulations served, then, as a substitute for reinterpreting or updating Islamic law. Reforming the Islamic legal system with an eye toward removing the incentives to use a foreign system was always an alternative to providing capitulations. Indeed, that was the choice made in other places that faced the analogous challenge of attracting foreign merchants. In thirteenth-century England, Italian merchants found local institutions inadequate to their needs. In response, English rulers opted to create new legal institutions available to domestic and foreign traders alike. They could have solved their immediate problem by showering Italians with privileges denied to the English. Instead, they undertook reforms without tilting the playing field against local merchants. In the process, Daniel Klerman proposes, England triggered a dynamic that enabled its merchants to become a global powerhouse in later centuries.[77]

All modern states grapple with the problem of reducing the contractual uncertainties of cross-border trade. One source of these uncertainties is the heterogeneity of national laws, another the pro-local biases of national courts. They are alleviated through institutions that exclude exporters and importers from the jurisdiction of national courts and allow them to trade under supra-national legal regimes. Thus, most export processing zones operate under supranational labor laws, and parties to a cross-border business deal may commit to resolving their disputes through legally binding international arbitration.[78] Modern states generally allow their own citizens to take full advantage of the privileges created to facilitate cross-border trade. They thus follow the precedent set by medieval English rulers, rather than that of the capitulations.

The Mamluk and Ottoman capitulations provided western merchants opportunities to conduct interregional commerce under institutions different from those prevalent in the Middle East. The privileges led to growing economic disparities. As western and Middle Eastern commercial institutions became increasingly dissimilar, Muslim merchants found themselves economically marginalized vis-à-vis foreigners and their protégés. Already apparent in the eighteenth century, this marginalization gained salience in the nineteenth century. Concentrated in traditional economic sectors, which still operated mainly under Islamic law, Muslim merchants of the nineteenth century were essentially left out of the newest and most innovative economic sectors—banking, mass transportation, mass production, and large-scale trade.

These long-term consequences were unintended. The sultans who agreed to the early capitulations for immediate political or economic gains may not have heeded the interests of Muslim merchants. Yet they did not aim to marginalize them vis-à-vis either indigenous minorities or foreigners. The observed outcomes depended on the subsequent institutional evolution of the West, which they could not have foreseen. Had western economic institutions stagnated after the sixteenth century, the privileges of foreign merchants would not have posed a major problem for the Middle East's indigenous merchants. Western-inspired institutional transplants would have been much less significant. Moreover, in the absence of an explosion in trade with the West, Muslim merchants and producers would not have lost market share to minorities and foreigners.

De-Islamization of Commercial Life through Legal Reforms

Another unintended consequence, of lasting significance, has been the de-Islamization of economic life in the Middle East. It started within the small enclaves of foreigners. The legal privileges of foreigners then set in motion a process through which Islam's role in the region's economic life diminished far beyond anything once imaginable. In encouraging western merchants to establish lasting commercial enterprises, the capitulations familiarized the region with business practices, organizational forms, and legal procedures without a basis in Islam. Judicial defeats such as the one that Mehmet bin Mahmut suffered against Heneage Finch taught the local population the advantages of documenting contracts in a world of expanding commerce and increasingly impersonal exchange. The growing powers of European representatives enabled their protégés to become less dependent on Islamic courts, at least on commercial matters. Most significant for the present, foreign economic successes gave Muslims an appreciation for institutions developed outside the realm of Islamic law. For example, they demonstrated the advantages of binding the tax-collecting hand of the state and of pooling savings within banks.

The capitulations set the stage, then, for momentous economic reforms of the nineteenth and twentieth centuries—momentous because they essentially severed the connection between daily economic life and Islamic law. Specialized commercial courts, corporate law, and stock markets—all of which presume largely impersonal exchange—were generally adopted and disseminated without even lip service to Islamic principles. In the twentieth century they would become part of the institutional fabric even in countries, like Saudi Arabia, whose economy is nominally under a divine and time-invariant law. Institutions and practices of foreign provenance became a visible part of Middle Eastern economic systems partly through emulation of prototypes already present in the region's most dynamic sectors, through the capitulations.

Until the de-Islamization of commercial life gathered steam, attempts to reverse the growing economic domination of foreigners resulted essentially in failure. The most notable program designed to increase Ottoman participation in trade with the West involved the creation of two cadres of Ottoman merchants protected by the Ottoman state. One of these, for non-Muslims, was called "Europe merchants" (*Avrupa tüccarı*); the other, for Muslims, was called "auspicious merchants" (*hayriye tüccarı*). In the first quarter of the nineteenth century these groups were given tax breaks extended to foreigners under the capitulations; and they were allowed, like foreigners, to have lawsuits involving sums over 4,000 aspers litigated in Istanbul in the presence of an official with duties resembling those of a European consul.[79] The auspicious merchants had little impact on the Muslim-controlled share of trade with western Europe, and the Europe merchants achieved successes only in the hinterlands of the Balkans and Anatolia.[80] Both patterns are consistent with the institutional interpretation developed here. Tax exemptions and the right to litigate cases before a special tribunal could not restore the competitiveness of Muslim traders in the absence of a legal system conducive to pooling capital within large and long-lived enterprises. As for the successes of the Europe merchants, it speaks volumes that they occurred in areas where foreign economic penetration was minimal. And if non-Muslims achieved successes in places where Muslims could not, the major reason, no doubt, is that only the former had relatives able to do business under a western system.

At what point did the Middle East begin to make the transition to impersonal exchange? The essential legal reforms would have to wait for the nineteenth century. But the earliest signs of the transition were present in the late seventeenth century, when, at least in the courts of Istanbul, the use of documents in lawsuits among Ottoman subjects began to rise. Growing interactions with foreigners may well have provided the necessary stimulus. A highly disproportionate share of the seventeenth-century Istanbul lawsuits involving foreigners are from the last quarter of the century, which testifies to the growing economic role of foreigners.[81] As foreign economic activity increased, local economic players would have grown more accustomed to documentation. Humiliating legal setbacks such as that suffered against Heneage Finch would have led to adaptations.

The last two chapters have focused on western–Middle Eastern commercial interactions that took place in the Middle East. It has not been necessary to examine the analogous interactions in western Europe, because before the nineteenth century few Middle Eastern merchants set foot in the West. An institution that symbolizes this asymmetry is the consulate, which supported foreign merchants in the Middle East. Until quite late, Middle Eastern merchants did not benefit from analogous institutions in western cities. From this new angle, we now return to an earlier theme, the origins of the long institutional divergence that turned the Middle East into an underdeveloped region.

13

The Absence of
Middle Eastern Consuls

magine a Turkish merchant based in Iskenderun around 1680. He has established a partnership with a wealthy person who is funding a commercial venture to Marseille. According to the plan, our traveling merchant will carry silk fabrics on the outbound trip, sell them in Marseille, and use the proceeds to buy woolens. When the woolens are finally sold in Iskenderun, the investing partner will recover his principal, and the profit will be shared. If this scenario appears fanciful, it is because in the seventeenth century few Muslim merchants ventured to the commercial centers of western Europe. Christian pirates and brigands discouraged them from traveling to the West, as did customs agents who preyed on their merchandise.

Within Europe itself, Christian merchants traded only in places with which they had formal security agreements. For instance, the Italians established merchant colonies in northwestern Europe only after obtaining credible guarantees against predation by local authorities—credible because of carefully crafted institutions, including courts with foreign judges and the means to respond collectively.[1] The Ottoman capitulations included formal security guarantees for Ottoman merchants venturing to the West. However, the credibility of these guarantees is open to question. In the absence of essential institutions, significant dangers awaited Ottoman visitors on land and at sea.

One danger lay in judicial biases. The decisions of European courts of the time tended to reflect local interests, and in cases pitting local parties against foreigners, the latter were often at a disadvantage.[2] A trader from Heidelberg or Exeter could not count on impartial justice in the courts of Marseille, and so it was for a lone Turk. Besides, if perchance a Turkish visitor won a case, Marseille's administration might refuse to enforce the verdict. Beyond physical insecurity and judicial bias, the Turk would endure communication problems. Lacking familiarity with local languages, he could not deal on his own with customs officials, innkeepers, or judges. He would need assistance also in hiring porters, negotiating deals, and appealing to authorities. Without assistance from a local Turkish community, he would have trouble finding trustworthy and competent helpers.

All these problems could have been mitigated by a merchant organization defending the interests of Ottoman, or specifically Turkish, traders on business in Marseille. If supported by sufficiently many merchants and headed by an official analogous to the European consuls posted in the Middle East, this organization could have protected its members from predators and retaliated collectively to abuses directed at individual members. It could have run a conflict resolution system of its own and worked to limit the biases of local courts. Such an organization would also have hired natives to serve as intermediaries between its members and the local population. Whereas a single merchant on a small commercial mission would have lacked the bargaining power to make local officials improve his trading conditions, an organization representing thirty such merchants might have negotiated effectively.

The challenge of this chapter is to explore why Middle Eastern merchants did not develop associations to support their commercial activities in western Europe. As Europe's share of global commerce expanded, such assistance would have become increasingly valuable. With minor exceptions, Middle Eastern merchants developed no associations for purely internal purposes either. Hence, resolving the puzzle requires identifying obstacles to mercantile collective action in general. As in previous contexts, the conditions that *did* generate merchant associations in the West can yield valuable insights into historical patterns in the Middle East. We will start by reviewing the structure and functions of the organizations that western merchants established in the Middle East.

The Organization of a Western Trading Community in the Middle East

In the seventeenth century Europeans already had merchant colonies in every major commercial center of the Mediterranean coastline, and in some inland towns as well. Each colony was formed by a "nation"—a group of traders with common geographic origins. The typical member of a merchant colony had a volume of business falling between that of a peddler and that of a "big time" merchant. A peddler was a trader who carried goods on his back, or in a box hanging from his neck, in search of customers. His capital was meager, just enough to maintain a single load. At the other extreme, major merchants such as the Fuggers and the Hochstätters had enough capital to finance the trading of goods by the shipload; some could deploy armed fleets of their own.[3] Members of the foreign trading communities in the eastern Mediterranean had considerably more capital than a peddler, but far less than a tycoon. This is evident in the loads of the ships that traveled in the seventeenth century between Marseille and Ottoman ports. Sailing in late 1612 from Iskenderun to Marseille, the *Sainte-Claire* carried sixty-two separate consignments. The largest included twenty-eight bales of silk and ten bags of galls; the smallest consisted of a box of medicine. The silk on the ship summed to 207 bales—an average of 3.34 bales per consignee.[4]

None of the merchants with goods on the *Sainte-Claire* operated on a scale large enough to provide his own security. Hence, it made sense for them to join forces. The associations that emerged from such needs were headed by a resident manager expected to assist members in their interactions with the host society. Depending on the vernacular, this manager was known as a *shāh bandar*, *wakīl al-tujjār*, *amīn al-tujjār*, *bezirgânbaşı*, *bailus*, or *podestà*, among other such designations. Over time, however, every one, regardless of nationality, came to be called a "consul." We will continue to use this term in a generic sense, to connote officials appointed by private groups to represent them and promote their interests in foreign lands. In the modern world, of course, consuls are commissioned by the state for the purpose of promoting the commercial affairs of citizens, in addition to issuing visas and renewing passports. In the period of interest here, states were represented by ambassadors rather than consuls.[5]

Although the functions of privately appointed consuls varied, certain tasks were standard. The consul collected and disseminated information on market conditions, investment opportunities, and individual reputations.[6] To lessen uncertainties and enhance returns, he cultivated ties with people capable of harming his constituents: customs collectors, tax assessors, judges, even outlaws.[7] Through his contacts he helped his constituents cope with customs formalities, resist arbitrary exactions, and collect debts. His duties included the safeguarding of capitulary privileges. If one of his co-nationals or protégés was charged a disallowed fee, he would complain to local authorities. In endeavoring to keep his nation and its property secure, a consul would administer a guarded compound ordinarily equipped with living quarters, warehouses, and trading facilities. Examples of such compounds for foreigners include Galata and Beyoğlu (Pera) in Istanbul, the street of the Franks in Izmir, and *funduqs* in Aleppo and Cairo.[8] Consular responsibilities included the management of estates and assistance to shipwrecked co-nationals.

A consul did not perform such duties alone. He had a permanent staff, including dragomans drawn from local minorities. His budget came principally from ad valorem consulage fees on the cargo of ships flying his country's flag.[9] He collected other charges for special services, such as estate management. In the eighteenth century a French consul delivered fifty-one distinct services for a known fee.[10] However, a consul was not merely a functionary delivering services on demand. He served also as a strategist authorized to impose responsibilities and engineer joint responses. He might bar his countrymen from dealing with a dishonest native and strive to make other consuls, including those of different nations, join the boycott. Used against locals of all faiths and even against foreigners, such retaliation was known as "battulation."[11] Another such strategic function involved risk sharing. A merchant faced with an arbitrary tax could appeal to his consul to have the burden spread among his fellow nationals.[12]

To recapitulate, consuls served critical roles in interregional trade. Their presence in Middle Eastern commercial centers helps to explain why western merchants found it profitable to dwell in the Middle East for years at a time.

Middle Eastern Trading Colonies in the West

During the period when western "nations" were forming in the Middle East under the leadership of consuls, Turks and other Muslims formed few trading colonies in the West. The exceptions themselves are revealing. As Spain fell under Christian governance, its new rulers established trading facilities known as *fondechs* to house Muslim visitors.[13] Evidently Spanish rulers considered this an efficient vehicle for both taxing and controlling Muslims. Little is known about the internal organization of these compounds, or about how their residents adapted to the evolving political landscape. Whatever their organizational particularities, no *fondech* survived beyond the early sixteenth century, when the Spanish Inquisition forced the remaining Muslims to convert or flee. By the time France received its initial capitulations from the Ottomans, Spain had extinguished its Muslim colonies.

Other Muslim mercantile colonies emerged around that time in Italy. In 1514, a building in Ancona became the *fondaco dei mercanti turchi et altri musulmani*, though only for a few years— evidence of a failed attempt at forming a colony.[14] The most significant exception is an exclusively Muslim neighborhood in Venice, established in the 1570s, at a time when Venice, having lost its Mediterranean commercial supremacy to France, was trying to regain trading privileges from the Ottomans. Known as the *fondaco dei Turchi*, it moved in 1621 to a new building that still bears the same name. At its peak, this building housed fifty to one hundred visiting Turkish merchants, with whom thirty-three native brokers were authorized to do business. The *fondaco dei Turchi* remained in operation until 1838, when its last resident left Venice.[15] Once again, not much is known about the internal organization of this mercantile colony. What is almost certain is that it had no officer commissioned to adjudicate disputes, gather commercial intelligence, or mediate problems with Venetian authorities. The compound was guarded by a Venetian soldier appointed to protect residents but also to keep them sequestered.[16] Evidently Turkish merchants in Venice enjoyed fewer rights and were less well organized than Venetians doing business in Ottoman realms. They were not allowed to form a local network, to say nothing of spreading their own institutions.

The literature contains references to Turkish or Iranian colonies in Antwerp, Vienna, Leipzig, and Lwow. Their participants consisted overwhelmingly of Jews, Greeks, Armenians, Serbs, and Macedonians.[17] Of these groups, the first three relied on preexisting ethnic diasporas. For example, in the sixteenth century, a Jewish merchant from Istanbul would stay in Venice's Jewish quarter, just as a Greek visiting Antwerp would receive hospitality from that city's resident Greeks. In interactions with the West, the geographic span of these diasporas gave minorities natural advantages over Muslims. Non-Muslim Middle Easterners did not have to establish protective organizations from scratch, as the English and French did in the Middle East, and Turks, Arabs, and Iranians would have needed to do in the West.

The Armenian commercial network based in New Julfa, mentioned in chapter 4, is one of two exceptions to the rule that Middle Easterners did not found trading colonies in the West. In the sixteenth century the New Julfa Armenians established a major presence in the terrestrial trade linking Iran with the Arab world, Turkey, the Balkans, and Italy. The New Julfa network, which a century later also included Holland and Scandinavia, operated like an autonomous merchant association. Its merchants had a chief representative (*ichkhanapet*) who negotiated with the Shah of Iran as well as visiting foreigners; lesser chiefs (usually *khodjas*) led far-flung colonies.[18] Evidently, the success of this network depended on its effectiveness at collective action. Around the time that the English crown was capitalizing on the growing organizational capabilities of English overseas merchants, in Iran Shah Abbas I (r. 1587–1629) used Armenians to expand his tax base, which had shrunk as a result of territorial losses to the Ottomans. Recognizing the advantages of supporting their organization, he gave them substantial commercial autonomy, in return for having them carry goods to Europe on his behalf.[19]

Neither Abbas, nor his successors on the Iranian throne, nor contemporaneous Ottoman rulers took steps to establish lasting merchant settlements in western commercial centers. They did not explore ways to enable their non-Armenian subjects, or more specifically their Muslim subjects, to trade with the West securely and profitably. They did not appoint consuls to facilitate the stays of their merchants in the West. Before the modern era, the only case of consuls that represented a Middle Eastern group is from the Venetian-administered part of Crete. In the 1570s, Ottoman Greek merchants had a consul who represented them in their dealings with Venice and its territories. These consuls were chosen from among Venetian Greeks, not Ottoman Greeks. They assisted their constituents on commercial matters, but did not have legal rights or duties. They could not represent Ottoman Greeks in court either as individuals or as a community. Moreover, they held no diplomatic rights, tax privileges, or legal immunities.[20] Evidently, they were appointed mainly to serve Venetian interests. Like the case of the New Julfa network, this second exception thus highlights the difference, rather than the similarity, between the organizational capacity of western- and Muslim-governed merchants. It is significant that neither exception involved Muslim traders.

To sum up, before the modern era very few Muslim merchants visited major commercial centers of the West. Moreover, no organizations emerged to facilitate Muslim mercantile activity in western cities. With two possible exceptions, neither did non-Muslim Middle Easterners form self-governing settlements in Western Europe. As a prelude to an interpretation, let us consider the explanations found in the historical literature.

Critique of Received Explanations

The most prevalent explanation is that opposition to Muslim merchant colonies formed part of a protracted defensive effort to arrest the spread of Islam.[21] Just as Muslim merchants helped to carry Islam across Asia and Africa, they might facilitate religious conversions in Europe. There was also the ubiquitous fear, initially of further Arab, and later of further Turkish, military conquests. Muslim merchant colonies could have provided a bridgehead for such advances. Proof of these European insecurities lies in contemptuous medieval tracts against Islam. Polemicists sought to fuel animosity toward Muslims and also to bolster Christian resistance to conversion.[22] Popes and kings participated in this defensive campaign through prohibitions against selling food and arms to "infidels."[23]

As an explanation for the absence of Muslim colonies, these observations admit several objections. Various religious bans were defied. The Italians sold forbidden commodities to Turks and Arabs. This is evident from the abundance of Italian ships docking at Muslim-controlled ports, as well as from incessant reiterations of the trade bans.[24] In any case, in western Europe political power was fragmented, and the authority to grant residence rights rested with cities. Had Muslim merchants offered irreplaceable services, some cities would have welcomed them, if only to gain a competitive advantage over rivals.

Religious intolerance was certainly a salient characteristic of medieval Christendom. It was on display in the Spanish Inquisition.[25] Its less extreme forms involved prejudice and mistrust toward Jews, Muslims, and even eastern Christians. But hostility toward religious outsiders was neither constant nor indiscriminate. Where economic interest was involved, fanaticism tended to recede. Venice's uneasy history with Jews offers an example. In 1550 Venice expelled its Jewish immigrants, including Ottoman subjects. The expulsion reduced the supply of credit, harming both merchants and the poor. It also lowered the competitiveness of Venetian exporters dependent on Jewish contacts abroad, partly because some of the expelled merchants settled in rival ports. Several Venetian constituencies demanded a policy reversal. Beginning in 1573, the expelled Jews were allowed to return.[26] Where a Muslim presence appeared useful, coalitions would probably have formed to welcome Muslims, too.

Another explanation invokes mercantilism—the policy of limiting competition to protect local commercial rents. One of its practical effects, it is said, was to keep Muslims away, thus discouraging western cities from building compounds to house them.[27] Like the explanation based on religious intolerance, this one overlooks both the possible benefits of a resident Muslim colony and the competition among European polities. Mercantilism was indifferent to faith. Had Muslims possessed scarce commercial skills or offered lucrative networking opportunities, one or more states would have broken ranks, through lobbying by groups with a stake in a Muslim presence.

A third explanation turns the spotlight on Muslim attitudes and policies. Muslims were averse to trading with enemies, it says, and to venturing into Christendom. If foreigners were begging to trade in Muslim dominions, why go to them? Foreigners could be allowed to conduct exchanges as an act of magnanimity, sparing Muslims the humiliation of submitting themselves, even temporarily, to corrupting influences.[28] Insofar as such prejudices were prevalent, and Muslims consciously avoided going to the West, Muslim consuls would have been superfluous. This line of reasoning collides, however, with evidence of Muslim commercial success in eastern trading emporia, including predominantly Hindu or Buddhist countries. In any case, evidence of aversion to visiting the West would not establish this as a cause of the observed Muslim passivity. Surely this aversion was not universal; and it would have taken a minuscule share of the Muslim Middle Eastern population to place a significant share of the cross-Mediterranean trade in Muslim hands.[29] The emphasis on Muslim religious sensitivity conflicts also with relaxed attitudes toward the importation of un-Islamic legal practices into places under Islamic rule. Although there existed Islamic justifications for denying foreigners special rights, these were widely disregarded, undoubtedly because of economic incentives to accommodate visiting traders. Muslim traders active in the West might have been equally pragmatic. But their small numbers would have dampened pressures to create Muslim commercial colonies.

Even together, then, Christian prejudices, mercantilism, and Muslim prejudices fail to illuminate why so few Muslim traders could be found in western commercial centers around, say, the late seventeenth century. Neither state policies nor communal attitudes are immutable. Insofar as they remained fixed, that is part of the puzzle at hand. That mercantilism developed only in the West is itself a fact that requires explanation.

One more interpretation merits consideration. Using medieval Genoese traders as a prototype for western traders and the Maghribi Jews who lived under Fatimid rule as a prototype for Middle Eastern traders, Avner Greif links the long-term successes of the former to intercommunal differences in "cultural beliefs." Specifically, Genoese were "individualists," in the sense that they could not be counted on to assist a fellow Genoese who had been cheated in the marketplace by boycotting the offender; whereas the Maghribis were "collectivists," in the sense that they treated the cheating of any one member as a collectively punishable offense against the community as a whole. As individualists, the Genoese risked less than the Maghribis in hiring agents from outside their own community. Hence, it was the Genoese who established colonies in the homeland of the Maghribis—the Islamic world—rather than the other way around.[30]

Although Greif's interpretation is consistent with the trajectory of Mediterranean commercial relations, it does not shed light on the successes of Middle Eastern traders, including Muslims, in sub-Saharan Africa, India, central Asia, and East Asia. The societies that Muslim traders encountered in those regions were all collectivist according to Greif's definition, so the individualist-collectivist distinction does not elucidate why the interactions resulted, in each case, in new Muslim settlements and the geographic spread of Islam. Something other than collectivism must have made Muslims more successful among peoples with cultural beliefs similar to their own. The asymmetry in question—greater success in eastern and southern trading emporia than in the western Mediterranean—developed and persevered, we shall now see, through the advantages that accrue to the initiator of a trade relationship.

The Advantages of Incumbency

Soon after the French received their first capitulations in 1535, most traders carrying goods across the Mediterranean were using French ships and paying consulage fees to a French consul. By virtue of its incumbency, the French-governed trading network faced no significant rival. The incumbency advantage, also known as the first-mover advantage, refers to the competitive edge one gains by being the first to market a product or service.[31]

In the present context, its sources included economies of scale. Below a certain limit, increasing the size of the colony would boost overall profits from interregional exchange, raising the returns available to local traders, members of the foreign colony, and the states that taxed these groups. This is because certain consular costs, such as those from information dissemination and local negotiations, would be spread over more traders. There were also countervailing size externalities. The larger the number of French traders in Iskenderun, the harder it would be to make them act collectively. Over a certain range, however, the positive externalities would dominate.[32]

Trading colonies also exhibited economies of scope. It was cheaper to have a single ship carry goods in both directions than to use separate ships for imports and exports. Likewise, it was cheaper to use a single vessel to transport both silk and medicine than to deploy a separate vessel for each commodity. Accordingly, the *Sainte-Claire* carried many different goods to Iskenderun and various others back to Marseille. Achieving a balance of trade required coordination among players at both ends. A salient theme in Mediterranean commercial history is the challenge of filling ships in a timely manner and matching exports with imports.[33] Apart from balancing payments, success lowered the average cost of transportation. A common language and legal system facilitated communication as well as collaboration.

These considerations imply the existence of a minimum efficient scale for a trading colony—a scale that minimized the sum of transaction and transportation costs. Without sufficient numbers and operational breadth, a foreign trading community could not become competitive on its own. Hence, merchants from countries with a modest presence in Middle Eastern commerce, such as Portugal and Malta, did not form colonies of their own. At least initially, they traded under the flag of another country and paid fees to its consuls. In the process, they delayed the formation of new networks to rival that of the French. In limiting the resources available to cover temporary losses, credit costs helped to deter entry.[34]

Another contributor to the prevailing incumbency advantage consisted of business methods and legal procedures of the French. Suppliers and clients of the French, wherever their location, would have valued the use of familiar templates that had gained clarity through litigation.[35] Local traders in Iskenderun were accustomed to dealing with the French, and they knew how local judges handled commercial disputes involving foreigners. By contrast, if merchants from Iskenderun somehow established a colony in Marseille, local French traders would lack familiarity with their methods. Nor would they know the types of probable disputes or have experience with settling them. This lack of familiarity would have limited the expected profitability of the new venture.

The expectations of buyers and sellers within the French network would have generated still another incumbency advantage. At each trading post, traders on both sides of the market invested in commercial relationships. They gathered information about their trading partners. Through repeated contacts, they also cultivated mutual trust. A member of the French network would pay a price, then, for switching to a new network centered, say, on merchants from Iskenderun. The switch would require him to develop new relationships from scratch. What holds for one person also holds for others, and this is common knowledge.[36] Consequently, members of the established French network would have considered the planned rival network unlikely to succeed. Switches could have failed to materialize for this reason alone.

In brief, the incumbent French network was insulated from competition by the entry costs of potential rivals, the lower average cost afforded by its volume of business, the switching costs of its existing clients and suppliers, and obstacles to coordinating on an alternative network. The resulting incumbency advantage of the

French points to path dependence in Mediterranean commerce—the dependence of success on past performance.[37] A dominant country could retain its supremacy indefinitely even if a new rival was now able to provide the same services more cheaply. Experience-based learning would have augmented the incumbency advantage. This advantage played a role, we shall now see, in the evolution of Mediterranean trade patterns.

Emerging Entry Opportunities

As a network expands, at some point it reaches a maximum efficient scale. Thereafter, rising coordination and communication costs increase the average cost of doing business through the network. For the period and trade emporium under consideration, there is no way to measure either the minimum or the maximum efficient scales, which would have changed with technological progress. Nevertheless, there is evidence that the relationships between the volume and costs of commerce affected the establishment and use of networks.

In 1535, when Süleyman the Magnificent extended trading privileges to the French, he also granted commercial permits to the English and Dutch. At the time, these nations did not conduct enough business with the Ottoman Empire to justify consular corps of their own.[38] Accordingly, they paid consulage to the French consul, acquiring the rights and duties of the French and becoming members of the French network. The capitulations granted in 1580 to England led to the establishment of several English consulates in Ottoman realms. Before long a dispute erupted over the flag under which nations without consulates would operate. With the French insisting that third nations continue trading under the French flag, the English favored the right to choose. The "flag dispute," which involved endless negotiations with Ottoman authorities, was a battle over network size, and the underlying motivation was the associated cost. The French wanted to protect their established network, in order to minimize its average cost per member. For their part, the English wanted to enlarge their own network, so as to spread the costs of their consulates over more merchants. In the course of the dispute certain merchants, including the Dutch, saw their "flag" change from French to English, then French again, until a 1609 agreement committed them to English protection.[39]

Revealingly, even as English consulates sprung up in certain Ottoman centers, English merchants remained under French protection elsewhere. Because Egypt's climate limited the demand for England's woollen fabrics, up to the mid-seventeenth century those in Alexandria and Cairo traded under the French flag.[40] English traders themselves resisted having a consulate of their own. In 1600, an attempt to install an English consul failed because of opposition from within the small English community. Justifying his resistance, an English merchant held that the fees required to maintain an English consul would "eat out all the profit" of their "small trade."[41]

The Dutch started to establish new consulates in 1612, and the English established a permanent consulate in Cairo in 1697.[42] In subsequent years, struggles over the management of nations without consulates followed the pattern of the Anglo-French flag dispute. Meanwhile, other countries entered the field. By the nineteenth century practically every western power had at least one consulate of its own (fig. 13.1). This trajectory matches the expansion of trade with the Ottoman Empire.[43] As we know from other contexts, market growth will erode whatever incumbency advantage may have existed, inviting new entry.[44]

Lack of Entry from the Middle East

As the expansion of Mediterranean trade created room for additional networks, at first there was no entry from the Middle East. Before the nineteenth century very few Middle Eastern consuls were posted in the West; and, except for those representing the New Julfa Armenians, none served merchants. Although Middle Eastern minorities became increasingly important players in inter-regional trade from the eighteenth century onward, their operations did not depend on organizational innovations of their own. In becoming

Figure 13.1 Square of the Consuls in Alexandria, Egypt, so-named because
many European consuls worked and resided there. Now it is known as Tahrir
Square. As the influence of this foreign enclave peaked in the nineteenth century,
Middle Eastern international traders were just beginning to benefit from
consuls. (Photo: Félix Bonfils. Courtesy of Thomas Weynants)

European protégés, they joined existing trading networks and began
benefiting from the consular services of their protectors. Even the
New Julfa Armenians who participated in the Mediterranean trade
did so under the Dutch flag. Evidently in this trading emporium
their own organizational capabilities were no match for those of
westerners. Even more tellingly, their heyday was over by the mid-
eighteenth century, in the face of British commercial advances in
India and Iran.[45]

The main reason for the lack of a Middle Eastern–run network
is that stagnant Islamic institutions posed a growing handicap in
international markets. The empirical bases for this claim were presented in previous chapters, so it will suffice to underscore their
relevance to the issue at hand. Insofar as establishing an overseas
trading post required long-term financing on a large scale, prior to
the arrival of western banking in the nineteenth century the east-

ern Mediterranean offered no suitable financial intermediaries. Islamic law did not accommodate long-lasting commercial ventures of a size comparable to the European overseas trading companies, or the financing of public goods for merchant communities abroad. The Middle East's indigenous communities had not developed organizational forms conducive to trading under the same name indefinitely. The last handicap alone could have made a difference. At the end of the seventeenth century English merchants in Aleppo were forming merchant houses. As we know, these were partnerships renewed routinely and thus considered effectively permanent.[46] By virtue of this continuity, English merchants developed time-tested reputations and enduring business connections that raised their profitability.

Most crucially, perhaps, Middle Easterners lacked organized mercantile communities. Again, except for New Julfa, there were no such associations even within the Middle East itself. Hence, there were no merchant leaders empowered to collect intelligence, cultivate ties, negotiate with rulers, and organize reprisals for the collective benefit of their constituents.

Origins of Western Commercial Dominance

Why were Middle Eastern merchants unorganized in the first place? For several centuries preceding the first French capitulations, the maritime cities of Italy dominated commerce between the Muslim- and Christian-governed shores of the Mediterranean.[47] They lost out to the French partly because of military conflict with the Turks.[48] The shifts occurred before the divergence of Middle Eastern and western commercial capabilities. Italian merchants of the fourteenth century could not form joint-stock companies or corporations; nor could they borrow from banks. True, they established enterprises that historians dubbed "medieval supercompanies," but the focus of these giant companies was not commerce with the Middle East. Even in the fifteenth century Italians on business in Istanbul or Tunis were financed through partnerships similar to those that local merchants formed under Islamic law.

Could other institutional factors have enabled a succession of western Christians, rather than Middle Easterners, to dominate this market? Italian merchants achieved domination because, unlike their Middle Eastern counterparts, they developed the means to pursue their collective interests. As early as the thirteenth century, merchants were forming organizations throughout western Europe. Several patterns had emerged. Venetian and Genoese merchants achieved political power and began using state institutions to promote their commercial interests. Elsewhere, merchants lacking political authority banded together to form durable organizations, which then negotiated with rulers for privileges, often including corporate status. The latter pattern was common in England. Displaying yet another pattern, small towns formed local mercantile organizations, which then built coalitions enjoying bargaining power. The best known case is the Hanseatic League of Germany, which contributed to Europe's medieval commercial expansion. Certain small Italian cities formed analogous coalitions.[49] All of these patterns balanced the advantages of greater numbers against the consequent coordination and collective-action problems.

Although the functionally similar organizations associated with the three patterns assumed various names, a "merchant guild" may serve as a generic term. Whether operating in the Baltic or the Mediterranean, a merchant guild had a leader who performed functions analogous to those of a consul posted in the Middle East. Most critically, he provided the means for collective action against predators, cheaters, and defaulters. He also pressured rulers to run courts equipped to enforce commercial contracts, or helped to establish merchant courts run jointly with other guilds. These forms of collective action were essential to commercial expansion in environments where aliens could not count on impartial justice.

In inhospitable environments, no form of reputation-based contract enforcement could induce foreigners to trade. Consider first bilateral enforcement, whereby a merchant keeps trading as long as his host society treats him well. He hopes that his hosts will refrain from abusing him, in order to ensure his return. Alas, as an individual his commercial contribution to his host society is too insignificant to deter his mistreatment. Knowing this, he will not initiate trade in the first place. Enforcement can also be multilateral. When multilateral enforcement is performing ideally, news of an offense spreads among foreign merchants, each of whom responds by ceasing trade. Group retaliation thus makes the host society pay an appreciable price for abusing visitors. The challenge is to ensure the cooperation of individual merchants. In a period of collective retaliation the host society's reservation prices are especially high, as are any given trader's gains from breaking ranks. Therefore, rulers can weaken the embargo through selective incentives. The merchant guild arose precisely because multilateral enforcement readily broke down in the absence of a coordinated response.[50] Established as a corporation, it gave merchants a collective power that they lacked as unorganized individuals.

The Middle Eastern Alternative
to the Merchant Guild

Middle Eastern merchants had no means to establish such permanent associations pursuing their collective interests. Although Middle Eastern guilds emerged in the fourteenth century, they lacked self-governance. As discussed in relation to the absence of the corporation, states tolerated guilds only insofar as they served political stability and facilitated taxation.[51] Most critical here, long-distance traders formed no guilds at all, probably because states saw nothing to gain from them.

Middle Eastern merchants shared the needs that motivated their western counterparts to form guilds. In trading in alien environments, they needed security guarantees and access to impartial adjudication. They must have developed a reasonably satisfactory solution, for long-distance trade within the Islamic Middle East, and with other parts of Eurasia and Africa, was a profitable pursuit. What made merchants in tenth-century Aden believe that they could profit from a trading mission to Cairo or Calicut? Only part of the answer lies in multilateral contract enforcement. Although Middle Eastern merchants may have been better equipped than Italians to respond collectively to an abusive ruler, the latter could have broken a trade embargo through targeted incentives to cooperative individuals. Three characteristic institutions of the region contributed to giving Middle Eastern merchants the confidence to trade in distant lands.

The first consisted of a vast web of caravanserais that enabled traders to secure their goods and themselves at night, often at subsidized rates. Situated a camel-day apart on major trade routes, these fortified inns were generally built and financed in a decentralized manner, through waqfs.[52] The founder of a waqf that supported a caravanserai obtained, as we know, social prestige and inner satisfaction, but also material security for himself and his descendants.

In protecting trade routes, the states of the region contributed to keeping trade profitable. To be sure, not even the most powerful premodern rulers could extinguish piracy and brigandage.[53] Also, Muslim rulers, like rulers elsewhere, were themselves tempted to abuse individual merchants and to subvert trade embargos. Yet competition among Muslim states weeded out those least respectful of private property.[54] An example lies in the Turkish conquest of Syria and Egypt in 1517, following a period when persistent Mamluk predation caused economic decline.[55] In both places the first century of Ottoman rule brought relative stability and prosperity, with massive commercial expansion. This is evident in the recovery and growth of towns located on trade routes.[56] Also telling is the mushrooming of new caravanserais and the physical expansion of markets.[57]

The third institution that helped Middle Eastern merchants in distant lands is the Islamic court system, which rulers regulated through the appointment of kadis. Rulers expected kadis to help with the maintenance of trade flows, both to protect their tax base and to keep cities content.[58] Although Islamic legal interpretations and procedures could vary across schools of law and according to local customs, on commercial matters there was sufficient uniformity to make adjudication predictable even in distant lands. A merchant from Aden could expect a Cairene kadi to accept the legality of a contract drawn according to Islamic law. That kadi would almost certainly have experience in handling commercial disputes among the people he might face. The legal predictability supplied in Europe through merchant organizations was thus provided through a state-staffed court system.[59]

The commonness of judicial corruption in Middle Eastern history indicates that adjudication was not necessarily impartial.[60] However, the frequent rotation of kadis must have lessened systematic biases against visitors. Unable to spread local roots, a kadi with a posting expected to last a year would have a limited financial stake in favoring locals; if he was ready to be bought off, the litigant bidding the highest would win, whether a local resident or a visitor. Hence, visiting traders had less need to worry about judicial biases than if kadis had long-term appointments.

The Middle Eastern traders who made the initial forays into sub-Saharan Africa, India, Central Asia, China, and Southeast Asia lacked the benefit of Muslim-provided security, incumbent kadis, and caravanserai. What made these forays profitable is that Islamic institutions were perceived as superior to the known alternatives. Local rulers and tribal leaders welcomed these commercial initiatives. Sometimes they even converted to Islam themselves, hoping to benefit from their visitors' organizational know-how, system of adjudication, and experience.[61] Middle Eastern trading colonies followed, and they were absorbed into an expanding trading zone regulated by Islamic law. Before long the Muslim traders who initiated this absorption started enjoying incumbency advantages akin to those that, in the Mediterranean, benefited first the Italians and then the French.

Solutions Compared

The Middle East and western Europe adopted distinct solutions to a common need: contract enforcement for merchants traveling to alien environments. Within the Islamic Middle East itself, physical security and conflict resolution were provided through a combination of institutions involving states and waqfs. Outside of Muslim-governed territories, Middle Eastern merchants deterred abuses by virtue of their commercial capabilities, which offered advantages over those of the communities into which they ventured; these advantages induced the diffusion of Islamic law, removing the need for alien institutions. In the West, the legal system was relatively more varied than in the Middle East, and it contained no built-in mechanism for limiting pro-local biases in litigation. For this reason alone, traveling merchants needed to get organized. In so doing they also gained leverage over rulers tempted to prey on them. The fragmentation of political authority in western Europe compounded the need to form mercantile organizations, as did the associated breakdowns of law and order.

Although the Middle Eastern solution worked reasonably well in parts of the world with inferior commercial institutions, it was less well suited than the western solution to legally alien territories already equipped with efficient commercial institutions. Precisely because it was designed to counteract local judicial biases, the western approach provided the means for bargaining with rulers over extraterritorial legal rights and privileges. When Venetian merchants negotiated collectively with Mamluks over legal protections, they did something to which they were already accustomed.[62] In the absence of an organization representing them, Muslim merchants could not negotiate with Christian rulers over contract enforcement. As individuals, they could not make Italian courts alleviate anti-foreign biases, or protect them from fraud. Moreover, because the Italians already possessed commercial institutions at least as sophisticated as those grounded in Islamic law, the problems of Muslim merchants were unlikely to disappear through the spread of Islamization.

Western merchants could also launch a collective trade embargo against a predatory Muslim ruler. In practice the embargo would be accompanied by a threat of military intervention. Venice was prepared to have its navy attack the coasts or ships of states that harmed its merchants.[63] However, commercial success depended on more than military might. Ottoman merchants did not establish a significant presence in western Europe even in the sixteenth century, when the Ottoman Empire projected formidable military power. Lack of mercantile organizations denied Ottoman merchants the clout to use that power for their own ends. Consequently, they remained highly vulnerable to being abused in European ports.

Free Riding on Foreign Institutional Advances

There remains the question of why Middle Eastern rulers did not compensate for the vulnerability of their merchants by extending judicial and protective services to their subjects on foreign soil. Ottoman sultans must have understood that their subjects would shun insecure places. In principle, they might have required beneficiaries of the capitulations to provide genuine reciprocal rights to Ottoman merchants, threatening to withdraw the privileges of any uncooperative nation. The exercise of reciprocity would have included the posting of kadis in the West to perform consular services, including dispute resolution. Competition among westerners eager to maintain their Middle Eastern colonies might have ensured some success. If Middle Eastern rulers avoided that path, this is mainly because western merchants, already organized, were prepared to fill any demand for commercial intermediation. It was cheaper to let French merchants operate in Iskenderun than to support a Turkish or Arab colony in Marseille by posting a kadi and furnishing military protection.

As the western incumbency advantage grew through institutional innovations, the incentive to leave Mediterranean trade to foreigners would have increased. In effect, rulers would have chosen to take free rides on the rising commercial efficiency of foreigners. These rulers had no particular commitment to any group of merchants, local or foreign, which is itself a byproduct of the lack of Middle Eastern merchant associations. In Italy, England, and Holland, merchants either controlled the state or were organized enough to make officials address their needs. For lack of organizations to coordinate their actions, Middle Eastern merchants were powerless to make domestic officials serve their interests.

Once trade was left essentially to western merchants, the pattern became self-enforcing. Few Ottoman subjects, and even fewer Muslims, traveled to the West; those who did, relied on the pre-existing business networks of their resident co-religionists. Thus, no demand emerged for a consul-like official providing physical protection, conflict resolution, assistance in dealing with local officials, and commercial information. The established pattern was also self-*re*inforcing, in that it became increasingly unrealistic to expect Muslim merchants to capture substantial market share. By virtue of their incumbency, the Venetians, and then the French, and eventually others extended their networks in the Middle East, solidified their local contacts, and improved their understanding of local peoples, resources, and cultures. Eventually they became indispensable to rulers, facilitating ever more generous capitulations. Meanwhile, it became progressively more difficult for Muslim merchants to gain a foothold in trade with western Europe.

As western enterprises expanded and gained longevity, the possibility of succeeding through traditional Islamic institutions shrank to insignificance. This eliminated the need to respond or adapt to western institutional innovations, at least until the nineteenth century, when institutional reforms became a matter of preserving political sovereignty. For an analogy, consider the modern Middle East's responsiveness to foreign technological advances. Local firms will quickly adapt to an advance in refrigeration technology. However, an improvement specific to manufacturing jumbo jets will fail to elicit a response, because in the absence of aircraft production, no one stands to benefit.

If in 1680 Turkish merchants were absent from Marseille, one reason is that Ottoman sultans did nothing significant to facilitate their ventures into western Europe. Yet this indifference was not an independent cause of the observed asymmetry in Mediterranean trade. Rather, it was among the responses to an organizational divergence initiated several centuries earlier. The long divergence included the establishment of merchant organizations all across Europe. The Middle East's failure to develop merchant organizations contributed to various contrasting patterns that symbolize its loss of economic prominence. One is the rise of mercantilism in the West alone. Another is that during commercial expansions of the second millennium, anti-Muslim prejudices in the West lasted longer, and took more virulent forms, than anti-western prejudices in the Middle East. The West had relatively less to lose from obstinacy. Finally, the capitulations became one-sided treaties because the expansion of Mediterranean trade required special accommodations only for those merchants who operated on foreign soil. No pressing need arose to assist the occasional Iskenderun resident seeking his fortune in Marseille.

PART IV

Conclusions

14

Did Islam Inhibit Economic Development?

I n seeking to explain why the Middle East—defined to include the Arab countries, Iran, Turkey, and the Balkans—entered the nineteenth century as an underdeveloped region, this book has focused on institutions that contributed to critical deficiencies. Until the eighteenth century, and in some respects even later, neither the people who lived under those institutions nor outside observers saw the unfolding problems. In the seventeenth century, not even foreigners whose organizational innovations were turning western Europe into an economic superpower understood that the Middle East's economic infrastructure would become dysfunctional. They did not foresee that the region would need to transplant from abroad an entire institutional complex. Although certain statesmen, businessmen, and other players may have noticed particular inefficiencies—frozen waqf assets, atomistic financial markets, courts unsuited to impersonal exchange—none comprehended how such features were mutually reinforcing, or how they were blocking transformations essential to global competitiveness.

Part of the problem is that, alongside inefficient institutions, observers also noticed institutions that were working admirably well. The region's bazaars carried a wide assortment of luxuries. Its commercial centers attracted fortune seekers speaking a babel of languages, much as Los Angeles and Paris do today. The capitulations allowed ambitious foreigners to operate in the region with increasing ease. Through waqfs, residents benefited from subsidized social services. Economic disputes were settled informally through arbitration or formally through courts that rendered judgments quickly.

Just as the region was not viewed as headed for underdevelopment, so until quite late its dominant legal system, Islamic law, was not considered harmful to economic progress. True, certain institutions identified as distinctly Islamic bothered local residents and foreigners alike. However, observers of Islamic law also saw evidence of its pragmatism. Its acceptance of interest-based contracts and interfaith cooperation were just the most obvious examples of business-friendly accommodation. Hence, had this book been written without the benefit of hindsight, from the perspective of a premodern observer, and relying solely on facts that appeared significant before the West achieved global economic domination, Islam's economic infrastructure would have seemed generally unproblematic. By the same token, the reasons why the Middle East fell behind would have remained a mystery. To explain the lag in the region's modernization, and Islam's role in this delay, we have had to focus on aspects of the Middle East's organizational heritage that turned into weaknesses gradually, through transformations elsewhere. We have also had to recognize that locally optimal solutions need not have been globally optimal, just as the highest peak in sight might be dwarfed by mountains beyond the horizon.

To identify those weaknesses and explain their persistence, we have needed to keep track of the mechanisms that fueled the ascent of the West. This methodology of comparative institutional analysis has led to emphases and conclusions that may rattle Middle Eastern specialists who concentrate on a premodern period, or a city's premodern history, without attention to unfolding global patterns. Deliberately ignoring what came later, such historians offer portraits of life in their chosen period and milieu, conveying an appreciation of the prevailing institutions. As in other contexts, ignoring facts that gain salience only later exacts a price: questions of relative and dynamic efficiency are set aside. To comprehend trends spanning centuries and shifts in global rankings, one must identify institutions that made a difference by inhibiting critical transformations. As a practical matter, the task requires tips available only in hindsight.[1] What have we learned, then, about whether Islam mattered to the Middle East's slip into underdevelopment?

How Islam Delayed Economic Modernization

In its early centuries, Islam developed a law of contracts that was sophisticated for the time. Facilitating the pooling of resources across family lines, Islamic partnerships stimulated commerce and helped merchants carry Islam to far corners of the globe. Islamic contract law allowed passive investors to shield their personal assets against liabilities incurred on behalf of the partnership. However, active partners carried full liability. Also, an Islamic partnership lacked entity shielding, in that any member could force its dissolution unilaterally, and its assets were exposed to demands from third parties. The death of a partner terminated the partnership automatically, giving his heirs an immediate claim on a share of the assets; all surviving members incurred costs. The number of heirs could be large, because Islam's inheritance law assigns mandatory shares to designated relatives of the decedent. The partnership termination rule, like the lack of entity shielding, thus discouraged the formation of large and long-lived partnerships. Merchants and investors would form small and short-lived partnerships in order to lessen the risks of untimely dissolution. In allowing polygyny, Islam compounded the incentives to keep partnerships atomistic and ephemeral. This is because merchants with multiple wives tended to have more heirs. Rarely did the business empires of the most successful merchants survive them, because their estates got divided into too many pieces to make recombination practical.

The stagnation in the size and longevity of Middle Eastern partnerships had dynamic consequences. Exchange remained largely personal, removing the need for transformations essential to the modern economy. No demand arose for standardized accounting or a business press. Incentives to trade shares were dampened. Finally, prior to the nineteenth century, oral rather than written contracting remained the norm, and adjudication relied mostly on oral testimony. In sum, several self-enforcing elements of Islamic law—contracting provisions, inheritance system, marriage regulations—jointly contributed to the stagnation of the Middle East's commercial infrastructure. From around the tenth century to the industrial era, commercial enterprises did not gain complexity, as they did in western Europe.

In the nineteenth century, the most heavily capitalized commercial enterprises of the global economy tended to be organized as corporations rather than partnerships. Meant to last indefinitely, they enjoyed legal personhood. The stagnation of the Middle East's commercial infrastructure could have been overcome through business corporations. Two factors precluded this option. For one thing, precisely because of the delay in economic modernization, the preconditions for making business corporations viable were lacking. In the absence of stock markets, standardized bookkeeping, and courts accustomed to large organizations, people would not invest in corporations. For another, the concept of a corporation was alien to Islamic law in general. Although the corporation was known to Middle Easterners even before the seventh century, early Muslims had limited legal standing to natural individuals. Hence, until well into the nineteenth century the corporate form was absent also from other domains of the domestic economy, including urban government, education, and charitable services. The resulting lack of experience made it impossible to introduce the corporation into commerce when the need presented itself. Thus, when technologies of mass production raised the demand for large-scale financing, banks could not be established under Islamic law to mobilize the required resources. Nor could the new technologies be exploited through appropriately capitalized manufacturing enterprises.

In the premodern Middle East, many services now generally provided through corporations were delivered through the waqf, a form of trust. A waqf was established by endowing income-producing property to provide a service in perpetuity. Like a corporation, it could outlive its founder and employees. However, it was not self-governing. Required to abide by its founder's wishes, as recorded in the deed, a waqf could not easily remake its internal rules or modify its objectives. This rigidity reduced its usefulness in the face of structural economic changes. The resulting resource misallocations became increasingly costly over time, because individuals had consistently strong pecuniary motives to establish waqfs. First of all, a founder could appoint himself as the caretaker of his waqf. Second, he could draw a salary for his services, and appoint its staff as well as his own successor. Finally, a widely held belief in the sacredness of its assets made the waqf a credible vehicle for sheltering wealth against arbitrary taxation and expropriation. Largely because of these advantages, vast resources flowed into waqfs. The founders included wealthy merchants. In establishing waqfs, they transferred wealth from a sector in which resources could be deployed flexibly to one in which uses were essentially fixed. They also depressed the already low need to develop more advanced commercial organizations.

None of the institutions that hindered the development of modern organizational forms was developed deliberately to impair commercial life. As far as one can tell, each emerged for other reasons. The provision that an Islamic partnership ended with the death of a partner protected the deceased partner's heirs. Egalitarian rules of the Islamic inheritance system dampened wealth disparities and gave women financial security. Limits on the freedoms of waqf caretakers addressed a principal-agent problem by making it difficult to depart from the founder's wishes. For yet another example, the absence of the corporation limited the destructiveness of tribalism by denying tribes the ability to form legally recognized organizations. As these Islamic provisions took shape more than a millennium ago, no one could have anticipated the evolutionary paths they would foreclose. Indeed, no one foresaw that the institutional evolution of a neighboring region would make it increasingly disadvantageous to conduct business under Islamic law.

Positional Losses against Foreigners and Indigenous Minorities

The organizational stagnation of the Middle East turned it into an underdeveloped region as modern forms of commercial organization emerged elsewhere, along with business practices essential to their viability. Precisely because it spearheaded this process of economic modernization, western Europe came to dominate the global economy. The global explorations that fostered western control over the new world, an explosion in global trade, and the formation of colonial empires all depended, for their financing and execution, on organizational innovations. Thus, the expansion of commerce between western Europe and the Middle East occurred largely at the initiative of western merchants who established trading colonies in the eastern Mediterranean. These expatriate merchants did business under treaties known as capitulations. Their privileges allowed them to have courts of their own, use new financing methods and organizational forms, and settle estates according to European laws. The advantages of operating outside of Islamic law grew in concert with Europe's institutional transformation. Modern banking arrived in the region through consortia headquartered in Europe. Middle Eastern cities started supplying modern utilities through western-style municipalities rather than waqfs, beginning in neighborhoods favored by foreigners.

The rise in the advantages of trading and producing under western institutions coincided with striking economic advances by the region's indigenous Christians and Jews over its Muslim majority. Non-Muslims leapt ahead of Muslims especially in economic sectors requiring major capital outlays: banking, mass communications, mass transport, and mass manufacturing. They did so usually under western legal protection. What enabled non-Muslims to do business under a western legal system was their choice of law in commerce and finance. As the modern economy took shape in western Europe, growing numbers of local Christians and Jews began exercising this long-standing privilege in favor of a western legal system, at least in their dealings with westerners. In the process, they jumped ahead of their Muslim neighbors, who were required to live by Islamic law. In limiting choice of law to non-Muslims, Islamic law thus contributed, inadvertently, to the recorded divergence between the economic fortunes of Muslims and non-Muslims.

Prior to the eighteenth century, the Middle East's minorities tended to do business under Islamic law. Three factors account for this earlier pattern. First, the decisions of Islamic courts were enforced more reliably than those of Christian and Jewish courts.

Second, Islamic law offered substantive advantages to certain groups, such as women, who received more from an estate insofar as the settlement conformed to Islamic inheritance regulations. Third, non-Muslims could exercise their choice of law unilaterally and at will, which meant that an agreement among them could be overturned in an Islamic court. Christian and Jewish legal authorities responded to these varied incentives by adapting their own laws to Islamic law.

Consequently, until the eighteenth century the Middle East's religious minorities generally invested, borrowed, and traded under the dominant legal system of the region. In enjoying all the advantages that Islamic law conferred on Muslims, they also endured the same disadvantages. Therein lies a key reason for the lack of major gaps in economic achievement, prior to the eighteenth century, among the principal religious communities. The sharing of legal practices also had far-reaching dynamic consequences. Until the rise of the West gave minorities new legal options, they found it as difficult as Muslims to accumulate private wealth and to preserve business enterprises across generations. Moreover, they remained as unmotivated to develop complex business organizations.

For around a millennium, then, Islamic legal pluralism kept Middle Eastern minorities, too, from developing advanced economic institutions. If this legal pluralism subsequently turned into a vehicle for modernization and enrichment, the reason lies in the evolution of foreign institutions. Jewish and Christian access to western institutions was intertwined with the progression of the capitulations. As capitulary privileges broadened, the consulates of the European powers began serving indigenous non-Muslims as well. Foreign courts, including those in the Middle East itself, began to accept cases involving local Christians and Jews. This effectively enabled the latter to take advantage of western institutional advances without worrying about the enforceability of their contracts under Islamic law. They could use banks, purchase insurance, and enter into agreements involving various new organizational forms, including joint-stock companies and corporations. In time, these opportunities allowed them to dominate the intermediation between foreign and indigenous merchants. Dealing with Muslims under Islamic law, they interacted with foreigners, and sometimes one another as well, under foreign laws. The arrangement generally suited western banks, shippers, producers, and merchants, who favored dealing with minorities over Muslims simply to avoid lawsuits in Islamic courts. In the late nineteenth century, the largest and most lucrative businesses in Salonika, Istanbul, Izmir, Beirut, and Alexandria, among other commercial hubs of the eastern Mediterranean, were very disproportionately owned and operated by Christians and Jews.

By that time, many Muslim manufacturers, merchants, and financiers, along with local political leaders, recognized the immense handicaps they endured on account of Islamic law. Starting in the mid-nineteenth century they launched successive legal reforms that enabled Muslims to conduct business under alternative institutions. The menu of available organizational forms thus expanded. Also, secular courts emerged to adjudicate conflicts involving modern business practices. Effectively narrowing the jurisdiction of traditional Islamic courts, the new courts set precedents for later curtailments.

The consequent westernization of commercial life in the region could not have eliminated the gap that had opened up between the economic fortunes of Muslims and minorities. For one thing, religious minorities were farther along in capital accumulation, which gave them advantages in the most lucrative economic sectors. For another, they enjoyed incumbency advantages on account of global ties forged over a period when they faced limited Muslim competition. In the nation-states formed in the early twentieth century, including those that emerged from the ashes of the Ottoman Empire, Jews and Christians by and large began with economic advantages stemming from their head start in adapting to new global transformations. That head start was an unintended consequence of an early Islamic institution designed to benefit Muslims: the choice of law accorded to non-Muslim communities who accepted Muslim rule. More than a millennium later, under very different global conditions, Islam's distinct form of legal pluralism turned into an enormous asset for non-Muslims. Indeed, it allowed local Christians and Jews to take advantage of modern economic institutions more than a century before Muslims began joining them en masse, as a result of legal reforms.

Early and Late Islamic Institutions

Of the institutions that played prominent roles in the Middle East's slip into underdevelopment, several are traceable to Islam's canonical Age of Felicity: the Quranic rules of inheritance, the permissibility of polygyny, the ban on *ribā*, the absence of the concept of corporation, choice of law for non-Muslims, the prohibition of apostasy, and the absence of Muslim merchant organizations. The remaining key institutions were born after Islam's initial few decades, or their development lasted much longer. The latter group includes Islamic contract law, which took shape over several centuries; the waqf, which emerged as a well-defined and distinctly Islamic institution in the eighth century; the Islamic court system, whose procedures took form gradually; and the capitulations, which Muslim rulers started to extend to foreign merchants early in the second millennium (table 14.1).

Under a restrictive definition of what qualifies as "Islamic," institutions in the latter group might appear as deviations from

TABLE 14.1
Islamic Institutions that Helped to Delay Economic Modernization

Present in Islam's first few decades	Developed mostly or entirely after Islam's initial period
Inheritance system	Contract law
Acceptance of polygyny	Waqf
Ban on *ribā*	Court system
Absence of corporation	Capitulations
Choice of law limited to non-Muslims	
Prohibition of apostasy	
Absence of merchant organizations	

Islam, or as contextually and temporally specific Muslim responses divorced from Islam's essence. Indeed, the capitulations are now widely condemned as both a strategic mistake and profoundly un-Islamic. Some Islamists reject the waqf as a perversion that allowed the circumvention of inheritance rules. Nothing in Islam limits the menu of commercial organizations to those enshrined in Islamic contract law, or fixes the procedures of Islamic courts. On such grounds the shortcomings of Muslim empires, including those of the Umayyads, Abbasids, Fatimids, Seljuks, Ottomans, and Safavids, are sometimes dismissed as irrelevant to the question of whether Islam contributed to the Middle East's economic backwardness. Likewise, the idea that institutions in the first category might have had negative economic effects is dismissed out of hand because no Muslim-governed state, except possibly the earliest, has implemented them uncompromisingly.

Such dismissals are akin to arguing that, because the Soviet Union failed to eliminate private property, its record says nothing about the economic merits of communism. To take them seriously would amount to abandoning meaningful social analysis. One cannot compare civilizations or institutional complexes if all data on their performance are considered too contaminated to yield reliable answers on causality. Whatever the analytic challenges, there is a huge demand, within and outside the region we call the Middle East as a short-hand, for insights into the question of whether the original institutions of Islam posed permanent obstacles to economic advancement or modernization, in themselves. Are the Islamic institutions in our first category—those known to Muhammad and the early caliphs—compatible with modern economic life?

Inheritance System

The Islamic inheritance system delayed organizational modernization only because, with the corporation precluded, the partnership remained the only possible starting point for developing durable and large commercial organizations. It is not inherently incompatible with modern organizational forms. Once partnerships with tradable shares and the corporation joined the menu of available organizational options, the Islamic inheritance system ceased to undermine enterprise continuity or longevity. Consider a corporation operating in a country that continues to practice the Islamic inheritance system. The corporation's ownership is divided into ten thousand shares. The owner of two thousand of these shares dies, prompting their division among his ten heirs, two hundred shares for each. This division need not make any difference to the survival of this corporation. Heirs who prefer cash to shares may transfer their entitlements without endangering the company.[2]

Marriage Regulations

By the same logic, polygyny need not harm enterprise continuity or longevity once modern organizational forms and their infrastructure exist. Ordinarily it makes no difference to a company's survival whether a given bloc of its shares belongs to one wife or is subdivided among four.

Opposition to Interest

The third of the seven problematic institutions present from the beginning, the ban on *ribā*, was a steady irritant to suppliers and users of credit. By requiring the use of stratagems, it raised credit costs. But the added costs must have been small. In any case, the ban never prevented transactions involving interest. If financial markets of the Middle East failed to modernize except through institutional transplants from the West, the reason is not, then, that dealing in interest was considered un-Islamic. Rather, obstacles to forming modern business organizations in general precluded the emergence of banks and stock markets. Just as inheritance systems based on Quranic directives continue to be practiced, today certain countries treat interest as illegal in principle. However, nowhere do Muslims find it difficult to borrow for a fee that amounts to interest. Also in major countries of the Middle East the capitalization of stock markets has been growing at double-digit rates.[3] The very fact that the late twentieth century saw the emergence of a massive "Islamic finance" sector testifies to the lack of any fundamental incompatibility between the ban on *ribā* and modern finance.[4]

Although Islamic banks ostensibly do only interest-free business, in reality they give and take interest through means resembling the stratagems used in medieval financial markets.

The Corporation

That the Islamic legal system emerged without a concept of corporation contributed to keeping Middle Eastern businesses atomistic. However, the Quran contains no explicit statement against the corporation, so if a demand for the corporate form had emerged and its institutional preconditions were in place, it could have been adopted without difficulty. In fact, as global modernization fostered an awareness of the corporation's uses, countries of the Middle East absorbed it into their domestic legal systems. The rapid diffusion of the corporate form signals that its absence from Islam's original organizational menu did not pose an insurmountable obstacle to its discovery or emulation later on. The lack of Islamist opposition to the corporation strengthens the point.

Choice of Law

The fifth original institution, choice of law, might have benefited the region by making courts compete for clients. In fact, in restricting Muslim options, allowing Islamic law to trump the legal systems of non-Muslims, and permitting anyone to sue in Islamic court at will, it depressed the competition faced by Islamic courts. This did not pose an appreciable handicap as long as economic life under Islamic law remained sophisticated by global standards. However, in time western institutional developments turned the prevailing choice of law into an instrument of economic advancement for minorities. Thus, the region as a whole benefited from the opportunities it provided for doing business under western institutions. On the downside, in limiting the new opportunities to Christians and Jews, faith-based legal rights caused Muslims to fall behind economically. Islam's distinct form of legal pluralism did play a major role, then, in the region's observed economic trajectory. However, it is no longer a significant contributor to economic performance. The establishment of nation-states with unitary legal systems, various institutional reforms, and the emigration of minorities has turned Islamic legal pluralism into an anachronism.

Apostasy

Both the Quran and the remembered sayings of Prophet Muhammad contain references to apostasy as a religious offense. On the basis of these references, Muslim jurists of the seventh century declared apostasy punishable by death. The severity of this punishment doubtless contributed to the outcomes of Islamic legal pluralism. In making it practically impossible for Muslims to do business under a non-Muslim legal system, or to take their disputes to a non-Muslim judge, Islam's apostasy law contributed to the economic ascent of the Middle Eastern religious minorities. Starting in the eighteenth century, it helped non-Muslims jump ahead by preventing Muslims from switching legal jurisdiction. Previously the same law contributed to keeping the various communities more or less equal in economic performance by ensuring that they all did business under the same institutions.

The Muslims of the Middle East began to embrace modern economic institutions collectively, through legal reforms spearheaded by governments. Christians and Jews were able to do so as individuals, simply by exercising their customary choice of law. Since those institutions have now been transplanted and are not controversial, does the apostasy law still matter to the Middle East's economic performance? Insofar as it makes Muslims refrain from proposing bold reforms, from criticizing policies and institutions identified with Islam, and from exerting pressure on conservative clerics, Islam's apostasy law must be retarding the region's economic development.

Merchant Organizations

The final problematic pattern that was present at the birth of Islam is the absence of merchant organizations serving them in foreign lands. Initially, this did not represent a handicap for Muslims in global markets, for nowhere else were merchants organized. It became a handicap in the Mediterranean trading emporium as western merchants formed guilds and then appointed consuls to represent and guide them. The lack of the corporate form and the persistent simplicity of Islamic partnerships hindered the emergence of Middle Eastern merchant organizations later. Such organizations would not have had to be created from scratch had they been part of Islam's original institutional complex. Now, of course, chambers of commerce and associations of industrialists exist throughout the Middle East. So the last of the original handicaps no longer remains an obstacle to economic development.

Summary

To recapitulate, the question of whether Islam's original institutions are compatible with modern economic life admits no categorical answer. The unavailability of merchant organizations and the corporate form became increasingly disadvantageous over time, and in any modern economy they would be crippling. However, the handicaps in question have been overcome through institutions alien to early Islamic civilization. Islam's distinct form of legal pluralism and its apostasy law also turned into sources of disadvantage as the global environment evolved. If they were enforced strictly today, Muslims would lack the flexibility to borrow institutions from abroad, and the region's economic performance would suffer. But legal practices have become westernized, and no serious obstacles now exist to further legal transplants. By the same token, the punishability of apostasy continues to limit flexibility and creativity.

Along with traditional institutions that are incompatible with economic success in the modern world, there are those that pose no significant problems. The Islamic inheritance system and its marriage regulations jointly hindered indigenous organizational modernization, but once modern organizations were transplanted from abroad, they ceased to harm economic performance. The ban on *ribā* never had much influence on economic behavior in the first place, and its current impact remains negligible.

Islam and the Persistence of Underdevelopment

With the possible exception of the Islamic apostasy law, not one of the institutions that turned the Middle East into an economic laggard by delaying its organizational modernization remains an obstacle to economic development in the twenty-first century. Reforms of the nineteenth and twentieth centuries allow the region's peoples to borrow from banks, invest in stock markets, establish corporations pursuing a wide range of objectives, and protect themselves from undocumented financial claims, among sundry other privileges of modernity.[5] Yet, the Middle East remains an economically backward region. Might this book have overlooked certain deeper causes of backwardness? Could economic underdevelopment have become a chronic condition because organizational capabilities were never critical in the first place? Even if the processes identified and analyzed in earlier chapters were once significant, the region's institutional history could well be irrelevant to explaining current patterns. My answer consists of three parts, each involving "path dependence"—the persistence of historical influences. A summary is given in table 14.2.

Missing Complementary Institutions

First of all, only a subset of the institutional complementarities critical to the effectiveness of particular reforms could be borrowed from abroad. Indeed, transplanting a legal code, organizational form, or business technique is not the same thing as appropriating the social system that produced, refined, and sustained it. The performance of a borrowed institution necessarily depends on preexisting local institutions, including norms and understandings. It depends also on capabilities of the receiving community.[6] Consider the transplant to the Middle East, starting in the 1850s, of commercial courts modeled after those of France. The judges appointed to serve on Turkish and Egyptian commercial courts did not become proficient at applying the French commercial code overnight. It took time to train competent lawyers. Local norms of fairness and liability did not change instantly. Only slowly did the notion

TABLE 14.2
How the Middle East's Institutional History Limits Its Present Economic
Performance

Obstacles to full modernization	Historical roots
1. Incomplete reforms	Modern organizational forms have been transplanted into societies with social norms inimical to their efficient use: relatively high corruption and nepotism, and low trust in organizations. These norms are among the legacies of traditional Islamic law.
2. Political systems with low capacity for innovation and experimentation	The weaknesses of private sectors and civil societies, which are rooted in the region's institutional history, breed complacency toward autocratic rule.
3. Economically counterproductive reactions to underdevelopment	Economic failures have created fertile ground for (a) inward-looking ideologies that limit adaptation to changing global realities and (b) Islamism, which fosters political uncertainty and limits experimentation in certain areas.

of attributing responsibility for an adverse externality to a judicial person, as opposed to a natural individual or group, take root in the region's legal culture.[7] If nepotism and judicial corruption have remained rampant, this is partly because at the time of the reforms state employees were accustomed to personalizing exchanges involving judicial persons. As officials, they dealt with the employees of other organizations as individuals rather than as functionaries representing an organization. To a greater extent than in parts of the world that modernized earlier, the pattern has persisted.

No reliable data exist on the extent of corruption in the 1850s. A source of data for recent years is the "Corruption Perceptions Index" of Transparency International, an organization that monitors the business climate in most countries. According to this index, businessmen consider corruption, defined as the abuse of public office for private gain, a greater problem in the Middle East than in western Europe. In 2009, on a zero to ten scale running from "least clean" to "most clean" government, the five most populous countries of western Europe received a population-weighted average score of 6.7 (Germany 8.0, United Kingdom 7.7, France 6.9, Spain 6.5, Italy 4.3). The corresponding average for the three most populous countries of the Middle East was 3.0 (Turkey 4.4, Egypt 2.8, Iran 1.8).[8] Modifying the region's business practices has proved more difficult than rewriting its formal laws.

These chronic problems are not independent of the mechanisms highlighted in this book. The judges appointed to serve on specialized commercial courts lacked proficiency because centuries of organizational stagnation removed the need for judges equipped with more sophisticated skills. There existed no law schools in the modern sense, because exchange remained largely personal, and a training in Islamic law remained adequate to handle the disputes that arose commonly among people transacting under traditional Islamic institutions. The region's commercial norms had co-evolved with its traditional organizational forms, contracting instruments, and means of enforcement. The prevalence of corruption is itself rooted in old patterns. Centuries of efforts to overcome inflexibilities of the waqf through illicit means contributed to what one may call a "culture of corruption"—norms of state-subject interaction involving nepotism, bribery, and rule bending as a matter of course. In the modern era, the Middle East's culture of corruption has undermined campaigns to modify and strengthen the rule of law.

Weak Civil Society

The second part of the answer to the question of whether the institutional history interpreted in previous chapters matters to the Middle East's present economic failures involves mechanisms that constrain present political possibilities. In addition to stimulating corruption, the waqf system helped to keep civil society weak through several channels: tying the hands of the caretakers who managed vast resources, disallowing mergers that might have facilitated political coalitions beyond direct state control, and requiring waqfs to remain apolitical. That the Middle East began to modernize without a strong civil society made it easier for states to take the lead in the development of sectors that might have advanced through decentralized private initiatives. The Middle East's initial indigenous banks provide a case in point: states founded them with foreign help.

The state-centered development programs prevalent in the region have been criticized for limiting private enterprise through over-regulation and mis-regulation. Yet, state-centrism, and the associated insensitivity to the needs of merchants, gained currency because the states formed after World War I had weak private sectors to start with; and that weakness itself was a legacy of Islam's traditional institutional complex. Whatever the accomplishments of state-centered development programs, they have reinforced the prevailing weaknesses of civil society. Furthermore, they have fostered a suspicion of organized dissent and political decentralization, both essential to self-correction and self-generated innovation. The commonness of autocratic rule in the region stands, then, among the continuing legacies of traditional Islamic law.

The very condition of sustained economic underdevelopment has created obstacles to reform. Making the region chronically vulnerable to foreign meddling, and many individual countries ever dependent on foreign protection, it has bred complacency toward autocracy. This complacency has rested on fears that steps toward democracy, by exposing suppressed political cleavages and inviting further foreign interference, could cause political instability and economic retrenchment.

At the start of the twentieth century, almost all large commercial enterprises in the Middle East were owned by either foreigners or religious minorities, both because various Islamic institutions hindered private capital accumulation and because Muslims embraced modern economic institutions with a lag. With the shrinkage of these entrepreneurial communities through nationalist movements partial to Muslims, population exchanges (most importantly, the Turkish-Greek population exchange of 1922–23), and emigrations associated with the founding of Israel, in the twentieth century the Islamic Middle East's private sectors tried to accumulate physical and human capital from low bases.[9]

Reactions to Economic Failures

We arrive, finally, at a third reason for why the Middle East's institutional history has cast a shadow on the present. In sowing social dislocations and political insecurities, the region's traditional legal system has induced economically harmful reactions to economic failures. In particular, the Middle East's loss of economic standing created fertile ground for the spread of economically protectionist ideologies, such as Turkish statism and Arab socialism. Over a longer time span it also triggered the rise of Islamism—the diffuse global movement that aims to restore the primacy of traditional Islam by shielding Muslims from selected transformative influences of globalization.[10] Inward-looking secular ideologies have done harm by reducing intellectual and economic competition, thereby discouraging innovation. For its part, in promoting the notion of an inexorable clash of civilizations, Islamism has fostered political uncertainty, which is inimical to investment.[11] It has induced policy makers and business leaders, including secularists, to eschew reforms, such as veritable freedom of the press, that might subject them to charges of impiety. It has also provided pretexts for intellectual suppression and hostility to experimentation. Islam's age-old prohibition of apostasy has compounded the resulting conservatism, all the more so in countries whose political regimes draw legitimacy from Islam.

By no means have the economic effects of Islamism been uniformly negative. Movements that fall under the Islamist rubric have stimulated various services to economically marginalized groups ill-served by state bureaucracies.[12] In any case, Islamists aim to restore premodern economic relations in only certain areas. They have little quarrel with the corporate form, or transfers of company shares through stock markets, or modern accounting, or publications that provide commercial intelligence, among other economic novelties of the past two centuries. Their opposition to economic modernization focuses on a few pet issues: the immorality of interest and insurance, the unfairness of certain inequalities, the mixing of sexes that accompanies tourism, and the destructiveness of unregulated advertising and consumerism. Even on these matters, Islamists are divided among themselves, with some accepting modern practices that others condemn as un-Islamic.[13] With the possible exception of the Taliban in Afghanistan, even militantly anti-modern Islamists have failed to restore economic patterns prevalent prior to the nineteenth century.

The Enduring Performance Gap

In remaining economically underdeveloped throughout the modern era, the Middle East has not stood still. Undergoing massive transformations in the twentieth century, it registered growth rates in line with the West.[14] To overcome underdevelopment it would have had to grow relatively faster, as Japan did, followed by other countries of East Asia. The region's institutional heritage, poor policy choices necessitated by that heritage, and assorted reactions, including Islamism, have all contributed to maintaining the gap that opened up centuries ago.

Islam and the Capacity for Change

For the Middle East, as for the rest of the non-western world, the economic transformation of the West presented both an immense problem and a golden opportunity. On the one hand, it created a host of military, political, and cultural challenges. On the other, it allowed the region to modernize in a hurry simply by borrowing institutions that in the West took shape in fits and starts, over many centuries. The Middle East was able to borrow modern institutions in their most advanced forms, without accepting "historical baggage"—collateral institutions that had outlived their usefulness.[15] From such observations one may infer, as some have, that something has denied the region the necessary flexibility. Could a conservative religious ethos that fosters resistance to learning and borrowing from abroad be a fundamental cause of why the catch-up process remains incomplete almost two centuries after the region set out to modernize economically? That possibility is worth reconsidering.

Were conservatism per se a significant factor, adjustments would lag across the board. In fact, the Middle East has undergone massive institutional changes over the past two centuries. In some places, beginning with the Republic of Turkey in the 1920s, Islamic law was abrogated in its entirety. Where it survived, as in the Arabian peninsula, it has been modified beyond recognition in areas of relevance here.[16] Now the corporation is not only acceptable but a popular organizational form. Banks form an integral component of every economy. Shares trade hands daily in Middle Eastern stock markets. Were an eighteenth-century merchant to come back to life, he would be impressed not by the sameness of Muslim economic practices but, rather, by the massive changes that took place over a span of two centuries.

Skeptics might point to the centuries of organizational stagnation that preceded the recent modernization as evidence of entrenched conservatism. They could add that the reforms came as a result of foreign prodding. If a sixteenth-century merchant came alive two centuries later, prior to the start of reforms, he would have been struck by the familiarity of the prevailing forms of contract, credit practices, and investment instruments. Yet military practices would have changed dramatically. The Ottoman Empire adjusted and readjusted its weaponry, tactics of warfare, and military organization.[17] Hence, it is not resistance to change itself that would have accounted for the sameness of commercial and financial practices. As this book has shown, key commercial and financial institutions were self-enforcing and mutually reinforcing. Jointly they generated incentives that prevented indigenous economic modernization, even as successive reforms took place in other domains, including the state bureaucracy.[18]

When economic modernization took off in the nineteenth century, states were in the lead on various fronts. The founding in 1851 of Şirket-i Hayriye, the Istanbul-based maritime transportation company, furnishes one example. The Ottoman and Egyptian adoptions of the French commercial code a few years later provide another. Still another consists of the establishment, again in the 1850s, of mainly foreign-funded state banks in the Ottoman Empire and Egypt, using transplanted organizational templates. Sizable literatures exist on all such state-driven reforms, partly because the relevant archival evidence is abundant and easily accessed. Far less studied and understood is that demands from below—from merchants, financiers, and investors—stimulated and shaped the modernization process. Communities all across the region invited banks to establish local branches.[19] Complaints about the inadequacies of traditional institutions, including courts, fostered a climate of opinion conducive to borrowing foreign commercial institutions.[20] At the founding of Şirket-i Hayriye, local Christians and Jews were already using modern organizational forms, and Muslims began doing so once complementary institutions fell into place.

These transformations reconfirm that communities of the region possessed a capacity for change. As the evolution of western economic institutions caused an increasingly visible divergence of living standards, first between Middle Easterners and westerners and then among religious communities within the Middle East itself, the urgency of reforms gained increasing acceptance. If major commercial centers led the way, one reason is that these twin contrasts were most glaring there. Two centuries earlier the motivation for institutional change was lacking even in the largest and most cosmopolitan cities. The region's traditional institutions removed the need for fundamental reforms, and the Middle East was not yet manifestly poorer.

It was not lost on anyone that the institutions transplanted to the Middle East had originated in Christian Europe. Although opposition arose to changes involving family life, gender relations, social hierarchies, and matters of identity, opposition to economic transplants has generally been insignificant. The anti-interest movement that spawned Islamic banking took off in the mid-twentieth century for reasons of identity protection rather than a commitment to traditional economic life.[21] Today, very few Muslims seek earnestly to purge interest from their economic transactions. Furthermore, even that minority is comfortable with modern banking, which has foreign origins. In sum, on economic matters the Middle East has demonstrated, time and again, that it can take advantage of new opportunities, including ones that emerge in secular realms and in overwhelmingly non-Muslim countries.

That Islam is compatible with cross-civilizational and cross-religious institutional borrowing is evident also in the origins of the principles, rules, and regulations that formed classical Islamic law. Most of these grew out of the Middle East's preexisting institutions, including those of the Romans, Persians, and the pagan, Jewish, and Christian tribes of Arabia. Even though many generations of Muslim interpreters have colluded to obfuscate the foreign origins of classical Islamic law, in fact it represented a vast, and in some respects magnificent, synthesis.

The Past and the Future

The foregoing interpretations carry an optimistic message for the future of the Islamic Middle East. They also carry a pessimistic message for its performance in today's global economy.

To start with the bad news, the region cannot be lifted from its present state of underdevelopment in a hurry. In leaving its private sectors and civil societies weak for centuries, the Middle East's premodern institutions set the stage for today's bloated state bureaucracies and, in many places, government policies and social norms harmful to creativity. Consequently, with a few exceptions, the countries of the region are uncompetitive in the global marketplace for industrial products and services; and, again with few exceptions, their civil societies are too poorly organized, and too beaten down, to provide the political checks and balances essential to sustained democratic rule. If the region's autocratic regimes were magically to fall, the development of strong private sectors and civil societies could take decades. Trust in strangers and in organizations, essential to impersonal exchange, is low by today's global standards; this stands as an obstacle to efficient economic cooperation. Also, new regimes would inherit bureaucracies accustomed to corruption.

Another unresolved difficulty is that, in spite of deep institutional reforms that implicitly recognized the unsuitability of classical Islamic law to modern needs, the region as a whole has not yet come to terms with the reasons why it turned into an economic laggard. The idea that outsiders are somehow responsible for the Middle East's underdevelopment resonates with much of the population, including secularists who consider Islamic law backward and obsolete. In particular, the role of classical Islamic law in blocking organizational modernization and stultifying Middle Eastern, and particularly Muslim, enterprise is hardly understood. This situation limits the rhetorical toolkit of Middle Eastern proponents of globalization and modernization. It also sustains sterile debates about the virtues of embracing Islam for solutions to poverty, mismanagement, and powerlessness. Not even the typical Islamist appreciates the limitations of Islamic law (generally known as the *sharī'a*) as a basis for social, economic, and political order in the twenty-first century.

The good news is that the region borrowed the key economic institutions of modern capitalism sufficiently long ago to make them seem un-foreign, and thus culturally acceptable, even to a self-consciously anti-modern Islamist. These institutions can be improved, recombined, and applied to new domains creatively without opposing Islam as a religion, or even dealing with it. They can be debated essentially in isolation from public controversies over what Islam represents and its relevance to the present. Furthermore, Islamic economic history offers abundant precedents for promoting free enterprise and limiting the government's economic role. In no period has private enterprise been lacking. Widely admired empires had shallow governments that left to waqfs the provision of social welfare, education, and urban amenities. A predominantly Muslim society is not inherently incompatible, then, with an economy based on free competition, openness to borrowing and innovation, and a government eager to support, rather than stifle, private enterprise.

Notes

～

CHAPTER 1. THE PUZZLE OF THE MIDDLE EAST'S
ECONOMIC UNDERDEVELOPMENT

1. Maddison, *World Economy*, pp. 51–52, estimates that in 1000 income levels in Europe were below those of Asia and North Africa.

2. Pamuk, "Urban Real Wages," tables 2, 3. For further indices, see Zanden, *Long Road*, pp. 270–74.

3. Pamuk, "Economic Growth since 1820." According to Angus Maddison's global per capita income comparisons (*Monitoring the World Economy*, table 1.3), in 1913 per capita income was $3,482 in the major industrialized countries, as against $979 in Turkey and $508 in Egypt (all in 1990 dollars).

4. Özmucur and Pamuk, "Standards of Living," table 1; Owen and Pamuk, *Middle East Economies*, p. 231. For further details on trends in Arab countries in particular, see Rivlin, *Arab Economies*.

5. For additional comparative statistics, see Rivlin, *Arab Economies*, especially chap. 4.

6. This definition is drawn from Berman, *Law and Revolution*, p. 2. Areas subsequently settled largely by westerners, such as North America, became part of the West.

7. The rationale for using this definition is that the analysis focuses on institutions. Muslim expansions into Spain and the Balkans imparted to these lands institutions characteristic of economic life under Islamic rule.

8. For an advanced treatment of the general definition, see Greif, *Institutions*, especially pp. 14–23.

9. İnalcık, *Ottoman Empire*, chap. 10; Gerber, *State, Society, and Law*, chaps. 1–4.

10. Imber, *Ebu's-Suʿud*; Düzdağ, *Ebussuûd Efendi Fetvaları*.

11. According to Daniel Lerner, an influential modernization theorist, Muslims have had to choose between "Mecca" and "mechanization." One of their options is to shed conservative attitudes rooted in religion and embark on modernization, another to uphold traditional Islam and remain mired in superstition. See his *Passing of Traditional Society*, p. 405.

12. Patai, *Arab Mind*, p. 310; Murray, *Human Accomplishment*, pp. 399–401.

13. In the World Values Survey, the question about perceived freedom of choice is viewed as an indicator of fatalism. On a 0–10 scale, low values connote fatalism and high values a feeling of self-control. In surveys conducted between 1999 and 2004 (http://www.worldvaluessurvey.org), the range of the means for Arab countries (5.47–7.26) overlapped substantially with those of OECD countries

(6.00–7.98). For interpretations, see Ajrouch and Moaddel, "Social Structure versus Perception"; and Acevedo, "Islamic Fatalism."

14. Hennigan, *Birth of Legal Institution*; Udovitch, *Partnership and Profit*.

15. Goldberg, "Origins of *Majālis al-Tujjār*."

16. Clay, "Modern Banking," especially p. 592.

17. The invention of tradition is a common phenomenon. See, generally, Hobsbawm and Ranger, *Invention of Tradition*; and Cowen, *Creative Destruction*.

18. Kuran, *Islam and Mammon*, pp. 7–19, 43–49; El-Gamal, *Islamic Finance*, pp. 7–25.

19. Mardin, *Young Ottoman Thought*, chaps. 3–6; Berkes, *Development of Secularism*, chaps. 12–14; Marsot, *Reign of Muhammad Ali*, especially chap. 8. For related insights, see also Curtin, *World and the West*, especially pp. 109–10.

20. Easterlin, *Growth Triumphant*, chap. 2. See also Maddison, *World Economy*, chap. 1.

21. United Nations Development Programme, *Arab Human Development Report 2002*, pp. 27–29.

22. Fischer, *Historians' Fallacies*, p. 178.

23. Diamond, *Guns, Germs, and Steel*.

24. Makdisi, *Rise of Colleges*; Huff, *Early Modern Science*, chaps. 5–6, 9; Mokyr, *Lever of Riches*, chaps. 7–11.

25. Faroqhi, *Approaching Ottoman History*, pp. 49–50, notes that the Ottoman central archives constitute by far the major resources for Ottoman historians. The organization of these archives reflects the administrative division of the Empire.

26. From different angles, Hayek, *Law, Legislation and Liberty*, and Scott, *Seeing Like a State*, explain how centrally managed social agendas get derailed by unfathomably complex social interdependencies.

27. Genç, *Devlet ve Ekonomi*, especially chaps. 3–4, 21.

28. Darling, *Revenue-Raising*; Coşgel, "Efficiency and Continuity."

29. Balla and Johnson, "Fiscal Crisis," develop this theme in comparing the fiscal capacity of the Ottoman Empire with that of France. See also Hoffman, Postel-Vinay, and Rosenthal, *Priceless Markets*, especially pp. 176, 286–91, who show how the modernization of French financial markets preceded various government reforms critical to economic performance.

30. Amin, *Arab Nation*, chap. 2; Ahmad, *Plagued by the West*; Avcıoğlu, *Millî Kurtuluş Tarihi*, vol. 1.

31. Greif, *Institutions*, chap. 10; North, *Process of Economic Change*, pp. 70–71.

32. Braude and Lewis, eds., *Christians and Jews*.

33. Based on figures in Behar, *Population of Ottoman Empire*, tables 1.2, 2.7; and Bakhit, "Christian Population of Damascus," table 2-5.

34. Clay, "Modern Banking."

Chapter 2. Analyzing the Economic Role of Islam

1. The story has been told many times. The most influential accounts include Mardin, *Young Ottoman Thought*; Berkes, *Development of Secularism*; Hourani, *Arabic Thought*; and Lewis, *What Went Wrong?*

2. Findley, *Bureaucratic Reform*, pp. 3–4.

3. This is consistent with the growing emphasis on justifying state policies through references to Islamic principles, and with the rising importance of the *şeyhülislam*, or chief Islamic officer. See İnalcık, *Ottoman Empire*, chap. 12.

4. This literature was initiated by North, *Structure and Change*. See also Greif, *Institutions*; Platteau, *Institutions*, chaps. 6–7; and Aoki, *Comparative Institutional Analysis*.

5. On the properties of social mechanisms and their analytical uses, see Hedström and Swedberg, eds., *Social Mechanisms*. The concepts discussed in this section are developed also by Elster, *Nuts and Bolts*, chaps. 10–16; and Coleman, *Foundations*. They are applied to historical phenomena by Bates et al., *Analytic Narratives*; and in my own *Private Truths, Public Lies*.

6. For variants of such interpretations, see Ülgener, *Zihniyet ve Din*, especially pp. 87–92; Landes, *Wealth and Poverty*, p. 398.

7. The evolution of every civilization has featured such surprises. For examples, see Lal, *Unintended Consequences*.

8. Hazlitt, *Economics in One Lesson*, pp. 3–4. Friedrich Hayek expounds on this tendency in his *Law, Legislation and Liberty*, especially chaps. 3, 9, 11, 18.

9. Landes, *Wealth and Poverty*, chaps. 4, 24. In concert with these interpretations, he claims (p. 215) that "in big things, history abhors accident."

10. See Gutas, *Greek Thought, Arabic Culture* on the translation movement in Abbasid Baghdad; Turner, *Science in Medieval Islam*, pp. 44–46, on the appropriation of Indian numerals and Hindu arithmetic; Bloom, *Paper before Print*, chap. 2, on the spread of papermaking across Islamic lands; and Ashtor, *Economic History*, pp. 95–112, on the adoption of diverse Chinese, Persian, and Byzantine commodities and production methods.

11. On path dependence generally, see Arthur, *Increasing Returns*; and David, "Institutions." On its significance for economic history in particular, see North, *Institutions*, especially chaps. 10–11.

12. Aghion and Howitt, *Endogenous Growth Theory*, chaps. 6, 9.

13. Acemoglu, Johnson, and Robinson, "Rise of Europe," use the same logic in explaining how British and Dutch merchants, once rich through Atlantic trade, gained political power and brought about political transformations that strengthened private property rights.

14. Marx, *Capital*; Darwin, *Origin of Species*.

15. Ashtor, *Social and Economic History*, especially chap. 7; Dols, *Black Death*, chap. 7.

16. Wallerstein, *Capitalist World-Economy*, especially pp. 26–30.

17. The West was not immune to outside developments. As İyigün, "Luther and Süleyman," shows, Ottoman advances in central Europe had political consequences throughout the continent.

18. Greif, *Institutions*, chap. 6, defines these terms formally. See also Rubin, "Lender's Curse," pp. 59–68.

19. This theme appears in studies of European and Latin American institutional evolution. See Engerman and Sokoloff, "Differential Paths of Growth"; Acemoglu, Johnson, and Robinson, "Reversal of Fortune."

20. Abdul-Rauf, *Muslim's Reflections*, pp. 21–22. See also Mawdudi, *Rise and Decline*; and Haffar, "Economic Development in Islam."

21. According to the best estimates available, between 1000 and 1820, per capita GDP in the Middle East fell slightly (Maddison, *Contours of World Economy*, table 4.3). The annual increase averaged 0.4% in 1820–70 and 0.7% in 1870–1913 (Pamuk, "Estimating Economic Growth," table 1). In each of these estimates the Middle East is defined to exclude North Africa and the Balkan peninsula.

22. Weber, *Economy and Society*, especially pp. 1231–34. For fuller analyses that build on his insight, see Cahen, "Corporations Professionelles"; and Stern, "Constitution of Islamic City."

23. Weber, *Economy and Society*, especially pp. 623–27.

24. Rodinson, *Islam and Capitalism*, pp. 12–14. Such verses of the Quran include 2:198, 28:77, 62:10.

25. Khan, *Teachings of Prophet Muhammad*, p. 36.

26. Rodinson, *Islam and Capitalism*, pp. 16–17.

27. Rodinson, *Islam and Capitalism*, pp. 28–35. For similar logic, see Akbar, "Ideology, Environment."

28. Hanna, *Making Big Money*, p. 59. For a similar focus on local optimality, see Gerber, *Islamic Law and Culture*, especially chaps. 3–5.

CHAPTER 3. COMMERCIAL LIFE UNDER ISLAMIC RULE

1. Rodinson, *Muhammad*, pp. 49–50.

2. Engineer, *Development of Islam*, pp. 33–35; Akbar, "Ideology, Environment," p. 139.

3. Finley, *Ancient Economy*, chap. 2; D'Arms, *Commerce and Social Standing*, chaps. 1–2, 7.

4. Quran 2:198, 28:77, 62:10.

5. Quran 2:197–98.

6. See, for example, Kamal, *Sacred Journey*; Sardar and Badawi, eds., *Hajj Studies*. A partial exception is Long, *Hajj Today*, chap. 6, which recognizes the event's contributions to the economy of Saudi Arabia.

7. Peters, *Hajj*, especially pp. 180–83, 291–93; Faroqhi, *Pilgrims and Sultans*, especially chap. 1.

8. Jews traveled to Jerusalem on sacred days to express religious devotion and strengthen communal consciousness (Safrai, "Pilgrimage," pp. 510–13). Christians went on pilgrimages to the Holy Land and other venerated places, usually to atone sins, cure an illness, or acquire relics (Sumption, *Pilgrimage*; Oursel, *Pèlerins du Moyen Age*; Coleman and Elsner, *Pilgrimage*, chaps. 4–5).

9. Quran 2:198.

10. Goitein, *Studies in Islamic History*, p. 8.

11. Crone, *Meccan Trade*, especially chaps. 1 and 6; Simon, *Meccan Trade*, especially chap. 1; Ibrahim, *Merchant Capital and Islam*, chap. 2.

12. Donner, "Mecca's Food Supplies."

13. Simon, *Meccan Trade*, chaps. 2–3.

14. Magnitudes were subject to renegotiation as conditions changed. See Faroqhi, *Pilgrims and Sultans*, chaps. 2–3, 7; and Barbir, *Ottoman Rule in Damascus,* chap. 3. Additional subsidies traditionally went to Mecca's underclass to

prevent disruptions of the huge bazaar formed in the pilgrimage season (Uzun-çarşılı, *Mekke-i Mükerreme Emirleri*, chap. 9). Insofar as these efforts were effective, their regimes gained legitimacy in the eyes of Muslims (Farooqi, "Moguls, Ottomans, and Pilgrims"; Brummett, *Ottoman Seapower*, especially chaps. 3–4).

15. See Faroqhi, *Pilgrims and Sultans*, pp. 46–47, which provides additional estimates from the Ottoman era.

16. In the thirteenth century the Seljuks operated an annual international fair known as the Yabanlu Bazaar (Bazaar of the Foreigners) at the intersection of several caravan routes (Sümer, *Yabanlu Pazarı*). In the Ottoman Empire, the sixteenth and seventeenth centuries saw the development of minor fairs along trade routes (Faroqhi, "Crisis and Change," especially pp. 489–93). Larger fairs were established in the eighteenth and nineteenth centuries, with state support (Şen, *Osmanlı Panayırları*). None produced institutional innovations of significance to the Middle East's economic trajectory.

17. Pirenne, *Economic and Social History*, especially pp. 96–102; Verlinden, "Markets and Fairs." On the institutions of the Champagne fairs, see also Greif, *Institutions*, pp. 328–38; Benson, "Spontaneous Evolution"; and Hunt and Murray, *History of Business*, chap. 4.

18. Chandler, *Scale and Scope*, pp. 389–92, develops such arguments in relation to family-owned British firms of the late nineteenth century, which grew more slowly than American firms administered by salaried managers. See also Cooter and Schaefer, "Law and Poverty," who consider the development of institutions conducive to cooperation among non-relatives central to economic modernization. Church, "Family Firm," identifies devices that family enterprises use to overcome their limitations.

19. Quran 62:10 and 4:29.

20. Cohen, "Economic Background," table C-1. The estimates relate to Islam's Arab heartland in the ninth and tenth centuries. Although most of the scholars who formed the 75 percent were sedentary artisans or producers, a significant share participated in commerce as investors, and 7 percent earned a living exclusively from trade or moneylending. On the power merchants wielded during Islam's initial half-century, see also Ibrahim, *Merchant Capital and Islam*.

21. Berman, *Law and Revolution*, chap. 11. As early as 1154, northern Italy had commercial courts consisting of merchant judges (*consules mercatorum*). See Mitchell, *Law Merchant*, chap. 3; and Milgrom, North, and Weingast, "Revival of Trade." On the development of medieval European commerce generally, see Lopez, *Commercial Revolution*.

22. Labib, "Capitalism in Medieval Islam," pp. 91–92.

23. Gedikli, *Osmanlı Şirket Kültürü*, pp. 140–47.

24. Udovitch, "Social Context of Exchange."

25. The two terms are from Hirschman, "Rival Views."

26. See Goitein, *Mediterranean Society: Abridgment*, especially chap. 10, for data from Cairo around the eleventh century; and Gedikli, *Osmanlı Şirket Kültürü*, especially chap. 4, for figures from sixteenth- and seventeenth-century Istanbul. The percentage for Istanbul is based on my own sample of 417 partnerships formed between 1602 and 1697, drawn from a large database described in chapter 4 ahead. Against such evidence, Panzac, "Maritime Trade," pp. 200–201, finds

that in the eighteenth century mixed partnerships were rare in the maritime trade of the Ottoman Empire; and Abdullah, *Merchants, Mamluks, and Murder*, pp. 91–92, reports that the same pattern held in coeval Basra.

27. If the merchant had contributed to the capital, he carried also the risk of capital loss.

28. Udovitch, *Partnership and Profit*, chaps. 4–6; Nyazee, *Islamic Business Organization*, chaps. 1 and 3.

29. For example, the investor's share could be set at 40 percent if the merchant transported wheat but 60 percent if he chose to carry cloth. See Udovitch, *Partnership and Profit*, pp. 74–75, 209–10, 257–58; Pryor, "Origins of *Commenda*," pp. 30–31; and Gedikli, *Osmanlı Şirket Kültürü*, pp. 129–32, 156–67. For an example of restrictions placed on expenses, see Galata court register 27, case 45b/4 (1605).

30. Wakin, *Function of Documents*, especially pp. 1–10, 37–70; Udovitch, *Partnership and Profit*, pp. 86–96, 131–36, 196–203.

31. Lopez and Raymond, *Medieval Trade*, pp. 174–84; Hunt and Murray, *History of Business*, pp. 60–63.

32. Weber, *Commercial Partnerships*, chap. 2.

33. Udovitch, *Partnership and Profit*, pp. 199–201.

34. Abu-Lughod, *Before European Hegemony*, especially chaps. 5–10; Lewis, "Agents of Islamization"; Chaudhuri, *Trade and Civilisation*, chap. 2; Hourani, *Arab Seafaring*, chap. 2; Constable, *Trade in Muslim Spain*; Goitein, *Mediterranean Society*, vol. 1; Ensminger, "Transaction Costs and Islam," especially section 3.

35. Curtin, *Cross-Cultural Trade*, pp. 49, 107.

36. Hiskett, *Islam in West Africa*, pp. 302–5.

37. Levtzion, *Islam in West Africa*, p. 27; Lewis, "Agents of Islamization," p. 20.

38. See Eaton, *Rise of Islam*; Bulliet, *Conversion to Islam*, chaps. 4, 11; Dale, "Trade, Conversion"; and Arnold, *Preaching of Islam*, especially chaps. 4, 9–11. In Africa, the Muslim demand for slaves stimulated conversions, for traders rarely enslaved Muslims (Horton and Middleton, *Swahili*, p. 51).

39. Levtzion and Pouwels, "Patterns of Islamization," especially pp. 3, 8; Bulliet, *Conversion to Islam*, chap. 4.

40. Last, "Economic Aspects of Conversion," quote at p. 241. See also Levtzion and Pouwels, "Patterns of Islamization."

41. For the club model of religious solidarity, see Iannaccone, "Sacrifice and Stigma"; and Berman, *Radical, Religious*, chaps. 2–3.

42. Hourani, *Arab Seafaring*, pp. 61–79; Chaudhuri, *Trade and Civilisation*, pp. 38, 44, 50–51.

43. Abu-Lughod, *Before European Hegemony*, pp. 241–42, 251–60; Chaudhuri, *Trade and Civilisation*, pp. 21–29, 48–49.

44. Chaudhuri, *Trade and Civilisation*, p. 188. Abu-Lughod, *Before European Hegemony*, especially pp. 340–48, offers a variant of this view, involving also such factors as epidemics, nativism on the part of rulers seeking legitimacy, and the fragmentation of the world trading system for reasons external to China.

45. Levathes, *China Ruled the Seas*, chaps. 5–10. The expeditions were led by Zheng He (1371–1435), a Muslim.

46. Polo, *Travels*, pp. 274–75.

47. Rossabi, "Central Asian Caravan Trade."

48. Ibn Battuta, *Travels*, vol. 3, pp. 747–48.

49. Ibn Battuta, *Travels*, vol. 2, pp. 374–78, 382–87; vol. 3, pp. 700–703; vol. 4, pp. 829, 840, 876, 913.

50. Ashtor, *Levant Trade*, pp. 270–76; Abu-Lughod, *Before European Hegemony*, pp. 227–30.

51. Parry, *Age of Reconnaissance*, chap. 8; Imamuddin, "Maritime Trade," pp. 67–77; Bouchon, "Trade in Indian Ocean."

52. Brummett, *Ottoman Seapower.*

53. Goitein, *Mediterranean Society*, vol. 1, pp. 164–79.

54. Chapra, *Just Monetary System*; Siddiqi, *Banking without Interest*. For critiques of the Islamist economic agenda, see El-Gamal, *Islamic Finance*, chap. 7; and Kuran, *Islam and Mammon*, pp. 7–14, 45–49.

55. The Maliki school allowed investment in the form of goods. See Udovitch, *Partnership and Profit*, p. 155.

56. Gedikli, *Osmanlı Şirket Kültürü*, pp. 76–77, 225–26. Under one of the four schools of jurisprudence, if more than one partner contributed to the principal, the currency had to be the same. If one contributed silver aspers, the other could not contribute Venetian ducats.

57. Rodinson, *Islam and Capitalism*, especially pp. 35–37, 43–46; Udovitch, *Partnership and Profit*, especially pp. 11–12, 63–64, 182–83. For an overview of the role that legal ruses played in the medieval Middle East, see Schacht, *Introduction to Islamic Law*, chap. 11.

58. Udovitch, *Partnership and Profit*, p. 183; Gedikli, *Osmanlı Şirket Kültürü*, pp. 175–83, 263.

59. There could also have been dynamic consequences favorable to commerce. All else equal, the greater the inconveniences of establishing a partnership, the larger were the incentives to develop alternative institutions.

60. Out of 417 partnerships that appear in 15 court registers (Istanbul 1, 2, 3, 4, 9, 16, 22, 23 and Galata 24, 25, 27, 41, 42, 130, 145), just six involved the investment of merchandise: Galata 25 (1604), 25b/1, Istanbul 3 (1617), 61a/2, Galata 42 (1617), 25b/1, Istanbul 4 (1619), 32a/1, Galata 130 (1683), 50b/2, and Galata 145 (1689), 69a/1. The reported share would be biased downward if disputes involving illegally formed partnerships were less likely to end up in court.

61. Udovitch, *Partnership and Profit*, pp. 48–51, 98–101. The sole exception to these rules arose with the unlimited commercial partnership (*mufāwada*). This contract required complete equality among partners in all financial matters. Hence, each member was considered partially liable for the actions of the others. Thus, to third parties it amounted to a single person. In this one respect, the unlimited partnership resembled a corporation. However, not even through agreement could its members modify their rules of operation. The consequent rigidity and the equality requirement kept it from gaining popularity.

62. Steensgaard, *Carracks, Caravans*, table 12, p. 168.

63. Hanna, *Making Big Money*, chap. 4; Hourani, *Arab Seafaring*, p. 84; Curtin, *Cross-Cultural Trade*, p. 158. In the 1500–99 period, 770 ships sailed to Asia from seven European countries. In 1600–1700, the figure was 3,161, and in

1701–1800, 6,661 (Maddison, *World Economy*, table 3.1). Over these periods, ships grew in size. The figures thus reflect the growing importance of European trade.

64. Maddison, *World Economy*, table A-6. The figures for the Middle East refer to "West Asia."

CHAPTER 4. THE PERSISTENT SIMPLICITY OF ISLAMIC PARTNERSHIPS

1. For examples of unilateral dissolution, see Istanbul court register 3 (1618), case 66b/2; Galata 42 (1617), 51a/1, and Galata 145 (1689), 75b/2.

2. Udovitch, *Partnership and Profit*, pp. 117–18; Gedikli, *Osmanlı Şirket Kültürü*, pp. 236–32.

3. Included in the count are all partnerships that entailed the use of one person's capital by another for commercial purposes. The court records characterize 89 of these as *mudârebe* and six others as *inân*. In the remaining 77.2 percent of the cases, the form of partnership is not specified. The literature on Islamic partnerships makes references to contracts with as many as 20 participants (Çizakça, *Business Partnerships*, pp. 66–77; Gedikli, *Osmanlı Şirket Kültürü*, pp. 237, 254, 259). But as table 4.1 confirms, these are clearly exceptions to the general rule.

4. Galata 25 (1604), 76a/1 and 62a/4, respectively.

5. In pairwise comparisons, the shares of 2-, 3-, and 4-person partnerships are statistically identical across subperiods ($t = 1.70, 0.09, 0.89$), and the share of partnerships with five or more members is statistically lower at the 95 percent confidence level ($t = 2.18$). The distributions themselves do not differ statistically ($\chi^2 (3) = 1.40$). The calculations disregard the 11 partnerships of unknown size.

6. All of the cases of relevance to this work are reproduced in the Latin alphabet, along with detailed summaries in English and modern Turkish, in Kuran, *Mahkeme Kayıtları / Court Records*. The partnership cases found in the 15 registers are in vol. 2 of this 10-volume set.

7. Nothing prevented the renewal of a successful trade mission. But even the longest-lasting cooperative mission ended with the retirement or death of a partner.

8. Goitein, *Mediterranean Society*, vol. 1, pp. 167–70, stresses this point.

9. Steensgaard, *Carracks, Caravans*, chap. 1; Chaudhuri, *Trade and Civilization*, especially chap. 10. The latter source (p. 205) reviews a commercial letter written by an Egyptian investor of the eleventh century. It refers to merchants carrying goods on the investor's behalf to various lands, suggesting that he fragmented his investments.

10. Steensgaard, *Carracks, Caravans*, chap. 1; Chaudhuri, *Trade and Civilization*, chaps. 9–10.

11. Ashtor, "Discussion on Udovitch," p. 549; Gedikli, *Osmanlı Şirket Kültürü*, p. 88.

12. For examples, see Abdullah, *Merchants, Mamluks, and Murder*, pp. 86–91; Raymond, *Cairo*, pp. 208–9.

13. Firestone, "Production and Trade"; Çizakça, *Business Partnerships*, chap. 1, 3; Gedikli, *Osmanlı Şirket Kültürü*; Marcus, *Middle East*, p. 183. See also Labib, "Egyptian Commercial Policy," p. 68.

14. The "military and bureaucracy" includes state administrators at various levels, tax officials, market inspectors, official accountants, government scribes, professional soldiers, and security forces. As for "education, law, and religion," it includes such professionals as scholars, judges, waqf supervisors, prayer leaders, private scribes, librarians, and preachers.

15. Smith, *Wealth of Nations*, book 1, chap. 1.

16. Calculated from lists in *Slater's Manchester Trades Directory, 1903*, part 3; and *Scholes' Manchester Trades Directory, 1794*.

17. Shatzmiller lists these professions as *muwakki, sāhib al sikka, mudarris taksīm*, and *akīd*, respectively.

18. Based on lists recorded by Shatzmiller, *Labour in Medieval Islam*, pp. 255–318.

19. Shatzmiller, *Labour in Medieval Islam*, pp. 68–82.

20. This is evident in legal interpretations and analyses covering periods before the nineteenth century, including all those cited in this book. None identifies a debate motivated by structural changes in commerce.

21. McCabe, *Shah's Silk*, especially chap. 7; Curtin, *Cross-Cultural Trade*, chap. 9; Kévonian, "Marchands Arméniens"; Matthee, *Trade in Safavid Iran*, pp. 84–89.

22. Çizakça, *Business Partnerships*, chaps. 2–4. Gedikli, *Osmanlı Şirket Kültürü*, offers supportive evidence. Even the largest partnerships had a simple form: many investors and a single active merchant. Also, the sums invested were minuscule by the emerging European standards.

23. The Bardi firm had assets 4.5 times greater than those of the English king. See Greif, "Evolving Organizational Forms," pp. 476–77; and Hunt, *Medieval Super-Companies*, especially chaps. 1–2.

24. Greif, "Evolving Organizational Forms," pp. 489–90.

25. De Roover, *Bruges*, pp. 34–36; Usher, *Deposit Banking*, pp. 12–14; Hunt, *Medieval Super-Companies*, especially pp. 12–13, 25, 260; Hunt and Murray, *History of Business*, pp. 105–6.

26. De Roover, *Medici Bank*, chap. 5; Greif, "Evolving Organizational Forms," pp. 494–97; Hansmann, Kraakman, and Squire, "Rise of the Firm," pp. 1370–72.

27. De Roover, *Bruges*, pp. 34–42; De Roover, *Medici Bank*, especially chap. 5.

28. De Roover, *Business, Banking, and Economic Thought*, chap. 3; Hunt, *Medieval Super-Companies*, chap. 4. For earlier advances in accounting, see Lee, "Italian Bookkeeping, 1211–1300."

29. Usher, *Deposit Banking*, chaps. 1, 4.

30. De Roover, *Medici Bank*, p. 95. See also Ashtor, *Levant Trade*, p. 366; and Kedar, *Merchants in Crisis*, chap. 3.

31. Strieder, *Jacob Fugger*, especially chaps. 7–10; Hunt and Murray, *History of Business*, pp. 222–25, 244. See also Jardine, *Worldly Goods*, especially pp. 322–24, 343–46.

32. Lamoreaux and Rosenthal, "Legal Regime," sect. 2; Harris, *Industrializing English Law*, pp. 19–21.

33. Harris, *Industrializing English Law*, pp. 142–43.

34. Steensgaard, *Carracks, Caravans*, chap. 3; Chaudhuri, *Trade and Civilization*, chap. 4; Chaudhury and Morineau, eds., *Merchants, Companies*.

35. Epstein, *English Levant Company*, p. 36.

36. Harris, *Industrializing English Law*, pp. 40–45.

37. Ireland, "Capitalism without the Capitalist"; Wee, *Antwerp Market*, pp. 333–68.

38. For more on the roles of consuls, see chap. 13.

39. Morineau, "Eastern and Western Merchants," pp. 125–30, provides evidence of petty traders in eighteenth-century Europe.

40. Harris, *Industrializing English Law*, especially p. 144.

41. For a wide variety of examples, see Lamoreaux and Rosenthal, "Legal Regime"; Lamoreaux, "Partnerships, Corporations."

CHAPTER 5. DRAWBACKS OF THE ISLAMIC INHERITANCE SYSTEM

1. Quran 4:11–12, 4:176.

2. Fyzee, *Muhammadan Law*, chaps. 11–13; Coulson, *Succession in Muslim Family*, especially chaps. 1–2, 8; Kimber, "Qur'anic Law of Inheritance." In either case, the entire estate of a person who dies intestate is divided among the legal heirs. Mallat, "Middle Eastern Law," part 1, pp. 708–15, ascribes the latter variations to differences between the Syrian variant of Roman law, from which the Sunnis borrowed, and Zoroastrian law, which influenced Shii institutions. But each interpretation assigns shares to all members of a decedent's immediate family, and usually also to distant relatives. Hence, the variations are of no consequence to the generality of the present argument.

3. Powers, *Qur'an and Hadith*, finds similarities between the Islamic and eastern Roman inheritance systems. He also shows that the Quranic verses on inheritance mark a smaller shift in Arabian practices than is usually presumed. On the pertinent debates, see Mundy, "Family, Inheritance, and Islam."

4. For example, a daughter receives half as much as a son, and a surviving mother half as much as a father.

5. Marcus, *Middle East*, pp. 209–10; Doumani, *Rediscovering Palestine*, pp. 70–71; Meriwether, *Kin Who Count*, chap. 4; Ergene and Berker, "Inheritance and Intergenerational Wealth." In certain sectors similar patterns have been observed in later times. A study on Egyptian landownership in the early twentieth century documents the fragmentation of arable land into uneconomically sized plots through the combined effect of population growth and the Islamic inheritance system (Baer, *Landownership in Egypt*, pp. 79–83).

6. Kunt, *Sultan's Servants*, pp. 44–56.

7. Barkan, *Türkiye'de Toprak Meselesi*, chap. 8; Cohen, "Mīrī"; İnalcık, "Land Problems," pp. 211–24; Cuno, *Pasha's Peasants*, chap. 4; Imber, *Ebu's-Su'ud*, chap. 5.

8. Mundy, "Family, Inheritance, and Islam," pp. 49–65, offers much evidence. See also Baer, *Landownership in Egypt*, especially pp. 115–16, 163–66; Meriwether, *Kin Who Count*, chaps. 4–5; Powers, "Islamic Inheritance System," pp. 19–27.

9. Meriwether, *Kin Who Count*, pp. 164–65, speaks of estates that remained undivided for as long as 30 years.

10. Çizakça, *Philanthopic Foundations*; Yediyıldız, *Institution du Vaqf*; Kuran, "Public Goods."

11. Of all the methods used to avoid wealth fragmentation, the most common, and economically the most important, was to found a waqf placed under the control of living and future family members.

12. Kuehn, "Inheritance," pp. 454–61; Platteau and Baland, "Impartible Inheritance," especially sections 2–3.

13. Thirsk, "European Debate on Inheritance," especially pp. 189–90. Accounts of the evolution of inheritance practices in England, France, and other European countries make strikingly few references to religion. See also Cecil, *Primogeniture*, chaps. 2–5.

14. Thirsk, "European Debate on Inheritance," fig. 1. See also Kuehn, "Inheritance," pp. 457–60; Goody, *Family and Marriage*, pp. 118–25; Brinkmann, "Primogeniture"; Fichtner, *Protestantism and Primogeniture*, especially pp. 14–21, 72–75; Cecil, *Primogeniture*, chaps. 2–5; Platteau and Baland, "Impartible Inheritance," especially section 3; MacFarlane, *English Individualism*, especially pp. 87–88, 176.

15. Fichtner, *Protestantism and Primogeniture*, pp. 72–73.

16. They include Genesis 49:3, Exodus 13:2, Deuteronomy 21:17, Numbers 3:13, 8:16, 1 Chronicles 5:1.

17. Platteau and Baland, "Impartible Inheritance," section 3.

18. Lloyd, *Succession Laws*, pp. 42–46, 53, 55–56, 79–82.

19. *Code Napoléon*, book 3, chap. 3, especially sections 1–3.

20. Goitein, *Mediterranean Society: Abridgment*, p. 190.

21. Bertocchi, "Law of Primogeniture," models the underlying process.

22. Wittfogel, *Oriental Despotism*, especially pp. 22–29, 78–81.

23. Quran 4:2–3, 4:129.

24. On early Islam, Stern, *Marriage in Early Islam*, chap. 9; on medieval Arab world, Bianquis, "Family in Arab Islam," pp. 622–23; on Ottoman Istanbul, Zarinebaf-Shahr, "Women, Law," p. 87; and on Ottoman Syria and Palestine, Tucker, *House of Law*, pp. 151–53.

25. The Christian ban is typically based on Matthew 19:4–7. See Cairncross, *After Polygamy*.

26. Zanden, *Long Road*, pp. 105–10.

27. Coulson, *Succession in Muslim Family*, pp. 2, 240.

28. Meriwether, *Kin Who Count*, pp. 94–95; Ergene and Berker, "Inheritance," tables 3 and 4.

29. Gedikli, *Osmanlı Şirket Kültürü*, especially pp. 117–18, 226–32, 256–60. For additional examples, see Istanbul court register 9 (1662), 20a/1; Istanbul 16 (1665), 42b/3; and Galata 130 (1683), 75a/3, 77a/2, 80b/1, 82b/1.

30. Marcus, *Middle East*, pp. 209–10.

31. Hattox, *Coffee and Coffeehouses*, chap. 2.

32. Hanna, *Making Big Money*, pp. 78–95.

33. Hanna, *Making Big Money*, pp. 161–64. For another example, see Galata court register 130 (1683), case 8a/1. In the two centuries following Abu Taqiyya, several other Egyptian coffee traders accumulated huge fortunes. They include Qasim al-Sharaybi (died 1734) and Mahmud Muharram (d. 1795). Neither created a business organization that outlived him (Raymond, *Cairo*, pp. 208–9).

34. Marcus, *Middle East*, p. 113. While Marcus mentions this possibility in relation to shares in real estate, it applies also to shares in a commercial partnership.

35. Hunt and Murray, *History of Business*, pp. 154–55.

36. Jardine, *Worldly Goods*, pp. 321–24.

37. Hunt and Murray, *History of Business*, review developments to 1550. For the subsequent evolution of western business structures, see Harris, *Industrializing English Law*; Ireland, "Capitalism without the Capitalist"; Freedeman, *Joint-Stock Enterprise*; Neal, *Rise of Financial Capitalism*.

38. Sommerville, *News Revolution*, chap. 2; McCusker and Gravesteijn, *Beginnings of Commercial Journalism*; McCusker, "Demise of Distance."

39. Kedar, *Merchants in Crisis*, pp. 25–26.

40. On accounting practices in the premodern Middle East, see Zaid, "Accounting Systems"; Solas and Otar, "Accounting in Near East"; and Güvemli, *Muhasebe Tarihi*, vol. 2. On the region's stock markets, see Fertekligil, *Borsa'nın Tarihçesi*, especially pp. 18–26; and Azzam, *Arab Capital Markets*, pp. 197–98, 229–30. On the beginnings of the news media in the Middle East, see Hanioğlu, *Late Ottoman Empire*, pp. 94–95; Rugh, *Arab Press*, pp. 1–8; and Ayalon, *Press in Middle East*, chap. 1. The first Middle Eastern newspaper in a language spoken by Muslims was the Turkish-Arabic *Al-waqā'i al-Misrīyah*, published in Cairo in 1828. Periodicals with a commercial focus came a few decades later.

41. The lack of private sources has contributed to the pronounced state-centric bias of modern scholarship on the Middle East. In a 262-page book devoted to historical sources, Faroqhi, *Approaching Ottoman History*, devotes less than a page to "private archives" (p. 58). As she points out, political disturbances must have contributed to the paucity of the surviving private sources. In regard to commercial records, a more basic reason is that very few archives were formed in the first place, let alone maintained.

42. Goitein, "Bankers Accounts"; Solas and Otar, "Accounting in Near East."

43. Napier, "Defining Islamic Accounting," pp. 123–24.

44. Cahen, "Déclin Commercial."

45. Chaudhuri, *Trade and Civilization*, chap. 10, especially p. 212.

46. Genç, *Devlet ve Ekonomi*, chaps. 1–4.

CHAPTER 6. THE ABSENCE OF THE CORPORATION IN ISLAMIC LAW

1. Tutel, *Şirket-i Hayriye*, pp. 18–24; Koraltürk, "Şirket-i Hayriye'nin Kuruluşu," pp. 97–101. The number of shares reached 2,000 in stages, over several years. At its founding, the company issued only 150 shares (T. C. Başbakanlık Devlet Arşivleri Genel Müdürlüğü, *Boğaziçinde Asırlık Seyahat*, pp. 17–18).

2. Kazgan, *Osmanlı'dan Cumhuriyet'e Şirketleşme*, pp. 39, 72; Akyıldız, *Ottoman Securities*, pp. 19, 48–51; Koraltürk, "Şirket-i Hayriye'nin Kuruluşu," pp. 97–101. Şirket-i Hayriye appears to have been the brainchild of two leading reformers of the age, Fuat Pasha and Cevdet Pasha. See the latter's *Tezâkir*, vol. 1, pp. 12–13.

3. The mid-1850s saw a parallel development in Egypt, where the khedive Said Pasha chartered two steamship companies whose shares were bought mostly by Egyptian dignitaries. See Landes, *Bankers and Pashas*, pp. 83–84, 149–54.

4. Hansmann, Kraakman, and Squire, "Rise of the Firm," pp. 1337–43.

5. Toprak, *Milli İktisat*, pp. 83–87. Akyıldız, *Ottoman Securities*, pp. 93–185, lists the founders and organizational form of 46 companies established in this period. Of this group, which includes all of the largest, 43 were founded as corporations primarily, and often exclusively, by foreigners and foreign-protected local minorities; hence, for some purposes they had access to foreign courts. Of the remaining three, one was Şirket-i Hayriye. The second, Şirket-i Hayriye-i Hamidiye, was another marine transport company founded in 1906 under imperial patronage as a corporation. The third, the Karamürsel Fez and Broadcloth Company, was established in 1891 by a group composed entirely of Muslim Turks, as a *komandit* with tradable shares (a form of unincorporated joint-stock company). Revealingly, the only privately established company with majority-Muslim ownership is the only one without legal personhood.

6. Toprak, *Milli İktisat*, chap. 7; Toprak, *İttihad-Terakki*, chap. 3. Akyıldız, *Ottoman Securities*, pp. 186–301, lists 58 traded companies established between 1908 and 1920. Of this group, 56 were corporations, including 28 founded exclusively by Muslims and 10 founded by confessionally mixed groups. The passage of a law of corporations marks a turning point also in the formation of non-profit organizations. Whereas 36 non-profit organizations (*derneks*) were founded in Istanbul in the decade leading to 1907, 438 were founded in the subsequent decade (Alkan, "İstanbul'da Sivil Toplum Kurumları, p. 144). See also Özbek, *Sosyal Devlet*, chaps. 8–10.

7. Tignor, "Banking in Egypt."

8. Hansmann, Kraakman, and Squire, "Rise of the Firm"; Ekelund and Tollison, *Politicized Economies*, pp. 209–16; Harris, *Industrializing English Law*, pp. 152–67, 230–86.

9. Kuhn, *Law of Corporations*, pp. 17–18.

10. Malmendier, "Roman Shares," pp. 32–40; Jolowicz and Nicholas, *Roman Law*, pp. 296–97.

11. Berman, *Law and Revolution*, pp. 215–16. On Justinian's code, generally, see Jolowicz and Nicholas, *Roman Law*, chaps. 29–30.

12. Malmendier, "Roman Shares," p. 40.

13. Kuhn, *Law of Corporations*, pp. 24–29.

14. Berman, *Law and Revolution*, pp. 69, 89–91, 98, 182, 215–16; Dagron, "Urban Economy," pp. 405–10; Haldon, *Byzantium in Seventh Century*, pp. 92–99, 280–86, 293–97. The Abbey of Cluny, founded in 910 in southern France, exercised all of these rights.

15. There is an unresolved debate on whether the corporations formed in medieval Europe drew on Roman precedents. Gierke, *Community*, pp. 196–214, 244–45, argues that medieval jurists presented the corporation as the revival of an institution found in Roman texts merely for purposes of legitimation. Whatever the practical links between the medieval corporation and Roman law, it is well established that the concept saw use under the Romans.

16. Ullmann, *Carolingian Renaissance*, pp. 111–34; Finer, *History of Government*, vol. 2, pp. 883–88.

17. This development is known as the Papal Revolution or the Gregorian Reform.

18. Berman, *Law and Revolution*, especially chap. 2; Jolowicz and Nicholas, *Roman Law*, chaps. 16–17.

19. Berman, *Law and Revolution*, chap. 12; Pirenne, *Medieval Cities*, pp. 121–51; Stephenson, *Borough and Town*, especially chaps. 2, 6.

20. Mumford, *City in History*, pp. 253–61; Pirenne, *Medieval Cities*, pp. 55–74, 153–67.

21. In 1330, more than 3,200 towns dotted the area north of the Alps and the Danube; of these, 94 percent had fewer than 2,000 inhabitants and only nine had more than 25,000 (Pounds, *Historical Geography of Europe*, table 6.5).

22. Crone, *Roman and Islamic Law*, especially chaps. 1, 5–6. The local forms of Roman law are known collectively as "provincial law." The degree to which they influenced the development of Islamic law is a matter of controversy. Hallaq, "Quest for Origins," proposes that Islamic law grew out of Arabian customs rather than derivatives of Roman law. He acknowledges, however, that those customs were themselves influenced by legal systems of the wider region. The various influences are not mutually exclusive. Just as students learn from multiple teachers, so in its evolution Islamic law most certainly absorbed elements from multiple legal traditions.

23. Haldon, *Byzantium in Seventh Century*, chap. 3; Stern, "Constitution of Islamic City," pp. 47–48.

24. Haldon, *Byzantium in Seventh Century*, pp. 293–94; Patrich, *Sabas*, pp. 32–33; Laboa, *Atlas of Christian Monasticism*, especially chap. 6.

25. Bulsara, ed., *Mâtîkân ê Hazâr Dâtastân*, especially p. 302, verse 23:X+100 and p. 500, n. 7.

26. This "tribal responsibility system" evokes the "community responsibility system," which, in twelfth- and thirteenth-century Europe, promoted the trust essential to the growth of long-distance commerce (Greif, "Impersonal Exchange"). As under the latter system, tribes were motivated to keep their members from cheating outsiders, lest the entire group suffer retaliation. Each system generated strategic uncertainty: retaliations could deter cheating or, alternatively, trigger spiraling counter-retaliations and encourage alliance building. The case of pre-Islamic Arabia points to multiple equilibria, implying that a communally based responsibility system may well harm economic exchange.

27. Goldziher, *Muslim Studies*, vol. 1, chap. 2; Shaban, *Islamic History*, vol. 1, chap. 1.

28. Quran 3:103.

29. Quran 3:104, 3:110, 3:114, 7:157, 9:71, 9:112, 22:41, 31:17.

30. For an exegesis, see Cook, *Commanding Right*, chap. 1.

31. On the practice of collective responsibility in Islamic criminal law, see Mallat, "Middle Eastern Law," part 1, pp. 702–3; and Schacht, "Kisās." On the early succession struggles, see Crone, *God's Rule*, chaps. 2–3. Regarding marriage among kin, see Goody, *Oriental, Ancient, and Primitive*, chap. 12; and Stern, *Marriage in Early Islam*, especially pp. 60, 65–66. In recent centuries 10–15 percent of Arab marriages have been between cousins, with even higher rates in wealthy communities. See Meriwether, *Kin who Count*, pp. 132–40. On conflicts between Arabs and non-Arabs in the formative era of Islam, see Bashear, *Arabs and Others*.

32. Greif, *Institutions*, especially pp. 247–55. See also Goody, *European Family*, pp. 27–29.

33. Feldman, *Islamic State*, especially pp. 140–41.

34. 1 Corinthians 10. For another such passage, see Galatians 3:26–28.

35. The biblical teaching is in Matthew 22:21.

36. For comparisons between Islam and Christianity, see Lewis, *Islam and the West*, pp. 3–5, 181; and Sherwani, *Muslim Political Thought*, pp. 248, 259–66.

37. Vogel, *Islamic Law*, pp. 14–32; Masud, Messick, and Powers, "Muftis, Fatwas"; Tyan, *Organisation Judiciaire*, chap. 2.

38. Ullmann, *Law and Politics*, chap. 3; Strauss, *Law, Resistance*, chaps. 1–2.

39. The distinction is customarily based on Quran 47:4. The Shafii school of jurisprudence includes a third category, the abode of truce (*dār al-sulh*).

40. Dallal, "Ummah"; Lambton, *State and Government*, pp. 13–14.

41. Kayalı, *Arabs and Young Turks*; Khalidi, Anderson, Muslih, and Simon, *Origins of Arab Nationalism*; McCarthy, *Ottoman Peoples*.

42. Cahen, "Darība," pp. 143–44; Cahen, "Kharādj."

43. In 736, an Egyptian judge created a register of waqfs. The oldest treatise on the waqf, Al-Khassaf's *Ahkām al-Waqūf*, was written around 870 (Verbit, *Law of Trusts*).

44. See Kuran, "Public Goods"; Yediyıldız, "XVIII. Asır Vakıf Müessesesi"; Çizakça, *Philanthropic Foundations*; Arjomand, "Philanthropy, Law"; Lev, *Charity, Endowments*.

45. Ibn Battuta, *Travels*, especially vol. 1, pp. 64–65, 148–49, and vol. 2, p. 450.

46. Kuran, "Public Goods," pp. 841–52; Çizakça, *Philanthropic Foundations*, pp. 15–21.

47. The collective waqf of guilds, discussed in the next chapter, forms an exception.

48. In seventeenth-century Istanbul, 3.7 percent of all court cases involving a waqf consisted of a formulaic lawsuit designed to establish a written record of fixity. For examples, see Istanbul 1 (1612) 38b/1, Galata 42 (1617), 45a/1, Istanbul 9 (1662), 243a/1, and Galata 145 (1689), 6a/1. The famous Ottoman jurist Ebussuûd endorsed this legal procedure (Imber, *Ebu's-Su'ud*, pp. 148–49).

49. Hennigan, *Birth of Legal Institution*, pp. 50–70; Köprülü, "Vakıf Müessesesi," pp. 3–5; Powers, "Islamic Family Endowment," pp. 1171–72; Jones, "Pious Endowments," pp. 23–26.

50. The information comes from a ninth-century treatise by Abu-Bakr al-Shaybani al-Khassaf (Verbit, *Law of Trusts*, pp. 21, 33–34). See also Leeuwen, *Waqfs and Urban Structures*, chap. 1. Of the hundreds of waqf-related sayings that have been attributed to Muhammad and his companions, most are probably fabrications designed to legitimize the waqf at a time when the new institution was under attack as incompatible with the inheritance rules of the Quran.

51. Akgündüz, *Vakıf Müessesesi*, pp. 257–70; Little, *Al-Haram al Sarif*, pp. 317–18. In the court records of seventeenth-century Istanbul, very rarely does one encounter a waqf deed that explicitly allows even limited modifications. For an example, see Istanbul 9 (1661), 167b/1.

52. Schacht, *Introduction to Islamic Law*, pp. 125–26.

53. There is evidence that waqf law and the madrasa influenced the early university (Gaudiosi, "Merton College"). However, the university quickly metamorphosed into a very different organization. Unlike the madrasa, the mature university enjoyed legal personhood. Where a university granted degrees as an organization, successful madrasa students received certificates of competency (*ijāza*) from individual teachers. See Makdisi, *Rise of Colleges*, pp. 140–52.

54. Makdisi, *Rise of Colleges*; Huff, *Early Modern Science*, chap. 5; Hoodbhoy, *Islam and Science*. For stark comparative statistics relating to the modern era, see the United Nations Development Programme, *Arab Human Development Report 2003*, chap. 3.

CHAPTER 7. BARRIERS TO THE EMERGENCE OF A
MIDDLE EASTERN BUSINESS CORPORATION

1. Epstein, *Genoa and the Genoese*, pp. 260–61, 277–81, 304–6; Kuhn, *Law of Corporations*, pp. 34–38.

2. For more on these advances, see Baskin and Miranti, *History of Corporate Finance*, chap. 2; Hunt and Murray, *History of Business*, especially chaps. 6–10; Carlos and Nicholas, "Giants of Earlier Capitalism"; Greif, "Evolving Organizational Forms."

3. Harris, "East India Company."

4. Because of its stake in the chartered company's profitability, the state sometimes supervised the appointment of its managers and apportionment of its dividends. If a rent failed to materialize, the state might revoke a charter. In 1600, when an unchartered group of merchants promised to pay higher taxes in return for the Levant Company's privileges, the Queen of England revoked the Levant charter, restoring it only in return for higher annual contributions (Wood, *Levant Company*, p. 36). See, generally, Ekelund and Tollison, *Politicized Economies*, especially chap. 6; Harris, *Industrializing English Law*, chap. 2; Wood, *Levant Company*, chaps. 1–7; Brenner, *Merchants and Revolution*, especially chaps. 1, 12; and Davis, *Corporations*.

5. Harris, *Industrializing English Law*, pp. 32, 146–47; and Kuhn, *Law of Corporations*, pp. 46–48.

6. Wood, *Levant Company*, pp. 23–24, 151. Not all members were engaged in trade; some were passive investors.

7. Gelderblom and Jonker, "Completing a Financial Revolution"; Blussé and Gaastra, "Companies and Trade"; Neal, "Venture Shares," pp. 166–71; De Vries, *Economy of Europe*, pp. 128–46.

8. Scott, *Joint-Stock Companies to 1720*, vol. 1, p. 439. The figure includes land owned by joint-stock companies. Because of the financial bubble generated by the South Sea Company, the share rose to 13 percent in 1720. In 1760, according to another estimate, the total capital of joint-stock companies reached 15 percent of England's net reproducible capital stock, and by 1840 this figure stood at 24.5 percent (Harris, *Industrializing English Law*, pp. 193–98).

9. Maddison, *World Economy*, table 3.1. For an account of how trade stimulated economic growth during the period in question, see Findlay and O'Rourke, *Power and Plenty*, especially chaps. 4–5.

10. Hansmann, Kraakman, and Squire, "Rise of the Firm," pp. 1348–50, 1378–79, 1401.

11. Harris, *Industrializing English Law*, pp. 282–85; Lamoreaux, "Partnerships, Corporations."

12. See Roy, *Socializing Capital*, especially chaps. 6–9; Chandler, *Visible Hand*, especially chaps. 12–14; Lamoreaux, "Partnerships, Corporations"; and Williamson, *Economic Institutions of Capitalism*, especially chaps. 11–12.

13. In England, where the corporation came to dominate business organization in the mid-nineteenth century, not until 1844 could corporations be formed without state permission. The chartering process led to extensive rent-seeking by incumbent corporations trying to limit competition. See Harris, *Industrializing English Law*, pp. 282–85. On general incorporation acts in the United States, see Wallis, "Constitutions, Corporations, and Corruption."

14. At the founding of Şirket-i Hayriye incorporation remained restrictive in France, the source of the commercial codes instituted in the Middle East in the nineteenth century. However, the advantages of incorporation were replicated by partnerships endowed with legal personhood. Also, French law treated entity shielding and owner shielding as continuous variables, not, as in the Anglo-American tradition, as a dichotomous choice. Partnership contracts included clauses that restricted partner liabilities and identified who could encumber the partnership. There could be supervisory committees and reporting requirements. Furthermore, partnerships could be organized with tradable shares (*commandites par action*). In short, French merchants and financiers could obtain most advantages of incorporation through finely tuned partnerships (Lamoreaux and Rosenthal, "Legal Regime," pp. 37–42).

15. For analyses that take the superiority of the corporation for granted, see Williamson, *Economic Institutions of Capitalism*, chaps. 11–12; Blair, "Benefits of Corporate Form"; and Tirole, "Corporate Governance." Lamoreaux and Rosenthal, "Organizing Middle-Sized Firms," model the trade-offs faced in choosing an organizational form.

16. The history of the business corporation is not unblemished. There have been scandals such as the South Sea Bubble of 1720 and the Enron meltdown of 2001. But each has triggered measures to safeguard the interests of shareholders through disclosure requirements.

17. Lamoreaux and Rosenthal, "Organizing Middle-Sized Firms."

18. By the standards of today's advanced economies, most companies of the early industrial era followed simple accounting practices; some did not even keep systematic records of financial transactions. Moreover, it was common for managers to manipulate their accounts in order to misinform shareholders or the wider public (Lamoreaux, "Transition to Capitalism"). Nevertheless, there was a move toward advanced and standardized accounting methods, particularly in the most capital-intensive sectors (Levenstein, *Accounting for Growth*, chaps. 2, 7). Not all corporations of the early industrial era raised capital in open markets. The shares of most changed hands among closely connected individuals. But those of the largest tended to be traded widely.

19. For an overview of the divisions and subdivisions, see Crone, *God's Rule*, chaps. 2, 4–9.

20. On racial divisions, see Lewis, *Race and Slavery*, especially chaps. 3–5; and on group-based economic inequalities, Marlow, *Hierarchy and Egalitarianism*, especially chaps. 4, 6–7.

21. For writings by Arab travelers to Europe in the seventeenth century, see Matar, *Lands of Christians*.

22. Davis, *Aleppo and Devonshire Square*, especially chap. 13.

23. Frangakis-Syrett, *Commerce of Smyrna*, p. 77.

24. See chap. 11 ahead.

25. Lewis, *Muslim Discovery of Europe*, especially chaps. 3–5; and Lewis, *What Went Wrong?* chap. 3, highlight various western developments that went unnoticed in the Middle East, inferring that curiosity was lacking in general. The failure to produce treatises on western science and dictionaries of European languages does indeed suggest incuriosity about the West. It shows also, however, that Middle Easterners considered it feasible to appropriate useful innovations without learning new languages or becoming broadly familiar with western cultures.

26. Stein, "Habsburg Financial Institutions," p. 237.

27. Barkan, "Din ve Devlet İlişkileri," especially pp. 70–83; Repp, "Qānūn and Sharī'a"; Zubaida, *Law and Power*, chap. 3; Imber, *Ebu's-Su'ud*, especially chaps. 2, 5–6.

28. These jurists belonged to the Shafii and Maliki schools of law. See Karaman, *İslam Hukuku*, p. 210. For additional possible starting points, see Zahraa, "Legal Personality," pp. 202–6.

29. Hatemî, *Vakıf Kurma Muamelesi*, pp. 22–23.

30. Greif, *Institutions*, especially chaps. 5, 7; Roland, "Understanding Institutional Change"; Kuran, "Economic Trajectories of Civilizations."

31. Generally, Liebesny, *Law of Middle East*, chap. 3; Anderson, "Law Reform in Egypt." For specific organizational reforms, see Fertekligil, *Borsa'nın Tarihçesi*, especially pp. 18–26; Akyıldız, *Merkez Teşkilâtında Reform*, pp. 129–33; Güvemli, *Muhasebe Tarihi*, vol. 3, chaps. 1–2, 4–5; Ziadeh, *Rule of Law*, chaps. 1–3; and Tignor, "Modern Banking in Egypt."

32. See Hanna, *Making Big Money*, pp. 125–26, 142, 147; and Meriwether, *Kin Who Count*, pp. 23, 182–83, 193. There were also non-pecuniary motivations for forming waqfs. See Kuran, "Public Goods," pp. 853–61.

33. Wehr, *Modern Written Arabic*, pp. 1091–94.

34. Fernandes, "*Istibdal*"; Lev, *Charity, Endowments*, pp. 56–57. For examples from the seventeenth century, see the court cases Galata 42 (1617), 76b/1; and Istanbul 9 (1661), 32b/1, 37a/1, 54a/1, 147a/2.

35. In the sixteenth century the Ottoman legal scholar Ebüssuûd ruled repeatedly that waqf caretakers needed the permission of a judge whenever they departed in any way from the waqf founder's stipulations (Imber, *Ebu's-Su'ud*, pp. 150–62). For evidence of caretakers seeking a judge's permission, see the cases Galata 25 (1604), 20b/2; Galata 42 (1617), 76b/1; Istanbul 9 (1661), 111 b/2.

36. Hoexter, "Adaptation," pp. 323–25.

37. The most ambitious quantitative study of the waqf system, that of Yediyıldız, "Vakıf Müessesesi," pp. 28–33, on eighteenth-century Turkey, finds that only 7 percent were strictly family waqfs. On the distinction between the two types and further evidence, see Kuran, "Public Goods," pp. 855–60.

38. The act of weighing investment options is widely considered legitimate. However, applying risk-return calculations to the allocation of medical care is not. Most people find repulsive the notion of withholding scarce physician time from terminally ill patients for the sake of assisting potentially curable children. Evidently, we make trade-offs in certain contexts more readily than in others. On the universality of compartmentalization, see Calabresi and Bobbitt, *Tragic Choices*; and Fiske and Tetlock, "Taboo Trade-offs."

39. On the underlying psychological and social mechanisms, see Kuran and Sunstein, "Availability Cascades," sections 2–4; and Sunstein, *Risk and Reason*, especially chap. 2.

40. Mumcu, *Osmanlı Devletinde Rüşvet*, especially pp. 295–96, 345–46; Lambton, "Awkāf in Persia," p. 305; Reid, "Exemplary of Excess," chap. 3; Fernandes, "*Istibdal*"; İnalcık, *Osmanlı'da Devlet*, pp. 53–54; and Shatzmiller, "Property Rights," especially pp. 58–62. The last source shows that muftis contributed to corruption through their power to issue opinions concerning the legitimacy of desired adaptations. The court records of seventeenth-century Istanbul provide evidence of kadis' ability to block waqf caretakers from making modifications. See the cases Istanbul 9 (1661), 111b/2, 167b/1.

41. Income-producing waqf assets could be transferred, though with the permission of the caretaker.

42. If the transfer involved a payment, it would also cross the line between charity and commerce.

43. Harris, *Industrializing English Law*, pp. 152–53; Sitkoff, "Trust Law," pp. 654–57.

44. The following court cases offer examples: Istanbul 4 (1619), 6a/1, 41b/2; Galata 130 (1683), 21b/2, 38b/1; Istanbul 22 (1695), 138a/1, 140b/1, 143a/1. See also Meriwether, *Kin Who Count*, p. 195. Shatzmiller, "Property Rights," pp. 51–53, provides further evidence concerning the ambiguity of property rights over waqf assets.

45. Imber, *Ebu's-Su'ud*, pp. 226–27.

46. Jones, "Statute of Mortmain."

47. Harris, *Industralizing English Law*, pp. 282–85.

48. Yi, *Guild Dynamics*; Baer, "Guilds"; Kuran, "Ottoman Guilds." In seventeenth-century Istanbul, collective taxation appears as a theme in 83 percent of the guild cases involving tax matters. For examples, see cases Galata 27 (1604), 5b/3; Istanbul 4 (1619), 34b/2; and Galata 130 (1683), 35b/3.

49. There is a huge literature on whether "Middle Eastern" or "Islamic" guilds were corporations. The preponderance of the evidence points to a negative conclusion. They enjoyed far less autonomy than did their west European counterparts (Cahen, "Corporations Professionelles"; Baer, "Guilds," pp. 17–22; Kuran, "Ottoman Guilds," pp. 46–53; Yi, *Guild Dynamics*, pp. 41–112, 237–42; Arjomand, "Transformation of Islamicate Civilization"). For the dissenting view, see Gerber, *State, Society, and Law*, pp. 113–26. Gerber's argument hinges on variations among guild policies and privileges. Such variations are consistent, however, with heavy state supervision. The forms of autonomy compatible with state objectives could change over time, across space, and according to context.

50. For examples of guild-driven appointments and dismissals, see the court

cases Istanbul 3 (1617), 25b/1, 39b/3, 34a/4, 55a/3; Galata 42 (1617), 4a/2; Galata 145 (1689), 77b/2; Istanbul 22 (1695), 84a/1, 124a/2.

51. Yi, *Guild Dynamics*, especially pp. 70–81, 196–212. Keeping urban populations content has been a government objective throughout history. In the Ottoman Empire this goal undergirded a major principle of governance: provisionism. Genç, *Devlet ve Ekonomi*, chap. 3, shows that provisionism entailed keeping the capital well-stocked with food, to deter uprisings.

52. Yi, *Guild Dynamics*, pp. 90–95, 177–79.

53. Yi, *Guild Dynamics*, pp. 61–62, 85. The fund amounted to 76,000 aspers at a time when the daily wage of a skilled construction worker was 29.5 aspers (Özmucur and Pamuk, "Standards of Living," p. 301). The calculation assumes 300 work days a year.

54. All else equal, a tax farmer could appropriate more rents insofar as his demands enjoyed legitimacy. Accordingly, rulers imposed tax schedules for tax farmers to follow. In imposing limitations, these schedules also put the state's authority behind levies respectful of the specified limits. On Abbasid tax farming practices, see Løkkegaard, *Islamic Taxation*, pp. 92–108; and on those of the Ottomans, Çizakça, *Business Partnerships*, chap. 5; Darling, *Revenue-Raising*, chaps. 4–5, 8; Coşgel and Miceli, "Tax Assignment"; and Coşgel, "Efficiency and Continuity."

55. Coşgel and Miceli, "Tax Assignment."

56. Bidders specified a down payment and a schedule of periodic payments.

57. Salzmann, "Ancien Régime," pp. 400–408; Çizakça, *Business Partnerships*, pp. 184–86; Özvar, *Osmanlı Maliyesinde Malikâne*.

58. Özvar, *Osmanlı Maliyesinde Malikâne*, pp. 84–85. The life of one partner, the principal, determined the farm's duration.

59. Çizakça, *Business Partnerships*, pp. 159–78.

60. Çizakça, *Business Partnerships*, pp. 184–86. In taking over the management of tax units, the Ottoman government started selling "profit shares" (*esham*). In the nineteenth century these turned into tradable bearer shares. Revealingly, the Ottoman state, having arrested the development of a market for privately issued shares, allowed the trading of government-issued shares.

61. That premodern Muslim-governed states, including the Ottoman Empire, blocked various private initiatives has been noted by scholars exploring the origins of authoritarianism, including Mardin, "Power, Civil Society"; and Ibrahim, "Civil Society." The present argument extends the received literature by proposing social mechanisms that delayed organizational development outside the state sector.

62. Balla and Johnson, "Fiscal Crisis," pp. 826–41; Salzmann, "Ancien Régime," p. 402.

63. There were substantial geographic variations. In the nineteenth century almost every family waqf in Tripoli, Syria was required to engage in charity. In Nablus, the figure was only 10 percent (Doumani, "Endowing Family," p. 15).

64. See McCabe, *Shah's Silk*, especially chap. 7; Matthee, *Trade in Safavid Iran*, pp. 84–89; Kévonian, "Marchands Arméniens."

65. Labib, *Handelsgeschichte Ägyptens*, p. 116.

66. Ashtor, "Kārimī Merchants," p. 55; Abulafia, "Asia, Africa," pp. 437–40.

67. Labib, "Marchands Kārimīs"; Ashtor, "Kārimī Merchants"; Abu-Lughod, *Before European Hegemony*, pp. 227–30.

68. Caeiro, "Islamic Tradition of *Iftā*'"; Repp, *Müfti of Istanbul*; Gerber, *State, Society, and Law*, chap. 3; Masud, Messick, and Powers, eds., *Islamic Legal Interpretation*; Tucker, *House of Law*, chap. 1.

69. Weber, *Economy and Society*, vol. 2, pp. 725–26; Cahen, "Corporations Professionelles"; Stern, "Constitution of Islamic City."

CHAPTER 8. CREDIT MARKETS WITHOUT BANKS

1. In 1850 the Ottoman Empire promulgated a variant of the French Commercial Code of 1807. Egypt followed suit in 1875. Both variants explicitly allowed interest. Even before these enactments, the mixed commercial tribunals that adjudicated cases between local and foreign traders were enforcing interest-based contracts. Around the same time, efforts got under way in Istanbul to prepare an Islamic civil code that would accommodate emerging needs. The resulting code book, the "Book of Rules of Justice" (*Mecelle-i Ahkâm-ı Adliye*), was published between 1870 and 1877. None of its 1851 articles touches on interest. Evidently the drafters avoided taking a position on whether interest, treated as legitimate by the nascent secular courts, should be banned. In avoiding the question, they tacitly allowed the established practices to spread and gain further legitimacy. On the legal reforms of the mid-nineteenth century, see Anderson, "Law Reform in Egypt"; Zubaida, *Law and Power*, chap. 4; Velidedeoğlu, "Kanunlaştırma Hareketleri," pp. 175–205; Ekinci, *Osmanlı Mahkemeleri*, pp. 97–124; and Onar, "İslâm Hukuku ve Mecelle."

2. Davidson and Rees-Mogg, *Great Reckoning*, p. 201; Sennholz, "Economic Doctrines of Islam"; Perkins, "Islam and Economic Development"; Richards, "Failure of Islamoeconomics."

3. Hoffman, Postel-Vinay, and Rosenthal, *Priceless Markets*, pp. 14–16; De Roover, *Business, Banking, and Economic Thought*, chap. 5.

4. Quran 2:274–80, 3:130, 4:160–61.

5. Rahman, "*Ribā* and Interest." For critical perspectives on controversies over the meaning of *ribā*, see also Wilson, *Question of Interest*, chap. 10; El-Gamal, *Islamic Finance*, chap. 3; and Kuran, *Islam and Mammon*, pp. 13–15, 105–8.

6. For references to early Islamic sources, see Qureshi, *Islam and Interest*, chap. 2.

7. On concerns over unjustified enrichment and lopsided uncertainty, see Saleh, *Unlawful Gain*, chaps. 1, 3.

8. Homer and Sylla, *History of Interest Rates*, p. 3.

9. Deuteronomy 23:19–20.

10. Exodus 22:25, Leviticus 25:35–37.

11. Luke 6:33–35.

12. Noonan, *Scholastic Analysis of Usury*, especially chap. 3; Langholm, *Aristotelian Analysis of Usury*.

13. The observation belongs to Barkan, "Edirne Tereke Defterleri," p. 31.

14. Lewis, *Race and Slavery*, chap. 1. Slavery ended in recent times as governments outlawed the practice, beginning with Turkey in 1830 and ending with Mauritania in 1980.

15. Benedick, *Industrial Finance*, p. 52, n. 9.

16. Udovitch, "Social Context of Exchange," p. 459.

17. Gerber, *Islamic Law and Culture*, pp. 128–30.

18. Gerber, *Islamic Law and Culture*, pp. 62–63.

19. Jennings, "Loans and Credit," quote at p. 183.

20. Jennings, "Loans and Credit," pp. 184–85.

21. Gerber, *Bursa*, chap. 7, especially pp. 127–29, 146–47. In the sixteenth century, the customary interest rate ranged between 10 percent and 15 percent (Barkan, "Edirne Tereke Defterleri," pp. 34–36).

22. Examples of such disputes resolved in favor of litigant claiming that the transfer was a loan: Istanbul 9 (1662), 73b/3; Istanbul 16 (1665), 67b/19; Galata 145 (1695), 50a/2. Examples resolved in favor of the litigant claiming that the transfer represented capital of a partnership: Istanbul 4 (1619), 32a/1; Istanbul 16 (1665), 8a/3; Galata 145 (1695), 112a/1. For additional examples, see Gedikli, *Osmanlı Şirket Kültürü*, especially pp. 79–80, 183–86.

23. Goitein, *Mediterranean Society*, vol. 1, pp. 197–200.

24. Goitein, *Mediterranean Society*, vol. 1, p. 199; Hanna, *Making Big Money*, pp. 83–84.

25. These and many other legal artifices are described by Barkan, "Edirne Tereke Defterleri," pp. 32–36; Khan, "Mohammedan Laws against Usury," pp. 241–44; Rodinson, *Islam and Capitalism*, pp. 35–44; and Schacht, *Introduction to Islamic Law*, chap. 11.

26. "Payment for cloth" is the most common euphemism. An example of each (in order of the list): Istanbul 2 (1615), 13b/1; Istanbul 16 (1665), 108a/1; Istanbul 4 (1619), 54b/1; Galata 41 (1616), 7a/4; Istanbul 9 (1662), 244b/3; Istanbul 16 (1665), 61a/1; Istanbul 4 (1619), 57b/1; Istanbul 16 (1665), 132b/3; Galata 42 (1617), 20b/2.

27. For example, both Abu Hanifa and Abu Yusuf considered it legitimate to use a double sale as a cover for interest. See Gerber, *Islamic Law and Culture*, pp. 103–4.

28. Khan, "Mohammedan Laws against Usury," pp. 238–39.

29. See note 22 above.

30. For examples, see the court cases Istanbul 1 (1612), 22a/3; Istanbul 9 (1661), 125 b/3; Istanbul 16 (1665), 88b/3; Galata 145 (1689), 24b/3; Istanbul 22 (1695), 24a/1; Istanbul 23 (1696), 61a/2.

31. Schacht, *Introduction to Islamic Law*, p. 83.

32. On the underlying logic, see Kuran, *Private Truths*, especially chaps. 10–11, and specifically for the case of underdevelopment in the Middle East, Kuran, *Islam and Mammon*, pp. 136–39, 143–47.

33. In seventeenth-century Istanbul, 21.8 percent of all waqf cases in the court registers involved *istiglâl* contracts. In addition, individuals used *istiglâl* in lending to other individuals. For examples of such contracts, see the court cases Istanbul 1 (1612), 37a/1; Galata 42 (1617), 25b/2, 72b/3; Istanbul 22 (1695), 59b/2, 68b/1.

34. For examples, see Istanbul 2 (1615), 3b/2, 5a/3, 30b/1; Galata 130 (1683), 67a/1; Istanbul 22 (1695), 73a/2, 95a/1. Gerber, *State, Society*, pp. 74–76, 104–5, references examples from the Bursa court registers.

35. Dien, "Suftadja," p. 770.

36. D'Ohsson, *Tableau Général*, vol. 6, p. 46.

37. On such grounds the Maliki school of law prohibited the bill of credit except in cases of grave necessity; the Hanbali school permitted it only if no fee was charged; the Shafii school allowed it solely in places where it was already common; and the Hanafi school permitted it as long as the fee was small and excluded from the contract. See Dien, "Suftadja," p. 770; and Ashtor, "Banking Instruments," pp. 567–70.

38. Goitein, *Mediterranean Society*, vol. 1, pp. 242–46; Ashtor, "Banking Instruments," pp. 554–67; Sahillioğlu, "Bursa Kadı Sicilleri."

39. Goitein, *Mediterranean Society*, vol. 1, p. 245; Raymond, *Artisans et Commerçants*, vol. 1, pp. 298–301.

40. Noonan, *Scholastic Analysis of Usury*, especially chaps. 7–9; Maloney, "Teaching of the Fathers"; Reed and Bekar, "Religious Prohibitions," sects. 2–3, 6; Rubin, "Lender's Curse," pp. 84–95.

41. Epstein, *Freedom and Growth*, p. 66.

42. Hunt and Murray, *History of Business*, pp. 209–12.

43. De Roover, *Business, Banking, and Economic Thought*, chap. 5, offers a succinct survey.

44. Hoffman, Postel-Vinay, and Rosenthal, *Priceless Markets*, chaps. 2, 5–7.

45. Hoffman, Postel-Vinay, and Rosenthal, *Priceless Markets*, fig. 3.4.

46. Delumeau, *Sin and Fear*, pp. 220–28.

47. De Roover, *Medici Bank*, pp. 12–13.

48. Schumpeter, *History of Economic Analysis*, pp. 82–115; Noonan, *Scholastic Analysis of Usury*, chaps. 10–20.

49. Udovitch, "Credit and Banking," pp. 19–20.

50. Udovitch, "Credit and Banking," p. 6. See also Udovitch, "Bankers without Banks," especially pp. 268–70. On uses of these instruments in later centuries, see Pamuk, *Monetary History*, chap. 5.

51. Issawi, *Economic History of Middle East*, chap. 9; Issawi, *Fertile Crescent*, especially p. 444; Masters, *Origins*, especially pp. 52, 136; Frangakis-Syrett, *Commerce of Smyrna*, especially p. 147; Shields, *Mosul before Iraq*, especially pp. 107–10.

52. Usher, *Deposit Banking*, chaps. 1, 4.

53. De Roover, *Bruges*, pp. 39–42.

54. As late as the 1820s, no English bank other than the Bank of England could have more than six partners, and nowhere in Europe could banks form as a joint-stock company.

55. Harris, *Industrializing English Law*, chap. 8; Landes, *Wealth and Poverty*, pp. 256–57.

56. North and Weingast, "Constitutions and Commitment," especially p. 824.

57. On the feats of Europe's private financiers in the fifteenth and sixteenth centuries, see Jardine, *Wordly Goods*, pp. 95–99, 292.

58. Mandaville, "Usurious Piety"; Çizakça, *Philanthropic Foundations*, chap. 3; Kuran, "Public Goods," pp. 873–75.

59. In the seventeenth century, 15.3 percent of all cases in the Istanbul and Galata court registers involved a waqf. Interest on cash loans was an income source for about half of the waqfs with identifiable sources of income. Not one of the cash waqfs mentioned in the registers was treated as illegitimate.

60. Çağatay, "Ribā-Faiz Konusu"; Masters, *Origins of Western Dominance*, pp. 161–63; Yediyıldız, *Institution du Vaqf*, pp. 118–22; Çizakça, *Philanthopic Foundations*, p. 48.

61. An added impetus to forming cash waqfs came from cash-rich individuals seeking to establish steady revenue streams to finance charitable services with roughly constant expected expenses, for example, a mosque or a school.

62. For examples from the seventeenth century, see Istanbul 1 (1612), 16a/2, 62a/2; Galata 41 (1616), 36b/3; Istanbul 3 (1617), 11b/1, 42b/1, 21a/1; Istanbul 4 (1619), 14b/1, 54b/1, 63b/1; Istanbul 9 (1662), 200a/1, 212a/1, 244b/3; Istanbul 16 (1665), 24a/1, 32b/2, 36b/1, 121a/2; Istanbul 22 (1695), 3b/2. Yediyıldız, *Institution du Vaqf*, p. 122, provides evidence from the eighteenth century.

63. Çizakça, *Philanthropic Foundations*, pp. 52–53.

64. Çizakça, *Philanthropic Foundations*, pp. 333–50.

65. See the court cases Istanbul 4 (1619), 62a/2 and Istanbul 9 (1661), 9a/4.

66. My data set of seventeenth-century Istanbul court cases includes 1,544 cases involving a waqf. Of all the waqfs mentioned in these cases, only a couple had two founders, and none had more. The exceptions: Istanbul 4 (1619), 4a/1 and Istanbul 16 (1665), 131a/1.

67. Kuznets, *Modern Economic Growth*, table 6.3; Maddison, *Monitoring World Economy*, p. 74. World trade grew 23-fold between 1780 and 1880.

68. The earliest successful initiative was the Camondo Bank in Istanbul, founded by a Jewish-Ottoman family in 1802 (Seni, "Camondos"). It was far smaller than the banks that came to dominate the region's financial markets beginning in the 1850s.

69. The most notable of the predominantly Muslim-financed banks were Bank Misr in Egypt and İş Bank in Turkey. On the origins of modern banking in the region, see Landes, *Bankers and Pashas*; Pamuk, *Ottoman Empire and Capitalism*, chap. 4; Issawi, *Fertile Crescent*, pp. 410–12; Black and Brown, *Modernization in Middle East*, pp. 73–77, 226–27; Clay, "Modern Banking"; Clay, "Western Banking"; Eldem, *History of Ottoman Bank*, chaps. 1–2; and Tschoegl, "Financial Integration," pp. 248–54. Elsewhere, Muslim-owned banks arose even later. The first Muslim-owned bank of India, the Habib Bank, opened after World War II (Tandon, *Banking Century*, p. 50).

70. Issawi, *Fertile Crescent*, pp. 410–11.

71. Clay, "Modern Banking," pp. 592–93.

72. Fawaz, *Merchants and Migrants*, pp. 66–67; Issawi, *Fertile Crescent*, p. 76; Kazgan, *Osmanlıda Avrupa Finans Kapitali*, p. 173.

73. Issawi, *Fertile Crescent*, pp. 411–12; Kazgan, *Osmanlıda Avrupa Finans Kapitali*, p. 173.

74. In 1908, the total capital of cash waqfs amounted to 90 million grush. In 1909, the Agricultural Bank advanced 563 million grush as credit, and the

Ottoman Bank 1,102 million grush (Çizakça, *Philanthropic Foundations*, pp. 52–53).

75. Kuran, *Islam and Mammon*, chap. 3; Rayner, *Theory of Contracts*, p. 84.

76. Qureshi, *Islam and Interest*; Siddiqi, *Banking without Interest*; Chapra, *Just Monetary System*.

77. Wallerstein, Decdeli, and Kasaba, "Incorporation"; Berque, "Colonial Economy"; Frank, *ReOrient*.

CHAPTER 9. THE ISLAMIZATION OF NON-MUSLIM ECONOMIC LIFE

1. The concept of faith-based courts conflicts with the modern concept of the nation-state. Significantly, the Islamic world began to abandon faith-based legal pluralism in the mid-nineteenth century. Secular courts of the modern Middle East serve people of all faiths.

2. Bosworth, "Concept of *Dhimma*," p. 37.

3. This pact has many variants. Some begin with a petition from Christian subjects, requesting security in return for submission; they conclude with Umar's favorable response. Omitting the letter, others consist of a decree from Umar. For prominent variants, see Lewis, *Islam*, vol. 2, pp. 217–23. Cohen, "Pact of 'Umar," investigates the Pact's origins, and Bosworth, "Concept of *Dhimma*," puts the relevant research in historical context.

4. In the fifteenth century the Pact was ceremonially reimposed on the dhimmis of Cairo (Cohen, "Pact of 'Umar," pp. 130–31). A century later, when Sultan Selim I added the Arab Middle East to the Ottoman dominions, he renewed legal rights and obligations of minorities on the basis of the Pact of Umar and the consequent policies of previous rulers (Arnakis, "Greek Church," p. 239).

5. On the Ottoman *millet* system, see Karpat, "*Millet*s and Nationality."

6. Lewis, *Islam*, vol. 2, pp. 220–21.

7. Saeed and Saeed, *Freedom of Religion*, especially chaps. 2–4.

8. Winter, "Inter-Madhhab Competition"; Winter, *Egyptian Society*, pp. 111–14.

9. Hanna, "Marriage among Merchant Families," p. 146.

10. Winter, *Egyptian Society*, p. 121; Wiederhold, "Legal Doctrines in Conflict," pp. 251, 255, 257–58.

11. Ebussuûd, the chief religious officer (*şeyhülislam*) of the Ottoman Empire between 1545 and 1574, reports that the Ottoman sultan banned school switching in Anatolia and the Balkans (Düzdağ, *Şeyhülislam Ebussuûd Efendi Fetvaları*, p. 44, ruling 80). Earlier, the Fatimid rulers of Egypt appointed judges belonging to a single school (Al-Azmeh, *Islamic Law*, pp. 204–5). See also Ekinci, *Osmanlı Mahkemeleri*, p. 304; Wiederhold, "Legal Doctrines in Conflict," pp. 251–53, 256, 258; and Aydın, *İslâm-Osmanlı Aile Hukuku*, pp. 71–75.

12. For examples, see Bakhtiar, *Encyclopedia of Islamic Law*, part 2.

13. Tyan, *L'Organisation Judiciaire*, pp. 342–57.

14. For surveys of the pertinent literature, see Merry, "Legal Pluralism"; and Griffiths, "Legal Pluralism."

15. Klerman, "Jurisdictional Competition"; Guzman, "Choice of Law"; O'Hara and Ribstein, "Choice of Law"; Posner, *Economic Analysis of Law*, pp. 645–46; 709–10; Kramer, "Rethinking Choice of Law."

16. Goitein, *Mediterranean Society: Abridgment*, chap. 11; Gil, "Jewish Merchants," pp. 227, 281, 288–89, 314; Shmuelevitz, *Jews of Ottoman Empire*, pp. 41–54, 137–38; Goodblatt, *Jewish Life in Turkey*, pp. 86–88. Because the Jewish court system was not organized hierarchically, it allowed for diversity in legal interpretation.

17. Eryılmaz, *Gayrimüslim Tebaanın Yönetimi*, pp. 46–47; Pantazopoulos, *Church and Law*, especially pp. 42–44; Sugar, *Southeastern Europe*, pp. 45–47. See also Runciman, *Greek Church in Captivity*, pp. 165–85, who remarks that the Turkish conquest did not weaken the legal powers of the Orthodox Church. "On the contrary," he writes (p. 181), "it was firmly established with new powers of jurisdiction that it had never enjoyed in Byzantine times."

18. Steensgaard, *Carracks, Caravans*, p. 26; Sanjian, *Armenian Communities in Syria*, p. 33.

19. Al-Qattan, "*Dhimmīs* in Muslim Court," p. 439.

20. Cohen, *Jewish Life under Islam*, chap. 6; Shmuelevitz, *Jews of Ottoman Empire*, chap. 2. Goitein, *Mediterranean Society: Abridgment*, pp. 172–79, 188–93, documents that the same pattern held for Egyptian Jews a half-millennium earlier. For a sampling of further evidence, see Çiçek, "Cemaat Mahkemesinden Kadı Mahkemesine"; Faroqhi, *Men of Modest Substance*, pp. 183, 191; and Bakhit, "Christian Population of Damascus," pp. 22–28.

21. Jennings, "Loans and Credit," pp. 181–82.

22. Al-Qattan, "Litigants and Neighbors," especially pp. 514–17.

23. In testifying before Islamic courts, minorities would not necessarily have reported the decisions of their communal courts, since those of a kadi would trump them. And if they did make references to them, the scribes of the Islamic courts might have omitted the information from their summaries. The records of the Islamic courts are not minutes but formulaic accounts.

24. Jennings, *Cyprus*, pp. 166, 193–94. The cases initiated by non-Muslims usually involved Muslims as defendants or as fellow plaintiffs.

25. The registers generally do not distinguish between Greek and Armenian Christians; nor, for that matter, do they allow the separation of Slavic, Albanian, and Arab Christians from the rest.

26. This logic recognizes that the confessional communities in question favored their co-religionists in their economic dealings (in other words, Greeks dealt with Greeks where possible, Muslims with Muslims, and so on). If individuals disregarded religion in choosing partners, customers, and suppliers, the bilateral shares of all two-party intra-Muslim trials among all trials would be $(0.588)^2 =$ 34.6 percent, that of all intra-Christian trials 12.1 percent, and that of all intra-Jewish trials 0.4 percent. Hence, the intra-Christian share of all intra-faith trials would be $0.121 / (0.346 + 0.121 + 0.004) = 25.7$ percent. The actual share of intra-Christian trials was lower than even this number.

27. In eleventh-century Cairo both Christians and Muslims occasionally agreed to settle disputes with Jews before a Jewish court (Goitein, *Mediterranean Society: Abridgment*, p. 193; Gil, "Jewish Merchants," p. 281). Marcus, "Real Estate Property," p. 114; and Shmuelevitz, *Jews of Ottoman Empire*, pp. 46–47, cite similar cases from the fifteenth through eighteenth centuries, noting that rabbis

settled some of them according to their own interpretation of Islamic law. The underlying circumstances are unknown.

28. Çiçek, "Cemaat Mahkemesinden Kadı Mahkemesine," pp. 47–48; Goitein, *Mediterranean Society: Abridgment*, pp. 190–92; Ivanova, "Marriage and Divorce," pp. 63, 67; Al-Qattan, "*Dhimmīs* in Muslim Court," p. 433; Faroqhi, *Men of Modest Substance*, p. 183; Shmuelevitz, *Jews of Ottoman Empire*, pp. 50–68, 75.

29. In the seventeenth century, Bulgarian priests charged more to perform a marriage than the region's kadis (Ivanova, "Marriage and Divorce," pp. 63–64). But the kadi courts were not consistently cheaper; there is evidence from Turkey that their fees escalated over time (Ergene, "Costs of Court Usage"; Uzunçarşılı, *Osmanlı Devletinin İlmiye Teşkilâtı*, chaps. 9–10). In eleventh-century Egypt, litigation before a Jewish court was relatively inexpensive, the only required payments being those to the scribe who drew documents (Goitein, *Mediterranean Society: Abridgment*, p. 306).

30. Çiçek, "Cemaat Mahkemesinden Kadı Mahkemesine," p. 41. Until the mid-nineteenth century, and in parts of the Middle East until much later, some judges drew their incomes largely, if not entirely, from such fees. However, the costs that mattered to litigants were not all pecuniary. The time required to adjudicate a case could also be a factor. According to Goitein, *Mediterranean Society: Abridgment*, p. 313, in eleventh-century Cairo certain Jewish courts had trouble assembling judges to litigate commercial cases, because the qualified individuals knew at least one litigant personally. Consequently, Jewish plaintiffs in a hurry for a settlement went to the kadi. Ivanova, "Marriage and Divorce," pp. 61, 63, 71, notes that in Bulgaria Islamic courts performed certain procedures more simply than Christian courts.

31. Cohen, *Jewish Life under Islam*, pp. 126–27; Argenti, *Religious Minorities of Chios*, pp. 208–9; Goodblatt, *Jewish Life in Turkey*, p. 92.

32. In the seventeenth-century court registers of Istanbul, 38.9 percent of all recorded partnerships were exclusively between Christians or exclusively between Jews. These partnerships conformed to Islamic law. For examples, see note 42 of this chapter.

33. Pantazopoulos, *Church and Law*, especially pp. 67, 83.

34. Radford, "Inheritance Rights of Women," especially pp. 159–63, 171–81. See also Neusner, Sonn, and Brockopp, *Judaism and Islam*, pp. 94–104; Goitein, *Mediterranean Society*, vol. 3, pp. 250–60, 277–92. The system was subject to persistent controversy, and applications varied.

35. See Goitein, *Mediterranean Society: Abridgment*, pp. 425–27; Pantazopoulos, *Church and Law*, p. 106; Shmuelevitz, *Jews of Ottoman Empire*, p. 66. In 1783, a Jewish resident of Damascus successfully sued her male relatives to obtain the share of her deceased son's estate to which she was entitled under Islamic law. Around the same time, a Jewish man sued his half-brother, also successfully, claiming that the division of their maternal inheritance violated Islamic law (Al-Qattan, "*Dhimmīs* in Muslim Court," p. 435). For cases from seventeenth-century Istanbul, see Galata 25 (1604), 70a/1 and 89b/2; Istanbul 1 (1613), 95a/2; Istanbul 9 (1662), 217a/3.

36. Libson, *Jewish and Islamic Law*, especially chap. 7; Goitein, *Mediterranean Society: Abridgment*, pp. 190, 425; Cohen, *Under Crescent and Cross*, pp. 94–96; Pantazopoulos, *Church and Law*, pp. 56–57; Shmuelevitz, *Jews of Ottoman Empire*, pp. 69, 181.

37. Goitein, *Mediterranean Society: Abridgment*, p. 192; Goodblatt, *Jewish Life in Turkey*, pp. 87, 92, 122. In his 1191 classic *Guide of the Perplexed*, Moses Maimonides scolds Jews who "imitate [Muslims] and follow their ways" (p. 191).

38. Ivanova, "Marriage and Divorce," pp. 55, 63.

39. Shmuelevitz, *Jews of Ottoman Empire*, pp. 41, 72; Goodblatt, *Jewish Life in Turkey*, pp. 122–23. To a pious person of the period, excommunication might have seemed worse than death (Çiçek, "Cemaat Mahkemesinden Kadı Mahkemesine," p. 48).

40. Çiçek, "Cemaat Mahkemesinden Kadı Mahkemesine," p. 46; Ivanova, "Marriage and Divorce," pp. 55, 63.

41. Some Egyptian kadis of the twelfth century referred cases by Jews to the Jewish courts; they also avoided retrying cases already adjudicated according to Jewish law, unless the rabbinate had annulled them (Goitein, *Mediterranean Society: Abridgment*, pp. 192–93).

42. For examples of Islamic partnerships formed by minorities in the seventeenth century, see Galata 24 (1602), 14a/1; Istanbul 1 (1612), 4a/4, 5b/1, 35a/1, 48a/4, 52b/1, 61a/1; Galata 42 (1617), 58b/3; Istanbul 16 (1665), 41b/2, 91b/1; Galata 130 (1683), 3a/4, 26a/2; Galata 145 (1689–90), 54a/1, 64a/1, 98b/1. For additional examples, including ones from the sixteenth century, see Gedikli, *Osmanlı Şirket Kültürü*, pp. 140–47.

43. Cohen, *Under Crescent and Cross*, chap. 5, especially pp. 94–96.

44. For evidence from seventeenth-century Istanbul, see the following court cases: Istanbul 1 (1612), 18a/1; Istanbul 9 (1661), 63a/2 and 75b/4; and Galata 130 (1683), 81b/3.

45. Bowen, "'Awārid"; Darling, *Revenue-Raising*, pp. 100–8.

46. Cohen, "Communal Legal Entities," pp. 77–79.

47. Cohen, "Communal Legal Entities," p. 80. Anticipating this sort of challenge, Jewish leaders typically cloaked their communal debt agreements in a legal fiction. Specifically, they listed all members of the community as co-debtors, whether or not they had consented. In claiming implicitly that every member had agreed to liability, they met the requirement that only natural persons have standing before the law. For their part, by accepting this fiction, kadis effectively recognized the existence of a collective entity empowered to impose its will upon individuals, in selected contexts.

CHAPTER 10. THE ASCENT OF THE MIDDLE EAST'S RELIGIOUS MINORITIES

1. Atay, *Çankaya*, p. 325. For more on the theme, see Mardin, *Türk Modernleşmesi*, especially pp. 23–81; and Aktar, "Economic Nationalism in Turkey."

2. Abu-Lughod, *Arab Rediscovery*, especially chap. 7.

3. See Karpat, *Politicization of Islam*, especially chaps. 8–9, 15–16; Kayalı, *Arabs and Young Turks*; Lewis, *Islam and the West*, especially chap. 1; and Landau, *Politics of Pan-Islam*.

4. Shields, *Mosul Before Iraq*, especially pp. 86–89; Ma'oz, "Communal Conflicts in Syria," pp. 96–98.

5. Goitein, *Mediterranean Society*, vol. 1, chap. 3.

6. Lapidus, *Muslim Cities*, pp. 117–30; İnalcık, "Bursa."

7. Jennings, "Loans and Credit," pp. 181–82.

8. Abdullah, *Merchants, Mamluks, and Murder*, chap. 4.

9. Panzac, "Maritime Trade," pp. 194–95, 202–3.

10. Panzac, *Commerce et Navigation*, pp. 98–101.

11. Goffman, *Ottoman Empire and Europe*, chaps. 15–16.

12. Risso, *Merchants and Faith*; Chaudhuri, *Trade and Civilization*, chaps. 2, 8.

13. For references to this view, see note 40, this chapter.

14. Panzac, "Maritime Trade," p. 193; Eldem, *French Trade*, chap. 8; Issawi, "Transformation." In Istanbul, the ascent of Christians and Jews may have been under way already in the seventeenth century. 59.9 percent of the partnerships in the court records included at least one non-Muslim at a time when the non-Muslim share of the city's population was 41.2 percent. The difference is significant at the 99.9 percent level ($t = 7.76$).

15. Owen, *Middle East*, pp. 96–97, 158, 276, 291; Raymond, *Artisans et Commerçants*, vol. 2, pp. 417–50, 464–82; Panzac, "Maritime Trade," especially p. 203; Eldem, *French Trade*, chap. 8.

16. Frangakis-Syrett, "Economic Activities." See also Frangakis-Syrett, *Commerce of Smyrna*, chaps. 4–8; and Akyıldız, *Anka'nın Sonbaharı*, p. 15. In the 1770s, two European travelers estimated the share of Greeks at around 20 percent (Kütükoğlu, *İzmir Tarihinden Kesitler*, p. 22). The Ottoman census of 1893 found the share to be 26 percent (Karpat, "Ottoman Population Records," p. 258). In 1921, while the city was under Greek occupation, the American Consulate in Izmir offered an estimate of 38 percent (Birge et al., *Social Conditions in Smyrna*, p. 5).

17. Başar, "Zaferden Sonra İktisadî Savaş," p. 53.

18. Owen, *Middle East*, pp. 98–99; Gilbar, "Changing Patterns," pp. 61–62. At the time, less than half of Beirut's population was Christian (Courbage and Fargues, *Christians and Jews*, p. 89). For additional statistics in this vein, see Al-Shamat, "Educational Divide," pp. 342–49.

19. Fawaz, *Merchants and Migrants*, pp. 97–98.

20. Bowring, *Commercial Statistics of Syria*, p. 80; Masters, *Christians and Jews*, p. 143; Ambrose, "English Traders at Aleppo."

21. Gilbar, "Changing Patterns," p. 61.

22. Issawi, "Transformation," pp. 271–72.

23. Turgay, "Trade and Merchants," pp. 294–95.

24. Başar, "Zaferden Sonra İktisadî Savaş," p. 53.

25. According to data in a 1912 yearbook (Marouche and Sarantis, *Annuaire Financier*, pp. 137–40), 74 of the 127 bankers identifiable by name were Greek, 42 were Armenian, 11 were Jewish, and 2 were Muslim Turkish.

26. Pamuk, *Monetary History*, pp. 200–4; Eldem, *Ottoman Bank*, chaps. 2–4; Kazgan, *Galata Bankerleri*.

27. Frangakis-Syrett, "Economic Activities," p. 31.

28. Al-Shamat, "Educational Divide," pp. 343–44.

29. Landau, *Jews in Egypt*, pp. 9–15.

30. Başar, "Zaferden Sonra İktisadî Savaş," p. 53.

31. Quataert, "Silk Industry of Bursa," pp. 292–96.

32. Aktar, "Bursa'da Devlet ve Ekonomi," p. 133.

33. Toprak, *Milli İktisat*, chap.7.

34. Until the twentieth century, all broad confessional groups consisted primarily of unskilled and impoverished workers. Thus, in the mid-nineteenth century Ottoman tax registers for Aleppo listed the majority of Jews and Christians as poor (Masters, *Christians and Jews*, p. 144). In late-nineteenth century Baghdad, where Jews achieved major successes in commerce and finance, only 5 percent of them were classified as rich in a British consular document, and 65 percent were classified as poor (Dumont, "Jews, Muslims, and Cholera," pp. 356, 371). Yet the percentage of wealthy people grew faster among non-Muslims than among Muslims.

35. Karpat, "*Millets* and Nationality," pp. 158–59.

36. On Istanbul, see Çelik, *Remaking of Istanbul*, especially pp. 37–39; on Cairo, Behrens-Abouseif, *Azbakiyya*, especially pp. 76–77, 89–100; and on Aleppo, Masters, "1850 Events in Aleppo," p. 16.

37. Eldem, *Ottoman Bank*, pp. 297–99; Hadziiossif, "Management Control," pp. 171–72. At the time, a bank account was a sign of wealth, and borrowing from a bank a sign of professional success.

38. Seni, "Camondos," p. 671.

39. Numerous observers of the nineteenth century advanced this argument (Salt, *Imperialism*, pp. 24–27). For recent renditions, see Issawi, *Cross-Cultural Encounters*, pp. 109–10; and Braude and Lewis, "Introduction," p. 33.

40. See, for example, Mantran, *İstanbul*, p. 448; Lewis, *Islam and the West*, p. 32. For additional quotes, see Toprak, *Milli İktisat*, pp. 99–100, 129, 151, 162.

41. See chapter 8, note 2.

42. An overwhelming majority of the cash waqfs that appear in court records of the seventeenth century had a Muslim founder and caretaker. See also Jennings, *Christians and Muslims*; and Rodinson, *Islam and Capitalism*, especially chaps. 3, 5.

43. Issawi, "Transformation," p. 270. Also true is that certain Christian communities did less well than the broader Christian population. For example, the Nestorians of Iran and Iraq did not share in the advances of other minorities, doubtless because their geographic distribution limited their contacts with westerners.

44. Masters, *Christians and Jews*, p. 190.

45. Lewis, *Islam and the West*, p. 81, observes: "In the seventeenth century the Turkish capital was probably the only city in Europe where Christians of all creeds and persuasions could live in reasonable security and argue their various schisms and heresies. Nowhere in Christendom was this possible."

46. Greif, "Cultural Beliefs"; Rauch, "Business and Social Networks."

47. Bağış, *Osmanlı Ticaretinde Gayrî Müslimler*, p. 28.

48. Masters, *Christians and Jews*, p. 152; Eldem, *French Trade*, especially pp. 281–83; Sonyel, "Protégé System"; Goffman, *Izmir*, p. 86.

49. Issawi, "Transformation," p. 273.

50. Dursteler, *Venetians in Constantinople*, p. 78.

51. Often these were shared with officials who expected bribes (Bağış, *Osmanlı Ticaretinde Gayrî Müslimler*, pp. 25–26).

52. Even if the fees made "western justice" more expensive than the "Islamic justice" available from kadis, merchants might have agreed to them for the sake of gaining competitiveness.

53. Sonyel, "Protégé System," p. 87; Bağış, *Osmanlı Ticaretinde Gayrî Müslimler*, pp. 29–30. The price rose from 2,500–6,000 kuruş to 10,000 kuruş.

54. Turgay, "Trade and Merchants," p. 298. For further evidence of consulage charges on protégés, see Frangakis-Syrett, *Commerce of Smyrna*, pp. 80–81, who shows that patented merchants were willing to change consuls to escape high fees; Sonyel, "Protégé System," pp. 58, 64; Anderson, *English Consul*, especially pp. 118–25; Wood, *Levant Company*, p. 135, n. 2.

55. Frangakis-Syrett, *Commerce of Smyrna*, pp. 111–12; Al-Shamat, "Educational Divide," pp. 344–45.

56. Sonyel, "Protégé System," p. 677; Masters, *Christians and Jews*, especially chap. 5; Eryılmaz, *Gayrimüslim Tebaanın Yönetimi*, pp. 147–50; Turgay, "Trade and Merchants," pp. 293–94; Haddad, *Syrian Christians*, pp. 29–49.

57. Bağış, *Osmanlı Ticaretinde Gayrî Müslimler*, pp. 30–31.

58. McGowan, "Age of Ayans," p. 696.

59. Quataert, "Commerce," p. 839. This figure, like the previous one, includes family members.

60. Rosenthal, "Foreigners and Municipal Reform," p. 243, n. 1. A quarter-century earlier the American embassy put the figure at 50,000 (Sonyel, "Protégé System," p. 64).

61. Landau, *Jews in Egypt*, p. 23.

62. İnalcık, "Imtiyāzāt," p. 1187. Masters, *Christians and Jews*, p. 125, estimates that there were "a few hundred European protégés" in Syria in the eighteenth century, "thousands" a century later.

63. Frangakis-Syrett, *Commerce of Smyrna*, chap. 4 and especially p. 111.

64. Masters, *Christians and Jews*, especially p. 81.

65. Quataert, "Commerce," pp. 839–40. For complementary evidence, see Clay, "Origins of Modern Banking," especially pp. 594–96; Kasaba, "Compradore Bourgeoisie"; and Issawi, *Economic History of Turkey*, pp. 62–71.

66. Ortaylı, *İmparatorluğun En Uzun Yüzyılı*, pp. 74–75; McGowan, "Age of Ayans," pp. 699, 702–03.

67. The term belongs to Eldem, *French Trade*, p. 217.

68. For related points, see Eldem, *French Trade*, especially pp. 170–71, 217; Panzac, "Maritime Trade," p. 203; Bağış, *Osmanlı Ticaretinde Gayrî Müslimler*, especially pp. 54–57; Davison, "*Millets*"; and Haddad, *Syrian Christians*, pp. 34–36.

69. Masters, "Aleppo," pp. 58–92; Ambrose, "English Traders at Aleppo," pp. 260–61; Quataert, "Commerce," pp. 837–41; Kazgan, *Osmanlı'dan Cumhuriyet'e Şirketleşme*, pp. 39–43.

70. Precisely because the merchant houses settled disputes outside the purview of the Islamic courts, the kadi registers contain little information on their modes of operation. Their transactions can be tracked through customs registers.

Masters, "Aleppo," p. 62, offers these observations with regard to houses established by Jewish and Catholic Arab families in Aleppo.

71. It is beside the point that the Pact of Umar and the capitulations emerged in response to different problems. Each provided local minorities legal options unavailable to Muslims.

72. As late as the early nineteenth century, Christian merchants had achieved few successes in Damascus, where no consuls had been posted (Masters, *Christians and Jews*, p. 120). Bowring, *Commercial Statistics of Syria*, p. 94, observes that "as a body" the Christian commercial houses of Damascus were "less opulent than those of the Mussulmans and Jews."

73. In an otherwise commendable book, Eldem, *Ottoman Bank*, pp. 14–15, writes: "A closer look at the French trade in the Levant in the eighteenth century reveals that any advantage or leverage western traders may have gained against strongly implanted local trading communities were due to extra-economic interventions—diplomacy, political pressure, capitulation treaties—rather than to a real economic domination." For similar claims, see Quataert, "Commerce."

74. Fawaz, *Merchants and Migrants*, p. 86. In matters of divorce and inheritance, incentives to use Islamic courts never disappeared.

75. Landau, *Jews in Egypt*, pp. 22–23.

76. Tiebout, "Theory of Local Expenditures."

77. For influential variants of this argument, see North, "Paradox of the West," especially pp. 26, 30; Mokyr *Lever of Riches*, pp. 206–8; and Jones, *European Miracle*, chaps. 6–7.

Chapter 11. Origins and Fiscal Impact of the Capitulations

1. Ahmad, "Ottoman Perceptions," especially pp. 18–19.

2. Avcıoğlu, *Millî Kurtuluş Tarihi*, vol. 1; Amin, *Arab Nation*, chap. 2.

3. This conflicts with the shrewdness that these rulers displayed in other economic contexts. Their tax policies, for instance, varied according to the relative costs of monitoring tax agents and identifying taxable wealth. See Coşgel and Miceli, "Risk, Transaction Costs."

4. Nicol, *Byzantium and Venice*, especially pp. 59–64, 248–49; Lane, *Venice*, pp. 68–69.

5. Mango, *Byzantium*, pp. 83–87; Depping, *Histoire du Commerce*, vol. 2, chaps. 8–9.

6. All of these concessions amounted to treating law as "personal" and therefore mobile, as opposed to "territorial," in other words, circumscribed by political frontiers. See Borel, *Origine et Fonctions des Consuls*, pp. 4–5, 13–14, 94–97; Puente, *Foreign Consulate*, especially pp. 11–13, 18–20; and Verlinden, "Markets and Fairs," pp. 128–29.

7. Goitein, "Rise of Near-Eastern Bourgeoisie," p. 596.

8. Fleet, *European and Islamic Trade*, especially pp. 71, 76, 94; Martin, "Venetian-Seljuk Treaty," pp. 326–30; Depping, *Histoire du Commerce*, vol. 2, chap. 9; Constable, *Housing the Stranger*, chap. 4, especially pp. 113–26; Sousa, *Capitulary Régime of Turkey*, pp. 47–48; Liebesny, "Western Judicial Privileges," pp. 312–15; Ashtor, *Social and Economic History*, p. 326.

9. Zachariadou, *Trade and Crusade*, pp. 155–56 and doc. 1337A, clause 13, pp. 191–92.

10. Reinert, "Muslim Presence in Constantinople," especially pp. 144–48; Sousa, *Capitulary Régime of Turkey*, pp. 46, 156–57; Le Tourneau, "Funduk"; Constable, *Housing the Stranger*, pp. 147–50.

11. On the operation of informal contract enforcement mechanisms, see Greif, *Institutions*, especially chaps. 3, 4, 9; and Platteau, *Institutions*, chap. 6.

12. For the Turkish text, see Kurdakul, *Ticaret Antlaşmaları ve Kapitülasyonlar* [hereafter *TAK*], pp. 41–48; and for an English translation, Hurewitz, *Middle East and North Africa* [hereafter *MENA*], doc. 1. Boogert, *Capitulations*, p. 10, notes that these texts are controversial; what have come down to us may differ from the original Turkish text. But it is clear that French traders began to enjoy the key privileges enumerated in versions available now.

13. Masson, *Commerce au XVIIᵉ Siècle*, especially pp. xv–xvi.

14. *TAK*, pp. 99–403; *MENA*, especially docs. 2–7, 9, 10, 14. In principle, no privilege extended beyond the reign of the grantor. However, it became routine for sultans to reinstate lapsed capitulations.

15. For the text of the convention, see Great Britain, *Parliamentary Papers*, 50 (1839), pp. 291–95.

16. Greece refused to recognize the capitulations in 1832, and Romania in 1878. Great Britain, which occupied Cyprus in 1878, opted not to enforce them. Italy, when annexing Libya in 1912, declared the capitulations abrogated. Hussein Ibn Ali, leader of the Arab revolt against the Ottomans in World War I, never recognized them. An exception was Bulgaria, where the capitulations remained in force until 1914, because it remained under Turkish suzerainty. Iran followed the Ottoman example by ending its own capitulations in 1928. See Bullard, *Privileges*, especially pp. 31–32, 37.

17. For the texts, see Wansbrough, "Venice and Florence" [hereafter *VF*], pp. 509–23.

18. Ashtor, *Levant Trade*, chap. 2. The Mamluks depended on southern Europe for arms, timber, and iron, all articles critical to self-survival. Egypt would continue to weaken, then fall to the Ottomans in 1517.

19. Over the previous two decades, Ottoman armies had conquered Syria, Palestine, and Egypt in the south, and parts of Serbia and Hungary in the north, reaching the gates of Vienna.

20. Lewis, *Political Language of Islam*, p. 84; Pakalın, *Osmanlı Tarih Deyimleri*, vol. 2, pp. 171–72. This perception had been validated by resistance to foreign demands. In 1368, for instance, Murat I turned down a Venetian request for land to establish a commercial colony similar to the Genoese colony in Byzantium [Thiriet, *Senat de Venise*, vol. 1, p. 118, no. 461].

21. *TAK*, pp. 41–48. The articles comprising the last category are 3–9, 12, and 16. The Mamluk concessions of the previous century harbor an even more extreme asymmetry. The Mamluk-Florentine treaty consists of 35 articles, all addressing concerns of Florentine merchants, without any mention of reciprocity. Nine of these address the predictability of customs duties and other fees. Seven aim to improve the enforcement of contracts with Mamluk subjects, and sometimes more specifically with Muslims. One article requires the notarization of

contracts between Florentine and Muslim merchants. Finally, two articles enable Florentine merchants to keep Muslims from suing them in regular Islamic courts, by having Muslim-Florentine disputes resolved through special tribunals [*VF*, art. 1, 7–8, 14, 17, 22, 26–28 (duties), 3–4, 6, 18, 33 (contracts), 5, 32 (courts), 2 (notarization).]

22. For example, the Austrian capitulations of 1718, art. 6 [Liebesny, "Judicial Privileges," pp. 322–23] and the Spanish capitulations of 1773, art. 7 [*TAK*, p. 162].

23. The capitulations of the eighteenth century gave Ottoman representatives in western Europe authority over judicial matters involving their own subjects. But the Ottomans had not yet appointed permanent representatives, let alone ones with judicial expertise. In any case, it is doubtful that the Ottomans could have operated Islamic courts in London or Paris, for other provisions allowed Ottoman representatives to exercise only those rights accorded to the diplomatic corps in general. By this time, these excluded extraterritorial jurisdiction. See Liebesny, "Judicial Privileges," pp. 322–24; and Frey and Frey, *History of Diplomatic Immunity*, chap. 6. In 1703, when an Arab merchant appeared in London with a document showing that he sold goods to the "Turkey Company" and demanded payment, English courts denied him the rights that Ottoman kadi courts gave to visiting English merchants. His quest for justice was hampered by the lack of an Ottoman consul in London. See Levant Company files, "The Humble Petition of Hadgi Mahomet Ebu Ismael" [Public Records Office, S. P. 3418].

24. On 1773, *TAK*, p. 82. On 1675, *MENA*, doc. 14, art. 30–32, 54–75; *TAK*, pp. 112–20. The latter capitulations set a per unit duty for certain commodities, probably because of frequent disputes over valuation.

25. MENA, doc. 1, art. 3–5, and doc. 4, art. 7.

26. On some matters, westerners were able to avoid prosecution in all local courts, religious and secular.

27. For variants of the geopolitical explanation, see İnalcık, "Ottoman Economic Mind," pp. 214–15; İnalcık, "Ottoman State," especially pp. 189, 366–67, 373; Shaw, *History of Ottoman Empire*, vol. 1, pp. 97–98; De Groot, "Organization of European Trade," especially pp. 232, 236; and Karpat, "Ottoman Views," pp. 138–39. A complementary explanation invokes the geopolitical objectives of beneficiaries. For example, Horniker, "William Harborne," especially pp. 299, 304–6, stresses that England sought Ottoman capitulations as its relations with Spain worsened.

28. Brummett, *Ottoman Seapower*, offers much evidence from the fifteenth and sixteenth centuries.

29. Alliance building does explain why the Mamluks provided broader privileges than the Ottomans did a century later. As mentioned earlier, the former negotiated from a weaker position, which would have made them more accommodating.

30. Genç, *Devlet ve Ekonomi*, especially pp. 84–85. See also Gilbar, "Muslim Big Merchant-Entrepreneurs," p. 16.

31. Fleet, *European and Islamic Trade*, especially p. 94; İnalcık, "Ottoman State," pp. 189–90. In theory, the elasticity of labor supply might have been greater for domestic traders than for foreigners. But there is no evidence to that effect.

32. On early Islam, Abu-Yusuf, *Kitāb al-Kharāj*, especially pp. 100–01; Løkkegaard, *Islamic Taxation*; Björkman, "Maks"; and Kuran, "Islamic Redistribution," pp. 276–80. On the Ottoman Empire, Coşgel and Miceli, "Tax Assignment"; Çağatay, "Vergi ve Resimler"; and Darling, *Revenue-Raising*, especially pp. 26–27, 87–89.

33. Genç, *Devlet ve Ekonomi*, pp.199–200; De Groot, "Organization of European Trade," p. 237; Bulut, "Commercial Integration," especially pp. 213–16; Özbaran, "Hindistan Yolu," especially parts 1, 7; İnalcık, "Ottoman Economic Mind," pp. 214–15.

34. Pamuk, *Monetary History*, p. 11; De Groot, "Organization of European Trade," p. 237.

35. *MENA*, doc. 80, art. 3, 6.

36. The etymology of the term remains controversial. See İnalcık, "Ottoman State," p. 191; Darling, *Revenue-Raising*, especially chaps. 1 and 3; and Bowen, "'Awārid."

37. North, *Life*, especially pp. 67, 74–84; Sanderson, *Travels*, pp. 122–23, 134–35, 138, 183; Rycaut, *Present State*, p. 51; Abbott, *Under the Turk*, pp. 218, 228–31, 292–93; Masson, *Commerce au XVIIIᵉ Siècle*, chap. 1; Bent, "English in Levant," pp. 660–61; Dursteler, *Venetians in Constantinople*, p. 30.

38. For 1673, see *TAK*, pp. 77–83. For 1675, see *MENA*, doc. 14, art. 30–32, 54–75; and *TAK*, pp. 112–20.

39. Kütükoğlu, *Osmanlı-İngiliz İktisâdî Münâsebetleri*, p. 27.

40. *MENA*, doc. 1, art. 7. The Mamluks had also provided protections against collective punishment. See *VF*, art. 25, and the related discussion of Wansbrough, "Safe-Conduct," pp. 33–35.

41. See *VF*, art. 9; *TAK*, p. 35; *MENA*, doc. 1, art. 9; and *MENA*, doc. 4, art. 9.

42. West European countries had a wide variety of inheritance systems, which complicated the consul's task.

43. Where such dangers existed, a consul might take measures to keep assets of the deceased out of the hands of officials. The goal could be accomplished by distributing the property among other expatriates. Goffman, *Britons in Ottoman Empire*, pp. 134–35, offers an example from Izmir in 1649.

44. North, *Life*, pp. 84–89; Abbott, *Under the Turk*, pp. 271–73; Boogert, *Capitulations*, chap. 4.

45. *TAK*, p. 94; Boogert, *Capitulations*, p. 127.

46. Two Sultanic decrees recorded in an early seventeenth-century court register (Galata 27 (1604) 86b/2, 88a/1) indicate that this practice was already customary.

47. *MENA*, doc. 14. Several articles stipulate a specific, rather than ad valorem, duty for certain commodities, probably because the English objected to giving customs officials discretion.

48. Bullard, "Privileges," p. 18. Bullard offers many additional examples, mostly from Egypt. See also Shaw, "Ottoman Tax Reforms," especially pp. 428–38.

49. Bullard, "Privileges," pp. 22–23.

50. Akyıldız, *Anka'nın Sonbaharı*, p. 186. This book, especially pp. 185–94, contains further examples of abuse.

51. Shaw, "Ottoman Tax Reforms," p. 439.

52. Olnon, "Classifying *Avanias*," analyzes two famous cases of allegedly extortionate taxation by Ottoman officials, showing that the charges in question fell within a reasonable interpretation of the prevailing law. Boogert, *Capitulations*, pp. 133–55, offers several other such cases.

53. Toprak, *Milli İktisat*, chaps. 1–2.

54. Baer, "Social Change in Egypt," p. 158.

55. Toprak, "Nüfus," p. 110; Dursteler, *Venetians in Constantinople*, p. 142.

56. Ubicini, *Letters on Turkey*, vol. 1, pp. 266–83; Shaw, "Ottoman Tax Reforms," p. 428; Marlowe, *Anglo-Egyptian Relations*, p. 185.

57. Kütükoğlu, *Osmanlı-İngiliz İktisâdî Münâsebetleri*, pp. 30–32.

58. Goffman, *Izmir*, p. 107. See also İnalcık, "Ottoman State," pp. 195–204; and Hanna, *Making Big Money*, p. 112.

59. Steensgaard, "Consuls and Nations," pp. 18–19. For the text of the Dutch capitulations of 1612, see De Groot, *Ottoman Empire*, app. 1; the rate reduction appears in articles 17, 46, and 64.

60. Faroqhi, "Venetian Presence," p. 339.

61. Masters, *Christians and Jews*, p. 126.

62. Shields, *Mosul Before Iraq*, pp. 106, 110–11. For similar examples of violations, see British Foreign Office, "Tariff of 1839," p. 3.

63. Goffman, *Britons in Ottoman Empire*, especially pp. 17, 30–31, 38. See also North, *Life*, pp. 93–98.

64. Like disputes between foreigners and tax collectors, certain disputes between foreign nations were settled by local authorities able to defy capitulary provisions and government directives. In 1619, reports Goffman, *Izmir*, pp. 100–101, the Venetian consul appealed to Istanbul when the English consul sought to collect consulage from Venetians shipping goods from Venice to Izmir on English vessels. Customs officials in Izmir disregarded the government's order and kept awarding the right to the English consul, probably as a result of a deal that has left no historical traces.

65. Frangakis-Syrett, *Commerce of Smyrna*, especially p. 117; Fleet, *European and Islamic Trade*, especially chap. 10.

66. This distinction is customarily based on Quran 47:4.

67. Typically the justification is Quran 9:6. See Khadduri, *War and Peace*, chap. 15.

68. Schacht, "Amān," pp. 429–30. Guarantees extended to groups must have economized on administrative costs.

69. Khadduri, *War and Peace*, pp. 163–64.

70. Goffman, *Ottoman Empire*, pp. 187, 196.

71. *TAK*, p. 47; *MENA*, doc. 1, art. 15. Wansbrough, "Safe Conduct," examines the rationales Egyptian jurists developed in support of Mamluk treaties.

72. In 1621 the Venetians formally won the right to live in Ottoman territories for many years without losing the advantages accorded to foreigners (Faroqhi, "Venetian Presence," p. 329).

73. See the court records, Istanbul 9 (1661), 19a/1; Istanbul 23 (1696), 7b/2.

74. Genç, *Devlet ve Ekonomi*, pp. 54–59; Kuran, "Ottoman Guilds," pp. 46–48.

CHAPTER 12. FOREIGN PRIVILEGES AS FACILITATORS OF IMPERSONAL EXCHANGE

1. Finch had probably provided surety for the debt. Under his tenure (1660–69) English representatives obtained the right to guarantee the liabilities of English subjects (Kütükoğlu, *Osmanlı-İngiliz İktisâdî Münâsebetleri*, p. 32).

2. Istanbul 15 (1665), 69b/1. Such cases are not common, but they span many decades. See also Istanbul 9 (1661), 222 b/1 and Istanbul 23 (1696), 7b/2. The last lawsuit pitted Ishak veled-i Abraham, a Jewish merchant, against the Englishman "Aved" (possibly Avery). Ishak appeared before an Islamic court in Hasköy, a largely Jewish neighborhood, to make Aved settle the debt of another Englishman, a merchant. Aved had agreed to serve as surety to his co-national, claimed Ishak. At the start of the trial, Aved referred to a decree by Sultan Mehmet IV (reigned 1648–87) and the supportive opinions (*fetvas*) of two of his chief religious officers (*şeyhülislams*). According to the decree, said Aved, a surety claim involving a foreigner must rest on a legally valid document. Learning that Ishak had no documentation, the kadi made him drop the case.

3. The movement from personal to impersonal exchange is a critical ingredient of economic growth and modernization. See North, *Process of Economic Change*, pp. 84–85, 119; and Greif, *Institutions*, chap. 10.

4. Porter, *Observations on the Turks*, pp. 139–43; Masters, *Origins of Western Dominance*, pp. 65–68.

5. See introduction to chapter 13.

6. For examples, see the following cases: Galata 25 (1604), 6b/2; Istanbul 1 (1612), 55b/5; Galata 42 (1617), 16a/2, 19b/1; Istanbul 9 (1662), 163 b/2, 207a/4; Istanbul 22 (1695), 80a/2; Istanbul 23 (1695), 15a/1. Variations in the evaluation of testimony are found also in the Syrian court data compiled by Al-Qattan, "*Dhimmis* in the Muslim Court," pp. 437–38.

7. Both figures are statistically greater than 50 percent, the former at the 97.5 percent level of significance ($t = 2.33$) and the latter at the 99.9 percent level ($t = 4.24$). The differences between them are statistically significant ($t = 5.05$).

8. Weber, *Economy and Society*, vol. 2, pp. 976–78. See Shapiro, *Courts*, chap. 5, for an alternative interpretation of the Islamic court system's distinctness. Its key feature, observes Shapiro, is its lack of appellate institutions. Appellate judges prevent the law from being one thing to one lower court and something different to another lower court.

9. Vogel, *Islamic Law*, chaps. 1–2, especially pp. 15–23.

10. Of the 6,494 registrations in the seventeenth-century court registers analyzed here, 49 involved at least one foreigner. Six of these were exclusively among foreigners: Galata 27 (1604), 23b/4, 28a/3; Galata 42 (1617), 14b/3, 53a/3, 53a/4; Galata 130 (1683), 39a/3.

11. Goffman, *Izmir*, p. 125–27; and Ekinci, *Osmanlı Mahkemeleri*, pp. 97–98, 328. The fees charged by Islamic and consular courts influenced individual choices of forum (Steensgaard, "Consuls and Nations," pp. 23–24).

12. For an example, see Dursteler, *Venetians in Constantinople*, pp. 135–36.

13. Hurewitz, *Middle East and North Africa* [hereafter *MENA*], doc. 1, art. 3; Kurdakul, *Ticaret Antlaşmaları ve Kapitülasyonlar* [hereafter *TAK*], p. 42.

14. *TAK*, pp. 34–35.

15. See, for instance, *MENA*, doc. 4, art. 17; and *TAK*, p. 162, art. 5.

16. Wansbrough, "Venice and Florence" [hereafter *VF*], art. 5, 32.

17. Tyan, "Judicial Organization," p. 236; Vikør, *Between God and Sultan*, pp. 168–70, 209–12.

18. For the text of a 1601 stipulation, and an account of the members and procedures of this council, see Boogert, *Capitulations*, pp. 47–52. A 1675 variant of the same stipulation is in *MENA*, doc. 14, art. 24.

19. *MENA*, doc. 25, art. 16.

20. On ruler's courts (*mazālim*) in Mamluk Egypt, see Nielsen, *Secular Justice*; and on Ottoman imperial courts, Üçok and Mumcu, *Türk Hukuk Tarihi*, pp. 206–13; and Uzunçarşılı, *İlmiye Teşkilâtı*, pp. 153–57.

21. In the Ottoman Empire, a kadi's tenure in any one place lasted between 3 and 20 months. See Ortaylı, *Osmanlı Devletinde Kadı*, pp. 16–17; and Uzunçarşılı, *İlmiye Teşkilâtı*, p. 94.

22. Abbott, *Under the Turk*, p. 294, notes that English ambassadors of the time "urged the Capitulations as seldom as possible, never entered into litigation on that basis, if they could avoid it, and suffered a small injury to pass unnoticed rather than bring it before the supreme tribunal."

23. Ekinci, *Osmanlı Mahkemeleri*, especially p. 43.

24. Goffman, *Izmir*, p. 127; Hanna, *Making Big Money*, chap. 8, especially pp. 172–73.

25. For their part, Muslims felt victimized, as evidenced by their bitter complaints about restrictions on suing foreigners in local courts. Masters, *Christians and Jews*, pp. 125–26, relates one such complaint from a Muslim merchant in Aleppo in 1764. For other such cases, see Goffman, *Izmir*, pp. 128–30.

26. Having a dual legal status was not a frictionless process. Complex disputes involving multiple contracts could generate struggles over jurisdicton. For instructive cases, see Boogert, *Capitulations*, pp. 179–99, 226–59.

27. This is a common theme in economic histories of the region. See Frangakis-Syrett, *Commerce of Smyrna*, pp. 91–92; Masters, *Origins of Economic Dominance*, especially pp. 65–68, 78–79; and Faroqhi, "Venetian Presence," p. 335.

28. *The Times*, 12 February 1870, p. 4. See also Akyıldız, *Anka'nın Sonbaharı*, especially pp. 185–94.

29. D'Ohsson, *Tableau Général*, vol. 6, pp. 97–98; Wakin, *Documents in Islamic Law*, p. 6; Cook, "Opponents of Writing"; Messick, *Calligraphic State*, pp. 25–28; Lydon, *On Trans-Saharan Trails*, pp. 287–95.

30. For examples of witnesses introduced to provide legal value to a written contract, see the following records: Istanbul 1 (1612), 20b/2; Galata 41 (1616), 28b/5; Galata 42 (1617), 2b/3; Istanbul 4 (1619), 23a/3; Istanbul 9 (1662), 170b/3; Galata 130 (1683), 69a/3; Galata 145 (1689), 32a/3, 32b/2. Masters, "Aleppo," pp. 43–44, offers examples from seventeenth-century Syria. See also Tyan, *Organisation Judiciaire*, pp. 236–52; Wakin, *Documents in Islamic Law*, pp. 6–8. In general, only Muslim witnesses could validate the records of an Islamic court.

31. One or more documents was presented in 351 lawsuits, of which 11 produced no verdict. In 148 of the cases, the opposing party opted not to contest the

document. In only 6 of the contested cases did the kadi rule in favor of the submitting party without authentication by witnesses: Istanbul 3 (1617), 13b/2, 32b/2, 78a/2: Istanbul 9 (1662), 16a/2; Galata 145 (1689), 103b/3, 104b/4.

32. Ergene, "Evidence in Ottoman Courts," pp. 476–79 makes the same observation with respect to the seventeenth- and eighteenth-century court registers of Çankırı and Kastamonu. For evidence from North Africa, see Lydon, *On Trans-Saharan Trails*, pp. 293–95; and Lydon, "Paper Economy of Faith," especially pp. 652–55.

33. Galata 41 (1616), 6b/1.

34. Galata 27 (1604), 18a/3. Reviewing 25 court registers of Çankırı and Kastamonu, Ergene, "Evidence in Ottoman Courts," p. 479, found that no attempt was made to use these registers as evidence even when it was possible.

35. Certified witnesses are present in every single case in the database from which this chapter's tables are drawn. On early Islam, Tyan, *Organisation Judiciaire*, pp. 236–52; Wakin, *Function of Documents*, pp. 7–10; on the thirteenth century, Ibn Khaldun, *Muqaddimah*, vol. 1, p. 462; on the high-Ottoman period, Ortaylı, *Osmanlı Devletinde Kadı*, pp. 51–61; El-Nahal, *Judicial Administration*, pp. 18–19.

36. These figures are statistically different at the 99.9 percent significance level than the corresponding win rates in the absence of documentary support ($t = 25.1$ and $t = 51.8$).

37. The kadi requested an oath in 428 of the 2,291 trials contained in the 15 registers in the sample.

38. See the cases Galata 25 (1604), 31a/2; Galata 27 (1604), 7a/5; Istanbul 1 (1612), 56a/1; Istanbul 2 (1615), 28a/1; Istanbul 16 (1665), 101a/1; Galata 130 (1683), 50b/2; Galata 145 (1689), 37b/2, 87b/2.

39. Fear of divine retribution may reinforce the informational value of an oath involving a holy book. In the premodern Islamic world, litigants included genuinely God-fearing individuals, who would not have taken an oath lightly. Even today, many Muslims believe that a false oath will bring divine retribution (Rosen, *Anthropology of Justice*, pp. 34–35).

40. Porter, *Observations on the Turks*, chap. 10; North, *Life*, pp. 45–47; Cevdet Paşa, *Tezâkir*, vol. 1, pp. 62–63; Ubicini, *Letters on Turkey*, vol. 1, p. 184; Masters, "Aleppo," pp. 43–44; Ekinci, *Osmanlı Mahkemeleri*, pp. 28–41.

41. As recorded by Arbel, *Trading Nations*, p. 122.

42. Of the 72 cases involving a foreign litigant in the Istanbul court sample frequently referenced here, not one involved a foreign-drawn document.

43. In modern courts paid experts testify on behalf of the litigants. Known to have special qualifications as well as particular biases, they are expected to side with the party covering their bill. The difference is that their opponents can protect themselves through documents.

44. İnalcık, "*Rûznâmče* Registers," p. 266. In the period under focus, other Ottoman chroniclers, including Koçi Bey (d. 1650) and Kâtib Çelebi (1609–57), complained of rampant corruption in the courts. For extensive quotes and additional evidence, see Uzunçarşılı, *İlmiye Teşkilâtı*, chap. 18. See also Mumcu, *Osmanlı Devletinde Rüşvet*, especially pp. 134–41, 182–202.

45. Porter, *Observations on the Turks*, p. 134.

46. Porter, *Observations on the Turks*, pp. 137, 145.

47. This is why historical studies of corruption draw their evidence mainly from anti-corruption drives, political scandals, and impressionistic accounts. See Tiihonen, *History of Corruption*.

48. To bribing by officials: Istanbul 9 (1662), 145a/2, 177a/3; Istanbul 16 (1664), 10b/1; Istanbul 23 (1696), 25a/3; Istanbul 22 (1695), 88b/1, 108b/1, 137b/1. To false witnessing, Istanbul 22 (1695), 93a/1.

49. Oldham, "Origins of Special Jury," pp. 167–71.

50. Fleet, "Turkish-Latin Diplomatic Relations," p. 611.

51. Klerman, "Jurisdictional Competition," especially pp. 1190–91; Baker, *English Legal History*, especially pp. 67–68, 324–25. According to De Roover, *Medici Bank*, p. 18, Medieval European finance showed a preference for oral transfer orders over written assignment, which was later called a check. In Barcelona, checks were forbidden up to the sixteenth century, and in Venice prior to the eighteenth century bookkeepers were not allowed to enter a transfer unless the order was dictated by the depositor or his attorney.

52. When a company share is traded through the stock market, the buyer and seller need not be aware of each other's identity, to say nothing about information concerning character.

53. Lydon, *On Trans-Saharan Trails*, p. 242.

54. Hoffman, Postel-Vinay, and Rosenthal, "Notaries," show how notaries helped to dampen informational asymmetries between borrowers and lenders.

55. Coing, *Europäisches Privatrecht*, p. 409; Dalrymple, *Law of Scotland*, p. 145; *Ordonnances*, pp. 146–47.

56. In the course of these developments scores of towns took steps to limit the evidentiary value of verbal testimony. See Rabel, "Statute of Frauds," pp. 174–78, 182–88; Simpson, *Common Law of Contract*, chap. 13; and Klerman, "Jurisdictional Competition," pp. 1190–91. By that time it had become customary for debtors to get a written receipt when a loan was repaid, to protect themselves against fraudulent allegations of default.

57. Biegman, *Turco-Ragusan Relationship*, pp. 70–71 and docs. 22–24. The guarantee was renewed in 1575.

58. *VF*, art. 2. The treaty is unclear on whether a lawsuit may proceed without presentation of a notarized contract.

59. *MENA*, doc. 1, art. 4; *TAK*, p. 42.

60. Faroqhi, "Venetian Presence," pp. 340–41.

61. *MENA*, doc. 1, art. 4; *TAK*, pp. 42–43.

62. For example, *MENA*, doc. 4, art. 10, 16.

63. Galata 145 (1690), 99b/2.

64. Galata 145 (1689), 78b/2. For evidence in favor of this interpretation, see Abbott, *Under the Turk*, p. 294.

65. Cevdet Paşa, *Tezâkir*, vol. 1, pp. 62–63; Ekinci, *Osmanlı Mahkemeleri*, pp. 49–50, 97–100; Steensgaard, "Consuls and Nations," pp. 22–23; Anderson, *English Consul*, p. 207.

66. Akyıldız, *Osmanlı Merkez Teşkilâtı*, p. 130. Up to the eighteenth century, Ottoman rulers, and later semi-autonomous Egyptian governors as well, refused to recognize this extension of the judicial rights specified in the capitulations

(Brown, *Foreigners in Turkey*, pp. 67–68; Watson, *American Mission in Egypt*, pp. 463–64). But some of the late capitulations, for example, those given by the Ottomans to the Russians in 1782 and by the Moroccans to the British in 1856, formalized the consular right to try cases among different nationalities [*TAK*, p. 182; *MENA*, doc. 107, art. 9]. On judicial applications of the latter capitulations, see Ryan, *Last of Dragomans*, pp. 240–44.

67. Greene, *Shared World*, pp. 171–72.

68. Quran 2:282.

69. Hallaq, "Model *Shurūt*."

70. No reliable estimates exist for the seventeenth century. However, a century and a half later, at most 5 percent of Egyptians received any formal education at all (Heyworth-Dunne, *History of Education*, p. 360).

71. In the seventeenth century a sheet of paper cost about 1 percent of a skilled worker's wage (computation based on Walz, "Paper Trade," p. 32; and Özmucur and Pamuk, "Standards of Living," table 1). For supportive information on the price of paper in world markets, see Febvre and Martin, *Coming of the Book*, chap. 1; and Spicer, *Paper Trade*, especially pp. 89–90.

72. Porter, *Observations on the Turks*, p. 143. For evidence of rent-seeking through taxation, see Darling, *Revenue-Raising*, especially chaps. 6, 8.

73. Ergene, "Evidence in Ottoman Courts," pp. 473–74. The difference is significant at the 99.9 percent level of statistical significance ($t = 6.54$).

74. Hallaq, *Authority, Continuity and Change*, p. 211.

75. Quran 2:185.

76. Hallaq, *Authority, Continuity and Change*, pp. 211–13. Expeditious adjudication was considered a supreme virtue of Islamic litigation. Historically, Islam's major schools of law differed in some respects with regard to the admissibility of documentary evidence (Lydon, *On Trans-Saharan Trails*, pp. 294–95). But before the modern era none gave them the evidentiary value that they have in modern courts.

77. Klerman, "English Commercial Law."

78. On international commercial arbitration, see Casella, "Market Integration"; and on institutional support for global exchanges in general, Gessner, *Contractual Certainty*, especially part 3.

79. Masters, "Sultan's Entrepreneurs," pp. 580–86. On this program, see also Kütükoğlu, "Avrupa Tüccarı"; Pakalın, "Avrupa Tüccarı"; and Pakalın, "Hayriye Tüccarı."

80. Masters, "Sultan's Entrepreneurs," especially pp. 586–94.

81. This inference is all the more plausible because it was in the late seventeenth century that foreigners gained the right to transfer their important cases to special tribunals. As much as 47.0 percent of the cases involving foreigners contained in the court data set discussed here are from after 1680, as against 21.4 percent of all cases ($t = 13.9$).

CHAPTER 13. THE ABSENCE OF MIDDLE EASTERN CONSULS

1. Greif, *Institutions,* chap. 4; De Roover, *Bruges*, pp. 13–16; Klerman, "English Commercial Law."

2. Greif, "Impersonal Exchange," pp. 118–19. See also Herrup, *Common Peace*, chaps. 4–6, who shows that in English cities non-residents were much more likely than residents to be convicted of a criminal charge.

3. Morineau, "Eastern and Western Merchants," pp. 123–29 discusses these variations in scale.

4. Morineau, "Eastern and Western Merchants," app. 2.

5. Private individuals occasionally appointed ambassadors to perform functions usually associated with consuls. Also, state-appointed ambassadors sometimes had overlapping functions with consuls who represented merchants. But by the sixteenth century, at least in Europe where the modern diplomatic system was taking shape, the two offices were becoming distinct in terms of both source of authority and functions performed. Eventually, consuls were absorbed into the civil services of states, though their responsibilities generally continue to include commercial functions. On the evolution of the offices of the consul and the ambassador, see Queller, *Office of Ambassador*, especially chap. 3; and Anderson, *Rise of Modern Diplomacy*, chap. 1.

6. In the eighteenth century, French consuls in North Africa prepared trimestrial tables on commercial activity in their territories (Panzac, *Commerce et Navigation*, p. 130). For examples involving British consuls in other centuries, see Anderson, *English Consul*, especially chap. 6; Shields, *Mosul*, pp. 115–16. Borel, *Fonctions des Consuls*, chaps. 3, 6, focuses on the duties of French consuls.

7. Goffman, *Britons in Ottoman Empire*, especially pp. 20–23; Barbour, "Consular Service," pp. 567–68; Anderson, *English Consul*, pp. 189–99.

8. Mantran, *Istanbul*, pp. 510–83; Goffman, *Izmir*, pp. 135–37; Dursteler, *Venetians in Constantinople*, chap. 1; De Groot, "Organization of European Trade," p. 239; Constable, *Housing the Stranger*, especially chap. 8.

9. Kütükoğlu, "Ahidnâmeler," p. 331; Wood, *Levant Company*, p. 29. Typically the rate was 2 percent.

10. Borel, *Fonctions des Consuls*, pp. 347–50.

11. Steensgaard, "Consuls and Nations," p. 23; Anderson, *English Consul*, pp. 204–5.

12. Olnon, "Classifying *Avanias*," pp. 19–21. The consul would not grant such requests automatically. If the victim was deemed to have provoked the exaction or invited it through carelessness, assistance would be denied. Evidently the consul sought to balance the goal of risk sharing with another goal, the avoidance of moral hazard. Making loss sharing contingent on prudent behavior gave his constituents incentives to avoid putting themselves in positions liable to invite extortion. It also encouraged them to put up resistance when nonetheless faced with an unexpected charge.

13. In the thirteenth century *fondechs* were built for visiting Muslims in the realms of Aragón. In the fourteenth and fifteenth centuries, similar facilities were established in Valencia, Játiva, and Zaragoza. After the fall of Granada, the same model was used there, too. See Constable, *Housing the Stranger*, p. 329; and Meyerson, *Muslims of Valencia*, pp. 48–49, 154–55.

14. Braudel, *Perspective of the World*, p. 480.

15. Sagredo and Berchet, *Fondaco dei Turchi*, pp. 23–28, 49–50; Turan, "Venedik'te Türk Ticaret Merkezi," especially pp. 257–62, 265–75; Kafadar,

"Death in Venice," especially pp. 200–204; Dursteler, *Venetians in Constantinople*, pp. 159–70. The Venetian decision to allow a compound was partly a response to Ottoman complaints about abuses suffered by visiting Ottoman merchants.

16. Turan, "Venedik'te Türk Ticaret Merkezi," pp. 259–60, 268–69.

17. De Groot, *Ottoman Empire*, p. 83; İnalcık, "Ottoman State," p. 189; McGowan, *Economic Life*, pp. 24–26.

18. Aghassian and Kévonian, "Armenian Merchant Network," pp. 75–76, 89–90; Matthee, *Trade in Safavid Iran*, pp. 29, 199; McCabe, *Shah's Silk*, chap. 9.

19. Aghassian and Kévonian, "Armenian Merchant Network," pp. 77, 87–88; Matthee, *Trade in Safavid Iran*, chaps. 3–4; McCabe, *Shah's Silk*, chaps. 4–5.

20. Greene, "Italian Connection," section 4.

21. Braude, "Venture and Faith," p. 537.

22. Daniel, *Islam and the West*, especially chaps. 9–10. See also Lewis, *Cultures in Conflict*, chap. 1; and Kedar, *Crusade and Mission*, chaps. 2–5.

23. Ashtor, *Levant Trade*, especially pp. 17–20, 44–48.

24. Fleet, *European and Islamic Trade*, especially chap. 9; Ashtor, *Levant Trade*, chap. 1.

25. Peters, *Inquisition*, especially chaps. 2–4.

26. Pullan, *Inquisition of Venice*, chap. 10. The expulsions, which included Christian converts suspected of dissimulation, served as an alternative to inquisitorial action. See also Lane, *Venice*, pp. 300–304.

27. Ekelund and Tollison, *Politicized Economies*, especially chaps. 3–4; Constable, *Housing the Stranger*, pp. 328–29.

28. For two variants of this claim, see Mantran, *Istanbul*, pp. 603–4; and Stoianovich, "Balkan Orthodox Merchant," p. 292.

29. Even in the sixteenth century, a foreign merchant colony in the Middle East contained at most a few dozen merchants and as many expatriate assistants.

30. Greif, "Cultural Beliefs"; Greif, *Institutions*, chap. 9. Collectivist beliefs also resulted in a lower agency wage, which compounded the incentives for Genoese merchants to hire Maghribi agents.

31. Farrell and Klemperer, "Coordination and Lock-in."

32. For the general arguments that underlie this stylized example and its interpretation, see Economides, "Economics of Networks," especially pp. 678–80.

33. McGowan, *Economic Life*, p. 16; Davis, *Aleppo and Devonshire Square*, pp. 26–35.

34. By themselves economies of scale and scope would not deter entry. As Baumol, Panzar, and Willig's *Contestable Markets* shows, if entry and exit were costless, a more efficient rival could enter immediately and displace the incumbent. In fact, Mediterranean commerce was not contestable, because the costs of entry, including credit costs, were substantial.

35. For the general argument, see Kahan and Klausner, "Path Dependence," especially pp. 350–58.

36. On common knowledge, see Chwe, *Rational Ritual*, especially pp. 13–18.

37. David, "Carriers of History"; Arthur, *Increasing Returns*; Bebchuk and Roe, "Path Dependence."

38. The English had a consul in Crete, decades before they obtained their first capitulations. See Bent, "English in the Levant," pp. 657–59.

39. Kütükoğlu, *Osmanlı-İngiliz İktisâdî Münasebetleri*, pp. 24–25, 38–45; Wood, *Levant Company*, pp. 29–30. From 1597 onward, the Dutch had a consul in Syria (De Groot, *Ottoman Empire*, pp. 88–90). At least until 1612, everywhere else they did business under some other flag.

40. Kütükoğlu, *Osmanlı-İngiliz İktisâdî Münasebetleri*, p. 47, n. 165; Wood, *Levant Company*, pp. 34–35, 76–79.

41. Sanderson, *Travels*, pp. 205–6, n. 2, and p. 211 (quote at 211).

42. Bulut, *Ottoman-Dutch Economic Relations*, pp. 121–22; Wood, *Levant Company*, p. 125.

43. Between 1830 and 1914, the volume of Ottoman trade rose more than tenfold at constant prices (Pamuk, *Ottoman Foreign Trade*, table 4.1 and p. 27). No comparable statistics are available for the preceding centuries. But diverse studies provide abundant fragmentary information pointing to massive growth in ports, fleets, tariff income, and the range of traded commodities. See, for instance, Genç, *Devlet ve Ekonomi*, pp. 118–47, on the tripling of Ottoman customs revenue from 1750 to 1800, and, on the growth of French commerce, Masson's two classic works, *Commerce au XVIIᵉ Siècle*, especially pp. 353–70; and *Commerce au XVIIIᵉ Siècle*, especially pp. 407–30.

44. The insight goes back at least to Stigler, *Organization of Industry*, chaps. 6–7. Presenting evidence over 1887–1986, Agarwal and Gort, "First Mover Advantage," find that the incumbency advantage of innovators fell, and the interval over which they retained a monopoly shrank, because of two factors: market growth and increasingly easy transfer of knowledge and skills across firms.

45. Aghassian and Kévonian, "Armenian Merchant Network," pp. 87, 93; Matthee, *Trade in Safavid Iran*, chap. 8; McCabe, *Shah's Silk*, especially chaps. 6, 9.

46. The "Aleppo house" of the Radcliffe brothers stayed in business 30 years (Davis, *Aleppo and Devonshire Square*, pp. 16–19).

47. Lane, *Venice*, chap. 7; De Roover, "Organization of Trade," pp. 59–66; Depping, *Histoire du Commerce*.

48. Sella, "Crisis and Transformation."

49. Mauro, "Merchant Communities," pp. 256–61.

50. On reputation-based contract enforcement and the functions of merchant guilds, see Greif, *Institutions*, chap. 4; and Platteau, *Institutions*, chap. 6.

51. See chapter 7 in this book, especially the section on "role of the state."

52. Orhonlu, "Kārwān," p. 677.

53. Braude, "Venture and Faith," pp. 522–23, 525–27.

54. The success of a ruler thus depended on his ability to forego immediate gains from predation in the interest of longer-run returns from restraint. This tension is the overarching theme of Ibn Khaldun's *Muqaddimah*, especially vol. 1, pp. 311–55, and vol. 2, pp. 89–91, 93–96, 137–56, 340–42. Writing in 1379, Ibn Khaldun observed that in the Islamic world power typically shifted hands when a dynasty started seeking enrichment through high taxation and expropriation rather than good governance. The incumbent dynasty would lose legitimacy, setting the stage for a new dynasty and an improvement in incentives to trade.

55. Ashtor, *Levant Trade*, chap. 2.

56. Raymond, *Great Arab Cities*, especially pp. 5–9.

57. There were 360 caravanserais in Egypt by the end of the second century of Ottoman rule, up from 58 toward the end of the Mamluks (Raymond, *Cairo*, p. 218). Over the same period, the economic center of Aleppo expanded from 4 to 9 hectares (Raymond, "Expanding Community," p. 89).

58. Genç, *Devlet ve Ekonomi*, calls these motivations provisionism and fiscalism. Though his evidence pertains to the Ottoman Empire, other premodern Muslim states shared them. See Kuran, "Islamic Statecraft," pp. 161–69.

59. Under classical Islamic law, the responsibility to deliver justice fell on the sovereign. In practice, he delegated judicial duties to kadis, who usually performed other duties as well. See Tyan, *L'Organisation Judiciaire*, pp. 100–112; Uzunçarşılı, *İlmiye Teşkilâtı*, pp. 83–145; and Ortaylı, *Osmanlı Devletinde Kadı*, pp. 7–16.

60. Mumcu, *Rüşvet*, especially pp. 118–55, 163–70. See also chapter 12, section on "court procedures and impersonal exchange."

61. For further details, see chapter 3, section on "contributions to global trade."

62. See chapter 6, section on "emergence of formal corporations."

63. Lane, *Venice*, p. 68.

CHAPTER 14. DID ISLAM INHIBIT ECONOMIC DEVELOPMENT?

1. In highlighting facts that gained importance only in retrospect, one must guard against hindsight bias—the cognitive tendency to see historical patterns as more predictable than they were before the patterns unfolded (Fischhoff and Beyth, "Remembered Probabilities"; Blank, Musch, and Pohl, "Hindsight Bias"). It is easy to notice facts consistent with identified historical patterns and to overlook those that might make them less comprehensible. Hindsight bias masks the weaknesses of institutions that ultimately triumphed. It also amplifies the strengths of those that eventually became disadvantageous.

2. The fragmentation of the company's ownership through inheritance could have implications for the monitoring of its managers, and thus its organizational efficiency. Specifically, incentives to monitor the managers could fall.

3. Stock market capitalization in the region's three largest countries doubled between 2003 and 2008. At the end of 2008, market capitalization stood at $118.3 billion in Istanbul, $85.2 billion in Cairo and Alexandria, and $48.7 billion in Tehran (http://www.world-exchange.org/statistics/annual).

4. As of 2009, the assets of the world's Islamic banks were thought to exceed $400 billion.

5. This is consistent with Frederic Pryor's comparative research aimed at identifying distinct economic systems based on indicators of institutions and outcomes. In *Economic Systems* he finds that majority-Muslim countries no longer represent a distinct institutional complex.

6. Berkowitz, Pistor, and Richard, "Transplant Effect"; and Rodrik, *One Economics, Many Recipes*, especially chaps. 1, 6. See also North, *Institutions*, chap. 5; Platteau, *Institutions*, chaps. 5–7; Greif, *Institutions*, especially chaps. 7, 9, 11.

7. Rosen, *Culture of Islam*, chap. 4; Christelow, *Muslim Law Courts*, especially chaps. 1,5; Mallat, *Middle Eastern Law*, chap. 9; Brown, *Rule of Law*, especially chaps. 1, 7–8.

8. http://www.transparency.org/policy_research/surveys_indices/cpi/2009.

9. Issawi, *Economic History*, chap. 5.

10. The relevant literature is immense. See, for example, Voll, "Fundamentalism"; Sachedina, "Activist Shi'ism"; and Saikal, *Islam and the West*.

11. Kepel, *War for Muslim Minds*, especially chaps. 4–6; and Akbarzadeh, *Islam and Globalization*.

12. Sullivan, *Voluntary Organizations in Egypt*, chap. 3; Benthall and Bellion-Jourdan, *Charitable Crescent*; Clark, *Islam, Charity, and Activism*, chaps. 2–4.

13. Haneef, *Contemporary Islamic Economic Thought*; Kuran, *Islam and Mammon*, chaps. 1–3, 5; Behdad, "Disputed Utopia."

14. Noland and Pack, *Arab Economies*, develop this point.

15. In his *Economic Backwardness*, chap. 1, Alexander Gerschenkron developed the best-known variant of this argument. Its key insight is that relative backwardness motivates institutional innovation, which may involve borrowings to substitute for the missing preconditions of growth.

16. Comair-Obeid, *Law of Business Contracts*; Wilson, *Banking and Finance*; Hamoudi, "Death of Islamic Law"; Vogel, "Contract Law of Islam," pp. 55–60.

17. Ágoston, *Guns for the Sultan*.

18. Abou-El-Haj, *Formation of Modern State*; Barkey, *Bandits and Bureaucrats*, chap. 6; Findley, *Bureaucratic Reform*, especially chap. 4.

19. Clay, "Modern Banking," pp. 592–93.

20. Toprak, *Milli İktisat*, chap. 6; Berkes, *Development of Secularism*, especially chaps. 1, 4–6; Baer, *Social History*, chap. 9; Ekinci, *Osmanlı Mahkemeleri*, pp. 43–50; Toledano, "Social and Economic Change"; Hanioğlu, *Late Ottoman Empire*, especially chap. 4.

21. Kuran, *Islam and Mammon*, chap. 4.

References

Abbott, George F. *Under the Turk in Constantinople*. London: Macmillan, 1920; original edition, 1674–81.

Abdullah, Thabit A. J. *Merchants, Mamluks, and Murder: The Political Economy of Trade in Eighteenth-Century Basra*. Albany: State University of New York Press, 2001.

Abdul-Rauf, Muhammad. *A Muslim's Reflections on Democratic Capitalism*. Washington, D.C.: American Enterprise Institute, 1984.

Abou-El-Haj, Rifaʿat ʿAli. *Formation of the Ottoman State: The Ottoman Empire, Sixteenth to Eighteenth Centuries*. Albany: State University of New York Press, 1991.

Abulafia, David. "Asia, Africa and the Trade of Medieval Europe." In *The Cambridge Economic History of Europe*, vol. 2, 2nd ed., edited by M. M. Postan and Edward Miller, pp. 402–73. Cambridge: Cambridge University Press, 1987.

Abu-Lughod, Ibrahim. *Arab Rediscovery of Europe: A Study in Cultural Encounters*. Princeton: Princeton University Press, 1963.

Abu-Lughod, Janet L. *Before European Hegemony: The World System A.D. 1250–1350*. New York: Oxford University Press, 1989.

Acemoglu, Daron, Simon Johnson, and James A. Robinson. "Reversal of Fortune: Geography and Institutions in the Making of the Modern World Income Distribution." *Quarterly Journal of Economics*, 118 (2002): 1231–94.

———. "The Rise of Europe: Atlantic Trade, Institutional Change, and Economic Growth." *American Economic Review*, 95 (2005): 546–79.

Acevedo, Gabriel A. "Islamic Fatalism and the Clash of Civilizations: An Appraisal of a Contentious and Dubious Theory." *Social Forces*, 86 (2008): 1711–52.

Agarwal, Rajshree, and Michael Gort. "First Mover Advantage and the Speed of Competitive Entry, 1887–1986." *Journal of Law and Economics*, 44 (2001): 161–77.

Aghassian, Michel, and Kéram Kévonian. "The Armenian Merchant Network: Overall Autonomy and Local Integration," translated by Cyprian P. Blamires. In *Merchants, Companies and Trade: Europe and Asia in the Early Modern Era*, edited by Sushil Chaudhury and Michel Morineau, pp. 74–94. Cambridge: Cambridge University Press, 1999.

Aghion, Philippe, and Peter W. Howitt. *Endogenous Growth Theory*. Cambridge, Mass.: MIT Press, 1998.

Ágoston, Gábor. *Guns for the Sultan: Military Power and the Weapons Industry in the Ottoman Empire*. Cambridge: Cambridge University Press, 2005.

Ahmad, Feroz. "Ottoman Perceptions of the Capitulations 1800–1914." *Journal of Islamic Studies*, 11 (2000): 1–20.

Ahmad, Jalal Al-e. *Plagued by the West (Gharbzadegi)*, translated by Paul Sprachman. Delmar, N.Y.: Caravan Books, 1982; original Persian edition, 1962.

Ajrouch, Kristine J., and Mansoor Moaddel. "Social Structure versus Perception: A Cross-national Comparison of Self-Rated Health in Egypt, Iran, Jordan and the United States." In *Values and Perceptions of the Islamic and Middle Eastern Publics*, edited by Mansoor Moaddel, pp. 181–208. New York: Palgrave Macmillan, 2007.

Akbar, Mohammad. "Ideology, Environment and Entrepreneurship: Typologies from Islamic Texts and History." *Journal of Entrepreneurship*, 2 (1993): 135–54.

Akbarzadeh, Shahram, editor. *Islam and Globalization: Critical Concepts in Islamic Studies*, vol. 3. London: Routledge, 2006.

Akgündüz, Ahmet. *İslam Hukukunda ve Osmanlı Tatbikatında Vakıf Müessesesi*, 2nd ed. Istanbul: OSAV, 1996.

Akın, Nur. *19. Yüzyılın İkinci Yarısında Galata ve Pera*. Istanbul: Literatür Yayınları, 1998.

Aktar, Ayhan. "Bursa'da Devlet ve Ekonomi." In *Bir Masaldı Bursa ...*, edited by Engin Yenal, pp. 119–43. Istanbul: YKY, 1996.

———. "Economic Nationalism in Turkey: The Formative Years, 1912–1925." *Boğaziçi Journal: Review of Social, Economic, and Administrative Studies*, 10 (1996): 263–90.

Akyıldız, Ali. *Tanzimat Dönemi Osmanlı Merkez Teşkilâtında Reform*. Istanbul: Eren, 1993.

———. *Ottoman Securities*. Istanbul: Türk Ekonomi Bankası, 2001.

———. *Anka'nın Sonbaharı: Osmanlı'da İktisadî Modernleşme ve Uluslararası Sermaye*. Istanbul: İletişim, 2005.

Al-Azmeh, Aziz. *Islamic Law: Social and Historical Contexts*. London: Routledge, 1988.

Alkan, Mehmet Ö. "1856–1945, İstanbul'da Sivil Toplum Kurumları: Toplumsal Örgütlenmenin Gelişimi." In *Tanzimat'tan Günümüze İstanbul'da STK'lar*, edited by Ahmet N. Yücekök, İlter Turan, and Mehmet Ö. Alkan, pp. 79–145. İstanbul: Tarih Vakfı, 1998.

Al-Qattan, Najwa. "*Dhimmīs* in the Muslim Court: Legal Autonomy and Religious Discrimination." *International Journal of Middle East Studies* 31 (1999): 429–44.

———. "Litigants and Neighbors: The Communal Topography of Ottoman Damascus." *Comparative Studies in Society and History*, 44 (2002): 511–33.

Al-Shamat, Hania Abou. "The Educational Divide across Religious Groups in Nineteenth-Century Lebanon: Institutional Effects on the Demand for Curricular Modernization." *Journal of Islamic Studies*, 20 (2009): 317–51.

Ambrose, Gwilym. "English Traders at Aleppo (1658–1756)." *Economic History Review*, 3 (1931): 246–67.

Amin, Samir. *The Arab Nation*, translated by Michael Pallis. London: Zed Press, 1978; original edition, 1976.

Anderson, M. S. *The Rise of Modern Diplomacy, 1450–1919*. London: Longman, 1993.

Anderson, Norman. "Law Reform in Egypt: 1850–1950." In *Political and Social Change in Modern Egypt*, edited by Peter M. Holt, pp. 209–30. London: Oxford University Press, 1968.

———. *Law Reform in the Muslim World*. London: Athlone Press, 1976.

Anderson, Sonia P. *An English Consul in Turkey: Paul Rycaut at Smyrna, 1667–1678*. Oxford: Clarendon Press, 1989.

Aoki, Masahiko. *Toward a Comparative Institutional Analysis*. Cambridge, Mass.: MIT Press, 2001.

Arbel, Benjamin. *Trading Nations: Jews and Venetians in the Early Modern Eastern Mediterranean*. Leiden: E. J. Brill, 1995.

Argenti, Philip P. *The Religious Minorities of Chios: Jews and Catholics*. Cambridge: Cambridge University Press, 1970.

Arjomand, Said Amir. "Philanthropy, the Law, and Public Policy in the Islamic World before the Modern Era." In *Philanthropy in the World's Traditions*, edited by Warren F. Ilchman, Stanley N. Katz, and Edward L. Queen, pp. 109–32. Bloomington: Indiana University Press, 1998.

———. "Transformation of the Islamicate Civilization: A Turning Point in the Thirteenth Century?" *Medieval Encounters*, 10 (2004): 213–45.

Arnakis, G. Georgiades. "The Greek Church of Constantinople and the Ottoman Empire." *Journal of Modern History*, 24 (1952): 235–50.

Arnold, Thomas W. *The Preaching of Islam: A History of the Propagation of the Muslim Faith*. London: Constable and Co., 1913.

Arthur, W. Brian. *Increasing Returns and Path Dependence in the Economy*. Ann Arbor: University of Michigan Press, 1994.

Ashtor, Eliyahu. "The Kārimī Merchants." *Journal of the Royal Asiatic Society*, 1–2 (1956): 45–56.

———. "Banking Instruments between the Muslim East and the Christian West." *Journal of European Economic History*, 1 (1973): 553–73.

———. *A Social and Economic History of the Near East in the Middle Ages*. Berkeley: University of California Press, 1976.

———. "Discussion on Abraham L. Udovitch, 'Time, Sea, and Society: Duration of Commercial Voyages on the Southern Shores of the Mediterranean during the High Middle Ages'." In *La Navigazione Mediterranea Nell'Alto Medievo*, vol. 2, pp. 546–63. Spoleto, Italy: Presso la Sede del Centro, 1978.

———. *Levant Trade in the Later Middle Ages*. Princeton: Princeton University Press, 1983.

Atay, Falih Rıfkı. *Çankaya: Atatürk'ün Doğumundan Ölümüne Kadar*, 2nd ed. Istanbul: Bateş, 1969.

Avcıoğlu, Doğan. *Millî Kurtuluş Tarihi: 1838'den 1995'e*, 3 vols. Istanbul: İstanbul Matbaası, 1974.

Ayalon, Ami. *The Press in the Arab Middle East: A History*. New York: Oxford University Press, 1995.

Aydın, M. Âkif. *İslâm-Osmanlı Aile Hukuku*. Istanbul: Marmara Üniversitesi İlâhiyat Fakültesi Vakfı, 1985.

———. "Batılılaşma, Hukuk." *Türkiye Diyanet Vakfı İslâm Ansiklopedisi*, vol. 5, pp. 162–67. Istanbul: Türkiye Diyanet Vakfı, 1992.

Azzam, Henry T. *The Emerging Arab Capital Markets: Investment Opportunities in Relatively Underplayed Markets*. London: Kegan Paul International, 1997.

Baer, Gabriel. *A History of Landownership in Modern Egypt, 1800–1950*. London: Oxford University Press, 1962.

———. "Social Change in Egypt: 1800–1914." In *Political and Social Change in Modern Egypt*, edited by P. M. Holt, pp. 135–61. London: Oxford University Press, 1968.

———. *Studies in the Social History of Modern Egypt*. Chicago: University of Chicago Press, 1969.

———. "Guilds in Middle Eastern History." In *Studies in the Economic History of the Middle East from the Rise of Islam to the Present Day*, edited by Michael A. Cook, pp. 11–30. London: Oxford University Press, 1970.

Bağış, Ali İhsan. *Osmanlı Ticaretinde Gayrî Müslimler*. Ankara: Turhan Kitabevi, 1983.

Baker, John H. *An Introduction to English Legal History*, 4th ed. Oxford: Oxford University Press, 2002.

Bakhit, Muhammad Adnan. "The Christian Population of the Province of Damascus in the Sixteenth Century." In *Christians and Jews in the Ottoman Empire, Vol. 2: The Arabic-Speaking Lands*, edited by Benjamin Braude and Bernard Lewis, pp. 19–66. New York: Holmes & Meier, 1982.

Bakhtiar, Laleh, editor. *Encyclopedia of Islamic Law: A Compendium of the Major Schools*. Chicago: ABC International, 1996.

Balla, Eliana, and Noel D. Johnson. "Fiscal Crisis and Institutional Change in the Ottoman Empire and France." *Journal of Economic History*, 69 (2009): 809–45.

Barbir, Karl K. *Ottoman Rule in Damascus, 1708–1758*. Princeton: Princeton University Press, 1980.

Barbour, Violet. "Consular Service in the Reign of Charles II." *American Historical Review*, 33 (1928): 553–78.

Barkan, Ömer Lütfi. "Edirne Askerî Kassamına Âit Tereke Defterleri (1545–1659)." *Belgeler*, 3 (1966): 1–46.

———. "Türkiye'de Din ve Devlet İlişkilerinin Tarihsel Gelişimi." In *Cumhuriyetin 50. Yıldönümü Semineri*, edited by Türk Tarih Kurumu, pp. 49–97. Ankara: Türk Tarih Kurumu, 1975.

————. *Türkiye'de Toprak Meselesi: Toplu Eserler 1.* Istanbul: Gözlem Yayınları, 1980.

Barkey, Karen. *Bandits and Bureaucrats: The Ottoman Route to State Centralization.* Ithaca: Cornell University Press, 1994.

Başar, Ahmet Hamdi. "Zaferden Sonra İstanbulda Başlayan İktisadî Savaş." *Barış Dünyası,* 54 (1966): 52–60.

Bashear, Suliman. *Arabs and Others in Early Islam.* Princeton: Darwin Press, 1997.

Baskin, Jonathan Barron, and Paul J. Miranti, Jr. *A History of Corporate Finance.* Cambridge: Cambridge University Press, 1997.

Bates, Robert H., Avner Greif, Margaret Levi, Jean-Laurent Rosenthal, and Barry R. Weingast. *Analytic Narratives.* Princeton: Princeton University Press, 1998.

Baumol, William J., John C. Panzar, and Robert D. Willig. *Contestable Markets and the Theory of Industry Structure.* San Diego: Harcourt Brace Jovanovich, 1982.

Bebchuk, Lucian Arye, and Mark J. Roe. "A Theory of Path Dependence in Corporate Ownership and Governance." *Stanford Law Review,* 52 (1999): 127–70.

Behar, Cem. *The Population of the Ottoman Empire and Turkey, 1500–1927.* Ankara: State Institute of Statistics, 1996.

Behdad, Sohrab. "A Disputed Utopia: Islamic Economics in Revolutionary Iran." *Comparative Studies in Society and History,* 36 (1994): 775–813.

Behrens-Abouseif, Doris. *Azbakkiyya and Its Environs: From Azbak to Ismāʿīl, 1476–1879.* Cairo: Institut Français d'Archéologie Orientale, 1985.

Benedick, Richard E. *Industrial Finance in Iran: A Study of Financial Practices in an Underdeveloped Economy.* Cambridge, Mass.: Harvard University Press, 1964.

Benson, Bruce. "The Spontaneous Evolution of Commercial Law." *Southern Economic Journal* 55 (1989): 644–61.

Bent, J. Theodore. "The English in the Levant." *English Historical Review,* 5 (1890): 654–64.

Benthall, Jonathan, and Jérôme Bellion-Jourdan. *The Charitable Crescent: Politics of Aid in the Muslim World.* London: I. B. Tauris, 2003.

Berkes, Niyazi. *The Development of Secularism in Turkey.* New York: Routledge, 1998; original edition, 1964.

Berkowitz, Daniel, Katharina Pistor, and Jean-François Richard. "The Transplant Effect." *American Journal of Comparative Law,* 51 (2003): 163–203.

Berman, Eli. *Radical, Religious, and Violent: The New Economics of Terrorism.* Cambridge, Mass.: MIT Press, 2009.

Berman, Harold J. *Law and Revolution: The Formation of the Western Legal Tradition.* Cambridge, Mass.: Harvard University Press, 1983.

Berque, Jacques. "The Establishment of the Colonial Economy." In *Beginnings of Modernization in the Middle East: The Nineteenth Century,* edited by William

R. Polk and Richard L. Chambers, pp. 223–43. Chicago: University of Chicago Press, 1968.

Bertocchi, Graziella. "The Law of Primogeniture and the Transition from Landed Aristocracy to Industrial Democracy." *Journal of Economic Growth*, 11 (2006): 43–70.

Bianquis, Thierry. "The Family in Arab Islam." In *A History of the Family*, vol. 1, edited by André Burguière, Christiane Klapisch-Zuber, Martine Segalen, and Françoise Zonabend, pp. 601–47. Cambridge, Mass.: Harvard University Press, 1996.

Biegman, Nicolaas H. *The Turco-Ragusan Relationship: According to the Firmāns of Murād III (1575–1595) Extant in the State Archives of Dubrovnik*. The Hague: Mouton, 1967.

Birge, J. Kingsley et al. *A Survey of Some Social Conditions in Smyrna, Asia Minor*. Izmir: International American College of Izmir, 1921.

Black, Cyril E., and L. Carl Brown, editors. *Modernization in the Middle East*. Princeton: Darwin Press, 1992.

Blair, Margaret M. "The Neglected Benefits of the Corporate Form: Entity Status and the Separation of Asset Ownership from Control." In *Corporate Governance and Firm Organization: Microfoundations and Structural Forms*, edited by Anna Gandori, pp. 45–66. New York: Oxford University Press, 2004.

Blank, Hartmut, Jochen Musch, and Rüdiger F. Pohl. "Hindsight Bias: On Being Wise After the Event." *Social Cognition*, 25 (2007): 1–9.

Bloom, Jonathan M. *Paper before Print: The History and Impact of Paper in the Islamic World*. New Haven: Yale University Press, 2001.

Blussé, Leonard, and Femme Gaastra. "Companies and Trade: Some Reflections on a Workshop and a Concept." In *Companies and Trade*, edited by Leonard Blussé and Femme Gaastra, pp. 3–13. Leiden: Leiden University Press, 1981.

Boogert, Maurits H. van den. *The Capitulations and the Ottoman Legal System: Qadis, Consuls, and Beratlıs in the 18th Century*. Leiden: Brill, 2005.

Borel, F. *De l'Origine et des Fonctions des Consuls*. St. Petersburg: A. Pluchart, 1807.

Bosworth, C. E. "The Concept of *Dhimma* in Early Islam." In *Christians and Jews in the Ottoman Empire, Vol. 1: The Central Lands*, edited by Benjamin Braude and Bernard Lewis, pp. 37–51. New York: Holmes & Meier, 1982.

Bouchon, Geneviève. "Trade in the Indian Ocean at the Dawn of the Sixteenth Century," translated by Cyprian P. Blamires. In *Merchants, Companies and Trade: Europe and Asia in the Early Modern Era*, edited by Sushil Chaudhury and Michel Morineau, pp. 42–51. Cambridge: Cambridge University Press, 1999.

Bowen, Harold. "'Awārid." *Encyclopaedia of Islam*, 2nd ed., vol. 1, pp. 760–61. Leiden: E. J. Brill, 1960.

Bowring, John. *Report on the Commercial Statistics of Syria*. London: William Clowes and Sons, 1840.

Braude, Benjamin. "Venture and Faith in the Commercial Life of the Ottoman Balkans." *International History Review*, 7 (1985): 519–42.

Braude, Benjamin, and Bernard Lewis, editors. *Christians and Jews in the Ottoman Empire*, 2 vols. New York: Holmes & Meier, 1982.

Braude, Benjamin, and Bernard Lewis. "Introduction." In *Christians and Jews in the Ottoman Empire, Vol. 1: The Central Lands*, edited by Benjamin Braude and Bernard Lewis, pp. 1–34. New York: Holmes & Meier, 1982.

Braudel, Fernand. *The Perspective of the World* (vol. 3 of *Civilization and Capitalism, 15th–18th Century*), translated by Siân Reynolds. New York: Harper & Row, 1982; original French edition, 1979.

Brenner, Robert. *Merchants and Revolution: Commercial Change, Political Conflict, and London's Overseas Traders, 1550–1653*. Princeton: Princeton University Press, 1993.

Brinkmann, Carl. "Primogeniture." *Encyclopaedia of the Social Sciences*, vol. 11, pp. 402–5. New York: Macmillan, 1933.

Brown, Marshall Philip. *Foreigners in Turkey: Their Juridical Status*. Princeton: Princeton University Press, 1914.

Brown, Nathan J. *The Rule of Law in the Arab World: Courts in Egypt and the Gulf*. Cambridge: Cambridge University Press, 1997.

Brummett, Palmira. *Ottoman Seapower and Levantine Diplomacy in the Age of Discovery*. Albany: State University of New York Press, 1994.

Bullard, Reader. *Large and Loving Privileges: The Capitulations in the Middle East and North Africa*. Glasgow: Jackson, Son, and Co., 1960.

Bulliet, Richard W. *Conversion to Islam in the Medieval Period: An Essay in Quantitative History*. Cambridge, Mass.: Harvard University Press, 1979.

Bulsara, Sohrab Jamshedjee, editor. *The Laws of the Ancient Persians as Found in the "Mâtîkân Ê Hazâr Dâtastân."* Bombay: Hoshang T. Anklesaria, 1937.

Bulut, Mehmet. *Ottoman-Dutch Economic Relations in the Early Modern Period, 1571–1699*. Amsterdam: Hilversum Verloren, 2001.

———. "The Role of the Ottomans and Dutch in the Commercial Integration between the Levant and Atlantic in the Seventeenth Century." *Journal of the Economic and Social History of the Orient*, 45 (2002): 197–230.

Caeiro, Alexandre. "The Shifting Moral Universes of the Islamic Tradition of Iftā': A Diachronic Study of Four Adab al-Fatwā Manuals." *Muslim World*, 96 (2006): 661–85.

Çağatay, Neşet. "Osmanlı İmparatorluğunda Reayadan Alınan Vergi ve Resimler." *Ankara Üniversitesi Dil ve Tarih-Coğrafya Fakültesi Dergisi*, 5 (1947): 483–511.

———. "Osmanlı İmparatorluğunda Ribā-Faiz Konusu ve Bankacılık." *Vakıflar Dergisi*, 9 (1971): 31–56.

Cahen, Claude. "Darība." *Encyclopedia of Islam*, 2nd ed., vol. 2, pp. 142–45. Leiden: E. J. Brill, 1965.

———. "Quelques Mots sur le Déclin Commercial du Monde Musulman à la Fin du Moyen Age." In *Studies in the Economic History of the Middle East*, edited by Michael A. Cook, pp. 31–36. London: Oxford University Press, 1970.

———. "Y a-t-il Eu des Corporations Professionelles dans le Monde Musulman Classique?" In *The Islamic City*, edited by Albert H. Hourani and Samuel M. Stern, pp. 51–63. Oxford: Bruno Cassirer, 1970.

———. "Kharādj, in the Central and Western Islamic Lands." *Encyclopedia of Islam*, 2nd ed., vol. 4, pp. 1030–34. Leiden: E. J. Brill, 1978.

Cairncross, John. *After Polygamy Was Made a Sin: The Social History of Christian Polygamy*. London: Routledge & Kegan Paul, 1974.

Calabresi, Guido, and Philip Bobbitt. *Tragic Choices: The Conflict Society Confronts in the Allocation of Tragically Scarce Resources*. New York: W. W. Norton, 1978.

Carlos, Ann M., and Stephen Nicholas. "Giants of an Earlier Capitalism: The Early Chartered Companies as an Analogue of the Modern Multinational." *Business History Review*, 26 (1988): 398–419.

Casella, Alessandra. "On Market Integration and the Development of Institutions: The Case of International Commercial Arbitration." *European Economic Review*, 40 (1996): 155–86.

Cecil, Evelyn. *Primogeniture: A Short History of Its Development in Various Countries and Its Practical Effects*. London: John Murray, 1895.

Çelik, Zeynep. *The Remaking of Istanbul: Portrait of an Ottoman City in the Nineteenth Century*. Seattle: University of Washington Press, 1986.

Cevdet Paşa. *Tezâkir*, 4 vols., edited by Cavid Baysun. Ankara: Türk Tarih Kurumu, 1986; original edition, 1855–95.

Chandler, Alfred D., Jr. *The Visible Hand: The Managerial Revolution in American Business*. Cambridge, Mass.: Harvard University Press, 1977.

———. *Scale and Scope: The Dynamics of Industrial Capitalism*. Cambridge, Mass.: Harvard University Press, 1990.

Chapra, M. Umer. *Towards a Just Monetary System*. Leicester, U.K.: Islamic Foundation, 1985.

Chaudhuri, K. N. *Trade and Civilization in the Indian Ocean: An Economic History from the Rise of Islam to 1750*. Cambridge: Cambridge University Press, 1985.

Chaudhury, Sushil, and Michel Morineau, editors. *Merchants, Companies and Trade: Europe and Asia in the Early Modern Era*. Cambridge: Cambridge University Press, 1999.

Christelow, Allan. *Muslim Law Courts and the French Colonial State in Algeria*. Princeton: Princeton University Press, 1985.

Church, Roy. "The Family Firm in Industrial Capitalism: International Perspectives on Hypotheses and History." *Business History*, 35 (1993): 17–43.

Chwe, Suk-Young Michael. *Rational Ritual: Culture, Coordination, and Common Knowedge*. Princeton: Princeton University Press, 2001.

Çiçek, Kemal. "Cemaat Mahkemesinden Kadı Mahkemesine Zimmilerin Yargı Tercihi." In *Pax Ottomana: Studies in Memoriam Prof. Dr. Nejat Göyünç*, edited by Kemal Çiçek, pp. 31–49. Haarlem, the Netherlands: Stichting Sota, 2001.

Çizakça, Murat. *A Comparative Evolution of Business Partnerships: The Islamic World and Europe, with Special Reference to the Ottoman Archives*. Leiden: E. J. Brill, 1996.

———. "Towards a Comparative Economic History of the *Waqf* System." *Al-Shajarah*, 2 (1997): 63–102.

———. *A History of Philanthropic Foundations: The Islamic World from the Seventh Century to the Present*. Istanbul: Boğaziçi University Press, 2000.

———. "Comparative Evolution and Cross-Cultural Borrowing of Institutions: Islamic World and the West from the Seventh Century to the Present." Unpublished paper, Bahçeşehir University, 2004.

Clark, Janine A. *Islam, Charity, and Activism: Middle-Class Networks and Social Welfare in Egypt, Jordan, and Yemen*. Bloomington: University of Indiana Press, 2004.

Clay, Christopher. "The Origins of Modern Banking in the Levant: The Branch Network of the Imperial Ottoman Bank, 1890–1914." *International Journal of Middle East Studies*, 26 (1994): 589–614.

———. "Western Banking and the Ottoman Economy before 1890: A Story of Disappointed Expectations." *Journal of European Economic History*, 28 (1999): 473–509.

Code Napoléon, 2 volumes, edited and translated by Bryan Bartlett. London: W. Reed, 1811.

Cohen, Amnon. *Jewish Life under Islam: Jerusalem in the Sixteenth Century*. Cambridge, Mass.: Harvard University Press, 1984.

———. "Mīrī." *Encyclopaedia of Islam*, 2nd ed., vol. 7, pp. 125–26. Leiden: E. J. Brill, 1993.

———. "Communal Legal Entities in a Muslim Setting, Theory and Practice: The Jewish Community in Sixteenth-Century Jerusalem." *Islamic Law and Society*, 3 (1996): 75–90.

Cohen, Hayyim J. "The Economic Background and the Secular Occupations of Muslim Jurisprudents and Traditionists in the Classical Period of Islam (Until the Middle of the Eleventh Century)." *Journal of the Economic and Social History of the Orient*, 13 (1970): 16–61.

Cohen, Mark R. *Under Crescent and Cross: The Jews in the Middle Ages*. Princeton: Princeton University Press, 1994.

———. "What Was the Pact of 'Umar? A Literary-Historical Survey." *Jerusalem Studies in Arabic and Islam*, 23(1999): 100–57.

Coing, Helmut. *Europäisches Privatrecht*, vol. 1. Munich: C. H. Bech'sche Verlagbuchhandlung (Oscar Beck), 1985.

Coleman, James S. *Foundations of Social Theory*. Cambridge, Mass.: Harvard University Press, 1990.

Coleman, Simon, and John Elsner. *Pilgrimage: Past and Present in the World Religions*. Cambridge, Mass.: Harvard University Press, 1995.

Comair-Obeid, Nayla. *The Law of Business Contracts in the Middle East*. London: Kluwer, 1996.

Constable, Olivia Remie. *Trade and Traders in Muslim Spain: The Commercial Realignment of the Iberian Peninsula, 900–1500*. New York: Cambridge University Press, 1994.

———. *Housing the Stranger in the Mediterranean World: Lodging, Trade, and Travel in Late Antiquity and the Middle Ages*. Cambridge: Cambridge University Press, 2003.

Cook, Michael. "The Opponents of the Writing of Tradition in Early Islam." *Arabica*, 44 (1997): 437–530.

———. *Commanding Right and Forbidding Wrong in Islamic Thought*. Cambridge: Cambridge University Press, 2000.

Cooter, Robert, and Hans-Bernd Schaefer. "Law and the Poverty of Nations." Unpublished book manuscript, 2009.

Coşgel, Metin M. "Efficiency and Continuity in Public Finance: The Ottoman System of Taxation." *International Journal of Middle East Studies*, 37 (2005): 567–86.

Coşgel, Metin, M., and Thomas J. Miceli. "Risk, Transaction Costs, and Tax Assignment: Government Finance in the Ottoman Empire." *Journal of Economic History*, 65 (2005): 806–21.

Coulson, N. J. *Succession in the Muslim Family*. Cambridge: Cambridge University Press, 1971.

Courbage, Youssef, and Philippe Fargues. *Christians and Jews under Islam*, translated by Judy Mabro. London: I. B. Tauris, 1997.

Cowen, Tyler. *Creative Destruction: How Globalization Is Changing the World's Cultures*. Princeton: Princeton University Press, 2002.

Cromer, Evelyn Baring. *Modern Egypt*, 2 vols. New York: Macmillan, 1909.

Crone, Patricia. *Meccan Trade and the Rise of Islam*. Princeton: Princeton University Press, 1987.

———. *Roman, Provincial, and Islamic Law: The Origins of the Islamic Patronate*. Cambridge: Cambridge University Press, 1987.

———. *God's Rule: Government and Islam*. New York: Columbia University Press, 2004.

Cuno, Kenneth M. *The Pasha's Peasants: Land, Society, and Economy in Lower Egypt, 1740–1858*. Cambridge: Cambridge University Press, 1992.

Curtin, Philip D. *Cross-Cultural Trade in World History*. Cambridge: Cambridge University Press, 1984.

———. *The World and the West: The European Challenge and the Overseas Response in the Age of Empire*. Cambridge: Cambridge University Press, 2000.

Dagron, Gilbert. "The Urban Economy, Seventh-Twelfth Centuries." In *The Economic History of Byzantium: From the Seventh through the Fifteenth Century*, edited by Angeliki Laiou, pp. 393–461. Washington, D.C.: Dumbarton Oaks, 2002.

Dale, Stephen F. "Trade, Conversion and the Growth of the Islamic Community of Kerala, South India." *Studia Islamica*, 71 (1990): 155–75.

Dallal, Ahmad S. "Ummah." *Oxford Encyclopedia of the Modern Islamic World*, vol. 4, pp. 267–70. New York: Oxford University Press, 1995.

Dalrymple, James. *The Institutions of the Law of Scotland*, 2nd ed., vol. 1. Edinburgh: Bell and Bradfute, 1882.

Daniel, Norman. *Islam and the West: The Making of an Image*. Edinburgh: Edinburgh University Press, 1960.

Darling, Linda. *Revenue-Raising and Legitimacy: Tax Collection and Finance Administration in the Ottoman Empire, 1560–1660*. Leiden: E. J. Brill, 1996.

D'Arms, John H. *Commerce and Social Standing in Ancient Rome*. Cambridge, Mass.: Harvard University Press, 1981.

Darwin, Charles. *On the Origin of Species*. London: John Murray, 1859.

David, Paul. "Why Are Institutions the 'Carriers of History'?: Path Dependence and the Evolution of Conventions, Organizations and Institutions." *Structural Change and Economic Dynamics*, 5 (1994): 205–20.

Davidson, James Dale and William Rees-Mogg. *The Great Reckoning*. London: Sidgwick and Jackson, 1991.

Davis, John P. *Corporations: A Study of the Origin and Development of Great Business Combinations and Their Relation to the Authority of the State*, 2 vols. New York: Capricorn Books, 1961; original edition 1905.

Davis, Ralph. *Aleppo and Devonshire Square: English Traders in the Levant in the Eighteenth Century*. London: Macmillan, 1967.

Davison, Roderic H. "The *Millet*s as Agents of Change in the Nineteenth-Century Ottoman Empire." In *Christians and Jews in the Ottoman Empire, Vol. 1: The Central Lands*, edited by Benjamin Braude and Bernard Lewis, pp. 319–37. New York: Holmes & Meier, 1982.

Delumeau, Jean. *Sin and Fear: The Emergence of a Western Guilt Culture, 13th–18th Centuries*, translated by Eric Nicholson. New York: St. Martin's Press, 1990; original French edition, 1983.

De Groot, Alexander H. *The Ottoman Empire and the Dutch Republic: A History of the Earliest Diplomatic Relations*. Leiden: Nederlands Historisch-Archaeologisch Instituut, 1978.

———. "The Organization of Western European Trade in the Levant, 1500–1800." In *Companies and Trade*, edited by Leonard Blussé and Femme Gaastra, pp. 231–41. The Leiden: Leiden University Press, 1981.

———. "Some Thoughts on the Nature of the Capitulations: The Historical Development of the Capitulary Regime in the Ottoman Middle East from the

Fifteenth to the Nineteenth Centuries." Turkology Working Paper, University of Leiden, 2003.

Depping, G. B. *Histoire du Commerce entre le Levant et l'Europe*, 2 vols. New York: Burt Franklin, 1970; original edition, 1828.

De Roover, Raymond. *Money, Banking, and Credit in Mediaeval Bruges*. Cambridge, Mass.: Mediaeval Academy of America, 1948.

———. *The Rise and Decline of the Medici Bank, 1397–1494*. Cambridge, Mass.: Harvard University Press, 1963.

———. "The Organization of Trade." In *The Cambridge Economic History of Europe*, vol. 3, edited by M. M. Postan, E. E. Rich, and Edward Miller, pp. 42–118. Cambridge: Cambridge University Press, 1965.

———. *Business, Banking, and Economic Thought in Late Medieval and Early Modern Europe*, edited by Julius Kirshner. Chicago: University of Chicago Press, 1974.

De Vries, Jan. *Economy of Europe in an Age of Crisis, 1600–1750*. Cambridge: Cambridge University Press, 1976.

Diamond, Jared. *Guns, Germs, and Steel: The Fates of Human Societies*. New York: W. W. Norton, 1997.

Dien, Mawil Y. Izzi. "Suftadja." *Encyclopaedia of Islam*, 2nd ed., vol. 9, pp. 769–70. Leiden: E. J. Brill, 1997.

———. "Wakāla." *Encyclopaedia of Islam*, 2nd ed., vol. 11, pp. 57–58. Leiden: E. J. Brill, 2002.

D'Ohsson, Mouradgea. *Tableau Général de l'Empire Ottoman*, 7 volumes. Istanbul: ISIS, 2001; original edition, 1824.

Dols, Michael W. *The Black Death in the Middle East*. Princeton: Princeton University Press, 1977.

Donner, Fred McGraw. "Mecca's Food Supplies and Muhammad's Boycott." *Journal of the Economic and Social History of the Orient*, 20 (1977): 249–66.

Doumani, Beshara. *Rediscovering Palestine: Merchants and Peasants in Jabal Nablus, 1700–1900*. Berkeley: University of California Press, 1995.

———. "Endowing Family: *Waqf*, Property Devolution, and Gender in Greater Syria, 1800 to 1860." *Comparative Studies in Society and History*, 40 (1998): 3–41.

Dumont, Paul. "Jews, Muslims, and Cholera: Intercommunal Relations in Baghdad at the End of the Nineteenth Century." In *The Jews of the Ottoman Empire*, edited by Avigdor Levy, pp. 353–72. Princeton: Darwin Press, 1994.

Dursteler, Eric R. *Venetians in Constantinople: Nation, Identity, and Coexistence in the Early Modern Mediterranean*. Baltimore: Johns Hopkins University Press, 2006.

Düzdağ, M. Ertuğrul. *Şeyhülislâm Ebussuûd Efendi Fetvaları Işığında 16. Asır Türk Hayatı*. Istanbul: Enderun Kitabevi, 1983.

Easterlin, Richard A. *Growth Triumphant: The Twenty-first Century in Historical Perspective*. Ann Arbor: University of Michigan Press, 1996.

Eaton, Richard M. *The Rise of Islam and the Bengal Frontier, 1204–1760.* Berkeley: University of California Press, 1993.

Economides, Nicholas. "The Economics of Networks." *International Journal of Industrial Organization,* 14 (1996): 673–99.

Egypt. *Recensement Général de l'Égypte, 1er Juin 1897,* vol. 1. Cairo: Government of Egypt, 1898.

————. *Statistical Yearbook of Egypt for 1909.* Cairo: Ministry of Finance Statistical Department, 1909.

————. *Annuaire Statistique de l'Égypte, 1925–26.* Cairo: Ministry of Finance Statistical Department, 1927.

Ekelund, Robert B., Jr., and Robert D. Tollison. *Politicized Economies: Monarchy, Monopoly, and Mercantilism.* College Station: Texas A&M University Press, 1997.

Ekinci, Ekrem Buğra. *Tanzimat ve Sonrası Osmanlı Mahkemeleri.* Istanbul: Arı Sanat, 2004.

Eldem, Edhem. *French Trade in Istanbul in the Eighteenth Century.* Leiden: Brill, 1999.

————. *A History of the Ottoman Bank.* Istanbul: Economic and Social History Foundation of Turkey, 1999.

El-Gamal, Mahmoud A. *Islamic Finance: Law, Economics, and Practice.* New York: Cambridge University Press, 2006.

El-Nahal, Galal H. *The Judicial Administration of Ottoman Egypt in the Seventeenth Century.* Minneapolis: Bibliotheca Islamica, 1979.

Elster, Jon. *Nuts and Bolts for the Social Sciences.* New York: Cambridge University Press, 1989.

Engerman, Stanley L., and Kenneth L. Sokoloff. "Factor Endowments, Institutions, and Differential Paths of Growth Among New World Economies." In *How Latin America Fell Behind: Essays on the Economic Histories of Brazil and Mexico, 1800–1914,* edited by Stephen Haber, pp. 260–304. Stanford: Stanford University Press, 1997.

Engineer, Ashgar Ali. *The Origins and Development of Islam.* Kuala Lumpur: Ikraq, 1990.

Ensminger, Jean. "Transaction Costs and Islam: Explaining Conversion in Africa." *Journal of Institutional and Theoretical Economics,* 153 (1997): 4–29.

Epstein, Mordecai. *The English Levant Company: Its Foundation and Its History to 1640.* New York: Burt Franklin, 1908.

Epstein, Stephan R. *Freedom and Growth: The Rise of States and Markets in Europe, 1300–1750.* New York: Routledge, 2000.

Epstein, Steven A. *Genoa and the Genoese, 958–1528.* Chapel Hill: University of North Carolina Press, 1996.

Ergene, Boğaç A. "Costs of Court Usage in the Seventeenth- and Eighteenth-Century Ottoman Anatolia: Court Fees as Recorded in Estate Inventories." *Journal of the Economic and Social History of the Orient,* 45 (2002): 20–39.

———. "Evidence in Ottoman Courts: Oral and Written Documentation in Early-Modern Courts of Islamic Law." *Journal of the American Oriental Society*, 124 (2004): 471–91.

Ergene, Boğaç A., and Ali Berker. "Inheritance and Intergenerational Wealth Transmission in Eighteenth-Century Ottoman Kastamonu: An Empirical Investigation." *Journal of Family History*, 34 (2009): 25–47.

Eryılmaz, Bilal. *Osmanlı Devletinde Gayrimüslim Tebaanın Yönetimi*, 2nd ed. Istanbul: Risale, 1996.

Farooqi, Naim R. "Moguls, Ottomans, and Pilgrims: Protecting the Routes to Mecca in the Sixteenth and Seventeenth Centuries." *International History Review*, 10 (1988): 198–220.

Faroqhi, Suraiya. *Men of Modest Substance: House Owners and House Property: Seventeenth Century Ankara and Kayseri*. Cambridge: Cambridge University Press, 1987.

———. "The Venetian Presence in the Ottoman Empire, 1600–30." In *The Ottoman Empire and the World-Economy*, edited by Huri İslamoğlu-İnan, pp. 311–44. Cambridge: Cambridge University Press, 1987.

———. *Pilgrims and Sultans: The Hajj under the Ottomans, 1517–1683*. London: I. B. Tauris, 1994.

———. "Crisis and Change, 1590–1699." In *An Economic and Social History of the Ottoman Empire, 1300–1914*, edited by Halil İnalcık with Donald Quataert, pp. 411–636. New York: Cambridge University Press, 1994.

———. *Approaching Ottoman History: An Introduction to the Sources*. Cambridge: Cambridge University Press, 1999.

Farrell, Joseph, and Paul Klemperer. "Coordination and Lock-In: Competition with Switching Costs and Network Effects." In *Handbook of Industrial Organization*, vol. 3, edited by Mark Armstrong and Robert Porter, pp. 1967–2072. Amsterdam: North-Holland, 2007.

Fawaz, Leila Tarazi. *Merchants and Migrants in Nineteenth-Century Beirut*. Cambridge, Mass.: Harvard University Press, 1983.

Febvre, Lucien, and Henri-Jean Martin. *The Coming of the Book: The Impact of Printing, 1450–1800*, translated by David Gerard. London: NLB, 1976; original French edition, 1958.

Feldman, Noah. *The Fall and Rise of the Islamic State*. Princeton: Princeton University Press, 2008.

Fernandes, Leonor. "*Istibdal*: The Game of Exchange and Its Impact on the Urbanization of Mamluk Cairo." In *The Cairo Heritage: Essays in Honor of Laila Ali Ibrahim*, edited by Doris Behrens-Abouseif, pp. 203–22. Cairo: American University of Cairo Press, 2000.

Fertekligil, Azmi. *Türkiye'de Borsa'nın Tarihçesi*. Istanbul: İstanbul Menkul Kıymetler Borsası, 1993.

Fichtner, Paula Sutter. *Protestantism and Primogeniture in Early Modern Germany*. New Haven: Yale University Press, 1989.

Findlay, Ronald, and Kevin H. O'Rourke. *Power and Plenty: Trade, War, and the World Economy in the Second Millennium.* Princeton: Princeton University Press, 2007.

Findley, Carter V. *Bureaucratic Reform in the Ottoman Empire: The Sublime Porte, 1789–1922.* Princeton: Princeton University Press, 1980.

Finer, Samuel E. *The History of Government,* 3 vols. Oxford: Oxford University Press, 1997.

Finley, Moses I. *The Ancient Economy,* 2nd ed. Los Angeles: University of California Press, 1985.

Firestone, Ya'akov. "Production and Trade in an Islamic Context: Sharika Contracts in the Transitional Economy of Northern Samaria, 1853–1943 (I)." *International Journal of Middle East Studies* 6 (1975): 185–209.

Fischer, David Hackett. *Historians' Fallacies: Toward a Logic of Historical Thought.* London: Routledge & Kegan Paul, 1971.

Fischhoff, Baruch, and Ruth Beyth. "'I Knew It Would Happen'—Remembered Probabilities of Once Future Things." *Organizational Behavior and Human Performance,* 13 (1975): 1–16.

Fiske, Alan P., and Philip E. Tetlock. "Taboo Trade-offs: Reactions to Transactions that Transgress Spheres of Justice." *Political Psychology,* 18 (1997): 255–97.

Fleet, Kate. *European and Islamic Trade in the Early Ottoman State: The Merchants of Genoa and Turkey.* Cambridge: Cambridge University Press, 1999.

———. "Turkish-Latin Diplomatic Relations in the Fourteenth Century: The Case of the Consul." In *The Ottoman Capitulations: Text and Context,* edited by Maurits H. van den Boogert and Kate Fleet, pp. 605–11. Rome: Istituto per l'Oriente, 2003.

France. *Annuaire Statistique,* vol. 30. Paris: Ministère du Travail, 1911.

———. *Annuaire Statistique,* vol. 58. Paris: Ministère des Finances, 1952.

Frangakis-Syrett, Elena. *The Commerce of Smyrna in the Eighteenth Century (1700–1820).* Athens: Center for Asia Minor Studies, 1992.

———. "The Economic Activities of the Greek Community of İzmir in the Second Half of the Nineteenth and Early Twentieth Centuries." In *Ottoman Greeks in the Age of Nationalism: Politics, Economy, and Society in the Nineteenth Century,* edited by Dimitri Gondicas and Charles Issawi, pp. 17–44. Princeton: Darwin Press, 1999.

Frank, Andre Gunder. *ReOrient: Global Economy in the Asian Age.* Berkeley: University of California Press, 1998.

Freedeman, Charles E. *Joint-Stock Enterprise in France, 1807–1867: From Privileged Company to Modern Corporation.* Chapel Hill: University of North Carolina Press, 1979.

Frey, Linda S., and Marsha L. Frey. *The History of Diplomatic Immunity.* Columbus: Ohio State University Press, 1999.

Fyzee, Asaf A. A. *Outlines of Muhammadan Law,* 3rd ed. London: Oxford University Press, 1964.

Gaudiosi, Monica M. "The Influence of the Islamic Law of *Waqf* on the Development of the Trust in England: The Case of Merton College." *University of Pennsylvania Law Review*, 136 (1988): 1231–61.

Gedikli, Fethi. *Osmanlı Şirket Kültürü: XVI.–XVII. Yüzyıllarda Mudârebe Uygulaması*. Istanbul: İz Yayıncılık, 1998.

Gelderblom, Oscar, and Joost Jonker. "Completing a Financial Revolution: The Finance of the Dutch East India Trade and the Rise of the Amsterdam Capital Market, 1595–1612." *Journal of Economic History*, 64 (2004): 641–72.

Genç, Mehmet. *Osmanlı İmparatorluğunda Devlet ve Ekonomi*. Istanbul: Ötüken, 2000.

Gerber, Haim. *Economy and Society in an Ottoman City: Bursa, 1600–1700*. Jerusalem: Hebrew University, 1988.

———. *State, Society, and Law in Islam: Ottoman Law in Comparative Perspective*. Albany: State University of New York Press, 1994.

———. *Islamic Law and Culture, 1600–1840*. Leiden: Brill, 1999.

Gerschenkron, Alexander. *Economic Backwardness in Historical Perspective: A Book of Essays*. Cambridge, Mass: Harvard University Press, 1962.

Gessner, Volkmar, editor. *Contractual Certainty in International Trade: Empirical Studies and Theoretical Debates on Institutional Support for Global Economic Exchanges*. Oxford: Hart Publishing, 2009.

Gierke, Otto von. *Community in Historical Perspective*, translated by Mary Fischer. New York: Cambridge University Press, 1990; original German edition, 1868.

Gil, Moshe. "The Earliest *Waqf* Foundations." *Journal of Near Eastern Studies* (1998): 125–40.

———. "The Jewish Merchants in the Light of Eleventh-Century Geniza Documents." *Journal of the Economic and Social History of the Orient*, 46 (2003): 273–319.

Gilbar, Gad G. "Changing Patterns of Economic Ties: The Syrian and Iraqi Provinces in the 18th and 19th Centuries." In *The Syrian Land in the 18th and 19th Century*, edited by Thomas Philipp, pp. 55–67. Stuttgart: Franz Weiner, 1992.

———. "The Muslim Big Merchant-Entrepreneurs of the Middle East, 1860–1914." *Die Welt des Islams*, 43 (2003): 1–36.

Goffman, Daniel. *Izmir and the Levantine World, 1550–1650*. Seattle: University of Washington Press, 1990.

———. *Britons in the Ottoman Empire, 1642–1660*. Seattle: University of Washington Press, 1998.

———. *The Ottoman Empire and Early Modern Europe*. Cambridge: Cambridge University Press, 2002.

Goitein, Shelomo D. "The Rise of the Near-Eastern Bourgeoisie in Early Islamic Times." *Cahiers d'Histoire Mondiale*, 3 (1956): 593–604.

———. "Bankers Accounts from the Eleventh Century A.D." *Journal of the Economic and Social History of the Orient*, 9 (1966): 28–66.

————. *A Mediterranean Society, 1: Economic Foundations*. Berkeley: University of California Press, 1967.

————. *Studies in Islamic History and Institutions*. Leiden: E. J. Brill, 1968.

————. *A Mediterranean Society, 3: The Family*. Berkeley: University of California Press, 1978.

————. *A Mediterranean Society: An Abridgment in One Volume*, revised and edited by Jacob Lassner. Berkeley: University of California Press, 1999.

Goldberg, Jan. "On the Origins of *Majālis Al-Tujjār* in Mid-Nineteenth Century Egypt." *Islamic Law and Society*, 6 (1999): 193–223.

Goldziher, Ignáz. *Muslim Studies*, 2 vols., edited by Samuel M. Stern. Albany: State University of New York Press, 1967; original edition, 1888.

Goodblatt, Morris S. *Jewish Life in Turkey in the XVIth Century as Reflected in the Legal Writings of Samuel De Medina*. New York: Jewish Theological Seminary of America, 1952.

Goody, Jack. *The Development of the Family and Marriage in Europe*. Cambridge: Cambridge University Press, 1983.

————. *The Oriental, the Ancient, and the Primitive: Systems of Marriage and the Family in the Pre-Industrial Societies of Eurasia*. New York: Cambridge University Press, 1990.

————. *The European Family: An Historico-Anthropological Essay*. Oxford: Blackwell, 2000.

Great Britain. "Papers Respecting the Tariff of 1839 with the Porte." Foreign Office 424/4.

Greene, Molly. *A Shared World: Christians and Muslims in the Early Modern Mediterranean*. Princeton: Princeton University Press, 2000.

————. "The Italian Connection: Ottoman Merchants in Italy." Unpublished paper, Princeton University, 2008.

Greif, Avner. "Cultural Beliefs and the Organization of Society: A Historical and Theoretical Reflection on Collectivist and Individualist Societies." *Journal of Political Economy* 102 (1994): 912–50.

————. "The Study of Organizations and Evolving Organizational Forms through History: Reflections from the Late Medieval Family Firm." *Industrial and Corporate Change*, 5 (1996): 473–501.

————. "Impersonal Exchange without Impartial Law: The Community Responsibility System." *Chicago Journal of International Law*, 5 (2004): 109–38.

————. *Institutions and the Path to the Modern Economy: Lessons from Medieval Trade*. New York: Cambridge University Press, 2006.

Griffiths, John. "What Is Legal Pluralism?" *Journal of Legal Pluralism and Unofficial Law*, 24 (1986): 1–55.

Gutas, Dimitri. *Greek Thought, Arabic Culture: The Graeco-Arabic Translation Movement in Baghdad and Early 'Abbāsid Society (2nd–4th/8th–10th centuries)*. London: Routledge, 1998.

Güvemli, Oktay. *Türk Devletleri Muhasebe Tarihi*, 4 vols. Istanbul: İstanbul Yeminli Müşavirler Odası, 1995–2001.

Guzman, Andrew T. "Choice of Law: New Foundations." *Georgetown Law Journal*, 90 (2002): 883–940.

Haddad, Robert M. *Syrian Christians in Muslim Society: An Interpretation.* Princeton: Princeton University Press, 1970.

Hadziiossif, Christos. "Issues of Management Control and Sovereignty in Transnational Banking in the Eastern Mediterranean before the First World War." In *Modern Banking in the Balkans and West-European Capital in the Nineteenth and Twentieth Centuries*, edited by Kostas P. Kostis, pp. 160–77. Aldershot, U.K.: Ashgate, 1999.

Haffar, Ahmad R. "Economic Development in Islam in Western Scholarship," 2 parts, *Islam and the Modern Age*, 6/2 (1975): 5–22 and 6/3 (1975): 5–29.

Haldon, John F. *Byzantium in the Seventh Century: The Transformation of a Culture.* Cambridge: Cambridge University Press, 1990.

Hallaq, Wael B. "Model *Shurūt* Works and the Dialectic of Doctrine and Practice." *Islamic Law and Society*, 2 (1995): 109–34.

———. *Authority, Continuity and Change in Islamic Law*. Cambridge: Cambridge University Press, 2001.

———. "The Quest for Origins or Doctrine? Islamic Legal Studies as Colonialist Discourse." *UCLA Journal of Islamic and Near Eastern Law*, 2 (2002–3): 1–31.

Hamoudi, Haider. "The Death of Islamic Law." *Georgia Journal of International and Comparative Law*, 38 (2010): 293–337.

Haneef, Mohamed Aslam. *Contemporary Islamic Economic Thought: A Selected Comparative Analysis.* Kuala Lumpur: Ikraq, 1995.

Hanioğlu, M. Şükrü. *A Brief History of the Late Ottoman Empire.* Princeton: Princeton University Press, 2008.

Hanna, Nelly. "Marriage among Merchant Families in Seventeenth-Century Cairo." In *Women, the Family, and Divorce Laws in Islamic History*, edited by Amira El-Azhary Sonbol, pp. 143–54. Syracuse, N.Y.: Syracuse University Press, 1996.

———. *Making Big Money in 1600: The Life and Times of Isma'il Abu Taqiyya, Egyptian Merchant.* Syracuse, N.Y.: Syracuse University Press, 1998.

Hansmann, Henry, Reinier Kraakman, and Richard Squire. "Law and the Rise of the Firm." *Harvard Law Review*, 119 (2006): 1335–1403.

Harris, Ron. *Industrializing English Law: Entrepreneurship and Business Organization, 1720–1844.* Cambridge: Cambridge University Press, 2000.

———. "The Formation of the East India Company as a Deal between Entrepreneurs and Outside Investors." Working paper, Social Science Research Network, September 2004.

Hatemî, Hüseyin. *Önceki ve Bugünkü Türk Hukuku'nda Vakıf Kurma Muamelesi.* Istanbul İstanbul Üniversitesi Hukuk Fakültesi, 1969.

Hattox, Ralph S. *Coffee and Coffeehouses: The Origins of a Social Beverage in the Medieval Middle East.* Seattle: University of Washington Press, 1985.

Hayek, Friedrich A. *Law, Legislation and Liberty,* 3 vols. Chicago: University of Chicago Press, 1973–79.

Hazlitt, Henry. *Economics in One Lesson,* 4th ed. New York: Harper, 1946.

Hedström, Peter, and Richard Swedberg, editors. *Social Mechanisms: An Analytical Approach to Social Theory.* Cambridge: Cambridge University Press, 1998.

Hennigan, Peter C. *The Birth of a Legal Institution: The Formation of the Waqf in Third-Century A.H. Hanafi Legal Discourse.* Leiden: Brill, 2004.

Herrup, Cynthia B. *The Common Peace: Participation and the Criminal Law in Seventeenth-Century England.* New York: Cambridge University Press, 1987.

Heyworth-Dunne, James. *An Introduction to the History of Education in Modern Egypt.* London: Luzac, 1938.

Hirschman, Albert O. "Rival Views of Market Society." In his *Rival Views of Market Society and Other Essays,* pp. 105–41. New York: Viking, 1986.

Hiskett, Mervyn. *The Development of Islam in West Africa.* London: Longman, 1984.

Hobsbawm, Eric, and Terence Ranger, editors. *The Invention of Tradition.* Cambridge: Cambridge University Press, 1983.

Hoexter, Miriam. "Adaptation to Changing Circumstances: Perpetual Leases and Exchange Transactions in *Waqf* Property in Ottoman Algiers." *Islamic Law and Society,* 4 (1997): 319–33.

Hoffman, Philip T., Gilles Postel-Vinay, and Jean-Laurent Rosenthal. "What Do Notaries Do? Overcoming Asymmetric Information in Financial Markets: The Case of Paris, 1751." *Journal of Institutional and Theoretical Economics,* 154 (1998): 499–530.

———. *Priceless Markets: The Political Economy of Credit in Paris, 1660–1870.* Chicago: University of Chicago Press, 2000.

Homer, Sidney, and Richard Sylla. *A History of Interest Rates,* 3rd ed. New Brunswick, N.J.: Rutgers University Press, 1996.

Hoodbhoy, Pervez. *Islam and Science: Religious Orthodoxy and the Battle for Rationality.* London: Zed Books, 1991.

Horniker, Arthur Leon. "William Harborne and the Beginning of Anglo-Turkish Diplomatic and Commercial Relations." *Journal of Economic History,* 14 (1942): 289–316.

Horton, Mark, and John Middleton. *The Swahili: The Social Landscape of a Mercantile Society.* Oxford: Blackwell, 2000.

Hourani, Albert H. *Arabic Thought in the Liberal Age, 1798–1939,* revised ed. Cambridge: Cambridge University Press, 1983.

Hourani, George F. *Arab Seafaring in the Indian Ocean in Ancient and Early Medieval Times,* revised and expanded by John Carswell. Princeton: Princeton University Press, 1995.

Huff, Toby E. *The Rise of Early Modern Science: Islam, China and the West*, 2nd ed. Cambridge: Cambridge University Press, 2003.

Hunt, Edwin S. *The Medieval Super-Companies: A Study of the Peruzzi Company of Florence.* Cambridge: Cambridge University Press, 1994.

Hunt, Edwin S., and James M. Murray. *A History of Business in Medieval Europe, 1200–1550.* Cambridge: Cambridge University Press, 1999.

Hurewitz, Jacob C. *The Middle East and North Africa in World Politics: A Documentary Record*, 2nd ed., vol. 1. New Haven: Yale University Press, 1975.

Iannaccone, Laurence R. "Sacrifice and Stigma: Reducing Free-Riding in Cults, Communes, and Other Collectives." *Journal of Political Economy*, 100 (1992): 271–91.

Ibn Battuta. *The Travels of Ibn Battūta (A.D. 1325–1354)*, 5 vols., edited by Hamilton A. R. Gibb. London: Hakluyt Society, 1958–2000.

Ibn Khaldun. *The Muqaddimah: An Introduction to History*, 3 vols., translated by Franz Rosenthal. New York: Pantheon, 1958; original Arabic edition, 1379.

Ibrahim, Mahmood. *Merchant Capital and Islam.* Austin: University of Texas Press, 1990.

Ibrahim, Saad Eddin. "Civil Society and Prospects for Democratization in the Arab World." In *Civil Society in the Middle East*, edited by Augustus Richard Norton, vol. 1, pp. 27–54. Leiden: Brill, 1995.

Imamuddin, S. M. "Maritime Trade under the Mamlūks of Egypt (644–923/1250–1517)." *Hamdard Islamicus*, 3 (1980): 67–77.

Imber, Colin. *Ebu's-Su'ud: The Islamic Legal Tradition.* Stanford: Stanford University Press, 1997.

İnalcık, Halil. "Land Problems in Turkish History." *Muslim World* 45 (1955): 221–28.

———. "Bursa: XV. Asır Sanayi ve Ticaret Tarihine Dair Vesikalar." *Belleten*, 24 (1960): 45–102.

———. "The Ottoman Economic Mind and Aspects of the Ottoman Economy." In *Studies in the Economic History of the Middle East*, edited by Michael A. Cook, pp. 207–18. London: Oxford University Press, 1970.

———. "Imtiyāzāt." *Encyclopaedia of Islam*, 2nd ed., vol. 3, pp. 1179–89. Leiden: E. J. Brill, 1971.

———. *The Ottoman Empire: The Classical Age 1300–1600*, translated by Norman Itzkowitz and Colin Imber. London: Weidenfeld and Nicolson, 1973.

———. "The *Rūznāmče* Registers of the *Kadıasker* of Rumeli as Preserved in the Istanbul *Müftülük* Archives." *Turcica*, 20 (1988): 251–75.

———. "The Ottoman State: Economy and Society, 1300–1600." In *An Economic and Social History of the Ottoman Empire, 1300–1914*, edited by Halil İnalcık with Donald Quataert, pp. 9–409. New York: Cambridge University Press, 1994.

———. *Osmanlı'da Devlet, Hukuk, Adâlet.* Istanbul: Eren, 2000.

Ireland, Paddy. "Capitalism without the Capitalist: The Joint Stock Company Share and the Emergence of the Modern Doctrine of Separate Corporate Personality." *Legal History* 17 (1996): 40–72.

Issawi, Charles. *The Economic History of Turkey, 1800–1914*. Chicago: University of Chicago Press, 1980.

———. *An Economic History of the Middle East and North Africa*. New York: Columbia University Press, 1982.

———. "The Transformation of the Economic Position of the *Millets* in the Nineteenth Century." In *Christians and Jews in the Ottoman Empire, Vol. 1: The Central Lands*, edited by Benjamin Braude and Bernard Lewis, pp. 261–85. New York: Holmes and Meier, 1982.

———. *The Fertile Crescent, 1800–1914: A Documentary History*. New York: Oxford University Press, 1988.

———. *Cross-Cultural Encounters and Conflicts*. New York: Oxford University Press, 1998.

Ivanova, Svetlana. "Marriage and Divorce in the Bulgarian Lands (XV–XIX c.)." *Bulgarian Historical Review*, 21 (1993): 49–83.

İyigün, Murat. "Luther and Süleyman." *Quarterly Journal of Economics*, 123 (2008): 1465–94.

Jardine, Lisa. *Wordly Goods: A New History of the Renaissance*. New York: Doubleday, 1996.

Jennings, Ronald C. "Loans and Credit in Early 17th Century Ottoman Judicial Records: The Sharia Court of Anatolian Kayseri." *Journal of the Economic and Social History of the Orient* 16 (1973): 168–216.

———. *Christians and Muslims in Ottoman Cyprus and the Mediterranean World, 1571–1640*. New York: New York University Press, 1993.

Jolowicz, Herbert F., and Barry Nicholas. *Historical Introduction to the Study of Roman Law*, 3rd ed. Cambridge: Cambridge University Press, 1972.

Jones, A.H.M. "Taxation in Antiquity." In *The Roman Economy: Studies in Ancient Economic and Administrative History*, edited by P. A. Brunt, pp. 151–86. Totowa, N.J.: Rowman and Littlefield, 1974.

Jones, Eric L. *The European Miracle: Environments, Economies, and Geopolitics in the History of Europe and Asia*, 2nd ed. Cambridge: Cambridge University Press, 1987.

Jones, Ernest D. "The Crown, Three Benedictine Houses, and the Statute of Mortmain, 1279–1348." *Journal of British Studies*, 14 (1975): 1–28.

Jones, William R. "Pious Endowments in Medieval Christianity and Islam." *Diogenes*, 109 (1980): 23–36.

Kafadar, Cemal. "A Death in Venice (1575): Anatolian Muslim Merchants Trading in the Serenissima." *Journal of Turkish Studies*, 10 (1986): 191–218.

Kahan, Marcel, and Michael Klausner. "Path Dependence in Corporate Contracting: Increasing Returns, Herd Behavior and Cognitive Biases." *Washington University Law Quarterly*, 74 (1996): 347–66.

Kamal, Ahmad. *The Sacred Journey, Being Pilgrimage to Makkah.* New York: Duell, Sloan and Pearce, 1961; original Arabic edition, 1952.

Karaman, Hayreddin. *Mukayeseli İslâm Hukuku.* Istanbul: İrfan Yayınevi, 1974.

Karpat, Kemal H. "Ottoman Population Records and the Census of 1881/82–1893." *International Journal of Middle East Studies,* 9 (1978): 237–74.

———. "*Millet*s and Nationality: The Roots of the Incongruity of Nation and State in the Post-Ottoman Era." In *Christians and Jews in the Ottoman Empire, Vol. 1: The Central Lands,* edited by Benjamin Braude and Bernard Lewis, pp. 141–69. New York: Holmes & Meier, 1982.

———. "Ottoman Views and Policies Towards the Orthodox Christian Church." *Greek Orthodox Theological Review,* 31 (1986): 131–55.

———. *The Politicization of Islam: Reconstructing Identity, State, Faith, and Community in the Late Ottoman State.* New York: Oxford University Press, 2001.

Kasaba, Reşat. "Was There a Compradore Bourgeoisie in Mid Nineteenth-Century Western Anatolia?" *Review: A Journal of the Fernand Braudel Center,* 11 (1988): 215–28.

Kaşıkçı, Osman. *İslâm ve Osmanlı Hukukunda Mecelle.* Istanbul: Osmanlı Araştırmaları Vakfı, 1997.

Kayalı, Hasan. *Arabs and Young Turks: Ottomanism, Arabism, and Islamism in the Ottoman Empire, 1908–1918.* Berkeley: University of California Press, 1997.

Kazamias, Andreas M. *Education and the Quest for Modernity in Turkey.* Chicago: University of Chicago Press, 1966.

Kazgan, Haydar. *Galata Bankerleri.* Istanbul: Türk Ekonomi Bankası, 1991.

———. *Osmanlı'dan Cumhuriyet'e Şirketleşme.* Istanbul: Töbank, 1991.

———. *Osmanlıda Avrupa Finans Kapitali.* Istanbul: Yapı Kredi Yayınları, 1995.

Kedar, Benjamin Z. *Merchants in Crisis: Genoese and Venetian Men of Affairs and the Fourteenth-Century Depression.* New Haven: Yale University Press, 1976.

———. *Crusade and Mission: European Approaches toward the Muslims.* Princeton: Princeton University Press, 1984.

Kepel, Gilles. *The War for Muslim Minds: Islam and the West,* translated by Pascale Ghazaleh. Cambridge, Mass.: Harvard University Press, 2004.

Kévonian, Kéram. "Marchands Arméniens au XVIIe Siècle." *Cahiers du Monde Russe et Sovietique* 16 (1975): 199–244.

Khadduri, Majid. *War and Peace in the Law of Islam.* Baltimore: Johns Hopkins University Press, 1955.

Khalidi, Rashid, Lisa Anderson, Muhammad Muslih, and Reeva S. Simon, eds. *The Origins of Arab Nationalism.* New York: Columbia University Press, 1991.

Khan, Muhammad Akram. *Economic Teachings of Prophet Muhammad: A Select Anthology of Hadith Literature on Economics.* Islamabad: International Institute of Islamic Economics, 1989.

Khan, Siadat Ali. "The Mohammedan Laws against Usury and How They Are Evaded." *Journal of Comparative Legislation and International Law*, 11 (1929): 233–44.

Kimber, Richard. "The Qur'anic Law of Inheritance." *Islamic Law and Society*, 5 (1998): 291–325.

Klerman, Daniel. "Jurisdictional Competition and the Evolution of the Common Law." *University of Chicago Law Review*, 74 (2007): 1179–1226.

———. "The Emergence of English Commercial Law: Analysis Inspired by the Ottoman Experience." *Journal of Economic Behavior and Organization*, 71 (2009): 638–46.

Köprülü, Fuad. "Vakıf Müessesesinin Hukukî Mahiyeti ve Tarihî Tekâmülü." *Vakıflar Dergisi*, 11 (1942): 1–35.

Koraltürk, Murat. "Kentleşme, Kentiçi Ulaşım, İstanbul ve Şirket-i Hayriye'nin Kuruluşu." *Marmara Üniversitesi İktisadi ve İdari Bilimler Fakültesi Dergisi*, 10 (1995): 53–113.

Kramer, Larry. "Rethinking Choice of Law." *Columbia Law Review*, 90 (1990): 277–345.

Kuehn, Thomas. "Inheritance, Western European." In *Dictionary of the Middle Ages*, vol. 6, edited by Joseph R. Strayer, pp. 454–61. New York: Charles Scribner's Sons, 1985.

Kuhn, Arthur K. *The Law of Corporations*. London: P. S. King, 1912.

Kunt, İ. Metin. *The Sultan's Servants: The Transformation of Ottoman Provincial Government, 1550–1650*. New York: Columbia University Press, 1983.

Kuran, Ercümend. *Avrupa'da Osmanlı İkamet Elçiliklerinin Kuruluşu ve İlk Elçilerin Siyasi Faâliyetleri, 1793–1821*. Ankara: Türk Kültürünü Araştırma Enstitüsü, 1968.

Kuran, Timur. *Private Truths, Public Lies: The Social Consequences of Preference Falsification*. Cambridge, Mass.: Harvard University Press, 1995.

———. "Islamic Influences on the Ottoman Guilds." In *Ottoman-Turkish Civilisation*, vol. 2, edited by Kemal Çiçek, pp. 43–59. Ankara: Yeni Türkiye Yayınları, 2000.

———. "The Provision of Public Goods under Islamic Law: Origins, Impact, and Limitations of the Waqf System." *Law and Society Review*, 35 (2001): 841–97.

———. "Islamic Redistribution through Zakat: Historical Record and Modern Realities." In *Poverty and Charity in Middle Eastern Contexts*, edited by Michael Bonner, Mine Ener, and Amy Singer, pp. 275–93. Albany: State University of New York Press, 2003.

———. *Islam and Mammon: The Economic Predicaments of Islamism*. Princeton: Princeton University Press, 2004.

———. "Islamic Statecraft and the Middle East's Delayed Modernization." In *Political Competition, Innovation and Growth in the History of Asian Civilizations*, edited by Peter Bernholz and Roland Vaubel, pp. 150–83. Cheltenham, U.K.: Edward Elgar, 2004.

————. "Explaining the Economic Trajectories of Civilizations: The Systemic Approach." *Journal of Economic Behavior and Organization*, 71 (2009): 593–605.

————. *Mahkeme Kayıtları Işığında 17. Yüzyıl İstanbul'unda Sosyo-Ekonomik Yaşam / Social and Economic Life in Seventeenth-Century Istanbul: Glimpses from Court Records*, 10 vols. Istanbul: İş Bankası Kültür Yayınları, 2010–11.

Kuran, Timur, and Cass Sunstein. "Availability Cascades and Risk Regulation." *Stanford Law Review*, 51 (1999): 683–768.

Kurdakul, Necdet. *Osmanlı Devleti'nde Ticaret Antlaşmaları ve Kapitülasyonlar*. Istanbul: Döler Neşriyat, 1981.

Kütükoğlu, Mübahat S. *Osmanlı-İngiliz İktisâdî Münasebetleri, 1 (1580–1838)*. Ankara: Türk Kültürünü Araştırma Enstitüsü, 1974.

————. "Avrupa Tüccarı." *Türkiye Diyanet Vakfı İslâm Ansiklopedisi*, vol. 4 (1991), pp. 159–60.

————. "Ahidnâmeler ve Ticaret Muâhedeleri." In *Osmanlı*, vol. 3, edited by Güler Eren, pp. 329–50. Ankara: Yeni Türkiye Yayınları, 1999.

————. *İzmir Tarihinden Kesitler*. İzmir: İzmir Büyükşehir Belediyesi, 2000.

Kuznets, Simon. *Modern Economic Growth: Rate, Structure, and Spread*. New Haven: Yale University Press, 1966.

Labaki, Boutros. "The Christian Communities and the Economic and Social Situation in Lebanon." In *Christian Communities in the Arab Middle East: The Challenge of the Future*, edited by Andrea Pacini, pp. 222–58. Oxford: Clarendon Press, 1998.

Labib, Subhi. *Handelsgeschichte Ägyptens im Spätmittelalter (1171–1517)*. Wiesbaden: Franz Steiner, 1965.

————. "Capitalism in Medieval Islam." *Journal of Economic History*, 29 (1969): 79–96.

————. "Les Marchands Kārimīs en Orient et sur l'Océan Indien." In *Sociétés et Compagnies de Commerce en Orient et dans l'Océan Indien*, pp. 209–14. Paris: S.E.V.P.E.N., 1970.

————. "Egyptian Commercial Policy in the Middle Ages." In *Studies in the Economic History of the Middle East*, edited by Michael A. Cook, pp. 63–77. Oxford: Oxford University Press, 1970.

Laboa, Juan María. *The Historical Atlas of Eastern and Western Christian Monasticism*. Collegeville, Minn.: Liturgical Press, 2003.

Lal, Deepak. *Unintended Consequences: The Impact of Factor Endowments, Culture, and Politics on Long-Run Economic Performance*. Cambridge, Mass.: MIT Press, 1998.

Lambton, Ann K. S. *State and Government in Medieval Islam*. Oxford: Oxford University Press, 1981.

————. "Awkāf in Persia: 6th–8th/12th–14th Centuries." *Islamic Law and Society*, 4 (1997): 298–318.

Lamoreaux, Naomi R. "Rethinking the Transition to Capitalism in the Early American Northeast." *Journal of American History*, 90 (2003): 437–61.

———. "Partnerships, Corporations, and the Limits on Contractual Freedom in U.S. History: An Essay in Economics, Law, and Culture." In *Constructing Corporate America: History, Politics, Culture*, edited by Kenneth Lipartito and David B. Sicilia, pp. 29–65. New York: Oxford University Press, 2004.

Lamoreaux, Naomi R., and Jean-Laurent Rosenthal. "Legal Regime and Contractual Flexibility: A Comparison of Business's Organizational Choices in France and the United States during the Era of Industrialization." *American Law and Economics Review*, 7 (2005): 28–61.

———. "Organizing Middle-Sized Firms in the United States and France, 1830–2000." UCLA working paper, September 2005.

Landau, Jacob M. *Jews in Nineteenth-Century Egypt*. New York: New York University Press, 1969.

———. *The Politics of Pan-Islam: Ideology and Organization*. Oxford: Clarendon Press, 1990.

Landes, David S. *Bankers and Pashas: International Finance and Economic Imperialism in Egypt*. Cambridge, Mass.: Harvard University Press, 1958.

———. *The Wealth and Poverty of Nations: Why Some Countries Are So Rich and Others So Poor*. New York: W. W. Norton, 1998.

Lane, Frederic C. *Venice: A Maritime Republic*. Baltimore: Johns Hopkins University Press, 1973.

Langholm, Odd. *The Aristotelian Analysis of Usury*. Bergen: Universitetsforlaget AS, 1984.

Lapidus, Ira M. *Muslim Cities in the Later Middle Ages*. Cambridge, Mass.: Harvard University Press, 1967.

Last, Murray. "Some Economic Aspects of Conversion in Hausaland (Nigeria)." In *Conversion to Islam*, edited by Nehemia Levtzion, pp. 236–46. New York: Holmes & Meier, 1979.

Lee, Geoffrey Alan. "The Development of Italian Bookkeeping, 1211–1300." *Abacus*, 9 (1973): 137–55.

Leeuwen, Richard van. *Waqfs and Urban Structures: The Case of Ottoman Damascus*. Leiden: Brill, 1999.

Lerner, Daniel. *The Passing of Traditional Society: Modernizing the Middle East*. Glencoe, Ill.: Free Press, 1958.

Le Tourneau, Roger. "Funduk." *Encyclopaedia of Islam*, 2nd ed., vol. 2, p. 945. Leiden: E. J. Brill, 1965.

Lev, Yaacov. *Charity, Endowments, and Charitable Institutions in Medieval Islam*. Gainesville: University Press of Florida, 2005.

Levathes, Louise. *When China Ruled the Seas: The Treasure Fleet of the Dragon Throne, 1405–1433*. New York: Simon & Schuster, 1994.

Levenstein, Margaret. *Accounting for Growth: Information Systems and the Creation of the Large Corporation*. Stanford: Stanford University Press, 1998.

Levtzion, Nehemia. *Islam in West Africa: Religion, Society and Politics to 1800*. London: Variorum, 1994.

Levtzion, Nehemia, and Randall L. Pouwels. "Patterns of Islamization and Varieties of Religious Experience among Muslims of Africa." In *The History of Islam in Africa*, edited by Nehemia Levtzion and Randall L. Pouwels, pp. 1–20. Athens: Ohio University Press, 2000.

Lewis, Bernard. "Berātlī." *Encyclopaedia of Islam*, 2nd ed., vol. 1, p. 1171. Leiden: E. J. Brill, 1960.

———, editor. *Islam*, 2 vols. New York: Walker and Company, 1974.

———. *The Muslim Discovery of Europe*. New York: Norton, 1982.

———. *The Political Language of Islam*. Chicago: University of Chicago Press, 1988.

———. *Race and Slavery in the Middle East: An Historical Enquiry*. New York: Oxford University Press, 1990.

———. *Islam and the West*. New York: Oxford University Press, 1993.

———. *Cultures in Conflict: Christians, Muslims, and Jews in the Age of Discovery*. New York: Oxford University Press, 1995.

———. *What Went Wrong? Western Impact and Middle Eastern Response*. Oxford: Oxford University Press, 2002.

Lewis, I. M. "Agents of Islamization." In *Islam in Tropical Africa*, 2nd ed., edited by I. M. Lewis, pp. 20–31. Bloomington: Indiana University Press, 1980.

Libson, Gideon. *Jewish and Islamic Law: A Comparative Study of Custom during the Geonic Period*. Cambridge, Mass.: Harvard University Press, 2003.

Liebesny, Herbert J. "The Development of Western Judicial Privileges." In *Law in the Middle East*, vol. 1, edited by Majid Khadduri and Herbert J. Liebesny, pp. 309–33. Washington, D.C.: Middle East Institute, 1955.

———. *The Law of the Near and Middle East: Readings, Cases, and Materials*. Albany: State University Press of New York Press, 1975.

Little, Donald P. *A Catalogue of Islamic Documents from al-Haram al Sarif in Jerusalem*. Beirut: Orient-Institute, 1984.

Lloyd, Eyre. *The Succession Laws of Christian Countries, with Special Reference to the Law of Primogeniture as It Exists in England*. London: Stevens and Haynes, 1877.

Løkkegaard, Frede. *Islamic Taxation in the Classic Period, with Special Reference to Circumstances in Iraq*. Copenhagen: Branner and Korch, 1950.

Long, David E. *The Hajj Today: A Survey of the Contemporary Makkah Pilgrimage*. Albany: State University of New York Press, 1979.

Lopez, Robert S. *The Commercial Revolution of the Middle Ages, 950–1350*. Cambridge: Cambridge University Press, 1976.

Lopez, Robert S., and Irving W. Raymond. *Medieval Trade in the Mediterranean World: Illustrative Documents Translated with Introductions and Notes*. New York: Columbia University Press, 1955.

Lydon, Ghislaine. *On Trans-Saharan Trails: Islamic Law, Trade Networks, and Cross-Cultural Exchange in Nineteenth-Century Western Africa*. New York: Cambridge University Press, 2009.

———. "A Paper Economy of Faith without Faith in Paper: A Reflection on Islamic Institutional History." *Journal of Economic Behavior and Organization*, 71 (2009): 647–59.

MacFarlane, Alan. *The Origins of English Individualism: The Family, Property, and Social Transition*. New York: Cambridge University Press, 1979.

Maddison, Angus. *Monitoring the World Economy 1820–1992*. Paris: Organization for Economic Co-operation and Development, 1995.

———. *The World Economy*. Paris: OECD Publishing, 2006.

———. *Contours of the World Economy, 1–2030 AD: Essays in Macro-Economic History*. Oxford: Oxford University Press, 2007.

Maimonides, Moses. *A Guide of the Perplexed*, translated and edited by Shlomo Pines. Chicago: University of Chicago Press, 1963; original edition, 1191.

Makdisi, George. *The Rise of Colleges: Institutions of Learning in Islam and the West*. Edinburgh: Edinburgh University Press, 1981.

Mallat, Chibli. "From Islamic to Middle Eastern Law: A Restatement of the Field," 2 parts. *American Journal of Comparative Law*, 51 (2003): 699–750 and 52 (2004): 209–86.

———. *Introduction to Middle Eastern Law*. Oxford: Oxford University Press, 2007.

Malmendier, Ulrike. "Roman Shares." In *The Origins of Value: The Financial Innovations that Created Modern Capital Markets*, edited by William N. Goetzmann and K. Geert Rouwenhorts, pp. 31–42. Oxford: Oxford University Press, 2005.

Maloney, Robert P. "The Teaching of the Fathers on Usury: An Historical Study on the Development of Christian Thinking." *Vigiliae Christianae*, 27 (1973): 241–65.

Mandaville, Jon E. "Usurious Piety: The Cash Waqf Controversy in the Ottoman Empire." *International Journal of Middle East Studies*, 10 (1979): 298–308.

Mango, Cyril. *Byzantium: The Empire of New Rome*. New York: Charles Scribner's, 1980.

Mantran, Robert. *İstanbul dans la Seconde Moitié du XVIIe Siècle*. Paris: Librairie Adrien Maisonneuve, 1962.

———. "Transformation du Commerce dans l'Empire Ottoman au Dix-Huitième Siècle." In *Studies in Eighteenth Century Islamic History*, edited by Thomas Naff and Roger Owen, pp. 220–35. Carbondale: Southern Illinois University Press, 1977.

Ma'oz, Moshe. "Communal Conflicts in Ottoman Syria during the Reform Era: The Role of Political and Economic Factors." In *Christians and Jews in the Ottoman Empire, Vol. 2: The Arabic-Speaking Lands*, edited by Benjamin Braude and Bernard Lewis, pp. 91–105. New York: Holmes & Meier, 1982.

Marcus, Abraham. "Real Estate Property and Society in the Premodern Middle East: A Case Study." In *Property, Social Structure and Law in the Modern Middle East*, edited by Ann Elizabeth Mayer, pp. 109–28. Albany: State University of New York Press, 1985.

——. *The Middle East on the Eve of Modernity: Aleppo in the Eighteenth Century.* New York: Columbia University Press, 1989.

Mardin, Şerif. *The Genesis of Young Ottoman Thought: A Study in the Modernization of Turkish Political Ideas.* Princeton: Princeton University Press, 1962.

——. "Power, Civil Society and Culture in the Ottoman Empire." *Comparative Studies in Society and History,* 11 (1969): 258–81.

——. *Türk Modernleşmesi.* Istanbul: İletişim, 1991.

Marlow, Louise. *Hierarchy and Egalitarianism in Islamic Thought.* Cambridge: Cambridge University Press, 1997.

Marlowe, John. *Anglo-Egyptian Relations, 1800–1953.* London: Cresset Press, 1954.

Marouche, P., and G. Sarantis. *Annuaire Financier de Turquie.* Istanbul: Imprimerie Levant Herald, 1912.

Marsot, Lutfi Al-Sayyid. *Egypt in the Reign of Muhammad Ali.* Cambridge: Cambridge University Press, 1984.

Martin, M. E. "The Venetian-Seljuk Treaty of 1220." *English Historical Review,* 95 (1980): 321–30.

Marx, Karl. *Capital,* 3 vols., edited by Frederick Engels. New York: International Publishers, 1967; original German edition, 1867.

Masson, Paul. *Histoire du Commerce Français dans le Levant au XVIIe Siècle.* Paris: Hachette, 1896.

——. *Histoire du Commerce Français dans le Levant au XVIIIe Siècle.* Paris: Hachette, 1911.

Masters, Bruce. *The Origins of Western Economic Dominance in the Middle East: Mercantilism and the Islamic Economy in Aleppo, 1600–1750.* New York: New York University Press, 1988.

——. "The 1850 Events in Aleppo: An Aftershock of Syria's Incorporation into the Capitalist World System." *International Journal of Middle East Studies,* 22 (1990): 3–20.

——. "The Sultan's Entrepreneurs: The *Avrupa Tüccarı* and the *Hayriye Tüccarı* in Syria." *International Journal of Middle East Studies,* 24 (1992): 579–97.

——. "Aleppo: The Ottoman Empire's Caravan City." In *The Ottoman City between East and West: Aleppo, Izmir, and Istanbul,* edited by Edhem Eldem, Daniel Goffman, and Bruce Masters, pp. 17–78. New York: Cambridge University Press, 1999.

——. *Christians and Jews in the Ottoman Arab World: The Roots of Sectarianism.* New York: Cambridge University Press, 2001.

Masud, Muhammad Khalid, Brinkley Messick, and David S. Powers, editors. *Islamic Legal Interpretation: Muftis and Their Fatwas.* Cambridge, Mass.: Harvard University Press, 1996.

——. "Muftis, Fatwas, and Islamic Legal Interpretation." In *Islamic Legal Interpretation: Muftis and Their Fatwas,* edited by Muhammad Khalid Masud,

Brinkley Messick, and David S. Powers, pp. 3–32. Cambridge, Mass.: Harvard University Press, 1996.

Matar, Nabil, editor and translator. *In the Lands of the Christians: Arabic Travel Writing in the Seventeenth Century*. New York: Routledge, 2003.

Matthee, Rudolph P. *The Politics of Trade in Safavid Iran: Silk for Silver, 1600–1730*. Cambridge: Cambridge University Press, 1999.

Mauro, Frédéric. "Merchant Communities, 1350–1750." In *The Rise of Merchant Empires: Long-Distance Trade in the Early Modern World 1350–1750*, edited by James D. Tracy, pp. 255–86. Cambridge: Cambridge University Press, 1990.

Mawdudi, Sayyid Abul-Ala. *Nations Rise and Decline—Why?* translated from Urdu. Lahore: Islamic Publications, 1950; original edition, 1948.

McCabe, Ina Baghdiantz. *The Shah's Silk for Europe's Silver: The Eurasian Trade of the Julfa Armenians in Safavid Iran and India (1530–1750)*. Atlanta: Scholars Press, 1999.

McCarthy, Justin. *The Ottoman Peoples and the End of Empire*. New York: Oxford University Press, 2001.

McCusker, John J. "The Demise of Distance: The Business Press and the Origins of the Information Revolution in the Early Modern Atlantic World." *American Historical Review*, 110 (2005): 295–321.

McCusker, John J., and Cora Gravesteijn. *The Beginnings of Commercial and Financial Journalism: The Commodity Price Currents, Exchange Rate Currents, and Money Currents of Early Modern Europe*. Amsterdam: NEHA, 1991.

McGowan, Bruce. *Economic Life in Ottoman Europe: Taxation, Trade and the Struggle for Land, 1600–1800*. Cambridge: Cambridge University Press, 1981.

————. "The Age of the Ayans, 1699–1812." In *An Economic and Social History of the Ottoman Empire, 1300–1914*, edited by Halil İnalcık with Donald Quataert, pp. 637–758. New York: Cambridge University Press, 1994.

Meriwether, Margaret L. *The Kin Who Count: Family and Society in Ottoman Aleppo, 1770–1840*. Austin: University of Texas Press, 1999.

Merry, Sally Engle. "Legal Pluralism." *Law and Society Review*, 22 (1988): 869–96.

Messick, Brinkley. *The Calligraphic State: Textual Domination and History in a Muslim Society*. Berkeley: University of California Press, 1993.

Meyerson, Mark D. *The Muslims of Valencia*. Berkeley: University of California Press, 1991.

Milgrom, Paul, Douglass North, and Barry Weingast. "The Role of Institutions in the Revival of Trade: The Medieval Law Merchant." *Economics and Politics*, 2 (1990): 1–23.

Mitchell, W. *An Essay on the Early History of the Law Merchant*. Cambridge: Cambridge University Press, 1904.

Mokyr, Joel. *The Lever of Riches: Technological Creativity and Economic Progress*. New York: Oxford University Press, 1990.

Morineau, Michel. "Naissance d'Une Domination: Marchands Européens, Marchands et Marchés du Levant aux XVIIIe et XIXe Siècles." In *Commerce de Gros, Commerce de Détail dans les Pays Méditérranéens, XVIe–XIXe Siècles*, Actes des Journées d'Études Bendor, 25–26 Avril 1975, pp. 145–84. Nice: Centre de la Méditérranée Moderne et Contemporaine, 1976.

———. "Eastern and Western Merchants from the Sixteenth to the Eighteenth Centuries," translated by Cyprian P. Blamires. In *Merchants, Companies and Trade: Europe and Asia in the Early Modern Era*, edited by Sushil Chaudhury and Michel Morineau, pp. 116–44. Cambridge: Cambridge University Press, 1999.

Mumcu, Ahmet. *Osmanlı Devletinde Rüşvet (Özellikle Adlî Rüşvet)*, 2nd ed. Istanbul: İnkilâp Kitabevi, 1985.

Mumford, Lewis. *The City in History: Its Origins, Its Transformations, and Its Prospects*. New York: Harcourt, Brace and World, 1961.

Mundy, Martha. "The Family, Inheritance, and Islam: A Re-examination of the Sociology of Farā'id Law." In *Islamic Law: Social and Historical Contexts*, edited by Aziz Al-Azmeh, pp. 1–123. London: Routledge, 1988.

Murray, Charles. *Human Accomplishment: The Pursuit of Excellence in the Arts and Sciences, 800 B.C. to 1950*. New York: HarperCollins, 2003.

Napier, Christopher. "Defining Islamic Accounting: Current Issues, Past Roots." *Accounting History*, 14 (2009): 121–44.

Neal, Larry. *The Rise of Financial Capitalism: International Capital Markets in the Age of Reason*. Cambridge: Cambridge University Press, 1990.

———. "Venture Shares of the Dutch East India Company." In *The Origins of Value: The Financial Innovations that Created Modern Capital Markets*, edited by William N. Goetzmann and K. Geert Rouwenhorts, pp. 165–75. Oxford: Oxford University Press, 2005.

Neusner, Jacob, Tamara Sonn, and Jonathan E. Brockopp. *Judaism and Islam in Practice: A Sourcebook*. London: Routledge, 2000.

Nicol, Donald M. *Byzantium and Venice: A Study in Diplomatic and Cultural Relations*. Cambridge: Cambridge University Press, 1988.

Nielsen, Jørgen S. *Secular Justice in an Islamic State: Mazālim under the Bahrī Mamlūks, 662/1264–789/1387*. Istanbul: Nederlands Historisch-Archaeologisch Instituut, 1985.

Noland, Marcus, and Howard Pack. *The Arab Economies in a Changing World*. Washington, D.C.: Peterson Institute for International Economics, 2007.

Noonan, John T., Jr. *The Scholastic Analysis of Usury*. Cambridge, Mass.: Harvard University Press, 1957.

North, Douglass C. *Structure and Change in Economic History*. New York: W. W. Norton, 1981.

———. *Institutions, Institutional Change and Economic Performance*. Cambridge: Cambridge University Press, 1990.

————. "The Paradox of the West." In *The Origins of Modern Freedom in the West*, edited by Richard W. Davis, pp. 1–34. Stanford: Stanford University Press, 1995.

————. *Understanding the Process of Economic Change*. Princeton: Princeton University Press, 2005.

North, Douglass C., and Barry R. Weingast. "Constitutions and Commitment: The Evolution of Institutions Governing Public Choice in 17th-Century England." *Journal of Economic History*, 49 (1989): 803–32.

North, Roger. *Life of Dudley North and John North*. London: John Winston, 1744.

Nyazee, Imran Ahsan Khan. *Islamic Law of Business Organization: Partnerships*. Islamabad: Islamic Research Institute, 1999.

O'Hara, Erin A., and Larry E. Ribstein. "From Politics to Efficiency in Choice of Law." *University of Chicago Law Review*, 67 (2000): 1151–1232.

Oldham, James C. "The Origins of the Special Jury." *University of Chicago Law Review*, 50 (1983): 137–221.

Olnon, Merlijn. "Towards Classifying *Avanias*: A Study of Two Cases Involving the English and Dutch Nations of Seventeenth-Century Izmir." In *Friends and Rivals in the East: Studies in Anglo-Dutch Relations in the Levant from the Seventeenth to the Early Nineteenth Century*, edited by Alasdair Hamilton, Alexander H. de Groot, and Maurits H. van den Boogert, pp. 159–86. Leiden: Brill, 2000.

Onar, Sıddık Sami. "İslâm Hukuku ve Mecelle." In *Tanzimat'tan Cumhuriyet'e Türkiye Ansiklopedisi*, vol. 3, pp. 580–87. Istanbul: İletişim Yayınları, 1985.

Ordonnances du Roi Charles IX, vol. 13. Paris: Librairie du Châtelets, 1787.

Orhonlu, Cengiz. "Kārwān." *Encyclopaedia of Islam*, vol. 4, pp. 676–79. Leiden: E. J. Brill, 1997.

Ortaylı, İlber. *Hukuk ve İdare Adamı Olarak Osmanlı Devletinde Kadı*. Ankara: Turhan Kitabevi, 1994.

————. *İmparatorluğun En Uzun Yüzyılı*. Istanbul: İletişim Yayınları, 1999.

Oursel, Raymond. *Les Pèlerins du Moyen Age: Les Hommes, Les Chemins, Les Sanctuaires*. Paris: Fayard, 1963.

Owen, Roger. *The Middle East in the World Economy, 1800–1914*, revised edition. London: I. B. Tauris, 1993.

Owen, Roger, and Şevket Pamuk. *A History of the Middle East Economies in the Twentieth Century*. Cambridge, Mass.: Harvard University Press, 1999.

Özbaran, Salih. "Osmanlı İmparatorluğu ve Hindistan Yolu." *İstanbul Edebiyat Fakültesi Tarih Dergisi*, 31 (1977): 65–146.

Özbek, Nadir. *Osmanlı İmparatorluğu'nda Sosyal Devlet: Siyaset, İktidar ve Meşruiyet (1876–1914)*. Istanbul: İletişim, 2002.

Özmucur, Süleyman, and Şevket Pamuk. "Real Wages and Standards of Living in the Ottoman Empire, 1489–1914." *Journal of Economic History*, 62 (2002): 293–321.

Özvar, Erol. *Osmanlı Maliyesinde Malikâne Uygulaması*. Istanbul: Kitabevi, 2003.

Pakalın, Mehmet Zeki. "Avrupa Tüccarı." In his *Osmanlı Tarih Deyimleri ve Terimleri Sözlüğü*, vol. 1, pp. 115–17. Istanbul: Millî Eğitim Bakanlığı Yayınları, 1993.

———. "Hayriye Tüccarı." In his *Osmanlı Tarih Deyimleri ve Terimleri Sözlüğü*, vol. 1, pp. 780–83. Istanbul: Millî Eğitim Bakanlığı Yayınları, 1993.

———. *Osmanlı Tarih Deyimleri ve Sözlüğü*, vol. 2. Istanbul: Millî Eğitim Bakanlığı Yayınları, 1993.

Pamuk, Şevket. *The Ottoman Empire and European Capitalism, 1820–1913: Trade, Investment, and Production*. Cambridge: Cambridge University Press, 1987.

———. *Ottoman Foreign Trade in the 19th Century*. Ankara: State Institute of Statistics, 1995.

———. *A Monetary History of the Ottoman Empire*. Cambridge: Cambridge University Press, 2000.

———. "Urban Real Wages around the Eastern Mediterranean in Comparative Perspective, 1100–2000." *Research in Economic History*, 23 (2005): 213–32.

———. "Estimating Economic Growth in the Middle East since 1820." *Journal of Economic History*, 66 (2006): 809–28.

Pantazopoulos, N. J. *Church and Law in the Balkan Peninsula during the Ottoman Rule*. Amsterdam: Adolf M. Hakkert, 1984.

Panzac, Daniel. "International and Domestic Maritime Trade in the Ottoman Empire During the 18th Century." *International Journal of Middle East Studies*, 24 (1992): 189–206.

———. *Commerce et Navigation dans l'Empire Ottoman au XVIIIᵉ Siècle*. Istanbul: ISIS, 1996.

Parry, John H. *The Age of Reconnaissance: Discovery, Exploration and Settlement, 1450 to 1650*. New York: Praeger, 1969; original edition, 1963.

Patai, Raphael. *The Arab Mind*, revised edition. New York: Charles Scribner's, 1983.

Patrich, Joseph. *Sabas, Leader of Palestinian Monasticism: A Comparative Study in Eastern Monasticism, Fourth to Seventh Centuries*. Washington, D.C.: Dumbarton Oaks, 1995.

Perkins, John. "Islam and Economic Development." http://www.faithfreedom.org/Articles/perkins30410.htm.

Peters, Edward. *Inquisition*. New York: Free Press, 1988.

Peters, Francis E. *The Hajj: The Muslim Pilgrimage to Mecca and the Holy Places*. Princeton: Princeton University Press, 1994.

Pirenne, Henri. *Economic and Social History of Medieval Europe*. San Diego: Harcourt Brace, 1937; original French edition, 1933.

———. *Medieval Cities: Their Origins and the Revival of Trade*, translated by Frank D. Halsey. Garden City, N.Y.: Doubleday Anchor, 1956; original edition, 1925.

Platteau, Jean-Philippe. *Institutions, Social Norms, and Economic Development*. Amsterdam: Harwood, 2001.

Platteau, Jean-Philippe, and Jean-Marie Baland. "Impartible Inheritance versus Equal Division: A Comparative Perspective Centered on Europe and Sub-Saharan Africa." In *Access to Land, Rural Poverty, and Public Action*, edited by Alain de Janvry, Gustavo Gordillo, and Jean-Philippe Platteau, pp. 27–67. Oxford: Oxford University Press, 2001.

Polo, Marco. *The Travels of Marco Polo [The Venetian]*, edited by Manuel Komroff. New York: Horace Liveright, 1926; original Italian edition, 1307.

Porter, James. *Observations on the Religion, Law, Government, and Manners of the Turks*, 2nd ed. London: J. Nourse, 1771.

Posner, Richard A. *Economic Analysis of Law*, 5th ed. Aspen, N.Y.: Aspen Law and Business, 1998.

Pounds, Norman J. G. *An Historical Geography of Europe, 450 B.C.–A.D. 1330*. Cambridge: Cambridge University Press, 1973.

Powers, David S. *Studies in the Qur'an and the Hadith: The Formation of the Islamic Law of Inheritance*. Berkeley: University of California Press, 1986.

———. "The Islamic Inheritance System: A Socio-Historical Approach." In *Islamic Family Law*, edited by Chibli Mallat and Jane Connors, pp. 11–30. London: Graham and Trotman, 1990.

———. "The Islamic Family Endowment (*Waqf*)." *Vanderbilt Journal of Transnational Law*, 32 (1999): 1167–90.

Pryor, Frederic L. *Economic Systems of Foraging, Agricultural, and Industrial Societies*. New York: Cambridge University Press, 2005.

Pryor, John H. "The Origins of the *Commenda* Contract." *Speculum* 52 (1977): 5–37.

Puente J. Irizarry Y. *Functions and Powers of the Foreign Consulate—A Study in Medieval Legal History*. New York: New York University School of Law, 1944.

Pullan, Brian. *The Jews of Europe and the Inquisition of Venice, 1550–1670*. Totowa, N.J.: Barnes & Noble, 1983.

Quataert, Donald. "The Silk Industry of Bursa, 1880–1914." In *The Ottoman Empire and the World-Economy*, edited by Huri İslamoğlu-İnan, pp. 284–308. New York: Cambridge University Press, 1987.

———. "Commerce." In *An Economic and Social History of the Ottoman Empire, 1300–1914*, edited by Halil İnalcık with Donald Quataert, pp. 824–42. New York: Cambridge University Press, 1994.

Queller, Donald E. *The Office of Ambassador in the Middle Ages*. Princeton: Princeton University Press, 1967.

Qureshi, Anwar Iqbal. *Islam and the Theory of Interest*, 2nd ed. Lahore: Sh. Muhammad Ashraf, 1967.

Rabel, E. "The Statute of Frauds and Comparative Legal History." *Law Quarterly Review*, 63 (1947): 174–87.

Radford, Mary F. "The Inheritance Rights of Women under Jewish and Islamic Law." *Boston College International and Comparative Law Review,* 23 (2000): 135–84.

Rahman, Fazlur. "*Ribā* and Interest." *Islamic Studies,* 3 (1964): 1–43.

Rauch, James E. "Business and Social Networks in International Trade." *Journal of Economic Literature,* 39 (2001): 1177–1203.

Raymond, André. *Artisans et Commerçants au Caire au XVIIIe Siècle,* 2 vols. Damascus: Institut Français de Damas, 1974.

———. *The Great Arab Cities in the 16th–18th Centuries: An Introduction.* New York: New York University Press, 1984.

———. *Cairo,* translated by Willard Wood. Cambridge, Mass.: Harvard University Press, 2000; original French edition, 1993.

———. "An Expanding Community: The Christians of Aleppo in the Ottoman Era (16th–18th centuries)." In his *Arab Cities in the Ottoman Period: Cairo, Syria and the Maghreb,* pp. 83–100. Aldershot: Ashgate, 2002.

Rayner, Susan E. *The Theory of Contracts in Islamic Law: A Comparative Analysis with Particular Reference to the Modern Legislation in Kuwait, Bahrain, and the United Arab Emirates.* London: Graham and Trotman, 1991.

Reed, Clyde G., and Cliff T. Bekar. "Religious Prohibitions against Usury." *Explorations in Economic History,* 40 (2003): 347–68.

Reid, Megan Hibler. "Exemplary of Excess: Devotional Piety in Medieval Islam, 1200–1450." Unpublished Ph.D. dissertation, Princeton University, 2005.

Reinert, Stephen W. "The Muslim Presence in Constantinople, 9th–15th Centuries: Some Preliminary Observations." In *Studies on the Internal Diaspora of the Byzantine Empire,* edited by Hélène Ahrweiler and Angeliki E. Laiou, pp. 125–50. Washington, D.C.: Dumbarton Oaks, 1998.

Repp, Richard C. *The Müfti of Istanbul: A Study in the Development of the Ottoman Learned Hierarchy.* London: Ithaca Press, 1986.

———. "Qānūn and Sharīʿa in the Ottoman Context." In *Islamic Law: Social and Historical Contexts,* edited by Aziz Al-Azmeh, pp. 124–45. London: Routledge, 1988.

Richards, Vernon. "The Failure of Islamoeconomics." Asia Times Online Community and News Discussion, http://forum.atimes.com/topic.asp?TOPIC_ID=857.

Risso, Patricia. *Merchants and Faith: Muslim Commerce and Culture in the Indian Ocean.* Boulder: Westview Press, 1995.

Rivlin, Paul. *Arab Economies in the Twenty-First Century.* Cambridge: Cambridge University Press, 2009.

Rodinson, Maxime. *Islam and Capitalism,* translated by Brian Pearce. New York: Pantheon, 1972; original French edition, 1966.

———. *Muhammad,* translated by Anne Carter. New York: Pantheon, 1980; original French edition, 1961.

Rodrik, Dani. *One Economics, Many Recipes: Globalization, Institutions, and Economic Growth.* Princeton: Princeton University Press, 2007.

Roland, Gérard. "Understanding Institutional Change: Fast-Moving and Slow-Moving Institutions." *Studies in Comparative International Development*, 38 (2004): 109–31.

Rosen, Lawrence. *The Anthropology of Justice: Law as Culture in Islamic Society*. Cambridge: Cambridge University Press, 1989.

———. *The Culture of Islam: Changing Aspects of Contemporary Muslim Life*. Chicago: University of Chicago Press, 2002.

Rosenthal, Steven. "Foreigners and Municipal Reform in Istanbul: 1855–1865." *International Journal of Middle East Studies*, 11 (1980): 227–45.

Rossabi, Morris. "The 'Decline' of the Central Asian Caravan Trade." In *Ecology and Empire: Nomads in the Cultural Evolution of the Old World*, edited by Gary Seaman, pp. 81–102. Los Angeles: Ethnographics/USC, 1989.

Roy, William G. *Socializing Capital: The Rise of the Large Industrial Corporation in America*. Princeton: Princeton University Press, 1997.

Rozen, Minna. "Strangers in a Strange Land: The Extraterritorial Status of Jews in Italy and the Ottoman Empire in the Sixteenth to the Eighteenth Centuries," translated by Goldie Wachsman. In *Ottoman and Turkish Jewry: Community and Leadership*, edited by Aron Rodrigue, pp. 123–66. Bloomington: Indiana University Turkish Studies, 1992.

Rubin, Jared. "The Lender's Curse: A New Look at the Origin and Persistence of Interest Bans in Islam and Christianity." Unpublished Ph.D. dissertation, Stanford University, 2007.

Rugh, William A. *The Arab Press: News Media and Political Process in the Arab World*. Syracuse: University of Syracuse Press, 1979.

Runciman, Steven. *The Greek Church in Captivity*. Cambridge: Cambridge University Press, 1968.

Ryan, Andrew. *The Last of the Dragomans*. London: Geoffrey Bles, 1951.

Rycaut, Paul. *The Present State of the Ottoman Empire*. London: John Starkey and Henry Brome, 1668.

Sachedina, Abdulaziz A. "Activist Shi'ism in Iran, Iraq, and Lebanon." In *Fundamentalisms Observed*, edited by Martin E. Marty and R. Scott Appleby, pp. 403–56. Chicago: University of Chicago Press, 1991.

Saeed, Abdullah, and Hassan Saeed. *Freedom of Religion, Apostasy and Islam*. Aldershot, U.K.: Ashgate, 2004.

Safrai, Shmuel. "Pilgrimage." *Encyclopaedia Judaica*, vol. 13 (1971), pp. 510–13.

Sagredo, Agostino, and Federico Berchet. *Fondaco dei Turchi in Venezia*. Milano: Stabilimento di Giuseppe Civelli, 1860.

Sahillioğlu, Halil. "Bursa Kadı Sicillerinde İç ve Dış Ödemeler Aracı Olarak 'Kitâbü'l-Kadı' ve 'Süftece'ler. In *Türkiye İktisat Tarihi Semineri: Metinler/ Tartışmalar, 8–10 Haziran 1973*, edited by Osman Okyar, pp. 103–44. Ankara: Hacettepe Üniversitesi, 1975.

Said, Edward W. *Orientalism*. New York: Random House, 1978.

Saikal, Amin. *Islam and the West: Conflict or Cooperation?* New York: Palgrave Macmillan, 2003.

Saleh, Nabil A. *Unlawful Gain and Legitimate Profit in Islamic Law: Riba, Gharar, and Islamic Banking.* Cambridge: Cambridge University Press, 1986.

Salt, Jeremy. *Imperialism, Evangelism and the Ottoman Armenians, 1878–1896.* London: Frank Cass, 1993.

Salzmann, Ariel. "An Ancien Régime Revisited: 'Privatization' and Political Economy in the Eighteenth-Century Ottoman Empire." *Politics and Society*, 21 (1993): 393–423.

Sanderson, John. *The Travels of John Sanderson in the Levant, 1584–1602*, edited by William Foster. Nendeln, Liechtenstein: Kraus Reprint, 1967.

Sanderson, Michael. *Education and Economic Decline in Britain, 1870 to the 1990s.* Cambridge: Cambridge University Press, 1999.

Sanjian, Avedis K. *The Armenian Communities in Syria under Ottoman Dominion.* Cambridge, Mass.: Harvard University Press, 1965.

Sardar, Ziauddin, and M. A. Zaki Badawi, editors. *Hajj Studies*, vol. 1. London: Croom Helm, 1978.

Schacht, Joseph. "Amān." *Encyclopaedia of Islam*, 2nd ed., vol. 1, pp. 429–30. Leiden: E. J. Brill, 1960.

———. *An Introduction to Islamic Law.* Oxford: Clarendon Press, 1964.

———. "Kisās." *Encyclopaedia of Islam*, 2nd ed., vol. 5, pp. 177–80. Leiden: E. J. Brill, 1986.

Scholes's Manchester and Salford Directory. Manchester: Bowler and Russell, 1794.

Schumpeter, Joseph. *History of Economic Analysis.* New York: Oxford University Press, 1954.

Scott, James C. *Seeing Like a State: How Certain Schemes to Improve the Human Condition Have Failed.* New Haven: Yale University Press, 1998.

Scott, William Robert. *The Constitution and Finance of English, Scottish, and Irish Joint-Stock Companies to 1720*, 3 vols. Cambridge: Cambridge University Press, 1910–12.

Sella, Domenico. "Crisis and Transformation in Venetian Trade." In *Crisis and Change in the Venetian Economy in the Sixteenth and Seventeenth Centuries*, edited by Brian Pullan, pp. 88–105. London: Methuen, 1968.

Şen, Ömer. *Osmanlı Panayırları (18.–19. Yüzyıl).* Istanbul: Eren, 1996.

Seni, Nora. "The Camondos and Their Imprint on 19th-Century Istanbul." *International Journal of Middle East Studies*, 26 (1994): 663–75.

Sennholz, Hans. "Economic Doctrines of Islam." http://www.sennholz.com/article.php?a=071403.

Shaban, Muhammad A. *Islamic History: A New Interpretation*, 2 vols. Cambridge: Cambridge University Press, 1971.

Shapiro, Martin. *Courts: A Comparative and Political Analysis.* Chicago: University of Chicago Press, 1981.

Shatzmiller, Maya. *Labour in the Medieval Islamic World*. Leiden: E. J. Brill, 1994.

―――. "Islamic Institutions and Property Rights: The Case of the 'Public Good' Waqf." *Journal of the Economic and Social History of the Orient*, 44 (2001): 44–74.

Shaw, Stanford J. "The Nineteenth-Century Ottoman Tax Reforms." *International Journal of Middle East Studies*, 6 (1975): 421–59.

―――. *History of the Ottoman Empire and Modern Turkey*, vol. 1. New York: Cambridge University Press, 1976.

Sherwani, Haroon Khan. *Studies in Muslim Political Thought and Administration*, 4th ed. Lahore: Sh. Muhammad Ashraf, 1963.

Shields, Sarah D. *Mosul Before Iraq: Like Bees Making Five-Sided Cells*. Albany: State University of New York Press, 2000.

Shmuelevitz, Aryeh. *The Jews of the Ottoman Empire in the Late Fifteenth and the Sixteenth Centuries: Administrative, Economic, Legal, and Social Relations as Reflected in the Responsa*. Leiden: E. J. Brill, 1984.

Siddiqi, Muhammad Nejatullah. *Banking without Interest*. Lahore: Islamic Publications, 1973.

―――. *Muslim Economic Thinking: A Survey of Contemporary Literature*. Leicester: Islamic Foundation, 1981.

Simon, Róbert. *Meccan Trade and Islam: Problems of Origin and Structure*, translated by Feodora Sós. Budapest: Akadémiai Kiadó, 1989.

Simpson, A.W.B. *A History of the Common Law of Contract: The Rise of the Action Assumpsit*. Oxford: Clarendon Press, 1987.

Sitkoff, Robert H. "An Agency Costs Theory of Trust Law." *Cornell Law Review*, 89 (2004): 621–84.

Slater's Manchester, Salford Trades Directory 1903. Manchester: Slater's Directory Limited, 1903.

Smith, Adam. *The Wealth of Nations*. New York: Modern Library, 1937; original edition, 1776.

Solas, Çiğdem, and İsmail Otar. "The Accounting System Practiced in the Near East During the Period 1220–1350 Based on the Book Risale-i Felekiyye." *Accounting Historians Journal*, 21 (1994): 117–35.

Sommerville, C. John. *The News Revolution in England: Cultural Dynamics of Daily Information*. New York: Oxford University Press, 1996.

Sonyel, Salâhi. "The Protégé System in the Ottoman Empire." *Journal of Islamic Studies*, 2 (1991): 56–66.

―――. *Minorities and the Destruction of the Ottoman Empire*. Ankara: Turkish Historical Society, 1993.

Sousa, Nasim. *The Capitulary Régime of Turkey: Its History, Origin, and Nature*. Baltimore: Johns Hopkins Press, 1933.

Spicer, Albert Dykes. *The Paper Trade*. London: Methuen, 1907.

Spufford, Margaret. "Literacy, Trade and Religion in the Commercial Centres of Europe." In *A Miracle Mirrored: The Dutch Republic in European Perspective*, edited by Karel Davids and Jan Lucassen, pp. 229–83. Cambridge: Cambridge University Press, 1995.

Steensgaard, Niels. "Consuls and Nations in the Levant from 1570 to 1650." *Scandinavian Economic History Review*, 15 (1967): 13–55.

————. *Carracks, Caravans and Companies: The Structural Crisis in the European-Asian Trade in the Early 17th Century*. Odense, Denmark: Studentlitteratur, 1973.

Stein, Joshua M. "Habsburg Financial Institutions Presented as a Model for the Ottoman Empire in the Sefaretname of Ebu Bekir Ratıb Efendi." In *Habsburgisch-Osmanische Beziehungen, Wien, 26.-30. September 1983*, pp. 233–41.

Stephens, Mitchell. *A History of News: From the Drum to the Satellite*. New York: Viking, 1988.

Stephenson, Carl. *Borough and Town: A Study of Urban Origins in England*. Cambridge, Mass.: Mediaeval Academy of America, 1933.

Stern, Gertrude H. *Marriage in Early Islam*. London: Royal Asiatic Society, 1939.

Stern, Samuel M. "The Constitution of the Islamic City." In *The Islamic City*, edited by Albert H. Hourani and Samuel M. Stern, pp. 25–50. Oxford: Bruno Cassirer, 1970.

Stigler, George J. *The Organization of Industry*. Homewood, Ill.: Richard D. Irwin, 1968.

Stoianovich, Traian. "The Conquering Balkan Orthodox Merchant." *Journal of Economic History*, 20 (1960): 234–313.

Stone, Lawrence. "Literacy and Education in England 1640–1900." *Past and Present*, 42 (1969): 69–139.

Strauss, Gerald. *Law, Resistance, and the State: The Opposition to Roman Law in Reformation Germany*. Princeton: Princeton University Press, 1986.

Strieder, Jacob. *Jacob Fugger the Rich: Merchant and Banker of Augsburg, 1459–1525*, translated by Mildred L. Hartsough and edited by N.S.B. Gras. Westport, Conn.: Greenwood Press, 1984; original German edition, 1925.

Sugar, Peter F. *Southeastern Europe under Ottoman Rule, 1354–1804*. Seattle: University of Washington Press, 1977.

Sullivan, Denis J. *Private Voluntary Organizations in Egypt: Islamic Development, Private Initiative, and State Control*. Gainesville: University of Florida Press, 1994.

Sümer, Faruk. *Yabanlu Pazarı: Selçuklular Devrinde Milletlerarası Büyük Bir Fuar*. Istanbul: Türk Dünyası Araştırma Vakfı, 1985.

Sumption, Jonathan. *Pilgrimage: An Image of Mediaeval Religion*. Totowa, N.J.: Rowman and Littlefield, 1975.

Sunstein, Cass R. *Risk and Reason: Safety, Law, and the Environment*. Cambridge: Cambridge University Press, 2002.

Tandon, Prakash. *Banking Century: A Short History of Banking in India and the Pioneer—Punjab National Bank*. New York: Penguin, 1989.

T.C. Başbakanlık Devlet Arşivleri Genel Müdürlüğü. *Boğaziçinde Asırlık Seyahat: Belgelerle Şirket-i Hayriye.* Istanbul: İDO, 2007.

Thiriet, F. *Régestes des Délibérations du Sénat de Venise Concernant la Roumanie.* Paris: Mouton & Co., 1958.

Thirsk, Joan. "The European Debate on Customs of Inheritance." In *Family and Inheritance: Rural Society in Western Europe, 1200–1800,* edited by Jack Goody, Joan Thirsk, and E. P. Thompson, pp. 177–91. Cambridge: Cambridge University Press, 1976.

Tiebout, Charles M. "A Pure Theory of Local Expenditures." *Journal of Political Economy,* 64 (1956): 416–24.

Tignor, Robert L. "The Introduction of Modern Banking into Egypt, 1855–1920." *Asian and African Studies,* 15 (1981): 103–22.

Tiihonen, Seppo, editor. *The History of Corruption in Central Government.* Amsterdam: IOS Press, 2003.

Tirole, Jean. "Corporate Governance." *Econometrica,* 69 (2001): 1–35.

Toledano, Ehud. "Social and Economic Change in the 'Long Nineteenth Century'." In *The Cambridge History of Egypt,* vol. 2, edited by M. W. Daly, pp. 252–84. Cambridge: Cambridge University Press, 1998.

Toprak, Zafer. *Türkiye'de "Milli İktisat" (1908–1918).* Istanbul: Yurt Yayınları, 1982.

———. "Nüfus, Fetih'ten 1950'ye." *İstanbul Ansiklopedisi,* vol. 6, pp. 108–11. Istanbul: Türkiye Ekonomik ve Toplumsal Tarih Vakfı, 1994.

———. *Milli İktisat—Milli Burjuvazi.* Istanbul: Tarih Vakfı, 1995.

———. *İttihad-Terakki ve Cihan Harbi: Savaş Ekonomisi ve Türkiye'de Devletçilik, 1914–1918.* Istanbul: Homer Kitabevi, 2003.

Tschoegl, Adrian E. "Financial Integration, Dis-integration and Emerging Re-Integration in the Eastern Mediterranean, c. 1850 to the Present." *Financial Markets, Institutions and Instruments,* 13 (2004): 244–84.

Tucker, Judith E. *In the House of the Law: Gender and Islamic Law in Ottoman Syria and Palestine.* Berkeley: University of California Press, 1998.

Turan, Şerafettin. "Venedik'te Türk Ticaret Merkezi (Fondaco dei Turchi)." *Belleten,* 32 (1968): 249–83.

Turgay, A. Üner. "Trade and Merchants in Nineteenth-Century Trabzon: Elements of Ethnic Conflict." In *Christians and Jews in the Ottoman Empire, Vol. 1: The Central Lands,* edited by Benjamin Braude and Bernard Lewis, pp. 287–318. New York: Holmes & Meier, 1982.

Turkey. *28 Teşrinievel 1927 Umumî Nüfus Tahriri,* number 3. Ankara: İstatistik Umum Müdürlüğü, 1929.

Turner, Howard R. *Science in Medieval Islam.* Austin: University of Texas Press, 1995.

Tutel, Eser. *Şirket-i Hayriye.* Istanbul: İletişim, 1997.

Tyan, Émile. "Judicial Organization." In *Law in the Middle East,* vol. 1, edited by

Majid Khadduri and Herbert J. Liebesny, pp. 236–78. Washington, D.C.: Middle East Institute, 1955.

———. *Histoire de L'Organisation Judiciaire en Pays d'Islam*, 2nd ed. Leiden: E. J. Brill, 1960.

Ubicini, M. A. *Letters on Turkey*, 2 vols. New York: Arno Press, 1973; original edition, 1856.

Üçok, Coşkun, and Ahmet Mumcu. *Türk Hukuk Tarihi*, 7th ed. Ankara: Savaş Yayınları, 1993.

Udovitch, Abraham L. "At the Origins of the Western *Commenda*: Islam, Israel, Byzantium?" *Speculum* 37 (1962): 198–207.

———. *Partnership and Profit in Medieval Islam*. Princeton: Princeton University Press, 1970.

———. "Reflections on the Institutions of Credit and Banking in the Medieval Islamic Near East." *Studia Islamica* 41 (1975): 5–21.

———. "Bankers without Banks: Commerce, Banking, and Society in the Islamic World of the Middle Ages." In *The Dawn of Modern Banking*, edited by the Center for Medieval and Renaissance Studies, UCLA, pp. 255–73. New Haven: Yale University Press, 1979.

———. "Islamic Law and the Social Context of Exchange in the Medieval Middle East." *History and Anthropology*, 1 (1985): 445–65.

Ülgener, Sabri F. *Dünü ve Bugünü ile Zihniyet ve Din: İslâm, Tasavvuf ve Çözülme Devri İktisat Ahlâkı*. Istanbul: Der Yayınları, 1981.

Ullmann, Walter. *The Carolingian Renaissance and the Idea of Kingship: The Birbeck Lectures 1968–9*. London: Methuen, 1969.

———. *Law and Politics in the Middle Ages: An Introduction to the Sources of Medieval Political Ideas*. Ithaca: Cornell University Press, 1975.

UNESCO. *Statistical Yearbook*, 1963, 1970, 1999. Paris: UNESCO, 1964–2000.

United Nations Development Programme. *Arab Human Development Report 2002: Creating Opportunities for Future Generations*. New York: United Nations Publications, 2002.

———. *Arab Human Development Report 2003: Building a Knowledge Society*. New York: United Nations Publications, 2003.

———. *Arab Human Development Report 2004: Towards Freedom in the Arab World*. New York: United Nations Publications, 2005.

Usher, Abbott Payson. *The Early History of Deposit Banking in Mediterranean Europe*, vol. 1. New York: Russell and Russell, 1967; original edition, 1943.

Uzunçarşılı, İsmail Hakkı. *Osmanlı Devletinin İlmiye Teşkilâtı*. Ankara: Türk Tarih Kurumu, 1965.

———. *Mekke-i Mükerreme Emirleri*. Ankara: Türk Tarih Kurumu, 1972.

Velidedeoğlu, Hıfzı Veldet. "Kanunlaştırma Hareketleri ve Tanzimat." In *Tanzimat I*, pp. 139–209. Istanbul: Maarif Matbaası, 1940.

Verbit, Gilbert Paul, translator and editor. *A Ninth Century Treatise on the Law of Trusts (Being a Translation of Al-Khassāf, Ahkām al-Waqūf)*. Philadelphia: Xlibris, 2008.

Verlinden, C. "Markets and Fairs." In *The Cambridge Economic History of Europe*, vol. 3, edited by M. M. Postan, E. E. Rich, and Edward Miller, pp. 119–53. Cambridge: Cambridge University Press, 1971.

Vikør, Knut S. *Between God and Sultan: A History of Islamic Law*. Oxford: Oxford University Press, 2005.

Vogel, Frank E. *Islamic Law and Legal System: Studies of Saudi Arabia*. Leiden: Brill, 2000.

———. "Contract Law of Islam and the Arab Middle East." In *International Encyclopedia of Comparative Law*, vol. 7, edited by Arthur von Mehren, pp. 1–77. Tübingen: Mohr Siebeck, 2006.

Voll, John O. "Fundamentalism in the Sunni Arab World: Egypt and the Sudan." In *Fundamentalisms Observed*, edited by Martin E. Marty and R. Scott Appleby, pp. 345–402. Chicago: University of Chicago Press, 1991.

Wakin, Jeannette A., editor. *The Function of Documents in Islamic Law: The Chapters on Sales from Tahāwī's* Kitāb al-Shurūt al Kabīr. Albany: State University of New York Press, 1972.

Wallerstein, Immanuel. *The Capitalist World-Economy*. Cambridge: Cambridge University Press, 1979.

Wallerstein, Immanuel, Hale Decdeli, and Reşat Kasaba. "The Incorporation of the Ottoman Empire into the World-Economy." In *The Ottoman Empire and the World-Economy*, edited by Huri İslamoğlu-İnan, pp. 88–97. Cambridge: Cambridge University Press, 1987.

Wallis, John Joseph. "Constitutions, Corporations, and Corruption: American States and Constitutional Change, 1842 to 1852." *Journal of Economic History*, 65 (2005): 211–56.

Walz, Terence. "The Paper Trade of Egypt and the Sudan in the Eighteenth and Nineteenth Centuries." In *Modernization in the Sudan: Essays in Honor of Richard Hill*, edited by Martin W. Daly, pp. 29–48. New York: Lilian Barber Press, 1985.

Wansbrough, John. "Venice and Florence in the Mamluk Commercial Privileges." *Bulletin of the School of Oriental and African Studies*, 28 (1965): 483–523.

———. "The Safe-Conduct in Muslim Chancery Practice." *Bulletin of the School of Oriental and African Studies*, 34 (1971): 20–35.

Watson, Andrew. *The American Mission in Egypt, 1854 to 1896*. Pittsburgh: United Presbyterian Board of Publication, 1898.

Weber, Max. *The History of Commercial Partnerships in the Middle Ages*, translated by Lutz Kaelber. Lanham, Md.: Rowman and Littlefield, 2003; original German edition, 1889.

———. *The Protestant Ethic and the Spirit of Capitalism*, translated by Talcott Parsons. New York: Charles Scribner's, 1958; original German edition, 1904–5.

————. *Economy and Society*, 2 volumes, edited by Guenther Roth and Claus Wittich. Berkeley: University of California Press, 1978; original German edition, 1956.

Wee, Herman van der. *The Growth of the Antwerp Market and the European Economy (Fourteenth-Sixteenth Centuries)*, vol. 2. The Hague: Martinus Nijhoff, 1963.

Wehr, Hans. *A Dictionary of Modern Written Arabic*, edited by J. M. Cowan. Beirut: Librairie du Liban, 1980.

Wiederhold, Lutz. "Legal Doctrines in Conflict: The Relevance of *Madhhab* Boundaries to Legal Reasoning in the Light of an Unpublished Treatise on *Taqlīd* and *Ijtihād*." *Islamic Law and Society*, 3 (1996): 234–304.

Williamson, Oliver E. *The Economic Institutions of Capitalism: Firms, Markets, Relational Contracting*. New York: Free Press, 1985.

Wilson, Peter W. *A Question of Interest: The Paralysis of Saudi Banking*. Boulder: Westview Press, 1991.

Wilson, Rodney. *Banking and Finance in the Arab Middle East*. New York: St. Martin's Press, 1983.

Winter, Michael. *Egyptian Society under Ottoman Rule, 1517–1798*. London: Routledge, 1992.

————. "Inter-Madhhab Competition in Mamluk Damascus: Al-Tartusi's Counsel for the Turkish Sultans." *Jerusalem Studies in Arabic and Islam*, 25 (2001): 191–211.

Wintle, Michael. *An Economic and Social History of the Netherlands, 1800–1920: Demographic, Economic and Social Transition*. Cambridge: Cambridge University Press, 2000.

Wittfogel, Karl A. *Oriental Despotism: A Comparative Study of Total Power*. New Haven: Yale University Press, 1957.

Wood, Alfred C. *A History of the Levant Company*. London: Oxford University Press, 1935.

Yediyıldız, Bahaeddin. "Müessese-Toplum Münâsebetleri Çerçevesinde XVIII. Asır Türk Toplumu ve Vakıf Müessesesi." *Vakıflar Dergisi*, 15 (1982): 23–53.

————. *Institution du Vaqf au XVIIIᵉ Siècle en Turquie: Étude Socio-Historique*. Ankara: Éditions Ministère de la Culture, 1990.

Yi, Eunjeong. *Guild Dynamics in Seventeenth-Century Istanbul: Fluidity and Leverage*. Leiden: Brill, 2004.

Zachariadou, Elizabeth A. *Trade and Crusade: Venetian Crete and the Emirates of Menteshe and Aydın*. Venice: Library of the Hellenic Institute of Byzantine and Post-Byzantine Studies, 1983.

Zahraa, Mahdi. "Legal Personality in Islamic Law." *Arab Law Quarterly*, 10 (1995): 193–206.

Zaid, Omar Abdullah. "Accounting Systems and Recording Procedures in the Early Islamic State." *Accounting Historians Journal*, 31 (2004): 149–70.

Zanden, Jan Luiten van. *The Long Road to the Industrial Revolution: The European Economy in a Global Perspective, 1000–1800*. Leiden: Brill, 2009.

Zarinebaf-Shahr, Fariba. "Women, Law, and Imperial Justice in Ottoman Istanbul in the Late Seventeenth Century." In *Women, the Family, and Divorce in Islamic History*, edited by Amira El Azhary Sonbol, pp. 81–95. Syracuse: Syracuse University Press, 1996.

Ziadeh, Farhat J. *Lawyers, the Rule of Law and Liberalism in Modern Egypt*. Stanford: Hoover Institution, 1968.

Zubaida, Sami. *Law and Power in the Islamic World*. London: I. B. Tauris, 2003.

Index